SOCIOLOGY
OF SPORT

SOCIOLOGY OF SPORT

Theory and Practice

Edited by

Dr.ROBYN L.JONES & Dr.KATHLEEN M.ARMOUR

Longman

Pearson Education Limited
Edinburgh Gate
Harlow
Essex CM20 2JE, England
and Associated Companies throughout the world

ISBN 0 582 41912 3

British Library Cataloguing-in-Publication Data

A catalogue record for this book is available from the British Library.

Set by 35 in 9.5/12pt Garamond
Produced by

To
Savanna, Seren and Siân,
and to
Charlie, Georgina and Jamie.

Contents

CHAPTER EIGHT *From athleticism to commercialism: Engaging with the future* 99

Alan Tomlinson

CHAPTER NINE *From theory to application in the sociology of sport* 114

Andrew Yiannakis

CHAPTER TEN *Discrimination: What do we know, and what can we do about it?* 134

Juan-Miguel Fernández-Balboa

CHAPTER ELEVEN *Issues of equity and understanding in sport and physical education: A North American perspective* 145

Paul G. Schempp and Kimberly L. Oliver

About the Contributors

Kathleen M. Armour, formerly of Brunel University, is now a Senior Lecturer in the Department of Physical Education, Sports Science and Recreation Management, at Loughborough University, UK. Her research interests centre on pedagogy in higher education and teachers' lives and careers. This book is an attempt to 'walk the talk' and to make the sociology of sport accessible and relevant to those intending to work in sport-related professions and occupations. Kathleen is also author (with Robyn L. Jones) of *Physical Education Teachers' Lives and Careers* (Falmer Press, 1998) and joint editor of SOSOL, the electronic journal *Sociology of Sport Online*. Other interests include three young children, a long-suffering husband, and exercising to ward off impending middle age!

Peter Donnelly is currently Director of the Centre for Sport Policy Studies, and a Professor in the Faculty of Physical Education and Health, at the University of Toronto, Canada. He was born in Chester, England, studied physical education as an undergraduate, and taught school for several years. In 1969 he moved to the United States where he completed undergraduate studies in New York City, and then received Master's and Ph.D. degrees from the University of Massachusetts. In 1976 he moved to Canada, taught at the University of Western Ontario from 1976–79, and McMaster University from 1980–98. His research interests include sport politics and policy issues (including the area of children's rights in sport), sport subcultures, and mountaineering (history). He has published numerous scholarly articles on those and other topics. Recent books include: *Taking Sport Seriously: Social Issues in Canadian Sport* (1997), and *Inside Sports*, with Jay Coakley (1999). His current sporting interests include rock climbing/mountaineering (continually proving the inverse relationship between age and risk taking), hiking and skiing; he is a novice golfer, and is now enjoying life as an 'empty nester'.

Juan-Miguel Fernández-Balboa received his doctorate in education from the University of Massachussetts, Amherst, USA. Presently an Associate Professor of Education at Montclair State University, in New Jersey, he teaches courses on curriculum development and change, democracy in education, and critical thinking. His scholarly interests focus on teacher development, critical theory, and critical pedagogy – themes about which he has written numerous theoretical and research-based articles in various international journals. He is also the co-author and editor of *Critical Postmodernism in Human Movement, Physical Education, and Sport* (Suny Press, 1997).

Grant Jarvie is Head of Department at the University of Stirling and holds Scotland's first Chair of Sports Studies. He previously held the Chair of Leisure Studies at Heriot-Watt University and was Head of the Department of Physical Education at the University of Warwick from 1991–1994. He researches in the fields of sport, history and sociology and has published a series of articles, books and edited collections some of which include: *Highland Games: The Making of the Myth* (Edinburgh University Press, 1991); *Scottish Sport in the Making of the Nation*, with G. Walker (Leicester University Press, 1994); *Sport, Leisure and Social Thought*, with J. Maguire (Routledge, 1994); *Sport in the Making of Celtic Cultures* (Cassell Academic, 1999), and *Sport, Scotland and the Scots*, with J. Burnett (Tuckwell Press, 2000). His interests include supporting Motherwell Football Club, hillwalking, squash, the Fabian Society and the Scottish Labour Party.

Robyn L. Jones, formerly of Brunel University, UK, is a Lecturer in the School of Physical Education at the University of Otago, New Zealand. He is the joint editor of the electronic journal *Sociology of Sport OnLine*, and the co-author with Kathleen M. Armour of *Physical Education Teachers' Lives and Careers* (Falmer Press, 1998). His research interests include knowledge acquisition and the nature of interaction within coaching, and more broadly, the Black experience in UK sport. His interests, apart from three daughters, involve being a devotee of Delta Blues music, a long-suffering fan of Everton Football Club, while still remaining active as both a football player and coach.

David Kirk is currently Beckwith Professor of Youth Sport at Loughborough University. His research interests include young people in sport, curriculum change in physical education, the body, schooling and culture, and situated learning in physical education and sport. His most recent book is *Schooling Bodies: School Practice and Public Discourse, 1880–1950* (Leicester University Press, 1998).

Doune Macdonald is an Associate Professor in the Department of Human Movement Studies, The University of Queensland, Australia. After teaching health and physical education in New South Wales and Queensland schools, she undertook doctoral studies in physical education teacher education. Since then she has developed an interest in school curricula and the place of health in physical education. She was an evaluator of the trial phase of the new physical education syllabus, and currently serves on state level Queensland Board of Senior Secondary School Studies (QBSSSS) committees. She would love to have interests outside work if she could find the time!

Greg Naughtin is Head of Department, Health, Physical Education and Sport, at Nambour High School in Queensland, Australia, and has been teaching physical education since 1983. He has been closely involved in the development of the Queensland Board of Senior Secondary School Studies physical education syllabus as a member, and subsequently Chair, of the syllabus writing team. He also serves as a District Review Panel Chair in Physical Education, coordinating the review of samples of student work in order to advise on the maintenance of syllabus standards and provide assistance to schools in curriculum development. His particular interest is the further development of the notions of integration and personalization of student learning, principles central to the Queensland version of physical education.

Kimberly L. Oliver is an Assistant Professor in Human Performance Studies in the area of teacher education, at the University of Alabama, USA, where she teaches in the graduate and undergraduate physical education programmes. She is currently completing a co-authored book with Rosary Lalik on adolescent girls' bodily knowledge. Her current research focuses on ways of working with adolescent girls to help them develop their abilities to resist forms and processes of enculturation that are destructive and disempowering to their health and well-being.

Victoria Paraschak is an Associate Professor in the School of Human Kinetics, University of Windsor in Canada. Her research explores the physical cultural practices of indigenous peoples in both North America and Australia, in terms of race and gender relations, human agency, identity, and cultural production more broadly. When possible, she heads outdoors. Most recently, that meant a dog mushing trip in Alaska, but running and paddling are enjoyed on a more regular basis.

Dawn Penney is a Senior Research Fellow at the Department of Physical Education, Sports Science and Recreation Management, Loughborough University. Dawn's work in the area of education policy sociology has focused upon contemporary developments in physical education and the development of the National Curriculum for Physical Education in England and Wales in particular. Her ongoing research has been the focus for many publications, including the book *Politics, Policy and Practice in Physical Education*, co-authored with John Evans and published in 1999 by E&FN Spon, an imprint of Routledge.

Irene A. Reid lectures at the University of Stirling, Scotland. She previously lectured at De Montfort University having completed graduate research at Queen's University, Canada. She has published widely in the fields of sport, history and sociology. Her most recent research articles and chapters have included work on sport and racism, sport in South Africa, a social history of shinty and sport and nationalism. Her interests include travelling, politics, Scottish culture and various recreational sports.

Paul G. Schempp is a Professor in the Department of Physical Education and Sport Studies at the University of Georgia, Athens, USA, where he directs the Sport Instruction Research Laboratory. Dr Schempp has studied and written extensively on the topic of teacher socialization, teachers' knowledge, and expertise in teaching. His research has appeared in such journals as *Research Quarterly for Exercise and Sport*, *American Educational Research Journal*, *Journal of Teaching in Physical Education*, and *Journal of Educational Research and Development*. He has served on the faculties of Kent State University, University of Oregon, and now the University of Georgia. In 1990–1991, he was a Senior Research Fulbright Scholar to the Institute for Sport Science at the University of Frankfurt, Germany.

Trevor Slack is Professor and Head of the School of Physical Education, Sport and Leisure at De Montfort University in Bedford, UK. He was previously at the University of Alberta in Canada and has been a Visiting Professor at Warwick University Business School. His research interests are in the areas of organizational strategy, particularly the role of sponsorship as a strategic initiative, and organizational change. His hobbies include travelling and listening to the Blues. He is an avid fan of Eric Clapton.

Andrew C. Sparkes is currently Professor of Social Theory in the School of Postgraduate Medicine and Health Sciences, Department of Exercise and Sport Sciences, University of Exeter, UK. His research interests are eclectic and include: interrupted body projects, identity dilemmas, and the narrative (re)construction of self; organizational innovation and change; and the lives and careers of marginalized individuals and groups. These interests are framed by a desire to seek interpretive forms of understanding, and a postmodern aspiration to represent lived experience using a variety of genres.

Alan Tomlinson is Professor of Sport and Leisure Studies, Chelsea School Research Centre, University of Brighton, England, UK. He studied humanities and sociology for his BA at the University of Kent, and took Master's and Doctoral degrees in Sociological Studies at the University of Sussex. He has written extensively on the social history and sociology of sport, leisure and consumption. His most recent books are: *FIFA and the Contest for World Football; Who Rules the Peoples' Game*, with John Sugden (Polity Press, 1998); *Great Balls of Fire; How Big Money is Hijacking World Football*, with John Sugden (Mainstream Publishing, 1999); *The Game's Up; Essays in the Cultural Analysis of Sport, Leisure and Popular Culture* (Ashgate/Arena, 1999), and *Sport and Leisure Cultures; Local and Global Dimensions* (University of Minnesota Press, 2000).

Naree Wittwer is Head of Health and Physical Education at Immanuel Lutheran College on Queensland's Sunshine Coast, Australia. She has taught for ten years at the school and been involved in the trial and pilot phases of the physical education syllabus for students in Years 11 and 12. She is currently a member of the Queensland Board of Senior Secondary School Studies (QBSSSS) State Review Panel and was a member of the sub-committee involved in writing the 1998 physical education syllabus. Her interests include basketball (refereeing, scoring and playing), netball, walking, cooking and reading.

Andrew Yiannakis is Professor and Director of the Laboratory for Leisure, Tourism and Sport at the University of Connecticut, USA. His work has been published in a variety of journals including the *Sociology of Sport Journal*, the *Annals of Tourism Research* and the *Journal of Sport Management*. He is also senior editor of *Applied Sociology of Sport*, with Susan Greendorfer (Human Kinetics Publishers, 1992) and *Sport Sociology: Contemporary Themes* (5th edn), forthcoming with Merrill Melnick. He enjoys travel, reading historical novels, horseback riding and the martial arts.

Preface

Why does sport need sport sociology? What practical purposes are served by sociological research in sport? How can athletes, coaches, teachers and enthusiastic sports participants benefit from sport sociology knowledge? This book seeks to locate sport sociology in the 'swampy lowland of practice' (Schon, 1987, p. 3) by addressing these thorny practical questions. Concerns about applicability and relevance are not new to sport sociology (Yiannakis and Greendorfer, 1992; Feingold, 1997; Martinek and Hellison, 1997) nor, indeed, to sociology itself. Taylor (1999) argues that sociology can make a real difference to people's lives, but only if sociological knowledge and research can be communicated more effectively. He identifies the key tasks of sociology as: to accurately represent the social world, to evaluate it, and to provide 'fresh, imaginative and exciting ideas about the human lived experience within that world' (p. 32). Similarly, Morgan (1998) presents a vision of sociology as 'an imaginative pursuit . . . that is capable of delighting and disturbing' (p. 648). Morgan, drawing heavily on the classic text by Mills (1959), also points to the potential of sociology to make a difference. In particular, he argues that sociology can help people to 'see the social world in a slightly different way, to see as problems topics that had previously been taken for granted' (p. 658). However, Morgan urges sociologists not to obscure their ideas in complex language. Like Taylor (1999), he stresses the importance of effective communication to ensure that sociology is accessible to the widest possible audience.

This is useful advice for sport sociologists too. There is still little understanding of the relevance of sport sociology within the broad field of sport sciences/sport studies/human movement. Whereas physiology, biomechanics and, increasingly, psychology can demonstrate a measurable impact upon sports performances, sociology can seem divorced from the practical world of the sports practitioner. Yet, as Jarvie (1991, p. 2) points out 'sport is, first and foremost, a social activity involving a complex set of social relationships'. Harris (1998) also identifies sport as a key site of social activity within a civil society. She argues that, as a result, it has the potential to reflect, produce and reproduce a wide range of social inequalities:

> We must remember that opportunities for participation in physical activities are not equally available to everyone. For example, ethnic and racial minorities, women, economically impoverished people, those with minority gender identities and sexual orientations, and those with personal disabilities frequently encounter inequitable social arrangements that make access difficult.
>
> (1998, p. 146)

Furthermore, Harris points out that media presentations of sport tend to perpetuate damaging stereotypes; that there is pressure on women to conform to an ideal body type; and that the dominance of a power and performance model of sport is limiting for many people. This is not to suggest that sport is mainly negative in impact; on the contrary, sport also has the potential to offer enormous benefits. However, Harris cautions against holding an overly naive and functionalist view of sport as good for everyone and equally available to all. For those of us who have benefited from all that sport can offer, this may be a challenging thought. However, if changes are to occur to improve the quality and accessibility of sport, and if readers of this book are to be involved in creating some of that social change, then a fresh vision of both the present, and potential new futures, will be required. Echoing both Taylor (1999) and Morgan (1998), Harris suggests that such change will require 'vision, creativity, resources and hard work' (p. 148) and she exhorts sport sociologists to take up the challenge.

Sociologists do not need to be convinced of the centrality of 'social things' (Lemert, 1997) in sport: others are more sceptical. This book, through the writings of leading practitioners within the broad field of the sociology of sport, seeks to demonstrate how sociological theory and research can be understood and applied in the practical worlds of sport and sport-related employment. For example, in elite sport, by placing the athlete as *person* at the centre of analysis, rather than seeing the athlete as merely a 'body' or 'mind' to be trained, sport sociology can help both coaches and athletes to work more holistically and, thus, more effectively. Similarly, in an educational context, sport sociology can help teachers to think critically about sport, about the social construction of identity and embodiment in sporting contexts, and about the impact of sporting practices upon pupils. Centrally, the book is founded upon the principle that it is incumbent upon sport sociologists to demonstrate that sociological knowledge can assist practitioners to achieve *their* goals.

The book is divided into two broad thematic sections. In the first section, contributors based in the UK discuss key issues from a British perspective. Chapter 1, by Kathleen M. Armour and Robyn L. Jones, establishes a framework within which the value of sociology within the practical world of sport can be claimed and assessed. Thus, it introduces the coherent thread that runs through the book: that of the relevance of sociology to the sport practitioner. The four following chapters (2–5) focus upon the ways in which sociology knowledge and research can be applied to key roles in sport: the athlete (Andrew C. Sparkes); the coach (Robyn L. Jones); the sports manager/administrator (Trevor Slack) and the physical education teacher (Dawn Penney). In the next three chapters (6–8), sport is located within wider social structures. Kathleen M. Armour analyses the ways in which sport and social class are interlinked, Irene A. Reid and Grant Jarvie consider the role of sport in the complex process of developing and expressing national identities, and Alan Tomlinson discusses commercialism and globalization from a sports perspective. The purpose of this section is to highlight ways in which such issues are situated within a British context yet, at the same time, are located within a global framework.

The second section of the book provides an international perspective on the ways in which the sociology of sport can be of value in a range of practical contexts. Authors are drawn from North America and Australia. Andrew Yiannakis sets the scene with a chapter on the history and development of applied sport sociology. The following three chapters (10–12) examine issues of equity and social justice within American and Canadian sport. Juan-Miguel Fernández-Balboa discusses discrimination and its impact upon sport; Paul Schempp and Kimberly L. Oliver focus upon issues of equity and understanding; and Victoria Paraschak analyses the experiences of indigenous peoples in sport in Canada. The final three chapters (13–15) focus on youth sport, and draw upon Canadian and Australian experiences. Peter Donnelly highlights some prevalent problematic issues in Canadian youth sport and explores social resolution strategies, while Doune Macdonald, Greg Naughtin and Naree Wittwer examine ways in which sport sociology is supporting learning in Australian secondary school programmes. Finally, David Kirk analyses an innovation that sought to make sport sociology relevant and applicable to the learning needs of human movement studies students at university level.

Who is the book written for?

This book is written for both the sport sciences/studies student (including human movement studies, kinesiology, etc.) and the sport-related practitioner. For the student, it can be read at a number of different levels. As an introductory text, the more general chapters can help those seeking to understand the role of sociology in the multidisciplinary study of sport, whereas some of the topic chapters will be of particular interest where they resonate with personal knowledge and experience. For the more advanced student, the book can both extend knowledge across a range of topics, and help to make the complex links between theory and practice. For the practising or aspirant sport-related practitioner, including sport managers/administrators, athletes, coaches and physical education teachers, the text can impact directly upon practice by encouraging a fresh and informed analysis of long taken-for-granted policies and practices.

Finally . . .

An edited collection such as this is inevitably the work of many, and is only as strong as its contributors. As editors we were delighted to secure the agreement of so many eminent scholars to work on the project and for keeping true to its theme. We believe that the quality of the contributions on a somewhat unique but crucial topic is the strength of the book. To the chapter authors thus, we owe a debt of gratitude. Finally, we'd like to thank Ian Little, our commissioning editor, for believing in the project from our first meeting, and supporting it through to publication.

Robyn and Kathleen

References

- Feingold R.S. (1997) 'Service-based scholarship: An introduction', *Quest* 49: 351–4.
- Harris J.C. (1998) 'Civil society, physical activity, and the involvement of sport sociologists in the preparation of physical activity professionals', *Quest* 15: 138–53.
- Jarvie G. (1991) 'Introduction: Sport, racism and ethnicity', in G. Jarvie (ed.) *Sport, Racism and Ethnicity*, London: Falmer Press, pp. 1–6.
- Lemert C. (1997) *Social Things: An Introduction to the Sociological Life*, New York: Rowman & Littlefield.
- Martinek T. and Hellison D. (1997) 'Service-bonded inquiry: The road less travelled', *Journal of Teaching in Physical Education* 17: 107–21.
- Mills C.W. (1959) *The Sociological Imagination*, Oxford: Oxford University Press.
- Morgan D. (1998) 'Sociological imaginings and imagining sociology: bodies, auto/biographies and other mysteries', *Sociology* 32(4): 647–63.
- Schon D.A. (1987) *Educating the Reflective Practitioner*, San Francisco, CA.: Jossey-Bass.
- Taylor S. (1999) 'Communicating sociology', *Network* 73, May: 32.
- Yiannakis A. and Greendorfer S. (eds) (1992) *Applied Sociology of Sport*, Champaign, Ill: Human Kinetics.

Chapter One

The Practical Heart Within: The Value of a Sociology of Sport

Kathleen M. Armour and Robyn L. Jones

Introduction

What is the point of sport sociology? For whom are its theories written and its research conducted? How can it help coaches to coach, teachers to teach, elite athletes to achieve their goals, and the more casual sports participants to achieve theirs? What can it offer to those attempting to organize and administer sport? This chapter provides a rationale for the practical value of a sociology of sport. In the first section, Lemert's (1997) analysis of 'social things' provides a broad sociological framework for understanding the ways in which 'sociological competences' underpin our lives, and for illustrating the place of the sociological in sport. The second section provides a brief overview of the historical development of the sociology of sport, based on Giddens' (1986, p. 4) argument that: 'the development of sociology and its current concerns have to be grasped in the context of changes that have created (it)'. This section, therefore, examines sport sociology as a subdiscipline of sport sciences, and considers its future directions. In the third section, the focus is upon the student of sport and the sports practitioner, demonstrating practical ways in which the study of sport, from a sociological perspective, can inform a wide range of personal goals and understandings.

Social things in sport

Most students of sport, albeit with very different practical and theoretical purposes, will find themselves engaging with disciplinary knowledge in relevant areas of physiology, biomechanics and psychology. In each of these three cases, it is relatively easy to see how the studies undertaken are applicable to the world of sport. Performers, coaches or teachers may even be able to apply such knowledge directly and successfully into a practical context. Unsurprisingly then, those with an interest in enhancing practical performance, at whatever level, tend to raise few questions about the 'point' of such knowledge. But what of sport sociology as part of sport sciences programmes and support services? Why is sociology both relevant and important for the sports student and sports practitioner?

The short answer is that we are, inescapably, social beings, and that sport is, undeniably, a social structure which is intimately connected to other social structures such as the economy, political networks, education, class and global considerations. What happens in the articulation between those broad social structures will have some impact upon each individual's ability to work and to succeed in a chosen sport or sport-related career. Two obvious examples are: the influence of international politics upon performers in elite sport, and the impact of national government policies upon the structure and content of physical education programmes in schools. As Cheffers (1997, p. 4) reminds us, 'no individual is an island', or as Lemert (1997) comments:

> Individuals are who they are only partly because of what they do with what they have. They are also who they are because of what the wider social world gives or takes away.
>
> (1997, pp. xi–xii)

In many ways, Lemert's comment explains both the attraction of natural science sub-disciplines, and the difficulty some sports students, academics, and practitioners have with accepting sociology as a legitimate area of sport sciences. In the natural sciences, the goal is for each individual to learn how to maximize 'what they have'. The implication is that the power to succeed is vested in the individual (as long as they have the biological and psychological potential) if only they will train hard enough and in the correct ways, or manage/coach effectively enough. It is a seductive thought, reflecting both the 'education as science' approach which has largely become the standard for pedagogy and research in the sport sciences (Schempp, 1998), and the generally high esteem in which the natural sciences are held in society (Brooker and Macdonald, 1995). The sociology of sport, on the other hand, tends to focus upon the power of wider social structures to 'give and take away'; a less attractive proposition for two reasons. First, it seems to set limits to the power of natural science research to provide universal 'truths' about sporting performance and participation. This challenges the hegemony of the positivistic approach by suggesting that an individual's chances of success can only be partially explained by such knowledge. Second, and following on logically, sociology highlights the powerlessness of individuals in certain contexts, a particularly difficult concept for many sports people in higher education who, by definition, have been very successful in achieving academic and possibly sporting goals. Unsurprisingly, they wish to take credit for their endeavours, but Lemert (1997, p. 145) reminds us that there is more to consider:

> Some do well and are fortunate; others don't or aren't. But the fortunes we have, or lack, are never *entirely* ours to keep or regret (our emphasis).

Or, as Schempp (1998) points out:

> the identity of an individual is not the fixed property of the individual, but rather a culture commodity whose value and constitution fluctuate in the reality of the socially lived experience.

The missing consideration, then, is that part that social structures have played, and continue to play, in an individual's successes and failures.

Lemert acknowledges that 'social structures' are hard to define, however, he argues that there are four characteristics which they all share and by which they can be recognized: social structures are '(1) organizing, (2) enduring, and (3) generally invisible, but (4) salient, social things we know by their effects' (1997, p. 139). Thus, they can be ignored when things are going well, yet are easy to spot when they constrain us. For example, the gendered structure of professional sport becomes readily apparent to sportswomen who attempt to obtain media coverage of their sport, and to women who are seeking to build their careers in sports organizations; the economic structures of sport intrude when sponsorship is available for some sports people and not others; and the impact of education is seen in the range of sports which have been made available to different individuals as pupils. The examples cited illustrate the power of social structures in all our lives; a dynamic power which Lemert describes thus:

> *Power* is the means by which social structures do this not-exactly-fair work of sorting people according to the few or many life-chances they get. Power may simply, if incompletely, be defined as the social energy of structures. Power is the determining force that causes some people to get less and some more of whatever is considered desirable in a social world.
>
> (1997, p. 129)

The problem, as Lemert (1997) explains, is that such power is not usually experienced directly, but indirectly, and he defines the critical elements of that power as *prestige, authority*, and *class reproduction*. Prestige, in a sporting context, explains why status attaches to some individuals and activities and not to others. Authority is that feature of society which ensures that, more often than not, we respect rules, regulations, norms and etiquette, even if we disagree with them. Clearly, authority is something we would recognize as a defining characteristic of sport. In terms of the class system, and the reproduction of that system, Lemert identifies an interesting paradox:

> The poor actively contribute to the reproduction of the economic and social unfairness of a society when they believe . . . that they are part of the problem. People who suffer from unequal opportunities are committed very early in their lives to the proposition that it is they that are no good, and no good because they cannot accomplish what they are taught to dream of.
>
> (1997, p. 141)

In the world of sport, class reproduction is evidenced by the range and type of sports available to different individuals and, more fundamentally, the impact of inequalities in health status which are still largely class-based, and which affect an individual's motivation and ability to become involved in exercise and sport (for a more detailed discussion on social class and sport see Chapter 6).

At this point, it is important to note that although a sociology of sport focuses upon the power of social structures to influence and order sport, it does not assume that individuals are always powerless. On the contrary, social structures are comprised of individuals who are acting *both as they choose and as they are influenced to choose*. As Lemert (1997) reminds us, 'In our lives we do what we must do, and we do most of what society expects of us' (p. 50). Thus, the power of social structures is experienced as both constraining and enabling (Giddens, 1986) and this dialectic can be readily understood by considering the academic student of sport. Entry into higher education was sometimes expected, sometimes convenient, sometimes surprising. But the value attached to a degree; a value promoted for various reasons by society, and the increasing expectation of a degree as a minimal qualification, were likely factors in the equation – as were each individual's choices about the most enjoyable and effective ways to spend a period of three or four years. A person's choice of sport provides another example. It is very difficult for a young boy to select football as his main sport, if his school teaches only rugby union (Evans and Davies, 1986). Not impossible, but difficult. Furthermore, it is difficult for that boy to succeed in county or representative football unless his parents have the interest and the economic resources to support him. At the same time, the boy's interest, enthusiasm and aptitude for football are powerful factors which must influence the eventual outcome. Substitute 'girl' for 'boy' in the same scenario however, and the whole social equation looks rather different. Essentially then, a key focus of a sociology of sport is an analysis of the actions of individuals which are 'simultaneously a result of the force of social rules and of their own individual flourishes' (Lemert, 1997, pp. 44–45).

Lemert's comprehensive discussion about 'social things' is a helpful starting point in an analysis of the value of a sociology of sport. Perhaps its key message is that we all live sociological lives and that we all possess a degree of, what Lemert terms, 'sociological competence' – indeed societies could not function otherwise. Similarly, Mills (1970) argued that individuals need a 'sociological imagination' in order to understand that personal troubles are often linked to broader public issues. The message from both these perspectives is that sociology is best viewed as, first and foremost, a practical skill. As such, and with study, we may be able to become more competent in our sociologies and, as a result, more able to achieve those goals which are within our possibilities.

A sociology of sport

Having discussed some of the more general social parameters of society and of sport, it seems appropriate to focus upon understanding something of the development of the discipline of sport sociology. Giddens (1986) argues that an understanding of history ought to underpin new developments in any field. For example, it is important to realize that sport sociology is a relatively 'young' discipline, having only been fully recognized as a distinct subdiscipline of sport-related courses since the late 1960s. Sage (1997) charted the development of the discipline from that point. Recognizing the earlier academic analyses of play, sport and games from a variety of other disciplines, and noting papers by two West German scholars who pleaded for a sociology of sport, Sage identifies the paper by Kenyon and Loy (1965) entitled 'Toward a sociology of sport' as a key stage in the discipline's history. Also, at that time, he notes that international sport sociology committees were formed for research and development purposes, and the number of academics working in the field increased too. During the 1970s and 1980s, academic journals devoted to sport sociology were emerging, and articles in the field of sport sociology were appearing in broader physical education and sport science journals. However, Sage reminds us that the first textbooks specifically written for sport sociology courses were not published until the 1970s. Today, there are numerous scholars working in the field, and work which is recognized as of international significance emanates from most regions of the world. For example, the highly regarded North American Society for the Sociology of Sport (NASSS) runs an electronic discussion group, sportsoc. Before it became a victim of its own success, and was restricted to NASSS members in 1997, it had a list of over 400 subscribers from 32 countries. Besides America, there was a particularly strong representation from Canada, Australia and Great Britain.

Although sport sociology has grown rapidly in the last 30 years, it has not always grown smoothly. From its early positivistic orientation, it now embraces a plethora of theoretical and methodological perspectives, with disagreement between academics regarding the 'best' and 'most appropriate' ways to study sport. Indeed Dunning (1992, p. 221) argued that although the discipline is 'multi-paradigmatic', there is a 'near certainty that adherents to different "schools" will misconstrue and perhaps even parody the work of others'. However, Giddens (1986, p. 3) points out that sociology is an 'inherently controversial endeavour', and rather than a sign of immaturity, such disagreements may simply be evidence of one of the defining characteristics of the discipline. What is certain, is that disagreements between proponents of different theoretical approaches abound and are vigorously argued. In the context of this book, one example is interesting. Some sociologists consider that a sociology of sport ought to be more clearly grounded in the theoretical discipline of sociology, while others consider that a focus upon practical application is more important. Rees and

Miracle (1986) sought to overcome this division. They noted that research in sport sociology had been criticized in terms of both its quality and quantity, and also the charge that such research ought to be more clearly grounded in social theory. However, the focus of their work was to 'encourage readers to start their search for answers to questions about sociology of sport from some theoretical perspective' with the ultimate aim of achieving 'wider acceptance of the utility of sociology of sport among sociologists and sport practitioners alike' (1986, p. vii). In other words, they felt that the former would lead to the latter. Arguably, sport sociology has made more progress in the first aim than the second. Research published in the last five years in a broad range of sport science and sport sociology journals indicates an increasing concern with theoretical considerations. Indeed, a general grounding in social theory has become increasingly important for students interested in pursuing studies in the sociology of sport. There are still some questions to be asked, however, about the practical application of sport sociology research.

Luschen, in 1986, argued that 'the topic of the practical uses of sport sociology is not often discussed' (p. 245) and he advocated the development of 'action knowledge' to inform policy and planning in sport-related fields. Yiannakis and Greendorfer (1992) advanced the case for applied research by clarifying the definition of 'applied' as 'providing *solutions* to questions of practical importance, assisting in *changing* behaviour, and contributing to the *amelioration* of the human condition' (p. 11). They also pointed to the need to disseminate research widely and effectively within the sports community. Although the value of an applied approach is queried by some academics (Ingham and Donnelly, 1990; Sage, 1997), specifically upon the grounds that it is in danger of seeking solutions, without first raising critical questions about the problems themselves, the broad principle of application appears to be gaining some ground. Chalip (1992) exhorts sport sociologists to work more closely with the sports community, urging a 'many valued community of scholars who work in collaboration with the persons, groups and communities they study' (p. 259). More recently, Feingold (1997) argued for 'service-based scholarship' in the study of sport. He bases this upon Boyer's (1990) vision of scholars in higher education who ought to:

> think about the usefulness of knowledge, reflect on the social consequences of their work and, in so doing, gain an understanding of how their own study relates to worlds beyond the campus.
>
> (1990, p. 69)

Feingold argues that such an approach must lead to 'integration of the subdisciplines [and] a more holistic view of our commitment' (1997, p. 353). Similarly, in the context of physical education, Martinek and Hellison (1997) advocate 'service-bonded inquiry' to improve physical activity for young people. Such inquiry would be driven by 'a combination of perception, passion and purpose' in scholars who have made a personal commitment to the task. Centrally, they argue that action-based research of this nature must be disseminated widely 'to be shared with practitioners . . . rather than being restricted to high-quality journals read by a few colleagues' (p. 116). Finally, Burt (1998) presented a highly effective conference paper structured along the lines of a hypothetical dialogue between kinesiology (one of the American titles for sport science courses) and the conference theme 'Organizing to meet society's needs'. He used the framework of a dialogue to raise questions about the social responsibility and commitment of the academic study of sport. During the course of the dialogue, it is suggested that, from the perspective of the broader society, kinesiology is too narrowly conceived in rigidly separated subdisciplines, too concerned with its own internal differences, and that it is often divorced from the central missions of the universities within which it operates – that mission being 'the elevation of humanity and human existence' (1998, p. 84). Kinesiology is urged, instead, to focus upon the quality of the practitioners it produces – in all relevant fields, and to reconsider both its commitment to societal problems, and its power to address and solve them. Using the examples of premature death, depression, well-being, the compression of morbidity and violence, the suggestion is made that kinesiology has untapped potential to contribute to overcoming real life problems. Instead, Burt argues, it has remained rigidly and narrowly conceived with academics 'teaching what interests them without regard to what's good for the future of the field' (p. 83).

These are strong charges, and they will no doubt influence future debate in sport sciences. However, there are also other important theoretical and practical considerations. For example, Hargreaves (1994) argues that theoretical analysis in sport sociology has too often ignored the experiences of women:

> a common characteristic of the various sport sociology perspectives is the marginal- ization of women's experiences and relationships of gender. In this respect, the history of sports sociology reflects the long history of male domination of modern sports and the dominant ideas about sexual difference.

> (1994, p. 7)

As another example, Dunning (1992) draws upon the work of Norbert Elias to present the case for a 'figurational' approach in the sociology of sport. He describes figurational, or process sociology, as one which focuses upon the 'interdependency chains and networks formed by acting human beings' (p. 242). Jarvie and Maguire (1994) summarize its scope as being based on the principles that:

> human beings are interdependent; . . . their lives evolve in the figurations they form with each other; . . . these figurations are continually in flux, undergoing changes of different orders, some quick and superficial, others slower but perhaps more endur- ing; and . . . the long-term developments taking place in figurations have been and continue to be largely unplanned and unforeseen.

> (1994, p. 130)

A practical example of such a process is provided by Waddington and Murphy (1992) in an analysis of the use of drugs in sport. They argue that the increased use of drugs by sportsmen and women can only be understood by reference to a complex chain of net- works and relationships in sport – ranging from the links between medicine and sport to the politicization and commercialization of sport. Jarvie and Maguire (1994) reinforce this notion of interdependency further when they point to the increasing impact of globaliza- tion processes upon sport. They argue that 'Every aspect of social reality – people's living conditions, beliefs, knowledge and actions – is intertwined with unfolding globalization processes' (p. 230). Thus, they caution against the use of 'monocausal explanations' for social phenomena (Maguire, 1994), reinforcing Lemert's (1997, p. xi) contention that we live in a 'complex social web'.

Looking ahead to the future of sport sociology, Sage (1997, p. 131) cites the 'growing community of scholars' and the 'growing popular and scholarly literature' as evidence of its advance as an academic discipline. Importantly, however, there is an increasing recog- nition among sport sociologists that issues about the relevance and application of sport sociology must be explicitly addressed, a factor which might be indicative of the 'coming of age' of the discipline. What is also certain, however, is that such advances in practical understandings must be accompanied by a range of theoretical advances. Jarvie and Maguire (1994, p. 258) identify the need for 'historical analysis combined with fruitful theorizing, but also a tighter fit between theory and evidence'. At times, it may be that the development of theory leads to new insights into practice. At other times, it is possible that new understandings about practice will stimulate theoretical development. In order to succeed in any practical goals, sport sociologists will need to be concerned with both.

But what of the student of sport, and of the sociology of sport? Burt (1998) argues that in higher education, 'Faculty exist to advance and impart the kind of knowledge that will result in high-quality practitioners' (p. 83). That being the case, how can the discipline of sociology of sport contribute to the eventual development of high-quality practitioners in sports performance/participation, coaching, teaching, administration, etc? How can practitioners, and the communities within which they practise, benefit from a sociology of sport?

You and the sociology of sport

The final task of this chapter is to consider the practical relevance of the sociology of sport to you, the reader, as practitioner. As someone who is interested in the study of sport, it is likely that you are, or hope to be, one or more of the following: a sports performer, a recreational sports participant, a coach, a physical education teacher, a sports manager/ administrator, an academic or, perhaps, just an avid televised sports fan. Given the range of your interests, experiences and aspirations, how can the study of the sociology of sport help you to achieve goals for yourself and for the wider community? The answers will undoubtedly lie in the chapters which follow, however, three examples are discussed here briefly. In each case, an example of some recent sociological research is used as an illustration.

The coach

Although coaching studies or, more recently, 'coaching science' as an area of investigation has largely developed along bio-scientific fragmentary lines, there is increasing evidence that the most successful professionals are not only technically and intellectually competent, but are also multiskilled, creative and adaptable, 'while practising in a socially responsible way' (MacDonald and Brooker, 1995, p. 99). Similarly, it is also increasingly acknowledged that the coaching process is vulnerable to differing pressures and constraints, including those which are ideological, institutional, cultural, ethical and national in nature (Cross, 1995). Such a growing awareness of the influence of social and cultural factors within the coaching domain, in effect putting the person before the body, is making it increasingly important for new and established practitioners to take account of such forces if the potentialities of individual athletes and teams are to be fully realized.

A review paper by Woodman (1993) draws upon the work of Dyer (1992) to summarize the essential nature of coaching:

> [He] demonstrates many areas in which the coaches' knowledge of sociocultural factors is vital to their effectiveness. He believes that the bond between athlete and coach is of primary importance, and that consideration of sociocultural factors is an appropriate extension of the coach's role. In the interest of improving performance, the effective coach will take into account a wide range of factors operating before and after competition.
>
> (1993, p. 9)

In effect, Woodman and Dyer are arguing that each coaching situation is a specific environment that requires the coach to take into account the unique factors of that environment if success is to be achieved. Such a view is echoed by the work of Douge and Hastie (1993), who similarly conclude that 'effective leadership qualities may be unique to a social fabric or situation' (p. 20). Schempp (1998) has explored and developed a rationale for this theme further, stating that 'our social worlds offer no immunity to sport fields or gymnasia (and that) actions, beliefs, traditions and perspectives that define how we live in the world also define how we live and learn in sport'. If the influences of such defining factors are not fully acknowledged, there is a tendency to routinize high-level social communicative tasks, leading to the de-skilling of the practitioner both in terms of cognitive and human interaction (MacDonald and Tinning, 1995). One effect of this is the development of mechanistic coaches all primed with the same knowledge, but finding it difficult to adapt that knowledge to the ever-changing complexities of the human environment. A sociological perspective, on the other hand, reminds coaches and teachers that the sociocultural dynamics which shape identities in the wider society also impinge upon teaching/coaching and learning in sport, and ultimately upon the ability to perform well. Indeed, it is only the individual who understands social settings in a thoroughly practical way who can possibly mediate tensions and overcome difficulties (Lemert, 1997). Viewed in this way, sport sociology knowledge is that knowledge which empowers coaches to act intellectually and reflexively, to critically evaluate information from a range of interested parties, and to take responsibility for decisions affecting their athletes (see also Chapter 3).

The teacher of physical education

The influence of the broad structure of politics upon the work of the individual physical education teacher is clearly illustrated by reference to the National Curriculum (NC) in England and Wales. The document *Physical Education in the National Curriculum* (DFE, 1995) provided the legal framework for all physical education taught in state schools. However, sociological research alerted teachers to the need to view that framework as a text which privileges one particular view of education and physical education; a view which might not be in the interests of all pupils. Penney and Evans (1997) argue that:

> the needs and interests of the economy (of capital accumulation) rather than children and teachers have taken precedence in the development of a national curriculum for state schools in England and Wales, in an endeavour to nurture particular forms of 'citizenship', skilling and social control.
>
> (1997, p. 21)

In a range of research papers examining the development and structure of the national curriculum for physical education (NCPE), these researchers raise important questions about the nature of physical education knowledge as it is represented in national curriculum texts, and about the process which led to the development of that curriculum. For example, during the consultation process within the physical education profession, and between the government and the profession, a number of ideological difficulties arose which have impacted upon the final curriculum. As Evans and Penney (1995) point out:

> The texts of the NCPE therefore embed a set of compromises and adaptation, containing elements of progressivism and restoration which together may subsequently pose either problems or possibilities for teachers in schools. Even as a Statutory Order, the text of the NCPE remains only a frame, in an important sense independent of the material conditions that constrain and make possible forms of social and cultural reproduction in schools.
>
> (1995, p. 42)

Penney and Evans (1997) also examine the links between the NCPE document and another government document related to sport: *Sport – Raising the Game* (Department of National Heritage, 1995). The purpose of this latter document was to promote sport at all levels in the community. However, as Penney and Evans point out, it is elite sport and 'traditional' sport which appear to be at the forefront of government thinking. For example, the document highlights the importance of competitive team games at the school level. Furthermore, taken in conjunction with the NCPE, it becomes clear that teachers are facing a powerful structural influence upon their thinking, both ideologically and legally. For example, *Sport – Raising the Game* (DNH, 1995) advocates closer links between physical education departments and local sports clubs. However, although this may have some advantages, Penney and Evans comment:

> Our fear is that the emphasis on 'coaching' and links with clubs may together presage an emphasis on sport performance and the needs of the able few.
>
> (1997, p. 28)

Penney and Evans (1997) acknowledge that teachers are 'not automatons or mere puppets' (p. 28) and that they will interpret policy as they see fit. However, the value of this research lies in the questions which it raises and the focus which it provides for a critical analysis of policy in the best interests of the pupil:

> Whilst not wishing to dismiss or temper any interest in sport in schools, we would encourage all to ask exactly what the government is providing support for, who is this support directed to, why the particular direction is being taken, and what the consequences of these initiatives will be for the identities and opportunities of children in schools.
>
> (1997, pp. 28–9)

If you are to become a fully professional teacher of physical education, you will be keen to analyse and interpret influential policy documents, from whatever source, in the interests of all your pupils. The wide range of views and standpoints emerging from sociological research in physical education can help to inform that analytical process and the resulting practice (see also Chapter 5).

The sports manager/administrator

Two important research papers about Canadian sport organizations, published in 1989, raised a number of issues about gender. The issues raised are of direct concern to women who are planning a career in sports organizations, and to men and women who have an interest in, or responsibility for, implementing equal opportunities in sport-related employment. The first paper by Whitson and MacIntosh (1989) is based on case study research which sought to determine why women were underrepresented in senior technical, administrative and volunteer positions in national sport organizations. The first hurdle the researchers faced was to find female interviewees who were employed at a decision-making level of responsibility. In the end, one third of the respondents was female. Whitson and MacIntosh's findings indicate that the main problem for women lies in the broader 'politics of gender'. This was illustrated by the endurance and influence of stereotypical views in the broader society about male and female abilities in employment. In particular, there were strong beliefs among respondents that women are hampered by family responsibilities which prevent them from making a full contribution to the workplace. Furthermore, they are unable, or unwilling, to gain the required qualifications to progress in, for example, coaching.

The second paper, by Hall, Cullen and Slack (1989) also looked at the gender structure of national sport organizations, and the underrepresentation of women, focusing upon the possibilities for a change to a more equitable gender balance. The researchers sought to understand 'the processes and dynamics which structure gender in organizations' and, like the previous paper, they used interviews as the main source of data. Their conclusions about the power structures in sports organizations are sobering for individuals who hope for organizational change:

> We need to understand this intermingling of power, sexuality and structure much more clearly before we can suggest, and observe, effective attempts at change . . . We hypothesise that as sport organisations become increasingly bureaucratised, and more of the decision-making authority is assumed by professionals, the role of women (in terms of memberships, professionals, volunteers, coaches and officials) will be adversely affected. The organisation itself will see no need to initiate any sort of affirmative action program or structure to address the needs of women, and will co-opt or subvert any requirement that it do so.
>
> (1989, p. 42)

The findings from these papers are equally applicable to women in the UK, an indication, perhaps, of the increasingly global nature of social structures. Thus, for the aspiring career woman in sports organizations, it raises important questions such as: What is the power structure of the organization I am hoping to enter? How are decisions taken? What are the criteria for promotion – are there any available for examination? Is there an unwritten expectation of a time commitment beyond the recognized hours? Are there any female role-models in positions of power? Will I need to be exceptional to progress in my job – do I want to be? (see also Chapters 4 and 10).

The sociological research proves that difficulties are likely to be faced by women in sports organizations, and it demonstrates that the problem lies both within and beyond the social structure of sport. Armed with such information, women can enter the workplace with a more focused understanding of the constraints and opportunities they will encounter.

Conclusion

This book is all about social living and about the practical ways in which a sociology of sport can help those trying to work, study, or perform in the social world that is sport. Sport sociology knowledge may be less obvious in its application than some other sub-disciplines of the sport sciences. Upon analysis, however, it becomes apparent that it is fundamentally rooted in practical concerns which have both direct and indirect impacts upon individuals' lives and careers. Lemert (1997) identifies the ultimate practical question as 'what must I know, feel and believe in order to act in ways which will make life better for me and mine, and more just for all?' (p. 156). The answer may lie in developing, refining and exercising sociological competencies so that individuals are better able to deal with the challenging, practical issues to be faced in sport and beyond.

Finally, having used Lemert's (1997) dynamic understanding of sociology as a framework at the beginning of the chapter, it seems appropriate to allow him the last word:

> Social living is the courage to accept what we cannot change in order to do what can be done about the rest.
>
> (1997, p. 191)

In the following chapters, this book seeks to provide specific examples of 'what can be done about the rest'.

References

● Boyer E. (1990) *Scholarship Reconsidered: Priorities of the Professorate*, Princeton, NJ: The Carnegie Foundation.
● Brooker R. and Macdonald D. (1995) 'Mapping physical education in the reform agenda for Australian education: Tensions and contradictions', *European Physical Education Review* 1(2): 101–10.
● Burt J.J. (1998) 'The role of kinesiology in elevating modern society', *Quest* 50: 80–95.
● Chalip L. (1992) 'Rethinking the applied social sciences of sport: Observations on the emerging debate', in A. Yiannakis and S. Greendorfer (eds) *Applied Sociology of Sport*, Champaign, Ill.: Human Kinetics, pp. 257–64.
● Cheffers J. (1997) 'No man is an island', *AIESEP Conference Proceedings*, Singapore, December, p. 4.
● Cross N. (1995) 'Coaching effectiveness in hockey: A Scottish perspective', *Scottish Journal of Physical Education* 23(1): 27–39.
● DFE (1995) *Physical Education in the National Curriculum*, London: HMSO.
● DNH (1995) *Sport – Raising the Game*, London: Department of National Heritage, DNHJ0096NJ.July 1995.70M.
● Douge B. and Hastie P. (1993) 'Coach effectiveness', *Sport Science Review* 2(2): 14–29.
● Dunning E. (1992) 'Figurational sociology and the sociology of sport: Some concluding remarks', in E. Dunning and C. Rojek (eds) *Sport and Leisure in the Civilising Process*, London: Macmillan, pp. 221–84.
● Dyer K. (1992) 'Sociocultural influences on athletic performance', *New Studies in Athletics* 7(4): 7–12.
● Evans J. and Davies B. (1986) 'Sociology, schooling and physical education', in J. Evans (ed.) *Physical Education, Sport and Schooling*, London: Falmer Press, pp. 11–37.
● Evans J. and Penney D. (1995) 'The politics of pedagogy: Making a National Curriculum Physical Education', *Journal of Education Policy* 10(1): 27–44.
● Feingold R.S. (1997) 'Service-based scholarship: An introduction', *Quest* 49: 351–4.
● Giddens A. (1986) *Sociology: A Brief but Critical Introduction*, 2nd edn, London: Macmillan.
● Hall A., Cullen D. and Slack T. (1989) 'Organisational elites recreating themselves: The gender structure of national sport organizations', *Quest* 41: 28–45.
● Hargreaves J. (1994) *Sporting Females*, London: Routledge.
● Ingham A.G. and Donnelly P. (1990) 'Whose knowledge counts? The production of knowledge and issues of application in the sociology of sport', *Sociology of Sport Journal* 7: 58–65.
● Jarvie G. and Maguire J. (1994) *Sport and Leisure in Social Thought*, London: Routledge.
● Kenyon G.S. and Loy J.W. (1965) 'Toward a sociology of sport', *Journal of Health, Physical Education and Recreation* 36: 24–5, 68–9.
● Lemert C. (1997) *Social Things. An Introduction to the Sociological Life*, New York: Rowman and Littlefield.
● Luschen G. (1986) 'The practical uses of a sociology of sport: Some methodological issues', in C.R. Rees and A.W. Miracle (eds) *Sport and Social Theory*, Champaign, Ill.: Human Kinetics, pp. 245–54.
● MacDonald D. and Brooker R. (1995) 'Professional education: Tensions in subject design and implementation', *Educational Research and Perspectives* 22(2): 99–109.
● MacDonald D. and Tinning R. (1995) 'Physical education teacher education and the trend to proletarianization: A case study', *Journal of Teaching in Physical Education* 15: 98–118.
● Maguire J. (1994) 'Sport, identity politics and globilization: Diminishing contrasts and increasing varieties', *Sociology of Sport Journal* 11(4): 398–427.

● Martinek T. and Hellison D. (1997) 'Service-bonded inquiry: The road less travelled', *Journal of Teaching in Physical Education* 17: 107–21.
● Mills C.W. (1970) *The Sociological Imagination*, Harmondsworth: Penguin.
● Penney D. and Evans J. (1997) 'Naming the game: Discourse domination in physical education and sport in England and Wales', *European Physical Education Review* 3(1): 21–32.
● Rees C.R. and Miracle A.W. (eds) (1986) *Sport and Social Theory*, Champaign, Ill.: Human Kinetics.
● Sage G.H. (1997) 'Sport Sociology', in J.D. Massengale and R.A. Swanson (eds) *The History of Exercise and Sport Science*, Champaign, Ill.: Human Kinetics, pp. 109–42.
● Schempp P. (1998) 'The dynamics of human diversity in sport pedagogy scholarship', *Sociology of Sport Online* 1(1). Available: http://www.brunel.ac.uk/depts/sps/sosol/sosol.htm (June 22, 1998).
● Waddington I. and Murphy P. (1992) 'Drugs, sport and ideologies', in E. Dunning and C. Rojek (eds) *Sport and Leisure in the Civilizing Process*, London: Macmillan, pp. 36–64.
● Whitson D. and MacIntosh D. (1989) 'Gender and power: Explanations of gender inequalities in Canadian national sports organizations', *International Review for the Sociology of Sport* 24(2): 137–50.
● Woodman L. (1993) 'Coaching: A science, an art, an emerging profession', *Sport Science Review* 2(2): 1–13.
● Yiannakis A. and Greendorfer S. (eds) (1992) *Applied Sociology of Sport*, Champaign, Ill.: Human Kinetics.

Chapter Two

Illness, Premature Career-termination, and the Loss of Self: A Biographical Study of an Elite Athlete

Andrew C. Sparkes

Introduction

According to Drahota and Eitzen (1998), the role transition of athletes to a new career has presented a challenge to sociologists of sport; 'We know that this is a difficult time for athletes because they *lose* what has been the focus of their being for most of their lives, the primary source of their identities, the physical prowess, the adulation bordering on worship from others, the money and the prerequisites of fame, the camaraderie with team-mates, and the intense "highs" of competition' (p. 263). With the growing academic interest in career transition issues among athletes, Grove, Lavallee, Gordon and Harvey (1998) suggest that, during the last 30 years, a growing body of empirical and theoretical research has emerged that focuses on the factors involved in the process of disengaging from elite-level sport. Unfortunately, as Lavallee *etl al.* (1998) note, even though the sport-scientific community has become increasingly interested in career transitions and the concept of symbolic loss, this phenomenon 'remains poorly understood, frequently over-looked, and generally mismanaged' (p. 241).

The issue of loss is often dramatically highlighted when an elite athlete experiences an injury or illness that prematurely terminates their sporting career. For Lavallee *et al.* (1998), one of the most common forms of symbolic losses experienced by injured athletes was the loss of some aspect of the self. In this sense, athletic injury can be a source of 'biographical disruption' (Bury, 1982) that interrupts the narrative coherence of a person's life (Sparkes, 1996a, 1999). For many athletes, in these circumstances, the integrity of the self is assaulted and threatened, earlier taken-for-granted assumptions about possessing a smoothly functioning body are shaken, previous assumptions about the relationships between body and self are disturbed, and the sense of wholeness of body and self is disrupted. Consequently, for some, the sense of self is undermined and various identity dilemmas are initiated. This is particularly so when, as Kleiber, Brock, Youngkhill, Dattilo and Cadwell (1995) point out, negative life events disrupt the ability to engage in preferred activities that have special relevance to a person's identity.

Talking of injured college athletes who shaped their life narrative exclusively around the body's performance in sport, Brock and Kleiber (1994) emphasized that, although any future self imaginable had a body, the importance of that body varied greatly from one life story to the next. For example, the life story in which the future self was envisioned as a successful parent was likely to differ markedly in the extent of concern with embodied performance from the life story that envisioned a future for the body engaged in a professional sport. This is particularly so when individuals ascribed a great deal of psychological significance to their involvement in sport and developed a strong athletic identity.

Athletic identity: An Achilles heel to the survival of self

In their overview of the experience of loss in sport, Lavallee *et al.* (1998) proposed that athletic identity played a major role in the experience of symbolic loss in competitive sport. According to Brewer, Van Raalte and Linder (1993), and Wiechman and Williams (1997), athletic identity is the degree to which an individual identifies with the athlete role. They note that a person with a strong athletic identity was more likely to interpret a given event in terms of its implications for that individual's athletic functioning than a person who only identified weakly with the athlete role. Based upon a review of the literature, Brewer *et al.* (1993) suggested that there were both positive and negative consequences associated with a strong athletic identity, so that it could act as either 'Hercules' muscles' or an 'Achilles heel'. The potential benefits included the development of a salient self-identity or sense of self, positive effects on athletic performance, and a greater likelihood of long-term involvement in exercise behaviours. In contrast, the potential risks for individuals with a strong athletic identity related to the difficulties they might encounter in sport career transitions such as being deselected, injured, or reaching the end of their playing careers. For example, a strong, exclusive athletic identity was thought to be a risk factor for emotional disturbance upon termination of an athletic career, because individuals with this kind of identity were less likely to explore other career, education, and lifestyle options due to their intensive involvement and commitment to sport. Such 'role engulfment' (Adler and Adler, 1991; Wiechman and Williams, 1997) and premature 'identity foreclosure' (Good, Brewer, Petitpas, Van Raalte and Mahar, 1993) create conditions that might lead to a crisis for the athlete upon retirement, particularly a forced retirement due, for example, to a career-ending injury or illness.

Further support for this position comes from a series of studies designed by Brewer (1993) to test the hypothesis that experiencing an athletic injury as a disruptive life event in the pursuit of self-defining activities would be associated with depressed mood. His findings confirmed that a strong and exclusive identification with the athlete role was related to the individual's depressive response to both hypothetical and actual athletic injury. Likewise, Leddy, Lambert and Ogles (1994) found in their study of the psychological consequences of athletic injury among high-level competitors, that injured athletes exhibited greater depression and anxiety and lower self-esteem than controls immediately following physical injury and at follow-up two months later. They believed that their findings supported the general observation that physically injured athletes experience a period of emotional distress that, in some cases, may be severe enough to warrant clinical intervention. Finally, Grove, Lavallee and Gordon (1997), in their study of how athletic identity shaped the experiences of career transition for 48 former elite-level athletes, suggest that their bivariate correlation results 'indicated that individuals who maintain a strong and exclusive identity up to the point of retirement may be vulnerable to career transition difficulties' (p. 198). The view that injuries are extremely disruptive to the sense of self for those who hold a strong athletic identity, particularly when the athlete lacks other sources of self-worth and self-identification, also has support from more qualitative and sociologically framed studies on the experiences of elite athletes who sustain career-threatening or career-ending injury (Brock and Kleiber, 1994; Sparkes, 1996a; Young and White, 1995; Young, White and McTeer, 1994).

In this chapter I want to explore the experiences of one elite athlete whose career was prematurely terminated by an illness. The data presented from this biographical study are intended to illuminate the complex ways in which a strong athletic identity can act as an Achilles heel in terms of shaping both an individual's reactions to a disruptive life event and the consequences of these reactions for personal long-term development. The analysis reveals how, as an individual descends from the heights of the extraordinary into the mundane world of ordinariness, the loss of certain selves enforces a heightened reflexivity and awareness of previously taken-for-granted aspects of the body–self relationship that are no longer attainable. The manner in which certain selves, at the apex of an identity hierarchy, exert pressure on the individual to seek a restored self, rather than opt for more attainable or realistic identities, is highlighted. The problems of restorying the self when an individual is constrained by limited narrative resources are also examined. Finally, some implications of the findings from this biographical study for coaches, teachers, administrators and health care professionals in general are considered.

The participant

Rachael (a pseudonym) is a physical education student in her early twenties. Compared to the 'average' member of the population, Rachael is physically very fit. She is captain of the university swimming team, training and competing with them on a regular basis. Rachael looks healthy. Her body, however, tells a different story. The long scars on her lower back, the limp when she is tired, the depression, and the tears shed, all provide a different script.

Born into a family in the North of England, Rachael has two sisters and one brother. Her mother was a physical education teacher, her father was a keen rugby player, and participation in sport has been a central feature of family life for as long as Rachael could remember. From an early age, Rachael's body began to be noticed and acknowledged in performance terms. For example, on entry into secondary school at the age of 11, she recalled winning the first cross-country race her class undertook and how, following this, in a biology lesson her teacher said in front of the class, 'Rachael, you got the fastest time ever by a first year and you haven't even come to practices. You *must* come'. From then on, Rachael became heavily involved in a variety of school sports as a strong athletic identity began to be constructed.

Rachael began riding at the age of 10. However, eventing is not allowed in England until the age of 16, so she devoted her attention to the tetrathalon, an event involving shooting, running, swimming, and riding. Accordingly, she described her weekly schedule between the ages of 12 to 18 as follows: Monday: Swim; Tuesday: Run (at the track); Wednesday: Swim or gymnastics; Thursday: Swim; Friday: Run (at home), shoot; Saturday: Swim/dance; Sunday: Competition (either horses or tetrathalon – shoot, swim, ride, and run); Every day: Ride horses for an hour, muck out and feed horses.

When she was 13 years old, Rachael was ranked eleventh in the country for the under 21 age group in the tetrathalon, and one year she came in seventh at the national championships. As Rachael got older she began to be successful in horse trials, and her attention turned more and more to this event. As part of this process, numerous hours were spent training the body to develop specific skills and enhance its performance capacities.

Several years ago Rachael was competing at the national level as a horse rider in 3-day eventing and had aspirations to ride for her country in the Olympics. However, since the age of 14, Rachael recalled experiencing a back problem where her pelvis and back felt 'very clustered' and extreme pain was caused by sciatica, 'I couldn't sleep at night because I just had this massive pain down my leg all the time. They [doctors] put it down to growing pains, or circulatory problems'. During her second year at university, the pain got so intense that Rachael confronted her local doctor who still refused to send her to see a specialist. Eventually, Rachael's parents paid for a private consultation with a specialist who sent her for a scan, which revealed a tumour 'the size of a grapefruit' at the base of her spine. Rachael's initial reaction was one of relief.

> It was almost a relief. Like, there was actually something wrong that can be fixed. I was worried that if it was something like a slipped disc that I wouldn't be able to ride. I went home and I casually told my parents, 'Well, at least I'll be able to ride once its gone'. Which was a bit of a silly thing to say really . . . Tumour, get rid of it, fight it, get on with life.

Unfortunately, things did not go to script. Surgical complications arose following the first operation two years ago to remove the tumour, which led to four more visits to the operating theatre. In addition, Rachael contracted meningitis during her stay in the hospital. The effect of the tumour on her hip girdle and lumbar spine makes it unlikely that she will ever compete as a rider at the top level again or jump horses without putting herself at great risk of permanent disability. Not surprisingly, the tumour, and its consequences, formed an epiphany or major turning point in Rachael's life. For Denzin (1989a), epiphanies are interactional moments and experiences which leave their mark on people's lives. They are often associated with moments of crisis that shatter a person's life and alter its fundamental meaning structures. As Rachael commented:

> This has been the biggest thing in my life, although I am only just appreciating it now . . . It's no good just riding horses out and looking after them, it's just so tame . . . I feel like I have lost my identity. I was a horse rider through and through, and I felt so at home when I was competing . . . I lived, ate, and breathed horses. Anything could go wrong and it just didn't seem to matter so long as I had the horse 'on the road' . . . I do wish that I could feel grateful for my lot, but I don't. It's no use pretending that life goes on, and there is more to life than horses, because in my opinion there isn't.

For the last two years the multiple meanings of this epiphany and its impact upon her life have been explored by Rachael and myself in a collaborative fashion.

Methodology

The broad methodological perspective underlying this study is that of symbolic interactionism and, more specifically, the development of this tradition by Denzin (1989a, 1989b) in the form of interpretive interactionism and interpretive biography. According to Denzin (1989a), the biographical method is the 'studied use and collection of life documents that describe turning point moments in an individual's life' (p. 69). For Denzin, interpretive interactionism refers to attempts to make the world of problematic lived experience of ordinary people directly available to the reader. He notes that the interactionist interprets these worlds by attempting to live his or her way into the lives of those involved in order to see the world, and its problems, as they are seen by the people who live inside them. In this process, a variety of research methods can be called upon. Accordingly, Mohr (1997) states that interpretive interactionism is a multiperspectival, qualitative research method that attempts to study the whole person in their historico/sociocultural and biological context by utilizing theoretical concepts from a variety of disciplines.

At a superficial level, I had already lived my way into Rachael's life in my role as her personal tutor during her time at the university and as someone who lectured to her on various courses as part of her degree studies. Following her second year at university, Rachael took a year out for 'medical reasons'. At the time, I did not know what these were but knew they must be serious for Rachael to interrupt her studies. On her return the next academic year, during the usual personal tutor–student meetings that took place at the start of term, she hinted at the seriousness of her illness and stated that it had put an end to her sporting aspirations in the domain of horse riding. At that time, I was developing my theoretical interest on interrupted body projects and the self (Sparkes, 1996a, 1996b, 1997, 1999). I outlined these interests to Rachael and invited her to take part in a series of interviews that would explore her experiences prior to, during, and after her illness.

During the same meeting, we also discussed the ethical principles that would undergird the process should Rachael agree to become involved. These included the following: the content of the interviews would be confidential; the interviews would be audiotaped; the only person to listen to the audiotapes of the interview and transcribe them would be me; it would be Rachael's decision at the end of the project as to whether the audiotapes were returned to her, wiped clean by myself, or remained with me for future analysis and reanalysis as part of an archive I hoped to develop on athletes' experiences of injury; that in any writing undertaken by me, Rachael, and any person named by her, would be given pseudonyms in order to protect their identity; that Rachael would see drafts of any paper written for public consumption in order to check on the accuracy of the data presented and the fairness of my interpretation; the publication of data would only take place after Rachael had completed her degree and left the university; finally, it was made clear that Rachael was free to terminate an individual interview, or the whole series, without the need to give any explanation to me and that such an action would have no effect on her university career or future employment. We agreed that Rachael should have time to think about my invitation and that I would contact her after two weeks to get her decision. When contacted, Rachael agreed to become involved in the project.

During the next two years, I interviewed Rachael nine times (18 hours in total). Each interview took place in my office at the university. As suggested by Wolcott (1995), the first interview began with a 'grand tour' question in which I invited Rachael to tell me something about herself. With this as a starting point, life course stages and experiences were explored in an open-ended manner as issues and themes emerged from her life story in relation to pivotal events. During the interviews, I had no desire to position myself as a detached, disinterested, and objective outsider, and I attempted to adopt the creative role of 'active listener'. As Wolcott (1995) explained, this implies taking an interactive role in order to make a more effective speaker out of the person talking.

Following Denzin (1989a), I took the interviews to be a process in which two people creatively and openly shared experiences with one another in a mutual search for greater self-understanding. As an active listener, therefore, I shared my experiences where I deemed it to be appropriate and when I was invited to do so. For example, I have my own personal experiences of having once inhabited a highly skilled, performing body that developed a chronic back problem which prematurely ended a promising sports career (Sparkes, 1996a). Often, these experiences were shared with Rachael during our interviews as I reacted to issues raised by her. This sharing of stories and insights into the lives of each other reduced the distance between us as lecturer and student as we became less and less protected by these roles. Consequently, as with another student I collaborated with on a different issue (Sparkes, 1994a, 1994b, 1998), each of us became more vulnerable to the other due to the insider knowledge that was gained and this helped us to develop a trusting relationship that formed the basis of our collaboration. As Denzin (1989a) pointed out, 'To listen only, without sharing, creates distrust' (p. 43).

Each interview in the series was audiotaped and transcribed by me in my role as academic researcher before the next interview took place. This allowed me to identify issues and themes as they emerged in Rachael's interpretation of events, and these were then reflected upon at subsequent interviews. As part of this process, Rachael also undertook several pieces of writing that focused upon the meanings of events associated with her illness and its influence upon her life. These pieces ranged in length from three sides of A4 paper single-spaced and typed to a more substantial piece that amounted to 50 sides of double-spaced typed text. Once again, these written pieces formed a resource for discussion in our meetings and have stimulated both of us to further reflect about our own lives in relation to each other. Following Brock and Kleiber's (1994) research on injured collegiate athletes, this process focused primarily upon Rachael's illness experience rather than her injury experience. They suggested that the sport injury is an experience for many, and engaged the athlete with physicians, coaches, and trainers. Stories told about this issue were seen to depict detailed attention to significant others, to the rupture of physiology (the injury) and to its treatment. In contrast, the illness – the rupture in the athlete's life narrative – as described in an illness narrative, was an experience for the athlete alone. While at times it is difficult to separate the two in an analytical sense, it is the latter that greatly affects an individual's sense of self and how they react and give meaning to the situation.

Data analysis and interpretation

According to Stake (1995), 'There is no particular moment when the data analysis begins. Analysis is a matter of giving meaning to first impressions as well as final compilations. Analysis essentially means taking something apart. We take our impressions, our observations, apart' (p. 71). Furthermore, even though some (e.g., Wolcott, 1994) have argued that analysis and interpretation are separate stages of the research process, I find it difficult to specify the moments in this biographical study when analysis finished and interpretation began. This is not surprising given the inductive approach to data analysis that was used.

Having transcribed an interview, I assumed the posture of indwelling as described by Maykut and Morehouse (1994). This entailed reading through the transcript several times in order to immerse myself in the data and understand Rachael's point of view from an empathetic rather than a sympathetic position. Next, I read though the transcript and identified narrative segments and categories within it. While I was doing this, I also wrote analytical memos as I made preliminary and tentative connections to various theoretical concepts that I thought might be related to the issues emerging from Rachael's narrative. The analytical memos along with the coding helped shape the questions and themes that were raised at the next interview as part of a cyclic process. The same procedure was applied to the pieces of reflective writing that Rachael undertook. As the interviews progressed and data were accumulated, I searched for connections across narrative segments and themes in an attempt to identify patterns and meanings as they emerged in Rachael's story.[1]

Interpretation, Wolcott (1994) suggests, is when the researcher 'transcends factual data and cautious analysis and begins to probe into what is being made of them' (p. 36). Here, as Cresswell (1998) notes, the researcher reconstructs the individual's biography and identifies factors that have shaped the life. Following this, an analytic abstraction of the case is produced that highlights the processes in the individual's life, the different theories that relate to these life experiences, and the unique and general features of the life. As part of this probing and reconstruction, three frameworks initially informed and shaped my interpretation.

First, there is the work of Charmaz (1987) on the struggles for self during chronic illness and the manner in which people aspired to maintain or regain preferred identities (identity goals) within specific identity hierarchies. Identity levels are the implicit or explicit objectives for personal and/or social identity that chronically ill people aim to realize and they reflect the kinds of self the person wishes to shape or select. Charmaz notes that particular individuals aimed towards different preferred identities representing different identity levels during specific phases of their illness and at particular points in their biographies. Various identity levels that together formed the hierarchy of preferred identities were categorized by Charmaz according to their relative difficulty of attainment and the scope of activity implied within them. These are as follows:

- The *supernormal identity* level assumes success, values social acclamation and struggle in a competitive world. Persons aiming for this identity level often attempt to participate more intensely in conventional worlds than nonimpaired others, despite the serious limitations their conditions impose.

- The *restored self* means the identity level in which ill persons expect to return to their former lives. Those pursuing it take for granted that this is the normal course of events, the natural sequence of even serious illness. People who aim for this identity level, not only aim to reconstruct a similar physical self as before, but also to assume continuity with the self before illness.

- A *contingent personal identity* is the identity level ill individuals define as questionable, but perhaps possible, in the future. Thus, from the start, they define risk and possible failure. These ill people typically first pursued a supernormal identity or a restored self but failed to realise it before they aimed for a contingent personal identity.

- A *salvaged self* is the identity level in which ill persons attempt to define self as positive and worthwhile, despite their reduced ability to function. They attempt to cast themselves in the best light possible despite the adverse circumstances of their present existence. By this time, they hold little hope of realizing typical adult identities in the outer world. They have become invalids.

(Charmaz, 1987, p. 287)

The second framing device for my interpretation of Rachael's experiences came from the five-stage model of dramatic self-change proposed by Athens (1995).

First, people must witness firsthand the splintering of their own selves during the fragmentation stage. In the second or provisionality stage, they must desperately struggle at assembling new, unified selves to replace the former ones that split apart. If this challenge is not enough, they must then somehow summon the courage and conviction to subject their newly unified selves to the 'test of experience' during the praxis stage. Should their newly unified selves withstand this test, then people must patiently await the social repercussions that they hope will follow in the wake of their feat in order to generate the psychological momentum needed for them to embrace fully their new unified selves during the consolidation stage. Finally, during the social segregation stage, people must invariably gravitate toward groups in which they will be most comfortable and away from the groups in which they will be least comfortable expressing their new selves. Thus, once started, dramatic self-change may never be completed.

(Athens, 1995, p. 571)

The third framing device comes from the work of Frank (1991, 1995) on the body's problems with illness and the manner in which specific types of body–self relationships connect to various narrative structures that shape the telling and experience of specific conditions.

He notes that stories have to repair the damage that illness has done to the ill person's sense of where she or he is in life, and where she or he may be going. In this sense, stories are a way of redrawing maps and finding new destinations. This reconstruction, via the telling of unique individual stories, not only reflects strong personal preferences, but also reflects, draws on, adapts, and combines various narrative types that cultures make available.

Frank (1995) identifies three narrative types. The most common in Western cultures is the *restitution narrative*. Here, the basic storyline is that yesterday I was healthy, today I'm sick, but tomorrow I'll be healthy again and be 'as good as new'. In contrast, the plot of *chaos narratives* imagines life never getting better. These stories are chaotic in their absence of narrative order. They are told as the storyteller experiences life: without sequence or discernible causality. Finally, *quest narratives* meet suffering head on, accepting illness and seeking to use it. Here, illness is the occasion for a journey that becomes a quest.

The manner in which the work of the Athens (1995), Charmaz (1987), and Frank (1991, 1995) has framed my analysis of how illness affected aspects of Rachael's sense of self as an elite performer, and the manner in which she has attempted to resolve a number of specific identity dilemmas as they emerged, will be made evident as I present data from the case and offer interpretations. In keeping with the ethical principles outlined earlier, it needs to be acknowledged that Rachael has read the final draft of this paper and agreed that the data presented are accurate, that my interpretations of her experiences are fair, and that my reconstruction of moments from her life provide an accurate portrayal of her feelings as they developed over time. It also needs to be acknowledged that we have discussed the problems of maintaining Rachael's anonymity with regard to the following issues. First, it is difficult to disguise somebody when they have had a national profile in a specific sport. Second, there is the tension between the need for thick description in a biographical study to provide a holistic portrayal of a life so that Rachael's epiphany can be contextualized and keeping Rachael's identity anonymous. That is, providing sufficient detail to make Rachael recognizable to herself also means making her recognizable to others. Rachael has considered both these problems and has given her permission for the details given about her in this paper to be made public.

The emergence of a high performance body

Rachael's experiences as a high-level sports performer who inhabited a particular kind of body provide a backdrop for understanding her sense of loss now that she can no longer take part in a sport she loves. As her engagement with various sports increased when she was younger, a *disciplined* body emerged that, according to Frank (1991), becomes predictable through its regimentation, 'So long as the regimen is followed, the body can believe itself to be predictable; thus being predictable is both the medium and the outcome of the regimentation' (p. 55).

Such predictability is an important feature of what Gadow (1982) called *primary immediacy*, a state of being when the body functions and performs tasks without conscious effort. In this state, an overriding unity of the body–self relationship prevails, where body and mind act in unison. Indeed, Leder (1990) argues that the body disappears from consciousness when it is functioning in this unproblematic state. As Rachael commented on her riding at big events:

> I don't actually think about what I'm doing when I'm going around it. It all happens so quickly. But you have got milliseconds if your horse makes a bit of a mistake at a jump, you've literally got a millisecond to throw your weight back so you don't fall over it's head when it trips. You just do it. It's automatic.

For athletes, as Kleiber *et al.* (1995) argue, this sense of primary immediacy is *cultivated* through the process of engagement with developmentally challenging incapacities in which a new unity of self and body is readily imagined and achieved. Once achieved, this cultivated immediacy is characteristic of much of the enjoyment-orientated self-expression, and the feelings of 'flow' experienced in sporting or leisure situations where the consciousness of self disappears as ability matches challenges and action merges with awareness (Jackson, 1996). In this regard, Rachael spoke of the ecstasy of 3-day eventing and the feelings of control she gained from performing at a high level.

> It's very difficult to describe in words . . . It's just the feeling of power, of the horse, and the excitement . . . It's like skiing when you are going down a hard slope, or a Black Run [expert slope], you are just turning to stay in control – just – and it's like that . . . If it's a complicated fence, like there are several bits to it, and you have got to pick a perfect line for your horse, and it just goes so smoothly and beautiful. It's really indescribable because it feels so smooth and professional. Everything just comes together at once, and there's this jump and you are off to the next one . . . It's a complete channelling of everything. I can remember tiny, tiny details as if it was slow motion, but in fact it's very fast. But it's like 'Boom', and you get in a rhythm. It's a very intrinsic sort of activity . . . It's a real buzz, incredible.

Feelings of loss and fragmentation

The following comment is but one among many made by Rachael that illustrated her feelings of loss regarding former body–self relationships and the impact this has had on her life.

> My body has failed me because it can no longer perform the function I want it to. To ride horses in competition is for me the most meaningful expression of my body's special capabilities. This restriction has become the focus of my life; it has hit at the inner core of my being.

With regard to this sense of loss, it appeared that two years after her operation, Rachael remained located in the fragmentation stage of dramatic self-change. Describing this stage, Athens (1995) notes how it involves the breaking apart of the old self via a traumatizing social experience that is so utterly foreign to the person that they cannot assimilate it because it shatters their previously taken-for-granted assumptions about the world, throwing them into a state of utter shock and disbelief and, finally, total disarray.

This state of disarray is evident in the following extract from a piece of reflective writing undertaken by Rachael in August, 1995.

> I feel like I'm on a journey. One minute I am speeding along the motorway in a top of the range Land Rover Discovery when suddenly all I can see is bleak lights in front of me. I am stuck in the most horrendous traffic jam miles from the next junction. Progress is very slow, stationary some of the time, and my always reliable vehicle has developed serious engine trouble and keeps breaking down. I just manage to keep it going though. It seems like an age before I even reach the sign which tells me the junction is one mile away, and another age before I actually reach it. I come off anyway, even though it is the wrong route. I just have to find my way through. I find myself going down a tiny one-track lane. There are really high banks and hedges and I never know what is around the corners. At one stage, the little lane runs parallel to the motorway for a few metres. The traffic is flowing at 70 miles an hour.

> I feel like driving through the fence that separates me from the open road but there is a huge drainage ditch, and anyway, I might damage the exterior of the Discovery. I could just climb over the fence and scramble across the ditch but what use is a motorway without a car? I carry on along the lane. I am really bored now, at first it was a bit of an adventure but now the lane seems endlessly uniform. Nobody has given me any directions or map to follow. Eventually, I come across a by-pass and for some reason people that I know pass on the other side and wave as they head towards the motorway. The problem is that there is nowhere to do a U-turn so I carry on as the road is not that bad and I will probably get to where I want eventually. The problem now though is that I don't seem to know where it is that I'm supposed to be going.

During one interview in December 1995, Rachael and I discussed some of the meanings behind this piece of writing. She explained to me that the Range Rover represented her high performance body as it used to be when she was sponsored by this company. In contrast, Rachael stated that the car she would equate her body to now would be 'one that you have to pedal yourself [laughs]. A Sinclair 5. An old Fiesta that can't go up hills . . . I had one and I've just sold it. It was so crap. It was only 950 cc, it wouldn't go up any hills. That's me'. The other girls in her story were her former team mates now going in the opposite direction to her, and the motorway represented life as it was before her illness. 'That was my life. Going along at 70 miles per hour. It was all plain sailing. It was easy, there weren't any hills. There weren't any corners, bends, traffic works, road works'.

Finally, the big fences were things that in a previous life as a rider she would have jumped with ease but now they formed a barrier that hemmed her in due to the condition of her pelvis. 'I haven't jumped a jump since I had the operation. Before, I could have just got on my horse and jumped the jump. Jumped the fence and got to the other side and carried on. Now I'm hemmed in . . . I could try and bash through but I'd injure my body. That's what would happen if I tried to jump the jump and landed up on my pelvis'. In total, Rachael felt like she was travelling without a map and these feelings of fragmentation were a source of anxiety that she had not expected. 'It's weird because I just didn't have any concept of how it would affect me mentally. Not a tiny little bit. I just thought "OK, just have the operation, get back and everything would be Hunky Dory". Instead, this is just a complete shock'. This complete shock and experience of fragmentation related to the rapid demise of two key aspects of Rachael's sense of self.

The demise of the disciplined body–self

According to Frank (1995), 'The disciplined body–self defines itself primarily in actions of self-regimentation; its most important action problems are those of control. The disciplined body experiences its gravest crisis in loss of control' (p. 41). Rachael experienced just such a crisis:

> I have always been in control of my body. I had always had great faith in my ability to control my body. I now realise that I have always felt a synchronization of body and mind. It wasn't until after the complications that I full appreciated the holistic feeling I had had previously between 'body and soul', but as with many things you don't even realize it is there until it has gone.

Following her stay in hospital and on leaving hospital to recuperate, Rachael's words reflected a situation of *disrupted immediacy*, in which the unity of the body–self relationship has been lost, control and predictability have diminished, and her sense of self has become defined in opposition to the body she now inhabited:

I was expecting to be ill and weak and to have difficulty walking and so on after the operation. After all, I was having major body alterations. I suppose I looked upon myself as a car that had broken down, gone into the garage to be fixed, and come out as good as new . . . It was when the complications set in that I felt the real loss of control of my body. The doctors had control over me, and more importantly I had to admit that, for the first time in my life, I had no choice but to totally rely on them to sort my body out. I had control over my mind, but usually my mind controlled my body. Someone else now had this control.

Since the operation, issues of bodily control and predictability have become a central concern for Rachael. Emphasizing her concerns over losing a controlled and disciplined body, Rachael noted:

I used to have ultimate control over my body. It was very fit, co-ordinated, confident. I was pleased with my body . . . Now I know what it is like to watch. It is hell. There is not a thing you can do when your horse is going around. The lack of control is a new experience for me. The whole thing has become an issue of control. I no longer have control over my physical body; I have no control over my life or destiny; I can't control my emotions.

This loss of control has dramatically altered Rachael's feelings towards her own body. Rachael's body, like the body in multiple sclerosis described by Toombs (1992), was now inescapably embodied as it defined and presented itself to her as an oppositional force which curtailed activities, thwarted plans and projects, and disrupted her involvements in the surrounding world. Therefore, in contrast to former feelings of unity and harmony, her body was now experienced as something essentially alien, as something that was 'other-than-me'. Indeed, as Leder (1990) comments, insofar as the body tends to disappear when functioning unproblematically, 'It often seizes our attention most strongly at times of dysfunction; we then experience the body as the very *absence* of a desired or ordinary state, and as a force that stands opposed to the self' (p. 4). On this issue, Rachael commented:

I've just got no trust in my body whatsoever now [laughs]. For example, in the morning, the first thing I do out of habit, is to check to see if my left leg works. Just in case suddenly it's not working. Because that's the leg that's the problem. I check my left leg . . . I don't like my body any more. I think it's really let me down because I have been really good to it. It's just turned around and got this great big tumour . . . I don't like my body now because it just won't do the things that I want it to. It's frustrating. I'm still really annoyed with my body [laughs]. It's a bit weird, but I am, it's difficult to explain I think . . . I'd like to swap bodies with someone . . . One that can ride horses. That can do the things I want to do. At one stage I thought 'I quite like my body. It's all right. It's not too fat or too thin. It's all right. It suits riding. It's quite athletic'. I wouldn't have swapped it for any other body. But now, I'd swap it for someone fat and short, anything as long as it can ride.

Rachael had invested thousands of hours of cultivation in order to take her sporting performances into the realm of primary immediacy. However, as Kleiber *et al.* (1995) pointed out in their study of the relevance of leisure in an illness experience in relation to people with spinal cord injury, this cultivated immediacy of an activity that was engaged in prior to the injury is simply lost. This was brought home to Rachael, when despite the risks involved, she jumped a fence on her horse again at home early in 1996. When asked how she felt about making the jump, Rachael explained that although she accomplished the task, she did not feel good about it as she kept missing her stride, something that she never did before or even had to think about:

> I've always been a jump jockey and I always get on any horse and jump it really well. That was my strength in riding. It's one of those things that I believe you can't teach. You've either got it or you haven't . . . I think that even after two years you should be able to get on a horse and jump it.
>
> The horse is a lunatic . . . he hasn't jumped for ages obviously, as I haven't been jumping because I can't handle it. So he was really excited and just charging at the fences . . . and because he was really bad, I felt that I was not as good a rider and that I couldn't jump. I was really disappointed. He was all right after a bit of work. But he was still nowhere near where he was when I used to have him. Which is very obvious because he hasn't done very good. I just expected it to click back into place . . . I felt really gutted afterwards. I hated it . . . I thought 'Oh no, I've lost it'.

The loss of cultivated immediacy when associated with self-expression through physical performance can be defined as a direct threat to personal fulfilment, and as Kleiber *et al.* (1995) emphasize, with any radical disruption, 'The prospects of cultivating a new body/self unity are likely to seem very remote' (p. 285). Rachael's words from her reflective writing echoed this point, 'You develop a sense of self from the ability to perform required tasks associated with the self. The body must be able to physically carry out these tasks. I have lost an aspect of myself, a self that I wanted to be, a part of me that was the single most important aspect of my conception of self'.

The demise of the gloried self

> I am a nobody at the moment. I have a desire to be someone. When I was riding I was someone. I was one of the best riders in the country of my age. It is a good feeling to know that you are good at something. I had measured myself against others and come out on top, and that feels good. I don't want to slip into obscurity. I don't want to be normal.
>
> It's just the fact that I thought maybe I was going to make it and be, not famous, well-known as a rider. I mean, I was well known anyway in the area. The people in your area always follow what you do. They send you good luck cards if you go into a big event. It's really nice. I don't think that I'm an attention seeker. But, it was nice.

The above comments by Rachael suggested the loss of another sense of self that Brock and Kleiber (1994) identify as being closely associated with the demise of the disciplined body and the loss of public recognition that comes with the inability to perform at a high level in major sporting events. This self is the *gloried self*, identified by Adler and Adler (1989) in their study of the changes in the selves of North American, elite college basketball players in the United States as they entered into a world of celebrity and fame. They note that experiencing glory was exciting for the athletes involved and created or expanded various aspects of their sense of self. They point out that, characteristically, the gloried self is a greedy, intoxicating and riveting self, that seeks to ascend in importance and to cast aside other self-dimensions as it grows.

> It was my identity completely. I wasn't bothered about what I wore or anything. I spent all my money on horse stuff. Any money that I had always went on equipment or entries. If someone didn't get me something horsy for my birthday I'd go mad and think 'God, it's a waste of money'. Like perfume, 'What use is that?' I want some brushing bits for my horse!

The above comment by Rachael also highlights how the gloried self encourages role engulfment or identity foreclosure to occur where energy and time are withdrawn from a variety of social roles in order to be focused upon the athlete role (see Adler and Adler, 1991; Good *et al.*, 1993). This transformation involves various forms of self-narrowing or self-erosion. As both Adler and Adler (1989), and Brock and Kleiber (1994) point out, athletes can sacrifice both the multidimensionality of their current selves and the potential breadth of their future selves as various dimensions of their identities are either diminished, detached, or somehow changed as a result of their increasing investment in a gloried self.

In terms of self-immediacy, Adler and Adler (1989) further note that one of the first consequences of the ascent of the gloried self was the loss of a future orientation and long-term planning as the future became defined as a direct continuation of the present. For example, Rachael acknowledged that she invested little effort in her academic work at school because she assumed that her future career would be that of a professional horse rider.

> I started when I was 16. I won my second event, which I didn't think was that good, but it was good and I didn't realize it [laughs]. I got the fastest time of the day on one of the sections. So I got picked to do the Juniors, which is 18 and under, and that's when I was doing 'A' levels. I was really hooked. I just didn't want to do them. I'd never really done much work at all, I didn't bother revising for anything.

Likewise, Rachael's choice to study physical education as the main subject for her degree, and her choice of university, were haphazard and motivated by her desire to maintain and develop her riding career. 'Well, before, it was like I'd come away for ten weeks [to university] and I'd go back and ride horses. It was just a bit of an interruption to my horse riding'. Indeed, in a piece of reflective writing, Rachael noted the narrow internal focus and preoccupation she had previously with horse riding had resulted in 'a lack of preparation, both for the state of being ill, and retirement from competition. I feel that I have put all my eggs in one basket and someone has come along and smashed them all. I don't even know who this someone is'.

It would appear that, for Rachael, via her socialization into the world of elite sport, a specific identity has emerged and ascended to a position of psychological centrality in her constellation of identities. As part of this process, other identities have been relegated to a subordinate status. An example of this relegation was evident in an interview where Rachael and I discussed her thoughts about teaching as a future identity and career she might adopt now that becoming an international horse rider was unlikely. Rachel did not find the proposition attractive. For her, teaching was a non-event. 'It's a kind of nobody thing to do' that lacked the glamour, excitement, and prestige of being a professional horse rider. Here, in a similar fashion to the athletes described by Adler and Adler (1989), and Brock and Kleiber (1994), Rachael receives less satisfaction from other available roles and has distanced herself from them in such a way she has lost both the desire and the ability to see the world through them. As a consequence, other roles and identities have become more or less unavailable for alternative lines of action. This is because, as Adler and Adler (1989) point out, 'The longer the gloried athletic self served as their master status, the harder the athletes found it to conceive of any other identity for themselves' (p. 308).

Holding on to past selves

The biographical data presented suggest, that for Rachael, the loss of the disciplined body and the gloried self had a major impact on the way she defined her body–self relationships over time. Prior to surgery, and when she was riding at the top level, Rachael (although expressing herself in dualistic mind–body terms), experienced a unitary and harmonious body–self relationship. Illness, surgery, and the long-term consequences of the tumour have changed all this, and now Rachael holds a fragmented, anxious, and disenchanted view of herself. Like many athletes, given their general excellent health and their public posture of physical invulnerability, Rachael feels her body has betrayed her, and not surprisingly, she resents this state of affairs (Young and White, 1995).

Despite this bodily betrayal, Rachael has yet to give up the idea of competing at horse jumping again:

> I will not accept that it is inevitable. For example, only the other day I was trying to persuade my Mum that I needed a bone scan done privately, my National Health consultant refuses as he is dead against me riding, to ascertain the extent of the pelvic and spinal bone damage. I also say things like, 'I'm sure 50-year-old menopausal women are allowed to ride, and they must have weak bones all over, in fact there is a special body protector on the market for them' . . . I need to find out what state the pelvis is in so that I can either resume riding with some sort of protection, or so I can see evidence that will convince me to give up the whole idea and get on with my life.

In the meantime, Rachael's sense of self remains fragmented and life is put on hold. Contributing to this situation is the manner in which, despite their demise, the disciplined body–self along with the gloried self are apparently able to maintain their position at the apex of Rachael's salience hierarchy of identities. Consequently, these 'phantom selves' as Athens (1994) calls them, act as a major constraint upon Rachael's thinking with regard to the development of future, altered and/or novel senses of self. Indeed, the phantoms of both the disciplined body–self and the gloried self seem to operate in tandem to fuel Rachael's desire to seek a restored self within the preferred identity levels spoken of by Charmaz (1987) in relation to chronic illness. More specifically, within the types of restored selves available, Rachael seems drawn towards an *entrenched self*:

> Restoring an entrenched self means being wedded to a self-conception situated in the past. These persons hold clear images of their self-concepts, which they can readily articulate. The entrenched self represents patterns of action, conviction, and habit built up over the years. These unchanged patterns had been a source of self-respect before illness. After illness, resuming these patterns becomes the person's major objective . . . restoring an entrenched self also has the imagery of a 'comeback'.
> (Charmaz, 1987, p. 302)

Charmaz (1994) emphasizes that failed attempts to recapture the past self can lead to invalidism and despondency, as all valued social and personal identities remain in the irretrievable past. Furthermore, being unable to measure up to the past self results in further preoccupation with it, and heightens identity dilemmas. As the distance increases between their past self (now reconstructed in memory in idealized form) and present identities, the former valued identities collapse and new ones are viewed as negative. Significantly, with each identity loss due to chronic illness, the preservation of valued past 'performing' identities becomes increasingly difficult. Rachael's words echo these points:

> It's almost like I dare not give it up because it was such a part of me. I just don't want to say goodbye to it. I'm too scared to say that this is a chapter in my life that's finished because it was so good. I was someone else. I don't want to be the person I am now. I don't want to be the predicted, projected person post-tumour, but the one anti. I value the person I was in the past; I don't like the person in the present

or future. The main reasons for this being that I'm bored, and I feel trapped in a body that has let me down big time. I was always good to my body; I never abused it, I kept it very fit, I never injured it, I ate what was good for it. There is nothing I can think of that will possibly fill in this big hole in my life. To create a new meaning for my life would feel like I was abandoning me in the past, and me in the past was someone I valued. I fill life now, I lived it then.

Such comments cast Rachael as a 'refugee' (Bateson, 1990), as someone with an undetermined future. Her words also indicate how Rachael's volition is dominated by concerns that any attempt to make her circumstances better in the long-term, carries the risk of making life even worse in the short-term (see Helfrich, Kielhofner and Mattingly, 1994). The comments further suggest that Rachael is firmly locked into the fragmentation stage of dramatic self-change and highlight the barriers that must be overcome before she can move on to the provisional stage. According to Athens (1995), this stage involves the agonizing ordeal of finding a suitable replacement for former selves. It requires that a novel, provisional self be founded on a 'new phantom community comprised of, at the minimum, some phantom companions who are different from those of the former phantom community' (p. 575).

Indeed, Rachael acknowledged the need to find a suitable replacement and alter the focus of her life. 'I ought to search for something else to immerse myself in. It has to be something exciting and I have to be good at it . . . I am physically and mentally unchallenged. I need to find another challenge of some sort'. Just what this challenge might be is less than clear, and movement towards other challenges and a differing senses of self seem limited. In part, these limitations are set in place and exacerbated by the restitution narrative that continues to shape Rachael's life.

Narrative constraints in reconstructing the self

With regard to chronic illness, the restitution narrative is the dominant tale of our time in Western cultures and acts as a *master* or *canonical* narrative (Bruner, 1990; Linde, 1986). Such narratives, as received stories, can be constraining. According to Jago (1996), they tend to advocate appropriate or correct behaviour, and thus, provide versions of the way the world *should* be. Consequently, in defining and prescribing behaviour, these narratives provide a powerful cultural frame though which individuals construe their lived experiences. As Frank (1995) pointed out, the basic storyline of the restitution narrative ties in closely with notions of a restorable body.

Frank (1995) suggests that, even though a belief that the sufferings of illness will be relieved is the preferred narrative for any body, some bodies display a greater affinity for restitution narratives than others. This is particularly so when notions of the restored and disciplined body are invoked and the teller of the tale wants the body's former predictability back again. In such conditions, Frank (1995) argues that,

the body that turns in upon itself is split from the self that looks forward to this body's restitution. The temporarily broken-down body becomes 'it' to be cured. Thus, the self is *dissociated* from the body . . . The restitution story is about remaking the body in an image derived either from its own history before illness of elsewhere . . . In the restitution story, the implicit genesis of illness is an unlucky breakdown in a body that is conceived on mechanistic lines. To be fixable, the body has to be a kind of machine . . . Restitution requires fixing, and fixing requires such a mechanistic view. The mechanistic view normalizes illness: televisions require fixing, and so do bodies.

(Frank, 1995, pp. 85–88)

The point made by Frank (1995), that different bodies have 'elective affinities' to different illness narratives, would appear to have some relevance to Rachael's case. That is, the kind of body Rachael has (or had) plays a key role in creating and confirming her sense of self, which, in turn, leads her to choose some storylines over others among those available in the cultural repertoire. These choices, and the manner in which they are embodied, frame the dilemmas experienced by her. Accordingly, the combined effect of the restitution narrative, the gloried self and the restored self, diminishes Rachael's ability to narratively reconstruct her sense of self by reducing her access to, and flexibility to engage with, the wider cultural repertoire of stories that are available for synthesis into personal stories (Williams, 1984). As Gergen (1994) reminds us, over the life course, people may develop greater sophistication in their potential for telling a variety of life stories and may develop the capacity to reconstrue their lives in ways that enhance their present situations, relationships, and needs. However, in terms of restorying the self, people cannot transcend their narrative resources.

Bury (1982) notes that one of the responses to biographical disruption is the mobilization of resources in the face of an altered situation. Herein, as Rachael's case indicates, lies a critical problem for many elite athletes. This problem relates to the availability of alternative narratives within specific subcultures on which to build alternative identities and notions of self that recognize and acknowledge, among other things, issues of vulnerability and fragility (see Sparkes, 1996a). It also raises questions about the willingness of individuals like Rachael, in terms of her habitus and tastes, to approach and engage with different narratives if, and when, they become available.

Of course, this is not to suggest that those who inhabit elite, disciplined and performing bodies should not attempt to restore their sense of self and achieve their former performance levels following injury or illness. This can, and does, happen. However, as Frank (1995) makes clear, problems arise when people become fixated on one kind of body and sense of self in circumstances where the restitution narrative is not appropriate. As Rachael's case indicates, under such circumstances individuals find it hard to remind themselves that other body–self narratives might have to be found and told. However, without an increase in her narrative resources, the space and opportunity for Rachael to craft who she wants to be and can be would appear to remain constrained and limited for the time being.

For Rachael, the issue of access to a variety of narratives is of no small importance. At the moment, she is not able to envisage a suitable replacement for the body–self relationship she had previously. In Hyden's (1995) terms, Rachael has not been able to use the disruption in her life as a 'platform' from which to reconstruct a sense of self. Indeed, she would rather not seek a replacement and would prefer to return to the person she was prior to the tumour and surgery. The odds, however, are heavily stacked against such a return. In view of this, Rachael is unable to proceed through all the remaining stages of dramatic self-change described by Athens (1995) so that a new self can be created to replace the old one that fragmented. However, as Athens (1995) made clear, 'After our prior self has fragmented, however, there is no guarantee that we will ever develop a new unified one to replace it' (p. 584). Clearly, for Rachael, the potential for dramatic self-change remains problematic with no guarantees available.

Concluding comments

The data presented suggest that, in Brewer et al.'s (1993) terms, a strong athletic identity has acted as an Achilles heel with regard to Rachael's reactions to a disruptive life event and the consequences of these reactions for her personal long-term development. For health care professionals, coaches and physical activity professionals wishing to assist Rachael and other elite performers like her, it is important to recognize that critical life events, such as career-ending injury or illness, are multidimensional events with many biological, social and psychological components (also see, Drahota and Eitzen, 1998; Grove *et al.*, 1998; Lavallee *et al.*, 1998). Consequently, there is a need to gain an understanding of the specific dynamics of the Achilles heel for the athlete in terms of the salience of specific identities within the identity hierarchy held by the individual, the kinds of self experienced as lost that may relate to actual physical performance (e.g., the loss of the controlled body–self and primary immediacy), and/or wider social relations (e.g., the loss of the gloried self). Finally, there is also a need for health care and physical activity professionals, particularly physical education teachers and coaches, to understand the narrative type (e.g., restitution, quest or chaos narrative) that is framing the athlete's storied response to injury or illness, and the limitations this might place on reconstructing the self over time.

An awareness of these issues would benefit the care of seriously injured athletes in the following ways. First, as Brock and Kleiber (1994) argue, soliciting, listening to, and gaining a sense of the structure of the complete illness/injury narrative told by the athlete would enhance the physical education teacher/coach/health care professional's ability to identify those whose illness experience will be most problematic. Anticipating the shape that this problematic experience might take would then enable prompt interventions to take place to modify the course of distress and lead to more rapid rehabilitation. Brock and Kleiber (1994) emphasize that, taken together as complementary, '[A]n analysis of the patient's illness narrative and a biomedical assessment can bring the suffering person fully into clinical focus and anticipate roadblocks to and avenues for healing' (p. 427).

Charmaz (1987) also notes how applying the concept of identity levels to concrete cases can provide medical and social researchers with opportunities for unique collaboration that could lead to a much more finely tuned analysis of the relationships between identity pursuits and disease processes. 'Such a study, could generate precise information about how disease processes affect motivation and, conceivably, how motivation in the form of identity objectives affects disease processes' (p. 317). Charmaz also emphasizes how the concept of identity levels focuses attention on identity shifts and changes over time. Such a focus would guard against the simplistic sorting of people into 'identity types' in a way that reifies sociological labelling and may prompt practitioner labelling so that an inaccurate picture is painted of the social reality being studied. Finally, Charmaz (1987) notes that the notion of identity levels presupposes different selves. Multiple selves accompany different levels and different preferred identities call forth different potential selves, 'Thus, self-images and self-conception become intertwined with the identity level towards which the person aims' (p. 318).

Understanding the dynamics of the Achilles heel for athletes in the terms previously described would assist in designing effective programmes that link the timing of a transitional experience, like a career-ending injury, to an appropriate intervention. In their discussion of an intervention framework for the transitions of student-athletes, Petitpas, Brewer and Van Raalte (1996) argue that the goal of any intervention programme with student-athletes in transition 'should be to enhance their ability to not only cope with transitions, but to grow through the experience' (p. 150). Accordingly, they emphasize the need for interventions that take place before a transition (enhancement strategies), during a transition (supportive strategies), and after a transitional event (counselling strategies).

Drawing upon developmental-educational theory, Petitpas *et al.* (1996) see enhancement as the primary intervention that would prepare student-athletes to cope with future events (e.g., a serious or career-ending injury) by assisting them to anticipate future transitions, help them identify transferable skills that can be used in nonsport domains, and teach them a variety of coping or life skills. Supportive interventions were those that took place during a transition. Here, the goal of support is to buffer the impact of any stressful aspects of the transition and to assist in mobilizing the transitional student-athlete's coping resources. In contrast, counselling interventions take place after a transitional event and are directed at assisting those who are having difficulty coping with or managing the aftermath of a transition. During this phase, Petitpas *et al.* (1996) suggest that athletic departments or support service personnel should identify specialists within the college or university, or local community, who can serve as referral resources for those individuals having difficulties coping with a transition. 'Ideally these referral sources are well versed in the problem areas . . . and espouse an educational rather then a remedial orientation. The goal is to assist the individual in identifying resources to better cope with the transition' (p. 146).

The ideal intervention programme for college student-athletes, according to Petitpas *et al.* (1996), needs to be multidimensional and include enhancement, support, and counselling components because transitions do not occur in isolation and vary by timing and duration. They note that the more events occurred simultaneously, the greater the need for multidimensional interventions. The nature of Rachael's illness experience and the identity dilemmas it has created for her would support the need for this kind of approach. That such intervention programmes are noticeable by their absence is a source for concern, and the provision of these programmes demands serious attention in the future.

Acknowledgements

This chapter is a modified version of a paper that first appeared in Sparkes, A. (1998) 'Athletic identity: An Achilles' heel to the survival of self', *Qualitative Health Research* 8(5): 644–64. I am grateful to Sage Publications Ltd for kindly giving their permission to reprint it here. I would also like to say a special thanks to Rachael for sharing her experiences with me and allowing me to write about them.

Note

1. In many ways this process might be seen as loosely connected to notions of grounded theory with its procedures of open-coding (Strauss, 1987) and axial coding (Strauss and Corbin, 1990). Clearly, I am sympathetic to forms of data analysis in which theory emerges from the data. However, my study does not adhere to the genuine interweaving of data collection and theorizing of the kind advocated by Glaser and Strauss (1967), nor does it fit into the grounded theory tradition as described by Cresswell (1998). As such, notions of 'saturation' in a strict sense are not applicable to my work even though I feel assured of the meaning and importance of the themes identified in Rachael's story. These points are made to avoid paying lip service to grounded theory and using it as an approving bumper sticker as, according to Bryman and Burgess (1994), so many qualitative studies seem to do.

References

- Adler P.A. and Adler P. (1989) 'The gloried self: The aggrandisement and the constriction of self', *Social Psychology Quarterly* 52(4): 299–310.
- Adler P.A. and Adler P. (1991) *Backboards and Blackboards*, New York: Columbia University Press.
- Athens L. (1994) 'The self as soliloquy', *The Sociological Quarterly* 35(3): 521–32.
- Athens L. (1995) 'Dramatic self change', *The Sociological Quarterly* 36(3): 571–86.
- Bateson M. (1990) *Composing a Life*, New York: Plume.

● Brewer B. (1993) 'Self-identity and specific vulnerability to depressed mood', *Journal of Personality* 61(3): 343–64.
● Brewer B., Van Raalte J. and Linder D. (1993) 'Athletic identity: Hercules' muscles or Achilles' heel?', *International Journal of Sport Psychology* 24: 237–54.
● Brock S. and Kleiber D. (1994) 'Narrative in medicine: The stories of elite college athletes' career-ending injuries', *Qualitative Health Research* 4(4): 411–30.
● Bruner J. (1990) *Acts of Meaning*, Cambridge, MA: Harvard University Press.
● Bryman A. and Burgess R. (1994) 'Developments in qualitative data analysis: An introduction', in A. Bryman and R. Burgess (eds) *Analyzing Qualitative Data*, London: Routledge, pp. 1–17.
● Bury M. (1982) 'Chronic illness as biographical disruption', *Sociology of Health and Illness* 4: 167–82.
● Charmaz K. (1987) 'Struggling for a self: Identity levels of the chronically ill', in J. Roth and P. Conrad (eds) *Research in the Sociology of Health Care: A Research Manual*, vol. 6, Greenwich, Connecticut: JAI Press Inc.
● Charmaz K. (1994) 'Identity dilemmas of chronically ill men', *The Sociological Quarterly* 35(2): 269–88.
● Cresswell J. (1998) *Qualitative Inquiry and Research Design: Choosing Among Five Traditions*, London: Sage.
● Denzin N. (1989a) *Interpretive Interactionism*, London: Sage.
● Denzin N. (1989b) *Interpretive Biography*, London: Sage.
● Drahota J. and Eitzen D. (1998) 'The role exit of professional athletes', *Sociology of Sport Journal* 15(3): 263–78.
● Frank A. (1991) 'For a sociology of the body: An analytical review', in M. Featherstone, M. Hepworth and B. Turner (eds) *The Body*, London: Sage, pp. 36–102.
● Frank A. (1995) *The Wounded Storyteller*, Chicago: University of Chicago Press.
● Gadow S. (1982) 'Body and self: A dialectic', in V. Kestenbaum (ed.) *The Humanity of the Ill: Phenomenological Perspectives*, Knoxville, TN: University of Tennessee Press, pp. 86–100.
● Gergen M. (1994) 'The social construction of personal histories: Gendered lives in popular biographies', in T. Sarbin and J. Kituse (eds) *Constructing the Social*, London: Sage, pp. 19–45.
● Good A., Brewer B., Petitpas A., Van Raalte J. and Mahar M. (1993) 'Identity foreclosure, athletic identity and college sport participation', *The Academic Athletic Journal*, Spring, pp. 1–12.
● Grove J., Lavallee D. and Gordon S. (1997) 'Coping with retirement from sport: The influence of athletic identity', *Journal of Applied Sport Psychology* 9: 191–203.
● Grove J., Lavallee D., Gordon S. and Harvey J. (1998) 'Account-making: A model for understanding and resolving distressful reactions to retirement from sport', *The Sport Psychologist* 12: 52–67.
● Glaser B. and Strauss A. (1967) *The Discovery of Grounded Theory: Strategies for Qualitative Research*, Chicago: Aldine.
● Helfrich C., Kielhofner G. and Mattingly C. (1994) 'Volition as narrative: Understanding motivation in chronic illness', *The American Journal of Occupational Therapy* 48(4): 311–17.
● Hyden L. (1995) 'In search of an ending: Narrative reconstruction as a moral quest', *Journal of Narrative and Life History* 5(1): 67–84.
● Jackson S. (1996) 'Toward a conceptual understanding of flow experience in elite athletes', *Research Quarterly for Exercise and Sport* 67: 76–90.
● Jago B. (1996) 'Postcards, ghosts, and fathers: Revising family stories', *Qualitative Inquiry* 2(4): 495–516.
● Kleiber D., Brock S., Youngkhill L., Dattilo J. and Cadwell L. (1995) 'The relevance of leisure in an illness experience: Realities of spinal cord injury', *Journal of Leisure Research* 27(3): 283–99.

● Lavallee D., Grove J., Gordon S. and Ford I. (1998) 'The experience of loss in sport', in J.H. Harvey (ed.) *Perspectives on Loss: A Sourcebook*, Washington DC: Taylor and Francis, pp. 241–52.

● Leddy M., Lambert M. and Ogles B. (1994) 'Psychological consequences of athletic injury among high-level competitors', *Research Quarterly for Exercise and Sport* 65(4): 347–54.

● Leder D. (1990) *The Absent Body*, Chicago: University of Chicago Press.

● Linde C. (1986) 'Explanatory systems in oral life stories', in D. Holland and N. Quinn (eds) *Cultural Methods in Language and Thought*, Cambridge: Cambridge University Press, pp. 343–66.

● Maykut P. and Morehouse R. (1994) *Beginning Qualitative Research*, London: Falmer Press.

● Mohr W. (1997) 'Interpretive interactionism: Denzin's potential contribution to intervention and outcomes research', *Qualitative Health Research* 7(2): 270–86.

● Petitpas A., Brewer B. and Van Raalte J. (1996) 'Transitions of the student-athlete: Theoretical, empirical, and practical perspectives', in E. Etzel, A. Ferrante and J. Pinkey (eds) *Counselling College Student-Athletes: Issues and Interventions*, 2nd edition, Morgantown, WV: Fitness Information Technology, pp. 137–56.

● Sparkes A. (1994a) 'Life histories and the issue of voice: Reflections on an emerging relationship', *International Journal of Qualitative Studies in Education* 7(2): 165–83.

● Sparkes A. (1994b) 'Self, silence and invisibility as a beginning teacher: A life history of lesbian experience', *British Journal of Sociology of Education* 15(1): 93–118.

● Sparkes A. (1996a) 'The fatal flaw: A narrative of the fragile body–self', *Qualitative Inquiry* 2(4): 463–94.

● Sparkes A. (1996b) 'Interrupted body projects and the self in teaching: Exploring an absent presence', *International Studies in Sociology of Education* 6(2): 167–90.

● Sparkes A. (1997) 'Reflections on the socially constructed physical self', in K. Fox (ed.) *The Physical Self: From Motivation to Well-being*, Champaign, IL: Human Kinetics, pp. 83–100.

● Sparkes A. (1998) 'Reciprocity in critical research? Some unsettling thoughts', in G. Shacklock and J. Smyth (eds) *Being Reflexive in Critical Educational Research*, London: Falmer Press, pp. 67–82.

● Sparkes A. (1999) 'Exploring body narratives', *Sport, Education and Society* 4(1): 17–30.

● Stake R. (1995) *The Art of Case Study Research*, London: Sage.

● Strauss A. (1987) *Qualitative Analysis for Social Scientists*, Cambridge: Cambridge University Press.

● Strauss A. and Corbin J. (1990) *Basics of Qualitative Research*, Newbury Park, CA: Sage.

● Toombs K. (1992) 'The body in multiple sclerosis: A patient's perspective', in D. Leder (ed.) *The Body in Medical Thought and Practice*, Netherlands: Kluwer Academic Publishers, pp. 127–37.

● Wiechman S. and Williams J. (1997) 'Relation of athletic identity to injury and mood disturbance', *Journal of Sports Behaviours* 20(2): 199–211.

● Williams G. (1984) 'The genesis of chronic illness: Narrative reconstruction', *Sociology of Health and Illness* 6: 175–200.

● Wolcott H. (1994) *Transforming Qualitative Data*, London: Sage.

● Wolcott H. (1995) *The Art of Fieldwork*, London: Sage.

● Young K. and White P. (1995) 'Sport, physical danger and injury: The experiences of elite women athletes', *Journal of Sport and Social Issues* 19(1): 45–61.

● Young K., White P. and McTeer W. (1994) 'Body talk: Male athletes reflect on sport, injury, and pain', *Sociology of Sport Journal* 11: 175–94.

Chapter Three

Toward a Sociology of Coaching
Robyn L. Jones

Introduction: Sociology and coach education: The need for change

During the past two decades, research into coaching and coach education has increased significantly. However, much of this work has reflected systematic and scientific approaches, which have naturally limited the focus to specific components. The result has been the development of a theory and methodology of training, which can be defined as 'a process of athletic improvement conducted on the basis of scientific principles underlying the physical, mental, technical and tactical development of the athlete' (Woodman, 1993, p. 1). Thus, despite claims that it is a unique occupation which combines a multiplicity of roles, coaching, as an academic and practical subject, has largely developed along bioscientific fragmentary lines, while the essential humanistic social nature of the total process has remained less well understood. Nevertheless, as MacDonald and Brooker (1995) point out, there is a growing realization that successful professional pedagogical practice is not only founded on technical competence, but also on flexibility, creativeness, intelligence and social responsibility. Similarly, it is becoming increasingly acknowledged that the coaching process is vulnerable to many and varied social pressures and constraints, including those which are ideological, institutional, cultural, ethical and national in nature (Cross, 1995). Consequently, these need to be taken into account when designing effective coaching programmes.

The purpose of this chapter is two fold. First, and principally, a case is made for the value of sociological knowledge to coaches. Specifically, following a rationale for a more critical approach to coaching, drawn mainly from pedagogical research, the relevance of differing sociological perspectives to coaching practitioners is discussed. The aim is not to explain the multidimensional coaching process in terms of a single sociological doctrine, but rather to reflect upon the principal strands of social thought and how they can be appropriately related to coaching; in short, to discuss the applicability of sociological theories and perspectives to an analysis of the coaching process. Second, the method employed to achieve such a goal in a practical setting, namely that of critical reflection, is discussed, before an example is given of such a strategy in action. The example is drawn from a module which has been run at Brunel University, UK. The practical objective, of both chapter and module, is to challenge student coaches to question their own practices and philosophies in the context of sociological perspectives. Conversely, the more theoretical aim is to become increasingly discursive about the practical sociology of coaching, and thus to utilize social thought to inform an ever increasing coaching body of knowledge.

The fragmentation of knowledge into specialized subjects, has been linked with an increasing product-orientated view of education (McDonald and Brooker, 1995). Those sport sciences contributing most frequently to coaching (or coaching 'science' as it has become termed) are sport physiology, sport psychology including motor control, and bio-mechanics. These fit closely into the area of athletic development as encapsulated into training theory. Coaching knowledge thus, is taken as an almost 'autonomous body of facts that is passed on through generations' (McKay, Gore and Kirk, 1990, p. 62), while the possibility of its socially constructed nature is barely considered. Such an approach tends to represent coaching as both technical and unproblematic, and coaches as 'merely technicians engaged in the transfer of knowledge' (McDonald and Tinning, 1995, p. 98). Additionally, such a framework suggests that knowledge is 'given', and that it is compart-mentalized rather than holistic.

While undoubtedly training theory must remain a major focus for the professional coach, if the preference for the scientific, fragmented and uncritical knowledge that currently underpins professional preparation continues, graduates from the system will remain ill-equipped to deal with the multidisciplinary, unique, uncertain social demands of their work. Furthermore, through the separation of theory from practice, including the 'tendency to routinize high level tasks' (McDonald and Tinning, 1995, p. 100), the 'de-skilling' of the practitioner, in terms of cognitive and human interaction, occurs. As a result, Noddings (1984) has argued that the 'human being, who is an integral composite of qualities in several domains, is thereby shaped into something less than fully human' (p. 172). Similarly, Turner and Martinek (1995) agree that an inherent problem with the rational approach to 'effective' coaching practice is that the learning is often decontextualized. Without the contextual frame of reference the learning has little relevance. What are produced, as a consequence, are two-dimensional coaches who, being driven by mechanistic considerations who are unable to comprehend and thus, adapt to the complex dynamic human context.

Alternatively, echoing the work of Aronowitz and Giroux (1985) in education, the premise is presented here that coaches, far from being 'merely technicians', need to be educated as intellectuals, with practical and cognitive skills and values. These include a comprehensive knowledge base, intellectual skills, practical competencies, and skills of critical reflection, collaboration and communication (McDonald and Tinning, 1995). Con-sequently, coaches should be encouraged to develop their independent and creative think-ing skills, particularly in relation to meaning-making, problem solving and integrating and reflecting upon knowledge and skills. The focus of coach education should, therefore, be shifted away from learning based on imitation and directed work, and be increasingly based on developing socially informed decision-making abilities.

Undoubtedly, a major task in coaching is to work to balance individual and collective needs and manage the dilemmas that arise (Rovegno and Kirk, 1995). Such complexities are inherent in coaching, and are further reflected in the multiple goals, realities and needs that inevitably exist within the wider instructional process. In developing coaching theory, we should, therefore, avoid the temptation to teach and apply 'ready-made' knowledge, as this oversimplifies our understanding of coaching and its varying goals. It is plain that the current 'smorgasbord of disconnected facts and experiences' (Locke, 1985, p. 10) that we feed our prospective coaches in coach education programmes is not appropriate to produce consistent excellence in a complex area of human relations such as coaching. What appears to be missing is the conscious aim to develop a quality of mind essential for grasping the interplay between other, society and self (Sage, 1987). Coaching exists (predominantly) not in sanitized classroom environments, but in the complexities and contradictions of modern sporting practice. It is a human activity with all the accompanying problems, thus, coach education programmes should reflect such realities. We need to move the mechanistic body as the focus of analysis aside, and bring in the social person.

Social thought and the coaching practitioner

Drawing on existing sociological thought, the following section attempts to address more concretely the question of how a study of sociology can assist coaches in their practical, everyday work. Specifically, following a general rationale for such a case drawn largely from the work of Lemert (1997), the centrality of 'power', as a sociological concept, to the coaching process is discussed. Finally, several principal sociological perspectives are briefly debated and their relevance outlined to the working coach.

According to Lemert (1997), the value of sociological knowledge is to increase social competence. This suggests developing a better understanding of the structures through which social power is exercised, and consequently to better deal with them. Thus, a recognition of the social influences that belie the actions of individuals is needed, as although the symptoms of certain behaviours may be psychological, the causes are often social; in effect, to comprehend the social rules that inform practice. Hence, awareness of social prejudices that cause individuals self-doubt and similar problems is required if the multiple roles of the coach are to be successfully accomplished. Similarly, coaches should be able to take stock of the practical realities of the local situation, particularly the life-situations of their athletes, if they are to understand the totality of the latter's performances. Additionally, an understanding of one's own position and possibilities, according to Lemert (1997), provides knowledge which is, in turn, capable of informing intellectual and political judgements; the result being improved understanding of social realities, social relations and the social environment.

Tomlinson (1998), in his brief but insightful recent review of 'power' literature, emphasizes the importance of power as a 'central dynamic of human societies' (p. 235), with 'power relations being inherent in social life' (p. 236). Thus, it is considered that its conceptualization in terms of understanding social situations is not an option (Tomlinson, 1998). Similarly, Locke (1985) has argued that any improvement in pedagogical practice must take account of the unique power structure of each particular situation, inclusive of varying and constantly changing measures of compliance and collaboration from 'charges'. Thus, resistance within those structures should also be considered as an expression of a form of power, which inevitably affects the ultimate outcome.

Examining the concept of resistance further, although power is considered as 'a structural characteristic . . . of all human relationships' (Elias, 1978, p. 74), it is also considered relative, dependent upon its strategic significance within the local situation. Hence, as long as one party has a function, and thus value, they are not powerless in any relationship, while the power chances of differing groups vary under differing conditions (Dunning, 1986). Indeed, an understanding of the nature of resistance is fundamental to comprehending the social situation and the relative nature of power. Thus, a need is emphasized to be sensitive to the varying forms of resistance that can be expressed within power relations if desired outcomes are to be achieved. Consequently, the coaching process could be viewed as one characterized by complex power relations which themselves are subject to the 'ebb and flow of influences, illustrative of the reflexive and generative capacities of human actors to confirm, adapt, negotiate and at times re-make their institutions and cultures' (Tomlinson, 1998, p. 238). The aim, therefore, of research and teaching into such socially dynamic areas as coaching, should not consist of the search for fundamental laws to cover every eventuality, but rather emphasis should be placed on models of structure and process;

in effect, to sensitize student coaches to understand the unique power dynamics of the local situation and act accordingly.

Durkheim, the acknowledged founder of modern structural-functionalism, a sociological theory which held popular status in the 1950s and early 1960s, believed that the aim of sociology was to 'attempt to establish the pattern that lies behind all observable phenomena' (Jarvie and Maguire, 1994, p. 5), with the related dominant themes of functionalist thought being primarily concerned with social cohesion. The social milieu is considered the determining factor behind human action. Unsurprisingly, if coaches are to truly maximize the potential of their athletes, an understanding of the social context which could influence behaviour seems obvious, whilst a grasp of the problematic nature of the social bonds that tie coach to athlete and athlete to athlete, would also appear necessary. Durkheim's analysis of the role of social interaction, through the use of certain rites and beliefs, in developing social solidarity and group integration, seems particularly relevant here. Indeed, an ability to insightfully address such questions as 'What selves, motivations and strategies do people bring to interaction; how do these affect the interaction itself; and how are they reinforced or altered by the interaction?' (Pope, 1998, p. 56) appear fundamental if the process of creating an appropriate team climate is to be adequately grasped. Similarly, the Durkheimian notion of sport having symbolic representation of personal identity for the social actor linked to a heightened sense of social significance (Jarvie and Maguire, 1994), further emphasizes the necessity for coaches to comprehend sociological concepts if they are to truly understand the athletes in their charge and help them to fulfill their potentials. Indeed, Lashuk (1992), in this context, has stated that the basic role of the coach is determined by the characteristics, needs and motives of the athletes; an understanding of which is a necessity if desirable outcomes are to be achieved. Consequently, if such and similar notions related to the relationship between individual athletes and their environments and role assignments are successfully grasped by coaches, they can more coherently account for their athletes as persons.

Functionalist research has also demonstrated the existence of a pattern in relation to the recruitment and occupation of leadership positions in sport (Jarvie and Maguire, 1994); a stratification that many believe mirrors that of the wider society. Particular attention in this regard has focused on playing positions in team sports being racially determined, a practice known as 'stacking'. An awareness of such discriminatory practices in team selection and a further critical questioning of the possible institutionalized nature of inequality (Jarvie and Maguire, 1994) are needed, if a positive, individualized and caring coaching environment is to be developed. Remaining with the issue of discrimination, Marxist sociologists have questioned the increasing involvement of Black athletes in sport as an expression of wider social racism and oppression (Stoddart, 1988; Hargreaves, 1986). Through analysis of the apparent Black obsession with sport in terms of the concepts of alienation, colonization, repression and liberation among others, an understanding of athlete participatory motivations can be somewhat gleaned. Again, through the recognition of such concepts and their influence, a more sensitive and individualized approach to athletes could be developed.

Additionally, Marx's concept of alienation appears a particularly relevant one in today's high pressured world of competitive sport; a world which is highly regimented, restrictive and controlled, with coaches involved as both repressors and repressed. Such a situation, manifest in lack of control over one's actions and destiny, is viewed as alienating athletes away from the activity and from their own humanity; an explanation often proffered for athlete burn out and drop out. Alternatively, Marx advocated a theory of de-alienation, a praxis which involved the abolition of the distinction between manual and mental labour (Jarvie and Maguire, 1994). Although in Marx's writings such notions as de-alienation were linked to issues of class and property, their relevance in the present context extends to coaches' ability to reconcile the humanistic with the mechanistic, thus developing a more complete understanding of their athletes and the coaching process in general. Indeed, according to George Lukacs, the founder of Western Marxism, the key to Marxism itself, 'the object of knowledge (is comprehending) the *social totality*' (Cuff, Sharrock and Francis, 1998, p. 185). Marxist thought, therefore, is seen as advocating the need to understand a particular thing in relation to the 'totality', with the deficiencies of positivism being highlighted as 'a restricted view of the whole' resulting in 'understanding being seriously distorted by an inability to connect and link (particular elements) into the whole' (ibid. p. 187). Similarly, Dunning (1986), in explaining Eliasian thought, has also criticized the conceptual tendency to 'separate "objects" of thought from the relationships in which they are involved' (p. 33), which can be seen as symptomatic of current coach education programmes. Such analysis, he argues, leads one to conceptualize the object as static and uninvolved in social relationships; in effect, separating the individual from society. Alternatively, the terms 'open men', which refers to the 'other directed character of interdependent individuals' (p. 34), and more significantly, 'figurations', which involve the 'actions of a plurality of separate people (which) intermesh to form an interwoven structure with a number of emergent properties such as power ratio's, axes of tension, class and stratification systems' (p. 34), are offered as more appropriate units of social analysis.

During the past 20 years a critical element has also emerged within the pluralistic sociological tradition, emphasizing social division, competing interests and overlapping commonalities (Jarvie and Maguire, 1994). The consequent notion of subcultures further reflects a greater awareness of social interests, together with a recognition that increasing sensitivity is needed to be given to minority voices in order for them to be adequately heard. An understanding of various subcultures from which such minority voices emerge is needed, if the identity and self position of an individual, incorporating their view of self and others, is to be understood. Examining the wider concept of culture creation from a team perspective, Fine (1986) contends that team members develop a culture based on a set of shared understandings that can be referred to by all. Such a culture aids in developing group cohesion and unity, which could also be termed 'team spirit'. Indeed, a sociological awareness of issues involving group prestige and structure has the potential to be the most effective means of developing 'team' as opposed to 'group' status (Murray, 1999). Furthermore, a recognition by coaches that the cultural preference of individuals and groups can serve both to unify with, and alienate from, others, in addition to affecting their relationship to the wider mainstream society, is required if the coaching process is to be individualized within a common team framework. Similarly, Luschen (1986) has emphasized the 'necessity of accounting for structure and group context' (p. 153) when analysing leader behaviour. It is thus argued, that a group's social and cultural composition has consequences for the structure of a team and, therefore, needs to be taken into account by coaches.

Interpretive sociologists, in building on the work of Weber, argue that society, as opposed to being moulded and driven by external factors, comprises the sum of interactions between active human beings (Jarvie and Maguire, 1994). These interactions, which include those of groups in a constant state of uneasy flux with each other, inevitably involve contradictions, and preclude understanding through purely mechanistic and rationalistic means. A comprehension of the nature of such 'inwardly plastic' (Scaff, 1998) relationships and interactions, or at least the framework in which they occur, would again be of benefit to coaches if they are to sincerely relate to their athletes and the relationships between them. Weber concluded that people have motives for their actions; that behaviour is guided by subjective meanings and that to understand the social action of an individual it must be examined in the wider context of its meaning. Sociological knowledge can assist in placing the individual act in a 'normative behavioural range', thus giving understanding to the action. Indeed, it is only the individual who understands social, and therefore sporting, 'settings in a thoroughly practical way that can possibly mediate and resolve tensions and overcome differences' (Lemert, 1997, p. 181).

Fine (1986), in making the case for greater symbolic interactionist research in sport, has argued that 'sport teams provide a sociologically significant setting for understanding interaction' (p. 159). Within this context, symbolic interactionists focus on the meanings created by, and for, individuals within the team environment and how these meanings influence play and performance. Thus, differing social meanings become apparent for the same players in differing situations; in short, sport means different things at different times, with the meaning in each case being socially generated (Fine, 1986). Through further analysis of such related concepts as the 'generalized other', which refers to the relationship between the individual player and team, and how the latter give the former 'unity of self' (Mead, 1934), the significance of such insights, particularly into the areas of team cohesion, becomes increasingly apparent. Indeed, as Fine (1986) concludes, 'in order to understand sports as a collective or team enterprise, it is necessary to recognize that not only do relationships exist among selves, [but that] there is also a relationship between a player's self-conception and his or her conception of the team' (p. 161).

Additionally, the social construction of 'momentum' appears particularly relevant in this regard (Adler and Adler, 1978, as cited in Fine, 1986). Momentum is viewed as being linked to the emotional tide associated with sporting activities, with a team perceived as having momentum likely to do better than one which doesn't. For momentum to occur it must be specifically related to past events, which must be appropriately defined as such by members. Momentum, therefore, becomes a result of how team members view their 'progress' and relative position, a constructed reality which is often linked to the rhetoric of the coach (Fine, 1986). Such rhetoric is, in turn, situationally generated, to create a reality conducive to providing desired future outcomes.

Finally, for Bourdieu, the ability to absorb appropriate actions, which can be seen as akin to Lemert's social competence, is the key for individuals to be at ease with themselves and others. According to Bourdieu, being a competent social actor and having a mastery over social practices involves a 'feel for the game' (Jarvie and Maguire, 1994) developed through the concept of 'habitus' (Wacquant, 1998). Habitus, in turn, refers to the internalization of social mores by an individual; an embodiment of the social game. An individual's action thus, is seen as neither exclusively objectively determined nor a product of free expression.

The concept of habitus, often expressed by the individual as subconscious or unconscious 'second nature' (Wacquant, 1998), has considerable significance for pedagogy and education programmes, in which the idea of knowledge as socially constructed looms large. Consequently, if coaching is to be viewed as a culturally contested site of social practices characterized by a series of power relations which shape individual identities within the wider society, the social and educational responsibilities of practitioners need to be highlighted. Acceptance of such a position, both in relation to the nature of coaching and of the role of the coach within it, would enable practitioners to recognize the liberating and constraining influences upon them, thus progressing to improved practices.

Applying sociology to coach education programmes

How then should we frame a sociological component to coach education? Although basic information concerning the fundamental sociological theories ought to be given, and their relevance to practical coaching outlined, these are likely to be most effective if integrated into a critical task-based reflective approach. Because such education programmes cannot possibly prepare coaches for every situation they may encounter, it is preferable to help coaches to become thoughtful, socially informed decision makers. Thus, drawing on the work of the philosopher John Dewey, and his writing on education and knowledge, the aim is to generate 'persistent and careful consideration of any belief or supposed form of knowledge in the light of the grounds that support it and the further conclusions to which it tends' (Dewey, 1933, p. 9). Such an approach falls broadly in line with postmodernist critique, which aims to question the processes by which coaches arrive at their opinions and the assumptions that underlie them (McLaren, 1994). Furthermore, given that coaching doesn't occur in a social vacuum, and that the 'identity of the individual . . . is a culture commodity whose value and constitution fluctuates in the reality of the socially lived experience' (Schempp, 1998), such societal influences on beliefs and behaviours, which construct the person of the coach, need careful and thoughtful consideration if coaches are to act in enlightened effective ways. In effect, to ensure that practice is informed by 'an understanding of the ways in which biography and history, individuals and society, are linked' (Pollard, 1988, p. 56). The goal here is to educate coaches to act in appropriate interpersonal ways, thus making them aware of the consequences of their actions. Pollard's (1988) work on the value of sociology to reflective teaching is particularly relevant in this context, in which sociology is viewed as 'intellectually liberating' for teachers. Similarly, an awareness by coaches of the value-laden nature of pedagogy would enable them to move beyond an exclusive focus on the symptoms apparent at the level of the sports field or gym, to an analysis of the larger social conditions partially responsible for those symptoms (Zeichner, 1981/2, as cited in Pollard, 1988).

Critical reflection is advocated as an appropriate teaching method in this context as not only does it imply an 'active concern with aims and consequences as well as technical efficiency' but also 'combines enquiry and implementation skills with attitudes of open-mindedness, responsibility and whole-heartedness' (Pollard, 1988, p. 52). Hence, through emphasizing constant self-appraisal, flexibility, rigorousness and social awareness, such an approach is able to take account of the complex social pedagogical decisions that coaches face daily, while also getting coaches to ask critical questions about coaching (Tsangaridou and Siedentop, 1995). Such an approach is grounded in the assumption that coaching is an entirely personal process, with the effective application of broad pedagogical principles requiring considerable insight, even artistry (Hellison and Templin, 1991). Thus, the goal is to get student coaches to reflect on what they actually do in practice without losing sight of the wider patterns of social life (Jarvie and Maguire, 1994). Hence, Pollard's (1988) point regarding the value of sociological thinking in reflective teaching, that is, linking the personal experiences of the individual to the social, economic and political structure of society (echoing Mills' [1959] classical sociological formulation) is realized. Through such a sociological analysis, perceptions and beliefs are opened to critique, examination and evaluation. Furthermore, Hellison and Templin's (1991) call to individualize the pedagogical process is well taken, with heightened self-awareness within the existing social confines resulting in a 'certain openness to new ideas, to alternatives, to improvement' (p. 9).

Within a general reflective framework, small group activity such as problem-solving is particularly appropriate here. The teaching strategy is, consequently, organized to maximize student involvement and to prompt critical questioning, not only of received wisdom, but also of its influence over individual coaching philosophies and practices. It is, therefore, attempted to actively engage the learners in the learning process and to give them a degree of responsibility for their own learning. The role of the teacher or tutor in this regard becomes much more that of facilitator, guiding and prompting the students into appropriate avenues of inquiry and reflection. It is, thus, to structure the learning environment into one where free and respectful discussion is allowed to flourish, in addition to setting challenging tasks for students as a framework within which appropriate topics can be explored.

The following section provides a brief example of how the teaching of social concepts can be incorporated into a practical coach education programme. The example is taken from a module recently run at Brunel University for M.Sc. sports coaching students entitled 'Social and ethical concerns in the coaching process'. In order to realize the module's aim ('To develop a critical understanding of the principal social and philosophical influences which impinge upon the coaching process . . . therefore enabling students to effectively analyse, evaluate and appraise their own coaching behaviour'), students were expected to reflect on their personal coaching philosophies in the light of predominant social structures and their role in shaping those structures.

To achieve this purpose, students were initially guided to explore the basis of their current conscious and reasoned knowledge, to understand their socialization and to deconstruct their assumptions. Thus, they were allowed 'the intellectual and emotional space to explore and understand their own philosophical grounding' (Zakus and Malloy, 1996, p. 552). Through such a reflective examination of the self, the students were encouraged to develop a critical consciousness of themselves and their constructed social world, consequently attaining a basis from which to critically evaluate social situations and the behaviour of others. This was done prior to introducing sociological concepts, because if merely a social 'how to' approach was handed out, then we would advance no further than the present status quo which we claim to be unsatisfactory (Zakus and Malloy, 1996).

Once such a starting point to the module was established, i.e. 'exploring the students' current subjective understanding, especially in terms of their axiological understanding' (Zakus and Malloy, 1996, p. 507), then, the wider issues of social stratification, the coaching of children, elite athlete coaching, athlete burn out and discrimination, including issues of ethnicity, gender and disability, could be examined. An example of a task employed within a lesson involved a series of thought-provoking questions being set for the students to reflect upon individually, before gathering in small groups of three or four for further meaningful discussion and debate. The predominant emergent issues from each group were then reported back to the main class for further consideration. Finally, in order to ensure that the discussion work proceeded to a form of conclusion, a summarized report of the principal points raised by the class was recorded, in addition to strategies being suggested in relation to tackling some of the problems associated with the issues raised. For example, such questions comprising a task concerning the topic of racial discrimination included:

1. Has the Black athlete been stereotyped? If so, how, and why? Have coaches played a part in creating and perpetuating this stereotype?

2. Is Black athletic overrepresentation in certain popular sports indicative of social egalitarian or racist policies?

3. Why are Black people not represented among the positions of coaching and administrative influence?

4. Is the Black experience in sport liberating or repressing?

5. 'Does the notion of meritocracy explain the sporting experiences of Black people?'.

(Jarvie, 1991, p. 4)

The purpose of such a task is to challenge the existing assumptions that the students may have about the Black athlete in sport. This challenge is portrayed 'as a social activity involving a complex set of primary relationships' (Jarvie, 1991, p. 2). Thus, it is encouraged that any stance taken on the participatory nature of sport 'must take account of social cultural contexts which could exert pressure on people's choices, options, experiences and actions' (Jarvie, 1991, p. 2). Similarly, the broader issues of power and social domination are introduced, with the arguments that emphasize the 'distributive' as opposed to the 'relational' aspects of sporting equality being investigated (Jarvie, 1991). Furthermore, such a task aims to help students to question the accuracy of the Black athletic stereotype within society, and to make them aware of the possibility of the concept of 'race' being predominantly a social, as opposed to biological, construct. The ultimate goal here is to stimulate reflection among students about their policies and practices through challenging the conventional wisdom and questioning the assumptions that currently operate in the field, thus becoming a means of refining judgements and decision making (Pollard, 1988).

Undoubtedly such an approach would not be seen as appropriate or applicable by many existing coach educators, while others may question the relevance for coaching of a sociological discipline, which is not only often characterized by abstract intellectualist language, but also ranges well beyond the coaching context. However, its rationale is grounded in the fact that coaching is essentially a social activity and that 'most [such] students do not wind up as technicians but as teachers of human beings, whose thoughts and predispositions they must often interpret in tacit and symbolic ways' (McKay, Gore and Kirk, 1990, p. 63). Therefore, what we need are 'dialetical as opposed to linear thinkers who can use [reflective] knowledge in their praxis' (Zakus and Malloy, 1996, p. 513).

Conclusion

It has been argued here that the principal point of coach education should be at the practical level focusing on the problems and realities of human interaction. It is a view that recognizes the 'complexities, uncertainties and creativity of people, and thus the inherent impossibility of precise verification' (Pollard, 1988, p. 55). The desire however, is not to deny the importance of equipping coaches with technical knowledge, but rather to take issue with the privileging of the technical over other, equally important, forms of knowledge and understanding. Consequently, individual perspectives, informed action and critical reflection, in addition to the existing technical literature, should be utilized to further understand and refine professional practice (McDonald and Brooker, 1995) in creating a dynamic and workable praxis. Indeed, 'as human beings we are not condemned to be swept along by forces that have the inevitability of the laws of nature. But this means we must be conscious of the alternative futures open to us' (Giddens, 1986, p. 22). To improve the quality of coaching, and to raise awareness of these futures, coach education programmes must be grounded in real life problems, and should principally aim to develop cognitive and creative interpretations of the fragmentary strands of knowledge that currently exist. These strands can then be integrated into the social context that should focus on the totality of humans (Rothig, 1985).

References

- Adler P. and Adler P. (1978) 'The role of momentum in sport', *Urban Life* 7: 153–76.
- Aronowitz S. and Giroux H. (1985) *Education Under Siege: The Conservative, Liberal and Radical Debate Over Schooling*, South Hadley, MA.: Bergin and Garvey.
- Cross N. (1995) 'Coaching effectiveness in hockey: A Scottish perspective', *Scottish Journal of Physical Education* 23(1): 27–39.
- Cuff E.C., Sharrock W.W. and Francis D.W. (1998) *Perspectives in Sociology*, 4th edition, London: Routledge.

● Dewey J. (1933) *How We Think*, Chicago: Dorsey.
● Dunning E. (1986) 'The sociology of sport in Europe and the United States: Critical observations from an "Eliasian" perspective', in R. Rees and A. Miracle (eds) *Sport and Social Theory*, Champaign, Ill.: Human Kinetics, pp. 29–56.
● Elias N. (1978) *What is Sociology*, London: Hutchinson.
● Fine G.A. (1986) 'Small groups and sport: A symbolic interactionist perspective', in R. Rees and A. Miracle (eds) *Sport and Social Theory*, Champaign, Ill.: Human Kinetics, pp. 159–70.
● Giddens A. (1986) *Sociology: A Brief but Critical Introduction*, 2nd edition, London: Macmillan.
● Hargreaves J. (1986) *Sport, Power and Culture*, Oxford: Polity Press.
● Hellison D. and Templin T. (1991) *A Reflective Approach to Teaching Physical Education*, Champaign, Ill.: Human Kinetics.
● Jarvie G. (1991) 'Introduction: Sport, racism and ethnicity', in G. Jarvie (ed.) *Sport, Racism and Ethnicity*, London: Falmer Press, pp. 1–6.
● Jarvie G. and Maguire J. (1994) *Sport and Leisure in Social Thought*, London: Routledge.
● Lashuk M. (1992) 'Coaching in the nineties', in T. Williams, L. Amond and A. Sparkes (eds) *Sport and Physical Activity: Moving Towards Excellence*, London: Spon, pp. 463–9.
● Lemert C. (1997) *Social Things: An Introduction to the Sociological Life*, Lanham, Md.: Rowman and Littlefield.
● Locke L. (1985) 'Research and the improvement of teaching: The professor as the problem', in G. Barrette, R. Feingold, R. Rees and M. Pieron (eds) *Myths, Models and Methods in Sport Pedagogy*, Champaign, Ill.: Human Kinetics, pp. 1–26.
● Luschen G. (1986) 'On small groups in sport: Methodological reflections with reference to structural-functionalist approaches', in R. Rees and A. Miracle (eds) *Sport and Social Theory*, Champaign Ill.: Human Kinetics, pp. 149–58.
● Macdonald D. and Brooker R. (1995) 'Professional education: Tensions in subject design and implementation', *Educational Research and Perspectives* 22(2): 99–109.
● Macdonald D. and Tinning R. (1995) 'Physical education teacher education and the trend to proletarianization: A case study', *Journal of Teaching in Physical Education* 15: 98–118.
● McKay J., Gore J.M. and Kirk D. (1990) 'Beyond the limits of technocratic physical education', *Quest* 42(1): 52–76.
● McLaren P. (1994) 'Multi-culturalism and the postmodern critique: Toward a pedagogy of resistance and transformation', in H.A. Giroux and P. McLaren (eds) *Between borders: Pedagogy and the Politics of Cultural Studies*, London: Routledge, pp. 192–222.
● Mead G.H. (1934) *Mind, Self and Society*, Chicago: University of Chicago Press.
● Mills C.W. (1959) *The Sociological Imagination*, New York: Oxford University Press.
● Murray P.F. (1999) 'The construction and validation of the facilitative coaching styles questionnaire (FCSQ), unpublished Ph.D. dissertation, University of Wolverhampton.
● Noddings N. (1984) *Caring: A Feminine Approach to Ethics and Moral Education*, Berkeley: University of California Press.
● Pollard A. (1988) 'Sociology and teaching: A new challenge for the sociology of education', in P. Woods and A. Pollard (eds) *Reflective teaching – The Sociological Contribution*, London: Croom Helm, pp. 54–75.
● Pope W. (1998) 'Emile Durkheim', in R. Stones (ed.) *Key Sociological Thinkers*, Basingstoke: Macmillan, pp. 46–58.
● Rothig P. (1985) 'Reflections on researching sport pedagogy', in G. Barrette, R. Feingold, R. Rees and M. Pieron (eds) *Myths, Models and Methods in Sport Pedagogy*, Champaign, Ill.: Human Kinetics, pp. 51–55.
● Rovegno I and Kirk D. (1995) 'Articulations and silences in socially critical work on physical education: Toward a broader agenda', *Quest* 47: 447–74.

● Sage G. (1987) 'The role of sport studies in sport pedagogy', in G. Barrette, R. Feingold, C.R. Rees and M. Pieron (eds) *Myths, Models and Methods in Sport Pedagogy*, Champaign, Ill.: Human Kinetics, pp. 29–40.

● Scaff L.A. (1998) 'Max Weber', in R. Stones (ed.) *Key Sociological Thinkers*, Basingstoke: Macmillan, pp. 34–45.

● Schempp P. (1998) 'The dynamics of human diversity in sport pedagogy scholarship', *Sociology of Sport Online* 1(1). Available: http://www.brunel.ac.uk/depts/sps/sosol/sosol.htm (June 22, 1998).

● Stoddart B. (1988) 'Sport, cultural imperialism and colonial response in the British empire', *Comparative Studies in Society and History* 30: 649–73.

● Tomlinson A. (1998) 'Power: Domination, negotiation and resistance in sports cultures', *Journal of Sport and Social Issues* 22(3): 235–40.

● Tsangaridou N. and Siedentop D. (1995) 'Reflective teaching: A literature review', *Quest* 47: 212–37.

● Turner A. and Martinek T. (1995) 'Teaching for understanding: A model for improving decision making during game play', *Quest* 47: 44–63.

● Wacquant L.J.D. (1998) 'Pierre Bourdieu', in R. Stones (ed.) *Key Sociological Thinkers*, Basingstoke: Macmillan, pp. 215–29.

● Woodman L. (1993) 'Coaching: A science, an art, an emerging profession', *Sport Science Review* 2(2): 1–13.

● Zakus D.H. and Malloy D.C. (1996) 'A critical evaluation of current pedagogical approaches in human movement studies: A suggested alternative', *Quest* 48: 501–17.

● Zeichner K. (1981/2) 'Reflective teaching and field-based experience in pre-service teacher education', *Interchange* 12: 1–22.

Chapter Four

Managing Voluntary Sport Organizations: A Critique of Popular Trends[1]
Trevor Slack

Introduction

In virtually every country of the world a large percentage of sports activities are structured and operated through a vast network of voluntary organizations. From the heights of international competition, where bodies such as Fédération Internationale de Gymnastique (FIG) and Fédération International de Natation Amateur (FINA) govern the way in which their respective sports are organized and played, to the clubs and community level groups which provide participation opportunities for young children and recreational athletes, the delivery of sport is highly dependent on voluntary organizations. Over the past 20 to 25 years these organizations have undergone considerable change. For example, in Australia, Hamilton and Turner (1997) talk about the shift from volunteer administration to professional management. In Sweden, Olson (1993) points out that businessmen (and he does mean men!) are being asked to sit on the boards of sport clubs in order to professionalize their operations. In France, Camy (1996) describes the rationalization of the organizational structures of sport governing bodies and the formation of a professional corps of managers; and in Canada, Kikulis, Slack and Hinings (1995) have written about the shift these organizations have made to a more professional and bureaucratic structure.

The impetus for the changes these writers describe has come primarily from three sources. First, a factor which became apparent in the 1960s and continued to strongly influence the structure and processes of sport organizations until the mid 1980s was the increasing role of the state in sport. Governments in many countries saw sport as a vehicle which they could use to support their domestic and foreign policy initiatives (Houlihan, 1991; Macintosh and Hawes, 1994). By providing national sport organizations with increased amounts of funding, politicians and government bureaucrats contributed to the adoption of corporate modes of operation in these organizations and the growth of sport science and sport management as a means of achieving organizational goals, most notably the winning of medals in major sporting events such as the Olympic and Commonwealth Games.

However, while state initiatives were the dominant force impacting on the structure and operation of voluntary sport organizations from the 1960s through to the mid 1980s, in the latter part of the 1980s and through the 1990s we have seen a transformation in the way in which many government agencies have dealt with sport. Most notable among these has been a reduction in state funding and an emphasis on the primacy of the market. The roots of this change have been seen as paralleling the rise to power of 'New Right' politicians such as Margaret Thatcher and Ronald Reagan (Henry, 1993). However, as Walsh (1995) points out, these types of changes cannot solely be attributed to those politicians influenced by liberal economic thinking, as a number of countries with left leaning governments have adopted similar reforms. In addition, such factors as fiscal pressures, the failure of the existing system, and the imitation of one government's actions by another, have all contributed to the type of changes that we have seen in public sector funding patterns.

For voluntary sport organizations the most notable impact of these changes has been the reduction of direct government grants to national governing bodies and their regional and local counterparts, and a rise in the consequent pressures for these organizations to turn to the private sector for support. In Canada, for example, there have been annual decreases in both the real and nominal levels of government funding for sport since 1987. In budget cuts announced in 1994, Sport Canada's contribution to individual national sport organizations dropped between 5 per cent and 15 per cent from 1993–94 levels. More recently, in 1995, some 22 federally funded sport organizations had their budget cut by a further 50 per cent, with a government commitment to eliminate their funding entirely in the 1996–97 budget (Slack and Berrett, 1996). As a result of these reductions, sport organizations are now increasingly seeking corporate support for their programmes and teams. As McKay and Miller (1991, p. 87) note about the situation in Australia, 'most amateur and semi-professional men's and women's sports have . . . become reliant on corporate support for player development, equipment, facilities, coaching, dissemination of information, publicity, and administrative costs'. Similar comments could be made about most Western countries as sport sponsorship has become a multi-billion dollar business (International Event Group, 1997). While the effects of this shift in sources of funding is not yet fully understood, it would appear that having to seek corporate support, as opposed to being granted government money, has not decreased the transformation that voluntary sport organizations are making to a more 'business like' organizational form.

In part, this may well be due to a third factor which has influenced the structure and processes of these organizations, namely strong institutional pressures to adopt and/or retain a business-like mode of operation. Institutional pressures are found in organizational networks where the control of resources is centralized in a small number of powerful organizations such as a state agency or a group of influential corporations (Zucker, 1987; Ritti and Silver, 1986). Dependent organizations usually respond to institutional pressures by rapidly incorporating the required elements, in our case more bureaucratic operating procedures and an increased number of professional staff, into their formal structure. This can help legitimize them in the eyes of their key constituents and, thus, ensure the continued flow of resources necessary for their survival. Slack and Hinings (1995) have shown evidence of such processes in voluntary sport organizations.

In this chapter, I explore the opportunities and constraints that the changes these pressures have brought about present for sport. I focus first on the structural changes that we have seen in voluntary sport organizations. Specifically, I examine the shift from the traditionally structured type of voluntary sport organization to a design that is more rational and perceived as being more business-like in its operation. I show that while this shift has opened up new possibilities for some groups, it also works to constrain the opportunities for involvement of others. I then focus on three managerial specialisms; strategic planning, leadership, and marketing. In many ways these have become the *sine qua non* of any legitimate voluntary sport organization. I use work from the sociology of organizations to show how conventional representations focus only on their enabling features. Yet a deeper and more critical analysis reveals that, while they enable certain types of organizational actors and activity, their emphasis on efficiency and motivation serve to mask aspects of organizational life such as inequality, domination, and manipulation. I hope to show that those individuals who operate and manage voluntary sport organizations (and commercial ventures in sport) can learn from the critical perspectives that emanate from the sociological study of sport organizations.

Structural Changes

Let us turn first to the structural changes we have seen in voluntary sport organizations. Traditionally, most of these organizations have operated with a set of structural arrangements which Kikulis, Slack and Hinings (1992) have termed 'a kitchen table' design, a reference to the fact that since their inception, many of these organizations have literally operated from the kitchen table of their volunteer president. They had little in the way of specialized roles, policies and procedures were virtually nonexistent and decisions were made informally by a volunteer board, a group of committed individuals who sought little more out of their involvement with the sport organization than a sense of personal satisfaction and camaraderie. The environment of these organizations was limited to other voluntary groups with missions similar to their own, while operating funds were primarily self-generated and came from membership fees and the occasional fundraising venture, usually something small scale. Rarely did these organizations have the resources to hire professional staff, with enthusiasm and time being the only prerequisites needed to sit on their boards.

Over the past two decades these types of structural arrangements have become increasingly deinstitutionalized as a legitimate way for these organizations to operate. Increased government funding and more recently corporate support has allowed these organizations to expand the number and type of programmes they provide and to hire staff to professionalize their operations. The result has been an institutionalized organizational form which Kikulis, Slack and Hinings (1992) have termed an 'executive office' design. An organization operating with these types of structural arrangements is highly specialized along technical and administrative lines. It will have formal policies and operating procedures and decisions will be made by professional staff working with the help of volunteer board members, many of whom will have been recruited primarily for their political and business contacts, not necessarily for their knowledge of a particular sport. This type of structure is somewhat akin to Mintzberg's (1979) 'professional bureaucracy' and has become the institutionally approved form for voluntary sport organizations in many countries (Camy, 1996; Slack and Hinings, 1995; Theodoraki and Henry, 1994).

There is no doubt that there are a number of benefits to the voluntary sport organizations that adopt this type of design. First, and in many ways most important for the organization, is that it is able to demonstrate its legitimacy to funding bodies such as government agencies and corporations. As sport has become increasingly important to government agencies as a policy tool or to corporations as a means of marketing their products, these organizations have demanded more and more accountability for the money they provide. One way of providing this accountability is by an organization conforming to the expectations of its institutional environment. By showing conformity an organization is able to demonstrate that it is acting on a collectively valued purpose, and by doing so it is able to increase its chances of being positively evaluated and thus ensure a continued flow of the resources necessary for its operation (Slack and Hinings, 1992). In short, by adopting the structural and operational characteristics of a 'business-like' organization sport bodies are able to more easily secure monies from funding agencies.

In addition, a more professional bureaucratic design is both appealing and enabling as a means of structuring a voluntary sport organization because it places operating power in the hands of the professional managers and coaches who work at the mid-level of the organization. These are the people who are seen to possess the specialist training within the organization and this type of structure allows them the autonomy to practise their trade, the production of elite-level athletes. The role of the volunteers, who, in the traditional structure carried out these tasks, is now limited to the setting of policy for the organization. For many this is an acceptable division of labour because as the task of producing elite-level performers has become more complex, increasingly scientific, and more time consuming, there is a feeling that it can only be handled by those who have the time, professional training, and resultant expertise to perform such a detailed task. These are attributes that many people believe are now beyond the scope of even the most dedicated volunteer.

The professional bureaucratic structure is also appealing because it is seen by many as democratic, disseminating power directly to those who are most closely concerned with the central work of the organization. The strategic direction of the organization remains in the hands of the volunteer board, but day-to-day operational decisions should be decentralized to the professionals who operate at the mid-level of the organization. This type of structure also presents the possibility for parallel but coordinated administrative hierarchies to exist (Mintzberg, 1979), something that is inherently appealing in voluntary sport organizations with their two main groups of operatives. The structure is appealing to professionals because it affords them the ability to control their own work and at the same time have input into the administrative decisions that affect them. This is most overtly seen in voluntary sport organizations through the involvement of professionals, along with volunteers, on the many committees that are deigned to structure and allocate work within these organizations.

The features of the bureaucratic structure that can be enabling for both volunteers and professionals are also the features that can constrain the actions and ambitions of each. This type of structure relies on the professional's training as its main means of coordination; direct supervision is seen as an infringement on her or his autonomy. Consequently, the professional sport scientists and sport managers who are at the heart of the organization's operations expect to run their organization with relative freedom. Such autonomy is anathema to many volunteers, who feel that the professionals work for them and by virtue of their voluntary labour they should have an equal, if not greater, say in its operation. The time volunteers can devote to this task and the greater expertise of the professionals are structural factors which militate against this type of arrangement. The professionals feel that because of their training in the subdisciplines of sport, it is they who are the experts and as such they should have the autonomy to operate as they see fit. These two countervailing positions have frequently led to conflicts in voluntary sport organizations. The quest for professional staff autonomy has also led to many volunteers being marginalized and/or feeling dissatisfied with their involvement, and subsequently leaving the organization.

The institutional pressures from governments and corporations for this type of organizational form have also led to an increasing requirement for those volunteers who do assume board positions in these organizations to hold the appropriate corporate credentials. In fact, Macintosh and Whitson (1990, p. 68), in their study of Canadian national sport organizations, found that 'it was financial and fund raising experience rather than sport experience that were . . . seen as the most important qualifications for volunteers who occupied senior positions on boards' and that the most important function for a volunteer director was no longer directly related to sport but 'to open corporate doors'. Such practices have led to the marginalization of certain volunteers who did not have the required corporate credentials and as Macintosh and Whitson note, this frequently meant women. Women were seen by many men, and some women, as not possessing the necessary qualifications (whether they did or not) to hold board positions. Some of Macintosh and Whitson's (1990) respondents even went as far as to suggest that women were not suited for such positions because issues at the board level were often decided by aggressive debating tactics and the most forceful debaters were 'men who are used to getting their own way in business' (p. 68). These constraining features of the professional bureaucracy for volunteers, particularly female volunteers, were also paralleled by a similar phenomenon in the staffing of professional positions. The emphasis in this type of organizational form, like many other types of state bureaucratic organizations (Grant and Tancred, 1992), was for men to assume positions of power with women relegated to support roles.

Also constraining in terms of the structure of the professional bureaucracy is the fact that 'it focuses all the discretion [for a particular job] in the hands of a single group of professionals, whose complex skills, no matter how standardized, require the exercise of considerable judgement' (Mintzberg, 1979, p. 373). If judgement is lacking, problems can occur. One of the most visible cases of such a situation is the one involving banned sprinter Ben Johnson and his coach Charlie Francis. Francis held a position of such authority that, despite considerable prior warnings, the Canadian Track and Field Association's volunteer board were unable to bring sanctions against him in his position as one of their coaches. Thus, while the professional bureaucracy is appropriate for professionals who are competent and conscientious, it can not easily deal with those who are not. The discretion that is afforded the professionals in this type of organization enables them to not only ignore the needs of clients (in this case the athletes) but 'it also encourages many of them to ignore the needs of the organization' (Mintzberg, 1979, p. 374).

We can see then that the professional bureaucratic form of organization which has become *de rigeur* for voluntary sport organizations to adopt can work both to enable the opportunities of the athletes, volunteers and professionals who constitute its members, and also to constrain them. Most notable is the limitations it places on volunteers who lack (or are seen to lack) the necessary qualifications to function in this type of milieu; many of these are women. The autonomy it gives professionals can also lead to dysfunctional actions if power is not exercised with the concerns of the clients and the organization in mind, and, in such situations, the members of the organization may be powerless to rectify the problem.

The enabling and constraining features of modern day voluntary sport organizations are not, however, limited to those that emanate from structural arrangements. The very processes which members of these organizations have come to hold in such high regard reflect the duality of action and constraint. In this chapter, I focus on three such processes; first, the issue of strategic planning.

Strategic planning

The development of a formally documented strategic plan has become as much a requirement of many voluntary sport organizations as the holding of an annual general meeting. In many countries, strategic plans have become the driving force behind the operation of many national sport organizations and for some the 'magic ingredient' in the production of medal winning athletes. In their work in Canada, Slack and Hinings (1992) found that many of the voluntary sport organizations they studied had produced, often at considerable time and expense, substantive documents that articulated a vision for the organization, a formally documented set of goals and objectives, and action steps and timelines for achieving these aims. Consultants were employed to assist in the development of these plans and many were more substantive than would be expected of a medium to large corporation. The rationale for the production of these plans was that this was a requirement of the state agency and funding was contingent upon the creation of such a document. Even more recently, when state requirements have been relaxed, institutional pressures have produced strong expectations that these organizations will have formally documented plans.

While the benefits of strategic planning are intuitively hard to question, it has become somewhat of what Abrahamson (1991) calls a 'managerial fad' for voluntary sport organizations to produce voluminous strategic plans outlining their aims and objectives. Although writing about corporations, the comments of one American management guru that North Americans get off on strategic management like the French get off on good food and romance could certainly be applied to voluntary sport organizations. The word 'strategy' which saw little use prior to the 1980s (Whipp, 1996) has, as Lyles (1990) notes, become a buzzword for establishing the importance of one's work. However, while there is scepticism about the use of the word, there can be little doubt that there are a number of enabling features associated with the act of strategic planning. From a managerial point of view, strategic planning is conceived in terms of strengthening the focal organization's command of its environment and the development of strategically conscious human resources who are knowledgeable about the content of such plans and committed to their successful implementation within the organization. Such plans, the adherents of the strategic planning process argue, aid managers in efficiently and effectively allocating their resources, provide direction to the members of the organization and to important outside groups, allow members of the organization to plan for the various programmes in which they wish to be involved, serve to provide the organization with legitimacy, direct and motivate employees, guide decision making and clarify performance expectations.

However, the concept of strategy, as it is used in most voluntary sport organizations, is monolithic and based on what Whittington (1993a) and others have termed the 'classical' approach. The roots of this are found in the discipline of economics and particularly the rational economic 'man'. From this perspective 'strategy is the product of a single entrepreneurial individual acting with perfect rationality to maximize "his" economic advantage' (Whittington, 1993a, p. 16). Originated by writers such as Alfred Sloan, the former President of General Motors, and Alfred Chandler, and more recently popularized by Michael Porter and Oliver Williamson, the classical approach to strategy fosters a mentality where objective criteria like profit, or in our case medal-winning athletes, are central, and a deeper understanding of organization development, is downplayed.

Such a way of seeing strategy tends to mask some of its constraining features. First, the Anglo-American origins of strategy may serve to constrain our understanding of what the concept actually means. As Whittington (1993a) notes, these two nations are heavily biased towards an individually-based free enterprise model of strategy where reliance on the state is frowned upon. This is in contrast to the traditional nationalism of the state which is found in countries like France and Germany and in Scandinavia, where the use of state resources is seen as a natural and important part of the strategy focus. Given the increasing Americanization of sporting practice (McKay and Miller, 1991), i.e., the adoption of American modes of operation, it is fair to say that the classical conception of strategy may not fit comfortably in voluntary sport organizations as they exist in other cultures. Shrivastava (1986, cited by Whittington, 1993a, p. 32) has even gone as far as to suggest that such orthodox approaches to strategic planning and management reflect an ideology 'that serves to normalize the existing structure of American society and universalize the goals of its dominant elite'. Those in voluntary sport organizations in countries outside the US and Great Britain who choose to use strategic planning as a method of operation, must be aware that both the concept of strategy and the way it is used are historically and socially constituted and, as such, if they fail to consider the social and economic systems in which the organizations they manage are embedded, they may find themselves constrained with a narrow choice of strategic options.

The process of strategy formulation in voluntary sport organizations (as in other organizations) is also constraining because, as employed in its classical mode, it takes for granted the institutionalized structures of power that exist within an organization. Most writers in the field of strategic planning and management take for granted that strategy 'is necessary and legitimately the domain of top management' (Alvesson and Willmott 1996, p. 136). Problematic in such a top-down approach is the frequent failure of strategists to account for the diversity that makes up their organization and to exclude such groups from consideration in the formulation of the strategy. Macintosh and Whitson (1990), for example, in their work on Canadian national sport organizations identified women, some volunteers, recreational athletes, and individuals from rural areas as groups which were disadvantaged by their exclusion from the strategic planning process. As Alvesson and Willmott (1996) point out, in orthodox approaches to strategy such groups 'have relevance only when the implementation of strategic plans is understood to depend upon their support or compliance' (p. 136). The issue for the strategist then becomes one of determining how support from these groups can be cost effectively engineered, rather than how to best appreciate and address their concerns.

Alvesson and Willmott (1996) even go as far as to suggest that what they refer to as 'strategy talk' can work to constrain the involvement of such groups and certain individuals from involvement in planning the direction of the organization, in that this discourse 'frames issues in a way that privileges instrumental reason [and] it tends to give the initiative to those who successfully claim to be strategists' (p. 136). Knights and Morgan (1991) make similar arguments about strategy as a discourse and suggest that participation in this discourse and identification with its practices are a source of power for organizational members. In the case of voluntary sport organizations, this has frequently meant that professional staff and those volunteers who have the required corporate credentials are able to legitimize their privileged position and gain influence and credibility by demonstrating the relevance of their role within the organization for obtaining the objectives it has that are deemed strategic (Alvesson and Willmott, 1996). Such control of discourse serves to construct and reinforce the taken-for-granted assumption that voluntary sport organizations should be strategically driven and those people outside the strategic core (usually lower-level professional staff, many of whom are women, volunteers without corporate credentials, and those who do not subscribe to the high performance ethos) should realize their limited ability to contribute to the future direction of the organization and subordinate themselves to those who can help achieve its objectives.

What this means then, is that while the formulation and implementation of strategic plans, which has become an accepted feature of voluntary sport organizations, can be seen as aiding the achievement of organizational goals, when we move beyond the narrow and rational approaches to strategy commonly used in these organizations, wider questions concerning the constraining nature of the classical process are uncovered. While there can be little doubt that the formulation and implementation of an appropriate strategy can enable the achievement of the goals of many members of an organization, the free enterprise logic of strategy, the discourse it presents, and its role as the domain of top management and/or selected groups of functionaries, all reveal its constraining features.

Leadership

Closely aligned to the formulation and implementation of strategy has been the concept of leadership, the second of the managerial specialisms I will examine in this chapter. It has been claimed that in terms of the study of sport organizations, more has been written about leadership than any other area (Paton, 1987). Certainly, the terms 'leader' and 'leadership' have been central to the vocabulary of politicians and state bureaucrats who have sought to make voluntary sport organizations more effective and efficient. The popular conception of leadership, which has been embraced within voluntary sport organizations, arises from the even more popular genre of books which describe how leaders such as Lee Iacocca at Chrysler, Thomas Watson at IBM, and Bill Gates at Microsoft built financial empires by exhibiting qualities of decisiveness, toughness, and risk taking. These popular press books present pictures of leaders inspiring followers with their vision, rugged in their individualism, ruthless in their directions, and vigorous in their quest to take their organization to unprecedented levels of success.

There can be little argument that, for both the corporation and the voluntary sport organization, having competent people in the so-called leadership positions can be enabling in assisting many members of the organization to achieve their goals. Leaders can after all influence the direction of the organization, they can motivate and inspire others, and serve a symbolic function both inside and outside the enterprise. It would be wrong, however, to see leadership as a panacea for all the ills of sport organizations, despite the image that is frequently presented. In fact, if we examine the concept and practice of leadership more critically, we can identify a number of its constraining features. First, like strategy, leadership is culture bound. As Whittington (1993a) notes, in comparison with continental Europe or the Far East, Anglo-Saxon cultures are 'peculiarly individualistic valuing autonomy and free enterprise above collective action and state interests' and, as such, 'the individualistic nature of leadership is consistent with prevailing American and English prejudices' (pp. 47–8). For those who function outside these areas, the concept of leadership as a route to organizational success may be less applicable.

Leadership may also be constraining in that it presents an overly voluntaristic view of organization, one that ascribes primacy to human agency. The focus is on the qualities of the individual and the power they can invoke. Such a perspective is in sharp contrast to much work in the sociology of organizations which has tended to present a far more deterministic view of the way in which leaders are able to shape strategic action. The former view takes no account of the social and historical conditions from which leaders arise. In our search for leaders, we are often blind to the manner in which the resources of an individual's background help the realization of leadership potential (Whittington, 1993b). Class, gender, race, and ethnicity can all be enabling or constraining features for leaders and several studies across several countries (Gruneau, 1976; McKay, 1997) have shown that women, individuals from lower social and economic backgrounds and ethnic and racial minorities are all underrepresented in leadership positions in higher-level voluntary sport organizations.

Czarniawska-Joerges and Wolff (1991) have, in fact, seen leadership as constraining for women, in that the very concept has become culturally defined as an inherently masculine role. Calas and Smircich (1991) go even further and suggest that, within the literature, the role of leader is described as liaising, probing, infusing, and potent and as such it's a seductive, sexual, and male role. Studies of leadership have frequently shown that men more frequently emerge as leaders than women (Carbonell, 1984); this is certainly the case in voluntary sport organizations (Hall, Cullen and Slack, 1989). Yet, many of those who work with and within these organizations still continue to extol the merits of leadership as a solution to many organizational problems.

Marketing

Also seen as a solution to many of the problems, particularly the financial problems, of voluntary sport organizations is the third managerial specialism that I consider in this chapter, marketing. In the world of the so called 'amateur' sports, the concept and practice of marketing have become centrally important as a perceived means of income generation. As Meenaghan and O'Sullivan (1999) note although 'professional sport was earliest to concern itself with marketing issues . . . the past decade has seen an extension of marketing approaches to the world of amateur sport' (p. 245). The discourse of sport marketing, which is promoted by government officials, politicians, and the professional staff and many volunteers who constitute some of the main stakeholders in amateur sport organizations, is about much more than the traditional quest to promote the development and successes of athletes. It is about selling sport and the values and images associated with it to future and existing customers. These customers may range from potential club members to multinational corporations.

In large part the increased interest in the marketing of amateur sport organizations has been the result of a reduction in state funding for these bodies and the resultant need for them to turn to the private sector for the shortfalls they are experiencing. However, the globalization of consumption and the ability of sport to transcend national boundaries has also contributed to its popularity as a marketing vehicle. The growth in the importance of marketing for amateur sport organizations is evidenced by the number of these organizations which employ in-house marketing personnel or hold contracts with external marketing agencies (albeit these individuals are often not as successful as they or their organization would like). It is also evidenced by the increased amount of corporate support given to sport (over $3.5 billion per year in North America – admittedly a significant proportion on professional sport), the growth of sport marketing as subdisciplinary area in sport studies and the emergence of such organizations as the Sport Marketing Council in Canada and the Institute of Sports Sponsorship in the UK.

Marketing, as a managerial activity, takes places primarily at two levels within voluntary sport organizations. First, sport managers attempt to market their sport to potential participants, usually young children whom they hope will take up the sport. Second, the organization can market properties, such as its name, logo, the events it holds or its athletes in order to obtain corporate support. I deal with each of these two levels in turn.

Marketing a sport in order to increase participation is an intuitively appealing and logical function for a voluntary sport organization. It is also a principle that is consistent with the tenets of mainstream management gurus who see marketing as being concerned with serving the interests of potential and actual consumers by satisfying their needs. The basic belief behind much marketing activity is that an increase in consumption leads to an increase in satisfaction. The basis on which this premise is founded is that an exchange relationship takes place, where, in sport, the voluntary organization operating the activity provides the opportunity for an individual to participate, and then she or he, in turn, provides loyalty to the organization through competing for them, paying membership fees, and being involved in social and related organizational activities. The basis of an exchange relationship is that each individual is unconstrained to select the option they want in a free and open marketplace. It does not take into account the fact that characteristics such as gender, race, geographical location, and family status can constrain an individual's ability to respond to marketing initiatives. As Alvesson and Willmott (1996) suggest, it presents an image of common-sense voluntarism, ignores the asymmetrical relations of power in [marketing] relationships, 'provides a deceptively easy-to-understand formulation of the complexities of human interaction and neglects to discuss how structures of domination and exploitation shape and mediate relationships' (p. 120).

While there can be little question of the fact that it is the responsibility of those who work for, and are members of, voluntary sport organizations to promote and publicize their sport and that this can be of benefit to both the organization and the participant, an excessive emphasis on marketing presents an image of the young athlete and potential athlete as a commodity. For some voluntary sport organizations they may be merely another membership fee to add to the coffers or another name on the membership list which is used to justify government and/or corporate funding of the sport.

The marketing image of sport that is presented to young potential athletes and their parents is consistent with the marketing image of other products and services in that it is about constructing myths. Involvement in sport is presented as healthful recreation and more often than not as providing the potential to achieve fame through athletic success. Such images tend to downplay the negative aspects of the activity such as drugs, injuries, eating disorders, and so forth. Also, they frequently focus on the object-ive criteria of winning and the pleasure that comes from such success as opposed to the more subjective satisfaction that can come from the aesthetics of performance and competing against oneself. The negative effects of such marketing can also include the reinforcement of gender stereotypes, the promotion of conformity, and an overemphasis on competitiveness.

Marketing in the form of seeking and obtaining corporate support is like the marketing of participation opportunities; an intuitively logical and appropriate activity for a volunt-ary sport organization to be involved in. The increased amounts of funding that have come through corporate support have had considerable benefits to many of the voluntary sport organizations that stage athletic events and to a number of the athletes who engage in them. Increased levels of corporate support have been linked to increased media coverage of sport, and now spectators in many parts of the world regularly see athletes they would not normally get to watch if it were not for such support. The athletes them-selves have benefited, no longer shackled by the bonds of amateurism, top performers in sports like track and field, cycling, skiing, figure skating, and volleyball have been able to receive compensation for their efforts. This has come about largely through the money that is obtained through corporate support in the form of sponsorship and advertising. We have also seen events, at all levels, that previously may not have been possible or would have been operated in a less grandiose fashion, sustain and increase their viability because of corporate support.

However, marketing and its related activities of sponsorship and advertising are not the neutral activities that their primary advocates would have us believe. The very discourse of marketing and its incorporation into voluntary sport organizations may be seen as helping transform them 'at their very roots into structures that fit more easily with the dominant market and marketing ethos of society' (Morgan, 1992, p. 143). It may appear that such a discourse can, as I noted above, promote the concept of exchange and the related ideas about freedom of choice (Copeland, Frisby and McCarville, 1996), but as Morgan (1992, p. 143) notes, it is also a discourse which 'conceals underlying inequalities of power which are produced and reproduced both inside and outside the market transactions'. First, and in many ways the most apparent of these inequalities, is the ability of some sport organizations to transact in the marketplace and secure corporate funding. In general, those organizations which have been the most successful in securing corporate money are those which are concerned with the larger and more visible sports. Copeland *et al.* (1996) found, for example, in their study of Canadian corporations that nearly 70 per cent of all their respondents were sponsoring professional or elite-level 'amateur' sport. Smaller sports and those which have a lower public profile are frequently unable to attract a high level of financial support from corporate bodies. Hargreaves (1986) has argued that even in those larger and more high profile organizations which do receive sponsorship this can lead to uneven development within the sport because there is no guarantee that the resources gained will filter down to the lower levels of the organization. With state funding as the primary source of income for these organizations, there is some degree of balancing between the 'haves' and the 'have nots'. The marketplace is less sensitive to these needs and a phenomenon where the rich get richer may be created. Work we have recently completed in Canada (Amis, Slack and Hinings, 1999) tends to suggest that this is the case. As voluntary sport organizations have lost state funding and have had to try to secure corporate help, a number of the smaller, lower profile bodies have had to restructure and return to the 'kitchen table' type of operation that they exhibited in the 1970s (not that this is necessarily bad for all organizations). They have been unable to retain the professional staff they had employed and a number have moved to less grandiose office facilities. Such changes to the funding patterns of these organizations creates instability and does not augur well for their effective operation.

Corporate funding of voluntary sport organizations may also be constraining in that it is a relatively fickle source of funding. A change in the CEO of a sponsoring company and/or a change in the company's strategic direction can result in rapid withdrawal of funds, again a factor which does not promote the long-term stability of these organizations. Involvement with corporate funders also means that the demands of the marketplace are given precedence over the needs of the athletes. Corporate sponsors who fund sport organizations and major sporting events expect a significant commitment from athletes, whose interests, in terms of their training and competition schedule, become subordinate to the sponsors' desire to have them participate in funded events. Star athletes now compete on sponsored circuits which Aris (1990) suggests may bring them more status (certainly more money!) than representing their country in a major event. Athletes are lured with prize money and/or appearance fees, so much so, that injuries may be ignored, educational opportunities are passed over in the search for success, and banned substances are employed to enhance performance. Top class athletes now no longer represent their club, country or even themselves; they are now the standard bearers of the sponsors who provide money for them and their sport. As Kidd (1988) points out, the expectations of the corporations who fund sport have 'become so commanding that they, in effect, have blocked the expression of the older, humanistic amateur based aspirations of Olympism and other similar values' (p. 302). Former Canadian Ski coach Currie Chapman noted it is not 'just them [the athlete] going down the mountain but it's also a bank, a drugstore, a car parts chain as well' (Kidd, 1988, p. 23).

It would appear, however, that such concerns have not halted or even slowed those who operate voluntary sport organizations as they have embraced marketing as the remedy to many of their financial woes. There can be no doubt that there are benefits to such involvement but it is always important for these people to keep in mind that the commodification of athletes also has its down side.

Conclusion

The growing importance of strategic planning and marketing and the perceived importance of good leaders in directing these processes will come as no surprise to anyone who has had any involvement with voluntary sport organizations in recent years. As I have noted in this chapter, there can be little question that there have been a number of benefits to these type of initiatives which have enhanced the status of sport in society and presented increased participation opportunities for the athletes, coaches, officials, and administrators who constitute the members of these organizations. Nevertheless, despite the obvious and oft cited benefits, it is incumbent on those who work within sport not to unwittingly accept at face value the technological rationality and efficiency of such changes. It is here, as I have briefly tried to show, that the sociological study of sport can play a role. There is a large body of literature on the sociology of organizations and also literature which has adopted a sociologically informed approach to such managerial specialisms as accounting (Richardson, 1987) and human resources management (Townley, 1994), which can be used to enhance our understanding of sport organizations. Utilizing such literature to inform our knowledge about sport organizations, and the changes they experience, will move us away from the overly managerial focus which has traditionally been adopted in work in sport management. It will present students and instructors with new paradigmatic approaches which challenge conventional wisdom, bring about a type of reflexivity that encourages a critique of managerial and organizational practices, and, as such, provide us with a deeper understanding of the opportunities and constraints that exist in sport organizations.

Note

1. A version of this chapter was presented as a keynote address at the 1997 International Committee for the Sociology of Sport Conference held in Oslo and parts of the section on marketing appeared in the electronic journal *Sociology of Sport Online* (SOSOL).

References

● Abrahamson E. (1991) 'Managerial fads and fashions: The diffusion and rejection of innovations', *Academy of Management Review* 16: 586–612.

● Alvesson M. and Willmott H. (1996) *Making Sense of Management: A Critical Analysis*, London: Sage.

● Amis J., Slack T. and Hinings C.R. (1999) *The Pace and Sequence of Organizational Change*, working paper.

● Aris S. (1990) *Sportsbiz: Inside the Sports Business*, London: Hutchinson.

● Calas M.B. and Smircich L. (1991) 'Voicing seduction to silence leadership', *Organization Studies* 12: 567–602.

● Camy J. (1996) 'Sport management in France', in J.-L. Chappelet and M.-H. Roukhadzé (eds) *Sport Management: An International Approach*, Lausanne: International Olympic Committee, pp. 53–62.

● Carbonell J.L. (1984) 'Sex roles and leadership revisited', *Journal of Applied Psychology* 69: 44–9.

● Copeland R., Frisby W. and McCarville R. (1996) 'Understanding the sport sponsorship process from a corporate perspective', *Journal of Sport Management* 10: 32–48.

● Czarniawska-Joerges B. and Wolff R. (1991) 'Leaders on and off the organizational stage', *Organization Studies* 12: 529–46.

● Grant J. and Tancred P. (1992) 'A feminist perspective on state bureaucracy', in A.J. Mills and P. Tancred (eds) *Gendering Organizational Analysis*, London: Sage, pp. 112–28.

● Gruneau R. (1976) 'Class or mass: Notes on the democratization of Canadian amateur sport', in R. Gruneau and J. Albinson (eds) *Canadian Sport: Sociological Perspectives*, Don Mills, Ontario: Addison-Wesley, pp. 108–41.

● Hall M.A., Cullen D. and Slack T. (1989) 'Organizational elites recreating themselves: The gender structuring of national sport organizations', *Quest* 41: 28–45.

● Hamilton L. and Turner P. (1997) 'Power in sport: A case study of Victoria soccer', in *Proceedings of the 2nd Annual Sport Management Association of Australia and New Zealand (Inc.) Conference*, pp. 95–114.

● Hargreaves J. (1986) *Sport, Power and Culture*, Oxford: Polity Press.

● Henry I. (1993) *The Politics of Leisure Policy*, Houndmills, UK: Macmillan.

● Houlihan B. (1991) *The Government and Politics of Sport*, London: Routledge.

● International Event Group (IEG) Sponsorship Report (1997) *1998 Sponsorship Spending: $6.8 Billion*, Chicago: International Event Group, 22 December.

● Kidd B. (1988) 'The philosophy of excellence: Olympic performance class power, and the Canadian state', in P.J. Galasso (ed.) *Philosophy of Sport and Physical Activity: Issues and Controversies*, Toronto: Canadian Scholars Press, pp. 11–31.

● Kikulis L., Slack T. and Hinings C.R. (1992) 'Institutionally specific design archetypes: A framework for understanding change in national sport organizations', *International Review for the Sociology of Sport* 27: 343–70.

● Kikulis L., Slack T. and Hinings C.R. (1995) 'Sector specific patterns of organizational design change', *Journal of Management Studies* 32: 67–100.

● Knights D. and Morgan G. (1991) 'Strategic discourse and subjectivity: Towards a critical analysis of corporate strategy in organizations', *Organization Studies* 12: 251–73.

● Lyles M. (1990) 'A research agenda for strategic management in the 1990s', *Journal of Management Studies* 27: 363–75.

● Macintosh D. and Hawes M. (1994) *Sport and Canadian Diplomacy*, Montreal and Kingston: McGill-Queen's University Press.

● Macintosh D. and Whitson D. (1990) *The Game Planners*, Montreal and Kingston: McGill-Queen's University Press.

● McKay J. (1997) *Managing Gender*, New York: State University of New York Press (Suny).

● McKay J. and Miller T. (1991) 'From old boys to men and women of the corporation: The Americanization and commodification of Australian sport', *Sociology of Sport Journal* 8: 86–94.

● Meenaghan T. and O'Sullivan P. (1999) 'Playpower – sports meets marketing', *European Journal of Marketing* 33: 241–49.

● Mintzberg H. (1979) *The Structuring of Organizations*, Englewood Cliffs, NJ: Prentice Hall.

● Morgan G. (1992) 'Marketing discourse and practice: Towards a critical analysis', in M. Alvesson and H. Willmott (eds) *Critical Management Studies*, London: Sage, pp. 136–58.

● Olson H.-E. (1993) 'Leisure policy in Sweden', in P. Bramham, I. Henry, H. Mommaas and H. van der Poel (eds) *Leisure Policy in Europe*, Wallingford, UK: CAB International, pp. 71–100.

● Paton G. (1987) 'Sport management research – what progress has been made?', *Journal of Sport Management* 1: 25–31.

● Richardson A. (1987) 'Accounting as a legitimating institution', *Accounting, Organizations and Society* 8: 341–56.

● Ritti R. and Silver J. (1986) 'Early processes of institutionalization: The dramaturgy of exchange in interorganizational relations', *Administrative Science Quarterly* 31: 31–42.

● Shrivastava P. (1986) 'Is strategic management ideological?', *Journal of Management* 12: 363–77.

● Slack T. and Berrett T. (1996) 'Seeking corporate sponsorship: some factors limiting the success of national sport organization initiatives', in J.-L. Chappelet & M-H. Roukhadzé (eds) *Sport Management: An International Approach*, Lausanne: International Olympic Committee, pp. 157–62.

● Slack T. and Hinings C.R. (1992) 'Understanding change in national sport organizations: An integration of theoretical perspectives', *Journal of Sport Management* 6: 114–32.

● Slack T. and Hinings C.R. (1995) 'Institutional pressures and isomorphic change: An empirical test', *Organization Studies* 15: 803–27.

● Theodoraki E. and Henry I. (1994) 'Organizational structures and contexts in British national governing bodies of sport', *International Review for the Sociology of Sport* 29: 243–68.

● Townley B. (1994) *Reframing Human Resources Management: Power, Ethics and the Subject at Work*, London: Sage.

● Walsh K. (1995) *Public Services and Market Mechanisms*, Houndmills, UK: Macmillan.

● Whipp R. (1996) 'Creative deconstruction: strategy and organizations', in S.R. Clegg, C. Hardy and W. Nord (eds) *Handbook of Organization Studies*, London: Sage, pp. 261–75.
● Whittington R. (1993a) *What is Strategy and Does it Matter?*, London: Routledge.
● Whittington R. (1993b) 'Social structures and strategic leadership', in J. Hendry, G. Johnson and J. Newton (eds) *Strategic Thinking: Leadership and the Management of Change*, Chichester, UK: John Wiley & Sons, pp. 181–97.
● Zucker L.G. (1987) 'Institutional theories of organization', *Annual Review of Sociology* 13: 443–64.

Chapter Five

Physical Education. . . . In What and Whose Interests?
Dawn Penney

Introduction

This chapter focuses upon the relevance and value of sociological study, concepts and understandings, to the development of policy and practice in physical education. In particular, I hope to illustrate that sociological concepts and understandings are not only highly pertinent to physical education teachers and sports coaches working with children, but furthermore, that as educationalists, we have a professional responsibility to address sociological issues and agendas and specifically, to engage in critical reflection and the development of our subject and professional practices. As I discuss further below, while we may not explicitly acknowledge it, in being involved in teaching and/or coaching, we are playing an active role in the development of future citizens and thus societies. Arguably there is a need for a far more proactive approach to this role. In this chapter, I therefore highlight the need to not only view the athlete or child as a person at the centre of analysis (Armour and Jones, 1999); but as citizens in, and of, society.

Why should we claim that sociology is important in the context of physical education? and, as a discipline, what has it to offer the study and development of physical education and sport?

To respond to the latter point first, sociology, as any discipline, is diverse. The ideas presented here can be regarded as drawing upon and broadly located within various bodies of work within the discipline. Many of the issues addressed can be associated with interpretative sociology, focusing attention upon the interpretations and meanings that individuals attribute to social and cultural worlds, and the ways in which those worlds are constructed (Evans, 1986). In addition, and particularly in relation to my focus upon addressing the potential for 'things to be different in physical education', I draw upon ideas forthcoming from more recent work that can variously be identified with 'critical sociology', 'postmodernism' and also 'poststructuralism'. Specifically, I make reference to the recent work of Michael Young (1998), and in the context of physical education, writings of, for example, Fernández-Balboa (1997); Tinning (1997); Evans and Davies (1986), and my own work with John Evans, centring upon policy and curriculum development (see for example, Penney and Evans, 1997, 1999). In drawing upon these works I hope to illustrate the ability of sociological inquiry to provide not merely a basis for extending understanding of contemporary policies and practices, but also, a basis for changing policies and practice in physical education.

Central to my discussions is an emphasis that, in looking at contemporary policies and practice in physical education from a sociological perspective, we need to address the *texts* of physical education (that as I explain below, encompasses not only formal and official curriculum documents, but also our expressions of those in the form of our own curriculum documents and physical education lessons), the *contexts* of policy and curriculum development and our professional practice, and the *processes* of policy and curriculum development. I argue that only by considering all three of these dimensions, their interrelationships and our own position and influence in relation to the form that they each take, can we consider prospects and potential for change in physical education. This is particularly the case in relation to the values and interests that policies and practice express and thus legitimate or equally exclude or marginalize. I also focus attention upon the concept of *discourse* as a means of exploring these issues and this potential.

Physical education, society and equity

Physical education and sport are a part of our social and cultural worlds. The relationship is dynamic, with the policies and practices of physical education reflecting, but also clearly shaping (reproducing and/or challenging), the values and interests of broader society. As Evans and Davies (1986) stressed, '. . . children do learn all sorts of things in the PE curriculum . . . schools do leave children with something' (pp. 15–16), and as they highlight, this may not always be positive. Pupils' experiences in, and of, physical education may well have been such that they feel that they have no place in the worlds of physical education and sport, and that those worlds have nothing to offer them (ibid., 1986). Issues such as these are, I believe, important ones for teachers and coaches of physical education to engage with, not merely with a view to critiquing present policies and practices, but also with a view to developing new or 'alternative' approaches. As teachers and coaches, we play a fundamental role in the development of skills, knowledge, understanding and attitudes of future citizens. Whether we choose to acknowledge it or not, we are, therefore, playing an active role in shaping future society. My own view is that we need to take a far closer look at that role, and critically reflect upon our policies, practices and pedagogies, in relation to it. But why should we be concerned to consider ways in which things could be different within the worlds of physical education and sport?

Michael Young (1998) explains that '. . . whereas the curriculum is always partly designed to enable students to acquire concepts and forms of understanding and learn how to apply them in different contexts, it is also always organised to preserve vested interests and maintain the status quo' (p. 5). Thus, Young prompts us to question whether curricula in their present form provide '. . . reliable frameworks for young people to make sense of the world they face' or, in contrast, are '. . . primarily a leftover of past traditions which have come to be seen as the only way of organising knowledge' (1998, p. 5). Furthermore, 'The issue is one of purposes and the extent to which the existing curriculum represents a future society that we can endorse or a past society that we want to change' (ibid., p. 21). Thus, one of the key concepts from sociology is that of 'socially organised knowledge' (see Young, 1998) and this relates directly to the title of this chapter. In short, my emphasis is that we need to be aware that *education is not neutral nor value free* and nor, more specifically, are any of our curricula, or teaching in physical education. Nor, I should add, is neutrality something that we should (or indeed can) seek. Rather, we need to be more aware that inevitably and unavoidably, education is *selective* in terms of the agendas, interests and values it includes, excludes, privileges, legitimizes and marginalizes, and that at various sites and in varying roles, all of us play an active part in this selection. Thus, in acknowledging selectivity, we also need to acknowledge exclusion; inequalities and inequities in, and of, (physical) education and our own role(s) in creating, reproducing, legitimating and/or challenging those (see also Evans and Davies, 1993). Physical education socializes children and schools their bodies, but it does so differentially. All curricula, any lessons, promote some interests over and above others and, in so doing, meet (and give value and status to) the needs and interests of certain individuals and not others. We can all reflect upon our physical education programmes and lessons in relation to these issues. We can identify pupils who perhaps 'got more out of the lesson' than others, and/or pupils for whom the experience was very positive, others for whom it was less so. Once we acknowledge the differences in pupils' experiences we can begin to discuss how we may contribute to developments in physical education that signal a conscious move towards greater equity, not only in education, but also in society more broadly. At this point, I should acknowledge that not all will share a desire or concern to identify equity as such a central concern in, and for, physical education; not everyone will perhaps feel that they have the interest or capacity to influence values in, and of, society. My point, however, is that even if we do not acknowledge it, we do not escape the role.

What are we referring to when talking of 'greater equity'? As teachers and coaches should we be concerned with it, should we engage in the debates, and what actions can we take to address inequities in, and of, physical education and sport?

Attempts to clarify the meaning of equity often tend to clarify what it is not, rather than leaving people with a clear vision of what a commitment to equity is really about. Hence, I will endeavour on this occasion, to start with the latter. In short, equity is concerned with giving value to, and celebrating social and cultural differences of individuals and in society. It is about seeing differences as a source of enrichment for all (Evans and Davies, 1993). Evans and Davies (1993) explain '. . . the issue must not be whether differences can be dissolved . . . but how they can be celebrated in ways which negate prejudice and stereotyping and at the same time respect individual cultural identity' (p. 19). Differences are, thus, regarded as important for both individuals and society and not as something to be denied, or a problem that has to in some way be 'overcome'. To be concerned with equity is thus to be concerned with social justice, and specifically, the matters of dignity, privileges and power that all individuals are entitled to (Byrne, 1985, cited in Evans and Davies, 1993).

This may still appear distinctly abstract and far removed from the curricula and teaching of physical education. However, if we briefly consider some of the actions and initiatives in physical education that have claimed to be promoting greater equality, we can perhaps appreciate how as a subject and profession we invariably continue to fall short of seriously addressing equity. For example, there have been moves in some schools in England and Wales to offer the same activities to both girls and boys, with for example, soccer being introduced as an activity for girls. However, to take an approach that centres on offering 'all the same' arguably not only denies the value inherent in individual differences, but also ignores what underlies important inequalities that students will experience both within and beyond physical education. While such moves may be a useful starting point in addressing the matters of equal opportunity and equity; alone, they will do little to further awareness and understanding of these issues, or to promote more equitable practices in physical education and society. Offering access to a particular activity does not in and of itself allow pupils to develop their very different talents and interests. Without accompanying changes in grouping strategies, teaching methods, language and assessment practices (in fact every aspect of our teaching), changes to physical education programmes may not only fail to address important inequalities and inequities, but may also further reinforce and legitimate them. To have a commitment to greater equity, therefore, demands that we look at all aspects of the design and delivery of physical education in relation to whose and what values are recognized, privileged and at the same time, marginalized or ignored. It is also to acknowledge that the inclusion and/or dominance of particular activities in our programmes have implications in these terms. In the UK, in extra-curricular physical education particularly, there is a tendency to provide (and thus focus attention upon and give status to) particular sports, and furthermore, focus upon particular standards of performance in the provision of these sports. Invariably, extra-curricular programmes centre upon (or are limited to) participation for the able few in team games (Penney and Harris, 1997). Is this situation educationally desirable and socially just? Similarly, in the design and structuring of lessons and assessment, we seek the development of particular skills, knowledge and understanding. What are we focusing upon and giving credit for? What other aspects of involvement and participation in physical education are we perhaps overlooking? How often do we think to question our 'common sense' notions of the 'good pupil', the 'able athlete', the 'good performance'? As Evans and Davies (1986) explain, 'By making problematic how we teach and what we teach, the new sociology of education demands that we begin to explore, or at least treat with caution, our organizing concepts of intelligence, physical ability, skill, educability, the slow learner, and the social ranking of subjects which might routinely be employed in PE contexts' (p. 26). Such need for a review and reconstruction of professional meanings, and particularly, what we regard as socially acceptable, desirable and 'healthy' bodies, in contexts of physical education and sport has recently been echoed by others (see Fernández-Balboa, 1997; Kirk, 1997).

So how can sociology help us to better understand the variety of interests in, and of, physical education, and our own roles in relation to them?

The concept of discourse is a very useful and powerful tool to employ here. It is a concept that enables us to examine the values and interests that professional texts in their various forms express and promote, and the alternatives that they overlook, marginalize or exclude. The concept centres upon language and meaning, emphasizing that our use of particular language comes with certain meanings and values. It positions people in certain ways, creates certain possibilities for thought, and excludes others. Discourses are, therefore, expressions of particular interests and values. They create and promote particular meanings and values and they endorse particular ways of thinking about issues. Discourse is thus not only about what is said, but also what is not said. Other possibilities for thinking and action are excluded by the absence of other discourses. Furthermore, all texts contain *multiple discourses*, some of which will be privileged over others. Texts always and inevitably represent and contain a number of discourses, that vary in visibility and status (see also Ball, 1990; Penney and Evans, 1997, 1999). Texts are thus an expression of competing interests; the contestation over what are the important interests, and ultimately, texts are a compromise between different interests. In recent years, this has been very apparent in physical education in the UK. In various contexts and at various times, the profession claims to be about, and to be seeking, many things, including for example, physical education being a foundation for the nation's sporting achievements, its health and the personal and social development of children. The Physical Education Association of the United Kingdom (PEA UK) articulates these multiple claims in its mission statement. It states that physical education '. . . enables young people to develop an appreciation of skilful performance', also that it 'aids the development of healthy lifestyles' and that it 'contributes to the spiritual, moral, social and cultural awareness of young people' (PEA UK, 1998, p. 4). Evident here are different interests, different discourses in and of physical education, illustrating the fact that 'subject communities . . . should not be viewed as homogenous groups whose members show similar values and definitions of role, common interests and identity' (Goodson, 1984, p. 40).

The development and implementation of the National Curriculum for Physical Education has vividly expressed the multiplicity of discourses both within and surrounding physical education, and the tension and contestation that can, therefore, arise in policy and curriculum development. In particular, we have seen the interests of performance in sport (and particularly games) come to the fore in the statutory texts, and arguably, also remain dominant in many curricula in schools (see Penney and Evans, 1997; 1999). While professional bodies may make many other claims about the educational value of the subject for children, at times it seems hard to see how these other aims and claims are being addressed in curriculum design and delivery. Do aspects of teaching and learning that we label as 'implicit' in all that we do, ultimately become invisible to the point of disappearance from that teaching and learning?

One of the key things to realize in considering these issues is that we are not all going to agree upon what the focus of attention should be, what aims our energies should be directed towards, and how these can best be achieved. That said, there is a need to be aware of the variety of discourses that potentially can, and perhaps should, find expression in our curricula and teaching. Similarly, we should also recognize that varying emphases will have different implications for whose and what interests are acknowledged, addressed or given status, and that there are then implications for what physical education promotes, who it engages with, or equally alienates and excludes. In addition, we should realize that the dominance of particular discourses can be contested, and perhaps the time for that is long overdue in physical education. Young (1998) prompts us to take a critical look at the link between subject-based specialisms and the contemporary worlds of work and leisure; between 'school' and 'non-school' skills and knowledge. He stresses the need for 'subjects to be used for curriculum purposes rather than to define those purposes' (p. 96), and identifies that this 'requires a vision of the kind of future for which we are preparing young people and for syllabi [and curricula] to be constructed with that vision in mind' (ibid., p. 96). In physical education, it seems difficult to contest his view that 'The National Curriculum and most GCSE and A-level subject syllabi are both based largely on a vision of the past' (ibid., p. 96). Young is not calling for a removal of specialisms, but rather, for a reconfiguration of them, to reflect changing times, but also to actively shape future society.

How can we embrace these ideas? How, as teachers and coaches, can we respond?

Certainly, none of this is easy. In recent years much research in the sociology of education has explored the complexity of the contemporary contexts in which teachers work, the curricula being developed, and has highlighted that the contexts of education are no more neutral than its texts. Research has drawn attention to the critical, dynamic tensions at various levels within the educational system, between texts and the contexts in which they are developed, and specifically, the influences of particular political, ideological and economic pressures. Work in education policy sociology has demonstrated very vividly the complexities, and the inequalities, inherent in policy and curriculum development in education and physical education specifically. Arising from the analysis is something of an ironic paradox for teachers and coaches. In particular, this work has emphasized that discourses are not only about what can and can not be said, and thought, but also about '*who can speak where, when and with what authority*' (Ball, 1990, p. 17; my emphasis). It has drawn attention to critical inequalities regarding matters of who has what say in relation to the discourses that are privileged, marginalized, included and excluded in education policies, curricula, teaching and learning. In the UK particularly, there has been much evidence to suggest that teachers have been 'disempowered' in relation to these matters, that teachers are far from totally autonomous in the process of curriculum development in physical education, and that they are perhaps moving towards the role of a technician rather than a critical and innovative professional (Evans and Penney, 1996; Penney and Evans, 1999).

At the same time, however, the concept of discourse has offered a very different vision. There are possibilities and potential for teachers to be central to, and proactive in, shaping curricula, teaching and learning in particular (and potentially 'different', 'new' or 'alternative') ways. With an appreciation that in all, and any, texts there are multiple discourses at play, and that there are tensions in texts as a result, there is acknowledgement that there is always, therefore, the potential for alternative readings and interpretations of texts. A variety of responses can emerge or be developed that give different emphases to different discourses (interests, values). Undeniably, by virtue of their position and relationship with pupils, teachers and coaches are empowered (even if less so in recent years) in the curriculum development process. Via their specific interpretations and expressions of policy, they play a central role in either reinforcing and legitimating, or alternatively, contesting and challenging, particular social and political agendas that are inherent in curricula. Thus I return to my earlier emphasis that the teachers' position is a privileged one, and one that can be seen as coming with particular social responsibilities. Previously, sociology may have been identified as drawing attention to the capacity of education and physical education in particular to not only educate, but also 'regulate' (see Tinning, 1997). Like Young (1998), I believe that there is now a need to emphasize the creative visions that sociological inquiry can generate. In the following section I turn attention to the possibilities and potential for all within the profession to think and act differently, with interests of future citizens and societies foregrounded in that thinking and action.

Shaping the future of physical education, sport and society

At this point, we should perhaps recall a number of key points that need to remain as parameters in our thinking; the realization that no aspects of education are neutral and that although we are active players in educational contexts, we are not autonomous in them. As teachers and coaches, our thinking and actions are variously bounded by social, cultural, historical, political and economic 'frames' (see Penney and Evans, 1999). Most notably for physical education teachers in England and Wales, there is the statutory frame of the National Curriculum for Physical Education. Our interest here, however, is in exploring the freedom to work creatively within that framework and in so doing, foreground discourses that, to date, have remained in the background or at the peripheries of our practices, and indeed, to look to introduce and embed new discourses in those practices. It should be emphasized that this is not a call for wholesale change, nor a claim that there is a need for that, but rather, that 'some change is both possible and highly desirable' (Evans, 1986, p. 7). We might question, for example, the degree to which interests of equity and social justice are expressed and embedded in the policies and practices of physical education, and the degree to which the subject serves the very varied and rapidly changing needs and interests of pupils set to enter life in the twenty-first century.

Central to this discussion is a belief that teachers and coaches are, and should be, far more than mere technicians; that their role should not be seen as the task of transmitting knowledge developed by others, but rather to play an active role in the creation of knowledge. In addition, however, I emphasize the desirability of an active and creative role for pupils in this process. If we are concerned to develop 'learning communities' and to inspire people to engage in 'lifelong learning', then education has to provide the skills, knowledge, understanding and experiences for this. Therefore in physical education there is a need to explore ways in which we can engage with and foster the creativity of pupils and allow them to experience a variety of roles and responsibilities. This is one of the notable characteristics of 'sport education' (see for example Almond, 1997; Alexander, Taggart and Thorpe, 1996), an initiative in which there is growing interest in the UK. Sport education involves pupils in all aspects of sport, including planning, organizing, staging and officiating sports competitions. However, like others (see Shehu, 1998), I would suggest a degree of caution in our response to sport education. In particular, there seems a need to reflect upon the extent to which it offers any potential to challenge long-standing and firmly established inequities in wider social and sporting worlds. In addition, there are perhaps dangers of a narrowing of physical education curricula and thus opportunities for pupils. This need not be the case. Rather, we can hopefully retain a diversity of experiences and opportunities within physical education (and thus, the valuing of the diversity in relation to physical activity, individuals and societies), while embracing in those diverse contexts, what we regard as the strengths of the sport education model.

In now looking in more detail at ways in which as teachers and coaches we can 'make a difference' to the social and sporting worlds that we are a part of, I focus attention on a framework presented by Figueroa (1993) in his work concerned with racism. The structure provided by Figueroa is useful for exploring the many ways in which inequities can be both reinforced but also challenged in, and through, physical education and sport in our schools, communities and societies. The framework also highlights that promoting greater equality and equity in sport and society is certainly not something that we can do alone, but rather, demands collective action. However, teachers and coaches have a position and authority in schools from which they can make a significant difference to the attitudes and values that pupils develop. They can also influence the views that colleagues and parents may have about physical education, physical activity and sport.

Figueroa (1993) identifies five dimensions or levels that we can associate with the reinforcement of inequity in society, or equally, see as a necessary target for any moves towards greater equity. Throughout, I have emphasized the need for us all to acknowledge our personal role in shaping society, so it is appropriate to begin with what Figueroa terms the *individual level*. This is concerned with our attitudes and prejudices, particularly as they relate to stereotypes. Once again, therefore, there is encouragement for critical reflection in relation to our thinking about sport and physical education, what we value and why, who we think certain activities are 'for' and why, and how receptive we are to new ideas or alternative emphases in curricula and extra-curricula programmes. The second level of Figueroa's framework reflects the direct ways in which our individual attitudes and prejudices shape our reactions to, and interactions with, others. At the *interpersonal level*, therefore, inequity is evidenced by the discrimination, avoidance and exclusion of particular individuals. Exclusion has to be acknowledged as a reality for some children in contexts of physical education and sport, and marginalization is probably a feeling many more would relate to. This level, therefore, prompts us to take a critical look at our relations with pupils, those between pupils, and the degree to which, in teaching and coaching, we can respond to each individual's needs and interests, and foster greater understanding of those varied needs and interests. The task is certainly far from easy, and it is also notable that a lack of development of differentiation has repeatedly been identified as a shortcoming of teaching in physical education.

The next level of the framework, the *institutional level*, is concerned with the way that society and its institutions, such as schools, function to advantage and disadvantage particular groups, by operating within particular (for example, racist, sexist) frames of reference, or by failing to acknowledge the specific needs of those not within the dominant social group(s). As indicated above, the design of curricula needs to be regarded in this light. By defining and structuring education primarily in relation to specific academic subjects, and then defining and shaping physical education in relation to specific activities, we are serving and promoting particular needs and interests, and marginalizing or excluding others. Certainly within physical education in England and Wales, the continued dominance of an activity-focused framework for curricula is probably the most significant institutional frame when contemplating changes in teaching and learning in physical education. My view is that without a change in this overarching framework, changes in thinking and practice will always be restricted. In England and Wales, the strength and dominance of the framework seems such that many within the worlds of physical education and sport struggle to envisage any alternative, but examples of curriculum developments in other countries show quite clearly that alternatives can and do exist (see also Penney, 1998).

In contemplating the development of alternatives, there is always a need, however, to reflect upon their likely acceptance not only within the profession, but beyond it. As Apple (1982, 1993) has emphasized, the 'discourses surrounding discourses' play a key role in shaping policies and practice in education (see also Penney and Evans, 1999). Figueroa's next two levels reflect these influences. First, he presents the *structural level*, addressing the way society is shaped by concepts such as race or gender, meaning that 'there is a differential distribution of resources, rewards, roles, status and power' (Figueroa, 1993, p. 93). Issues of resourcing and status will be all too familiar to many physical education teachers, who may feel that they, and their subject, are invariably marginalized in relation to others within schools. While this remains a concern, we should equally acknowledge the differential distribution of resources, rewards and status within our subject and within sport. Once again, decisions that we make about what and who to invest in are not neutral. The questions to pose continually relate to the basis upon which we are making particular decisions, the implications of them in relation to the opportunities that we are facilitating for whom, and whether we can and have considered alternative patterns of provision. I have referred here to the provision of particular activities for particular individuals or groups of individuals. However, in considering the matters of resources, rewards, roles, status and power (Figueroa, 1993), we should also be addressing our teaching of any lesson, and how this can be perhaps seen as reflecting a differential distribution of our own resources (energy, time, interest) in ways that reflect wider inequities in, and of, society. Here we see some of the potential links and dynamics between the various levels that Figueroa presents. The final level in that framework can be regarded as the most powerful, having a great influence upon all others. It is the *cultural level*, referring to socially shared sets of assumptions, beliefs, values and behavioural norms, that operate at a taken-for-granted level and, in so doing, constrain and direct our perceptions and actions. Figueroa's other levels can then be seen as addressing the ways in which inequity at this cultural level is expressed by societies and individuals. At the same time, however, we need to emphasize the dynamic nature of the relationships at play here and remember that the influences are not only one-way; for it is the dynamic that presents us with the opportunities and potential as individuals to make a difference.

Conclusion

This chapter has highlighted the potential for sociological concepts to be a basis for critical questioning of contemporary policies and practices in physical education and sport. It has been argued that if we are interested in actively shaping future society, such questioning should be a basis for not only a better understanding of the social implications of particular policies and practice, but also for changing them. Evans (1986) has previously emphasized that teachers '. . . tend to know more clearly what they are changing from, than changing to' (p. 8), and this is almost certainly still the case as we enter the twenty-first century. Hopefully, more teachers and coaches may be encouraged to now develop visions of 'alternative futures' and be supported in moving towards them in contexts of physical education and sport.

References

● Alexander K., Taggart A. and Thorpe S. (1996) 'A spring in their steps? Possibilities for professional renewal through sport education in Australian schools', *Sport, Education and Society* 1(1): 5–22.
● Almond L. (1997) *Physical education in schools*, London: Kogan Page.
● Apple M.W. (1982) *Education and Power*, London: Ark Paperbacks.
● Apple M.W. (1993) *Official Knowledge*, London: Routledge.
● Armour K. and Jones R. (1999) 'The practical heart within: The value of a sociology of sport', in R.L. Jones and K.M. Armour (eds) *Sociology of Sport*, London: Pearson Education Ltd, pp. 1–10.
● Ball S.J. (1990) *Politics and Policy Making in Education: Explorations in Policy Sociology*, London: Routledge.
● Byrne E. (1985) 'Equality or equity?: A European view', in M. Amot (ed.) *Race and Gender*, Oxford: Pergamon Press, pp. 97–113.
● Evans J. (1986) 'Introduction: "Personal troubles and public issues": Studies in the sociology of physical education', in J. Evans (ed.) *Physical Education, Sport and Schooling: Studies in the Sociology of Physical Education*, London: The Falmer Press, pp. 1–10.
● Evans J. and Davies B. (1986) 'Sociology, schooling and physical education', in J. Evans (ed.) *Physical Education, Sport and Schooling: Studies in the Sociology of Physical Education*, London: The Falmer Press, pp. 11–37.
● Evans J. and Davies B. (1993) 'Equality, equity and physical education', in J. Evans (ed.) *Equality, Education and Physical Education*, London: The Falmer Press, pp. 11–27.
● Evans J. and Penney D. (1996) 'The role of the teacher in PE: Towards a pedagogy of risk', *British Journal of Physical Education* 27(4): 28–35.
● Fernández-Balboa J.-M. (1997) 'Introduction: The human movement profession – from modernism to postmodernism', in J.-M. Fernández-Balboa (ed.) *Critical Postmodernism in Human Movement, Physical Education and Sport*, New York: State University of New York Press, pp. 3–9.
● Figueroa P. (1993) 'Equality, multiculturalism, anti-racism and physical education in the National Curriculum', in J. Evans (ed.) *Equality, Education and Physical Education*, London: The Falmer Press, pp. 90–102.

● Goodson I.F. (1984) 'Subjects for study: Towards a social history of curriculum', in I.F. Goodson and S.J. Ball (eds) *Defining the Curriculum: Histories and Ethnographies*, London: The Falmer Press, pp. 25–45.

● Kirk D. (1997) 'Schooling bodies in new times: The reform of school physical education in high modernity', in J.-M. Fernández-Balboa (ed.) *Critical Postmodernism in Human Movement, Physical Education and Sport*, New York: State University of New York Press, pp. 39–63.

● Penney D. (1998) 'Positioning and defining physical education, sport and health in the curriculum', *European Physical Education Review* 4(2): 117–26.

● Penney D. and Evans J. (1997) 'Naming the game: Discourse and domination in physical education and sport in England and Wales', *European Physical Education Review* 3(1): 21–32.

● Penney D. and Evans J. (1999) *Politics, Policy and Practice in Physical Education*, London: Routledge.

● Penney D. and Harris J. (1997) 'Extra-curricular physical education: More of the same for the more able?', *Sport, Education and Society* 2(1): 41–54.

● Physical Education Association of the United Kingdom (1998) 'PEA UK Mission Statement', *British Journal of Physical Education* 29(2): 4–7.

● Shehu J. (1998) 'Sport education: Ideology, evidence and implications for physical education in Africa', *Sport, Education and Society* 3(2): 227–35.

● Tinning R. (1997) 'Performance and participation discourses in human movement: Toward a socially critical physical education', in J.-M. Fernández-Balboa (ed.) *Critical Postmodernism in Human Movement, Physical Education and Sport*, New York: State University of New York Press, pp. 99–119.

● Young M.F.D. (1998) *The Curriculum of the Future: From the 'New Sociology of Education' to a Critical Theory of Learning*, London: The Falmer Press.

Chapter Six

'We're All Middle Class Now.' Sport and Social Class in Contemporary Britain

Kathleen M. Armour

Introduction. The concept of 'social class'

The concept of 'social class' can seem somewhat elusive, even irritating, as we enter the new millennium. It threatens to categorize us in ways that we don't necessarily support or recognize. It hints at the enduring influence of overbearing social structures and seems to undermine our autonomy, our initiative and our tenacity. Indeed, some people would argue that 'social class' represents a series of outdated working/middle/upper-class labels that are virtually meaningless today, whereas others claim that most people are middle class or, even better, that we have become a 'classless' society. Adonis and Pollard (1997, p. xiii) strongly disagree. They argue that 'Britain cannot be understood apart from its class system, which separates its people as clinically today as it did half a century ago'. They acknowledge that the class groupings have changed in nature, but claim that the barriers between classes are the same as ever: 'education, family and occupation (or lack of them)'. Some of the evidence is compelling – and disturbing. For example:

> Our study of the health system is a graphic account of class inequalities: a child from an unskilled social class is twice as likely to die before the age of 15 as a child from a professional family, while the life expectancy of a child with parents in the unskilled manual class is more than seven years shorter than for a child with parents from the professional class.
>
> (1997, p. xiii)

> One in five seven year olds in London state schools scores zero in reading tests. In secondary schools serving the poorest areas, less than 15 per cent of pupils achieve five or more GCSE grades A to C, and the best schools in such areas achieve average GCSE scores which are just one-third that of schools in more advantaged areas.
>
> (1997, p. xvi)

Furthermore, evidence from abroad suggests that social class inequality is not a peculiarly British concern. For example, Sage (1998) points out that for many Americans 'the notion that we live in a society of social classes is quite foreign; more than that, it is so objectionable that one can encounter strong resentment by even suggesting there are classes in America' (p. 39). However, Sage argues that although the precise nature of the class categories might be debatable, it is undeniable that in America, as elsewhere, 'social class is one of the most pervasive variables determining life chances . . . and patterns of social interaction' (p. 36). Marshall, Swift and Roberts (1997) support Sage's claim. They found that, like Great Britain, the United States has a very high association between class of origin and class of destination for individuals with educational qualifications. Sage also reminds us that the class system is fundamentally about power and the unequal distribution of power. Indeed, Lemert (1997) identifies the power of the class structure as one of three key defining constituents of social power, the others being prestige and authority. He argues that class structures 'organize the social opportunities allocated to various groups according to a group's greater and lesser access to scarce goods, particularly income and other sources of wealth' (p. 139). In this context, Donnelly (1996) states unequivocally that: 'Poverty represents a real class barrier to participation in sport' (p. 234). Hence, those planning to work in sports coaching, teaching or administration would do well to take heed of the implications of such evidence. In fact, our 'clients', be they pupils, youths or adult exercisers, are likely to be both enabled and constrained by their social class positions. Moreover, social class is only one of the social characteristics that influence an individual's life-chances. Opportunity in sport is also fundamentally determined by, for example, gender, race, ability and sexuality. Whereas space does not allow this chapter to specifically address all these issues, it is accepted that social class is inextricably bound-up with them. Hall (1985) argues that 'class cannot be understood except in connection with gender and vice versa' (p. 113). Inevitably then, a chapter such as this may be useful for raising general awareness, but it also has important limitations.

Central to any analysis of class is the notion of inequality – itself a central concept in sociology. Crompton (1993) states that 'all complex societies are characterized, to varying extents, by the unequal distribution of material and symbolic rewards' (p. 1) and reminds us that inequality has only been viewed as a problem relatively recently. For example, in traditional societies, inequalities were seen as 'natural' and 'divine' in nature. However, from the seventeenth century onwards, and with the advent of the Enlightenment, it was proposed that 'by virtue of their humanity, all human beings were born equal, rather than unequal' (p. 3). This belief led to a foundational question for sociology: if equality is the natural state, why is there so much inequality? In nineteenth-century classical sociology, Karl Marx analysed the sources of social class inequality and began to differentiate between classes in terms of differential access to the means of industrial (capitalist) production. Today, 'inequality' means different things to different groups – and has different consequences. Donnelly (1996) draws upon Figler (1981) to define a spectrum of beliefs about social inequality that ranges from:

> the right wing view that social inequality is inevitable (social Darwinism) or necessary to create incentive (conservatism), to the left wing view that social inequality is wrong and should be eradicated by democratic (social democracy) or revolutionary (Marxist) means.
>
> (1996, p. 221)

Donnelly (1996) also identifies a range of responses to inequality – from total eradication at all levels, to the establishment of a meritocracy which allows everyone to start equal in some notional way, and then make their way as best they can. Needless to say, both approaches are fraught with difficulties. The difficulties with attempting the former are seen in the objections raised to positive discrimination programmes (see, for example, Walden, 1989). The difficulties with the latter can be illustrated by drawing an analogy with a competitive race. Placing all the competitors on the starting line together will do little to redress, for example, their differential health and nutritional statuses. The advantages inherent in the backgrounds of some competitors will predominate in most cases (Evans and Davies, 1993). As Sage (1998) points out 'the very idea of equality of opportunity is meaningless unless there is a corresponding "equality of conditions"' (p. 44). However, even though resolving inequalities seems elusive and fraught with problems, many within sport still feel they ought to try. In the context of numerous sport-related jobs, where the goal is to widen access to allow others to experience the myriad benefits of sports participation, we appear to have no option. Indeed, in an expanding field of work in America, Lawson (1997, 1999) and Martinek and Hellison (1997) argue persuasively for the centrality of 'social responsibility' as a key feature of all professions, and particularly those involved in teaching or coaching sport to young people.

For those who benefit from current social and economic arrangements there is, of course, little incentive to support sweeping social change or redistribution. Lemert (1997) argues that 'economic structures in capitalist societies . . . usually work very well for, say, the top 40 per cent, or, increasingly, the top 20 per cent. Those who benefit from the way economic, or class, structures are organized seldom complain' (p. 141). Similarly, Adonis and Pollard (1997) identify a new 'super class' in Britain which 'like every economic elite in history . . . is steering more and more income towards itself, and claiming this to be for the public good' (p. 69). What is surprising is not the existence of such elites, but the lack of sustained, effective resistance to them. A logical question here may be: given that the super class is a relatively small group within society – how can it continue to predominate in this way? Two responses are interesting. First, is Lemert's (1997) explanation of the 'sneaky' nature of power in the context of class structures. Put another way, those who fail to achieve a high social status tend to be convinced that it is their own fault – it is they who are deficient – so there is no point in rebelling. The second response is also related to the workings of power and it lies in the popular belief that we are all of one class now – the middle class. As the *Sunday Times* reported on Britain in 1998:

> We are all middle class now. The government is to redefine Britain's class structure
> for the first time in nearly 80 years because so many people have joined the ranks
> of the upwardly mobile middle classes . . . The rapid growth in the middle class – up
> from a third of the population in the 1970s to a half today – has forced the govern-
> ment to adopt a new system of classification.
>
> (Norton, 1998, p. 9)

In 1999, the *Sunday Times* reported that the Labour Prime Minister, Tony Blair, was enthusiastic about the expansion of the middle class into a 'new, larger, more meritocratic middle class' (Woods and Norton, 1999, p. 10). However, the problem, as the paper reports, is that it has become increasingly difficult to identify what the term 'middle class' means in Great Britain today: 'At best, it describes a large section of the population that now has enough money to enjoy a certain amount of freedom – the cash-in-the-bank-class' (ibid.). Certainly, it does appear difficult to derive a meaningful understanding of Britain's class system using the traditional labels of 'working' and 'middle' class. On the other hand, it is generally agreed that the *perceived* expansion of the 'middle' classes is a feature of the contemporary class landscape. Indeed, Kelley and Evans (1995) found in their research that 'The predominance of middle-class self-image holds at all levels . . . rich and poor, well educated and poorly educated, high-status and low-status, all see themselves near the middle of the class system, rarely at the top or bottom' (p. 166). The authors explain this by drawing on the concept of 'reference group processes' that lead us to view ourselves and our immediate social group as unexceptional – as 'normal'. A further consideration is that in proclaiming class identity, 'a middle-class identity is a statement that you are not working class' (Gerteis and Savage, 1998, p. 271). This suggests that to be considered 'working class' is no longer a source of pride. However, as Adonis and Pollard (1997) point out, we need to beware of an overemphasis on the labels, which can act as a distraction from the key manifestation of social classes as powerful, enduring structures. They argue that a focus on class *systems*, rather than on labels, is a more helpful analytical starting point in a shifting class landscape. In this context, Crompton (1993) identifies key features of the modern class landscape:

- the decline of traditional manual labour
- the decline of jobs in general
- little evidence of 'class consciousness' (except, perhaps in the new super class as identified earlier)
- the rise of new social movements and interest groups which cut across traditional class boundaries (for example environmental groups and animal rights groups)
- the changes in gendered patterns of work
- the power of consumption

However, even when such changes are taken into account, Crompton concludes that, as a minimalist summary, 'it still makes sense to describe late capitalist society as being dominated by a "ruling class" which is economically dominant and has the capacity to influence crucially political and social life' (p. 18). Rose (1998) argues that even for those who claim that social class is a 'dead sociological issue', there is still agreement that 'social stratification remains central to the concerns of macro-sociology' (pp. 755–6) and, as Travers (1999) concludes, postmodernist suggestions that social class is no longer a relevant concept are 'at odds with our everyday experience' (section 12.8).

Paradoxically, the notion of 'classlessness' is also relevant here. Classlessness is an ethos that was eagerly promoted by the previous (Conservative) UK government. It seems to imply that there are no clear class distinctions of any note – hence the tendency to opt for a 'middle' label for everyone. However, as Adonis and Pollard (1997), Jones (1997) and Saunders (1996) argue, such a brand of classlessness is best understood as 'an opportunity society' based on traditional notions of meritocracy. It can be summed up in the adage that everyone can aspire to be Prime Minister – a view based on the previous Prime Minister John Major's personal experience of achievement from relatively humble roots. Only in this light can we understand the importance of academically-selective grammar schools and the former Conservative Government's 'assisted places' policy which sought to allow bright pupils from working-class backgrounds to attend top public (private) schools. However, social mobility appears to be an elusive goal. Prandy's (1998) study of social mobility between fathers and sons concludes: 'there is a continuum of social advantage . . . such that the location of the father can be used to predict, with a high degree of accuracy, the position, on average, of the son . . . At all levels, differences in resources operate to bring about differences in outcomes for offspring' (pp. 359–60). Add to this the tendency for those in high-status occupations/classes to marry from a similar group, and the power of the new super class is highlighted yet again. Perhaps the most interesting feature of the debate on class is the fact that 'classlessness' is somehow seen as a virtue, and something to which any society ought to aspire. Nonetheless, Adonis and Pollard (1997) dismiss it as a myth, arguing that 'like the most powerful social myths, its potency rests on the belief that it is coming and that it is irresistible' (p. xxiv). Furthermore, Novak (1997) points to the paradox of 'classlessness' in the increasing use of the term 'underclass':

> If we are to see ourselves as a classless society, then the abundant and growing evidence of class inequalities, their destructive impact on the lives, opportunities and aspirations of many of the young, and the moments of defiance or frustration that this provokes, need to be hidden under a rhetoric that blames members of the so-called 'underclass' for their situation and justifies their neglect or punishment on the ground that they are not a part or product of society but a class outside it.
>
> (1997, p. 34)

Currently in Britain, a wide-ranging review of the way in which we conceptualize and classify social classes is being conducted. Governments use social class based statistics for a variety of purposes, including to inform social and economic policy decisions and to analyse health differentials. However, the class indices in existence may no longer be appropriate for contemporary society which has changed dramatically from the 'male-breadwinner model' of households upon which most are based. Some of these may be familiar, for example that which classifies social classes according to broad job-related criteria, from Class I which represents professional workers to Class VII which represents unskilled manual workers (Goldthorpe, 1987). Another approach of this type is the Cambridge Scale that seeks to place occupations on a continuum of social stratification (Sewert, Prandy and Blackburn, 1980). Neither should be confused with a classification used for the purposes of advertising and marketing which allocates people into five groups from A–E on a wide range of income and life-style factors. In the new project, sociologists were asked to consider existing official classifications to determine whether such classifications are still of use, and if they are, to devise a new single social classification to be ready for use in the 2001 Census (O'Reilly and Rose, 1998). Developed from Goldthorpe's work, and still ongoing, a new Socioeconomic Classification (SEC) has been proposed which divides Britain into 14 levels, or classes (see Rose, 1998). Importantly, in the context of this chapter, the classification is based upon employment relations and conditions and, therefore, it rates occupations on key questions about forms of remuneration, promotion opportunities and autonomy. These are, undoubtedly, sensitive issues for many employees in sport and leisure-related occupations and they are considered again in the final section of this chapter.

Unsurprisingly, the new SEC is not without its critics, even at this early stage of its development. For example, Prandy (1998) argues that classes are more complex than the occupation indictor implies, and Blackburn (1998) contends that class analysis of this nature is 'primitive'. Indeed, the range of conditions in sport-related employment, even when considering one group such as professional athletes would appear to confound any simple classification. However, Rose (1998) counters:

> Occupation, when combined with employment status, is a reasonable indictor of overall social position. This is because the life-chances of individuals and families depend mainly on the positions they occupy in the social division of labour, and thus, on the material and symbolic advantages or disadvantages which derive from position in the labour market.
>
> (1998, p. 758)

If Rose's argument is accepted, then social class and sport must be conceptualized at a bewildering number of levels. For example, we need to consider the 'social position' of the sport-related professional (teacher, coach, athlete, manager) both as an individual and as a role holder which has a social status; the social class of clients; implications of the traditional class-status of the specific sport, etc. In order to develop such an analysis, we now need to focus more specifically upon some of the ways in which sport and social class are interlinked.

Social class and sport: Social construction and mutual reinforcement

Despite the historical links between sports and social classes in Britain, it is surprising to note that relatively few sport sociologists have written extensively on social class. Gruneau's (1999) book *Class, Sports and Social Development* is one of the exceptions. In a foreword to the new edition of the book, Connell (1999) praises Gruneau's work for recognizing that sports are 'contained within institutions, themselves embedded in large-scale social structures' and suggests 'that we can understand the activities and experiences at a personal level only by examining the dynamics of the structures at the societal level' (p. ix). For instance, economic, class-related influences may be readily apparent in the ways that individuals have been constrained or enabled to achieve in a particular sports. In addition, factors such as status and prestige may also be apparent. These latter factors are more difficult to quantify – but are a powerful presence in our lives nonetheless. Yet, as Connell argues, in order to develop the analysis further, we need to connect our personal experiences and understandings to broader structural considerations (Mills, 1959) to examine the ways in which those large-scale social structures might impinge upon and facilitate our current and future work in sport. That, in a nutshell, is the point of studying social class in a sport science degree. Without an understanding of the ways in which class systems operate to reflect and reproduce society, and to influence the life chances of ourselves and those with whom we wish to work, we might naively assume that everyone is equal in sport – that it is the ideal 'classless' pursuit. However, as was noted earlier, 'classlessness' is a slippery concept and it can be argued that although social class links with sport are changing, there is little evidence that they are disappearing. Four dimensions of the relationship are particularly relevant in this context: the weight of history and tradition, the social status of specific sports; the role of social structures in shaping class within sport; and the role of sport in structuring class within society.

History

In seeking to understand the complex ways in which social class and sport are interlinked in contemporary society, we will find it impossible to ignore history. In the guise of tradition, history constitutes a powerful and enduring influence in and over sport. As Bourdieu reminds us 'the separation of sociology and history is a disastrous division and one totally devoid of epistemological justification: all sociology should be historical and all history sociological' (Wacquant, 1989, p. 37). In this vein, there are numerous historical accounts detailing the development of sport in the context of, for example, the education system, the political system and the economic system (see, for example, Jones, 1988; Holt, 1989; Gruneau, 1999). Whereas it is not the purpose of this chapter to reproduce such texts, it is interesting to note that they tend to focus on such topics as the legacy of the Victorians, the role of religion, the influence of public schools, play and leisure, sport and the working class; and sport and politics. Furthermore, there are two important considerations that should inform the reading of historical texts. First, Holt alerts us to the fact that 'The history of sport in modern Britain is a history of men' (1989, p. 8), echoing Hall's (1985) earlier point about the intersection of gender and class. For a history of sport that specifically focuses upon women, it is helpful to access dedicated texts such as that by Mangan and Park (1987). Second, Gruneau argues that history must be regarded as a 'set of ongoing constitutive processes' (1999, p. 115) which allow us to recognize that dominant groups and structures are not immutable – they can be challenged and, as a consequence, that social change is possible. Clearly this latter point is particularly relevant in any consideration of a social responsibility role for sport professionals.

Social status of specific sports

There have been a number of attempts to link specific sports to social classes in a range of cultural contexts. In a rather unusual approach, Adonis and Pollard (1997) write about sport in Britain under the heading of 'lifestyle' which also includes media and food/holidays/style. They declare that 'Every sport has its class labels' (p. 229) and they divide sports into three classes. In the top class they place sports such as real tennis, polo and three-day eventing because they are 'hardly mass participation sports. That is their point' (p. 229). In the middle they place cricket and golf, which have a wide, if often segregated appeal, and in the bottom class, they place sports with working-class origins such as football, darts and boxing. Sugden (1996) supports the low-class status of boxing, claiming that it represents the 'exploitation of disadvantage'. He argues: 'there is little doubt that a survey of amateur and professional boxing is one of the quickest ways of discovering which groups are the poorest of the poor in the modern industrial world' (p. 187). Other studies have identified similar social class links. Renson and Careel (1986) point to a range of research that matches high socioeconomic status with individual, non-contact sports, and low socioeconomic status with team or individual contact sports. In a Belgian context, they were able to identify upper-class sports that 'symbolize the old noble values of "distance" and "finesse"' (p. 155); upper-middle-class sports that are essentially 'nature sports'; lower-middle-class sports using balls, nets and targets (described as a mixed, 'transit' layer); and lower-class sports expressing a 'toughness ethic, asceticism and "hard" manual labour' (p. 155). Goodger (1986) argues, similarly, that social processes are 'highly significant' in choice of sport and manner of participation. He cites Bourdieu (1978) who claimed that sports were either middle class or working class in orientation, depending upon the attitudes which different social groups take towards the body and physical activity. Indeed, Bourdieu's emphasis upon the importance of the body in society is illuminating in the context of sport and social class. He argues that in order to understand the role of the body, we must see 'society written into the body, into the biological individual' (cited in Jarvie and Maguire, 1994, p. 186). This view contrasts with a tendency to underplay the body within some social structures, such as education, where 'academic' achievements have been prioritized. Thus, sport and physical activities have been deemed of low worth; a factor that might contribute to a perception that sport is somehow outside of the important social structures of society and, therefore, absolved of social responsibility (Armour, 1999). If, however, the body is viewed as central, as Bourdieu suggests, then this perception is called into question. As Jarvie and Maguire (1994) state: 'Class attitudes to the use of the body influence the kinds of sports taken up, the kinds of style associated with a sport and the cultural status of the specific sport' (p. 198). It will come as little surprise, therefore, that in a recent study of youth sport in Ireland, coaches suggested that sports were viewed as either middle class or working class, and that they believed this to have a powerful influence on young people's choice of sport (Duncan, 1997).

Undoubtedly, at an intuitive level, it is possible to list sports and attach class labels for all sorts of reasons. Indeed, at the extreme ends of the social spectrum, this may be relatively easy to do. Yet many sports today would defy such a simplistic approach and Goodger (1986) cautions against seeking rigid social compartments for contemporary sports. Here again, our experience is likely to endorse this. So, perhaps there are more complex issues worthy of our attention. Attaching class labels to sports is interesting – but also limiting. We need to delve deeper.

Social structures shaping class within sport

Sage (1998) argues that understanding the class system in America is fundamental to understanding sport because class inequality permeates and structures sport and physical recreation. He identifies four processes through which this structuring of inequality takes place: patronage, access, control and social mobility. Thus, many sports have enduring links with their historical upper-class roots, they restrict access for the working class through time and financial constraints, and they are largely controlled by wealthy groups. We can recognize much of what Sage has to say in the British context, with the sport of tennis providing one example. More cynically, the myth of social mobility through sport is taken as evidence of equality of opportunity *in* sport. Myth it is though, as Sage concludes: 'Social mobility through sports, in terms of a significant, measurable rise in social class status of large numbers of athletes, is more illusory than real' (p. 53). What is less clear is how the myths about social mobility through sport are perpetuated.

Analysis of the mass media presentation of sport undoubtedly provides one answer. The role of the media as a social structure that shapes sport is well documented. Davis (1993) points out that the media 'help create, reproduce, legitimate and occasionally subvert relations of domination in racist, sexist, capitalist countries' (p. 165), and Hall (1977) describes the media as 'socially, economically, and technically organized apparatuses for the production of messages' (p. 343). The 'messages' to be produced and transmitted are those that reflect the views of the owners of media, and those that are likely to be palatable to the target audience. Undoubtedly, in recent years, sport has become a media commodity even, as Kellner (1996) argues, becoming a 'major spectacle of media culture' (p. 458). Kellner defines 'spectacles' as those phenomena of media culture that 'embody the society's basic values, serve to enculturate individuals into its way of life, and dramatize the society's conflicts and modes of conflict resolution' (p. 458). In this context, the following extract from a British newspaper, *The Daily Telegraph*, provides a pertinent example. It is an account of the football World Cup, held in the USA in 1994.

> The mood of this World Cup has been quite unlike that of football as we have known it. And the reason, I would suggest, is that USA '94 took a working-class winter sport and turned it into a middle-class, summer entertainment . . . This has been a tournament of tactical subtlety and occasional flashes of brilliant movement. It has been a game best appreciated over a cool glass of white wine rather than a steaming cup of Bovril and gristle pie . . . The appointment of Barry Davies, rather than John Motson, as the BBC's commentator for the final is proof of the transformation. Davies is the voice of sporting sophistication, a man who gives the impression that he perceives the aesthetic, even philosophical dimensions of the game. He is, both socially and intellectually, several rungs up the ladder from the trainspotting Motson, however amiable the latter may be . . . But will the brave new world of sanitised football be quite as enticing as it seems? A decade or two from now, the roar of the crowd may well have dwindled to an appreciative murmur as up-scale audiences applaud the subtle interplay of footballers moving with balletic grace . . . But as dusk approaches, the ghosts of footballing legends . . . will look down from on high. They'll remember the passion . . . They'll think of the steam as it rose from a pulsating, shouting, singing crowd, who watched hard men play a hard man's sport'.
>
> (Thomas, 1994, p. 17)

This extract introduces a fascinating array of class-related issues. Social class, as it relates to football, is linked to a whole range of social and cultural concepts that, on the surface at least, appear to have little to do with the game itself. The contrasts are between a cool glass of white wine and Bovril and gristle pie; Barry Davies and John Motson; balletic grace and hard men; up-scale audiences and pulsating, singing crowds; appreciative murmurs and passion. Importantly, the extract reflects the prevailing view that there is an expansion of middle-class values, while reflecting fondly (if somewhat patronizingly) upon the game's working-class heritage. It also offers a fascinating illustration of Bourdieu's earlier claim that social class differences in sports involvement are linked to different understandings about the body. Furthermore, the extract performs the function that Whannel (1992) argues is a key role of popular culture: 'it treads and retreads the ground of common sense, drawing upon the language, axioms, aphorisms, beliefs and superstitions of everyday life and working them into the form of more elaborated systematic practical ideologies' (p. 126). Most importantly, perhaps, the extract hints at a much more socially dynamic role for sport than has been discussed thus far. It hints at the possibility that sport is not only shaped by broader social structures, but that (with the help of other social structures such as the media) it takes a part in the shaping.

Sport perpetuating social class inequalities

In an appendix to his work on sport and social class in Britain, Holt (1989) urges us to view sport as 'a social process through which cultural meanings are produced' which, he argues, leads us 'into the thick of the sociological argument' (p. 359). This suggests a dynamic vision of sport as producing and reproducing social class inequalities. Moreover, if sport is viewed as active in this way, then real opportunities exist for resistance and change (Donnelly, 1996). For some readers this will be challenging for several reasons. First, and as was noted in an earlier section, those who benefit from the current arrangements in sport (identified by Donnelly as White, heterosexual, able-bodied males from the middle and upper classes) have little incentive to initiate and support change. Moreover, the nexus of class, gender, race and other social characteristics locates individuals in a range of relatively advantaged/disadvantaged positions in different sport-related contexts. To add to the complexity, we are often unaware that sporting opportunities are unequal. Goodger (1986) puts the case well: 'where individuals typically spend their lives in one particular social and cultural context, or within broadly similar contexts, the process of socialization is typically understood by individuals as the progressive discovery of the "way things are"' (p. 139). He goes on to argue that the only way to 'know' about the experiences and values of others is to be presented with contrasts, comparisons, ambiguities and tensions. However, once we 'know', it becomes more difficult to ignore the inequalities that we are helping to perpetuate. Fernández-Balboa (1993, p. 249) reminds those aspiring to be physical education professionals that they are also citizens and argues, like Lawson (1999), that they have responsibilities to 'struggle for justice and democracy' and to 'become human agents of change'. Given the role of the education system in reinforcing social class inequalities, this must certainly be a consideration for teachers – but not only for teachers. A personal story about a coach is illustrative.

> My son's eighth birthday. Twelve excited boys are resplendent in the gaudy, clashing, cluttered, shiny strips of their favourite football teams. They head for the pitch where the coach is waiting to run the 'football' part of the football birthday party. They look in awe at the coach. They know he runs the youth programme at one of the top professional clubs, and they are determined to excel. They work at a furious rate for the next 70 minutes. As I watch, I decide that perhaps football isn't so bad after all. I think some of the boys look quite good and I am curious about their level of ability in comparison to that of the elite youths selected by the clubs. At the end of

the session, the boys are exhausted and exhilarated, the coach is pleased with their responsiveness, and we head off to McDonald's for fuel. A successful party.

On the following Monday, I meet the coach. I can't wait to ask for his professional opinion of the boys and their potential. A small, nagging part of me hopes he will single out my son for particular praise. Instead, he comments on their willingness, their enthusiasm and their listening skills. He declares that they were a joy to teach but that they will never make 'real' footballers. I am surprised, a little disappointed, and then jolted by his explanation: apparently, they are all too middle class for football. They just wouldn't cope in the youth football environment. They're too . . . 'nice' – not hungry enough!

Maybe the coach was right. Few players in the top professional football leagues have a public school background. Whereas rugby union is becoming less exclusive in its player profile, football still appears to seek its players in a notional working class. Indeed, if the expectations of my child's coach are matched elsewhere, boys who don't fit a certain social class profile may be effectively barred from excelling in football. It's not the usual tale of inequality – but it is cautionary. Nor is the case of football simple, however. Lurking within conceptual notions of football players as notionally working class is a harsh economic dimension: whereas the audiences for many sports, particularly television audiences, are drawn from all sectors of society, live audiences are likely to be more restricted. The high cost of tickets is making the thrill of live football matches a rare event for those on low incomes. Indeed, Adonis and Pollard (1997) argue that football spectators are 'of one class – the comfortably off' (p. 238), seeming to echo the earlier point made about the rise of the 'cash-in-the-bank' class.

Taken together, the issues raised in the first two sections of this chapter point to a complex relationship between sport and social class. In order to understand such a relationship therefore, it seems clear that a multilayered, analytical approach is advisable. Thus far, the discussion has demonstrated that social class is an important issue for aspirant sport professionals, and that sport is both shaped by, and shaping of, social class inequalities. In the final section, attention is focused upon student learning on this issue and a learning framework proposed for teaching students about social class is applied to sport-related contexts.

Linking the personal to the social: Understanding social class and sport

Earlier in this chapter, it was noted that Connell (1999) argued for personal knowledge and experience of sport to be recognized and understood within the dynamics of broad social structures. The challenge, therefore, is to consider ways of learning and teaching about sport and social class which both draw upon, and extend, personal class-based knowledge. Travers (1999) suggests that the key to understanding social class is to analyse how people 'understand and produce social divisions and identities' and to recognize the pivotal role of "status"' (section 8.6). Even more strongly, Rose (1998) states that social class is an essential link to the way we understand 'the central dynamics of society' (p. 757). Indeed, it is currently being argued that focusing more upon analysing and sharing lived experiences of social class, and less upon traditional, large-scale surveys and macro-structural approaches, will result in better understandings of social class issues (Travers, 1999; Devine, 1998). But how could such an analysis be conducted; and how can it provide practical information for those who aspire to work within one of the many sport-related occupations? Travers suggests that a four-stage process based upon ethnomethodology can provide helpful insights. He uses this particular approach because ethnomethodology has a 'thorough-going commitment towards addressing the actor's point of view' (section 9.1) and it helps us in 'viewing aspects of the world that we normally take for granted as research topics' (section 11.1). Clearly, if we are largely unaware of the complex and enduring power of social class in sporting contexts, a learning approach that helps us to question 'taken-for-granted' assumptions will be useful. Travers points out that there are numerous ways in which such learning could be organized, but he proposes four linked 'projects': an autoethnographic study; ethnographic research; examining social mobility; and looking at groups who have a professional interest in class. What follows is an outline of the purpose of each project and some brief suggestions about the ways in which each can be applied to sport.

An autoethnographic study

This is a deceptively straightforward task. Travers (1999) suggests that it should begin by:

> describing something mundane or obvious in the world around us . . . we can see class around us in innumerable ways in the daily round of our everyday lives: in Britain it is still relatively easy to identify someone precisely in class terms by their dress, the newspaper they read, their diet, their accent or whether they have private health insurance.
>
> (1999, section 11.3)

It could be argued that the earlier newspaper description of the football World Cup (page 75) qualifies as a type of ethnomethodological account – albeit using rather more artistic licence than is strictly required. For sociology of sport students, one way to start might be to describe, vividly, the defining characteristics of two sports that would be placed at opposite ends of the social class spectrum. As the analysis becomes more detailed and in-depth, this should be followed by an analysis of why particular sports were selected, and how they came to have class-linked characteristics. Inevitably this will require historical evidence – a good illustration of Bourdieu's earlier point about the links between sociology and history (see p. 73). There are, of course, numerous directions that a task of this nature could take. The initial description could focus on individuals in sport, particularly well-known figures, or teams within sports, or teachers/coaches of note who are identified from personal biographies. The key, however, is that the descriptions must be detailed. They could certainly form the basis of some early and lively discussion work, follow-up reading, structured seminar work and assignments.

Ethnographic research

This is described as 'spending time in a number of settings in which one would expect to find members of a particular social class' (Travers, 1999, section 11.4). The task could be done as a small research project, either by individuals or by groups. The essence of this phase is that it is ethnography, therefore immersion in a recognized sports culture is essential. Obvious choices of site would include a tennis club, a boxing club, youth football, mini-rugby, women's rugby, etc. During the research process, students are likely to be involved in participant observation and more- or less-formal interviews. The purpose of this phase is not to attach class 'labels' to different sports contexts, but to try to gain some understanding of the ways in which social class manifests itself, and is experienced and understood by those in a particular setting. Key to this will be the recognition that social class is never easily defined, nor can it be isolated from gender, race, or even geographical considerations. In order that students can share findings from a range of different sport-related settings, poster presentations would be one way of presenting this phase of work.

The experience of mobility

In the context of sport, this project could be particularly revealing. It is suggested that the focus should be upon 'the experiences of those who have joined a different class' (Travers, 1999, section 11.8). If Sage (1998) is to be believed, such social mobility is rare. However, debate and discussion will inevitably result in claims for particular social-class positions for high-profile sports people. This, in turn, could lead to some thorny questions about the relevance of personal background, the importance of money/the irrelevance of money, status and life-style, etc. The purpose of this project is to generate debate and discussion about some key assumptions underpinning our knowledge of social class. Here again the nexus of gender, race, class (and other factors such as sexuality) will undoubtedly be revealed.

Professionals and class

This phase involves looking at groups 'with a technical or professional interest in class' (Travers, 1999, section 11.9) and implies drawing upon wider literature and research on social class. As an example, the positions which aspiring sport professionals might hope to fill – teachers, coaches, sports managers or professional athletes – could be located within the new occupation-based social class index discussed earlier (Rose, 1998). Hargreaves (1986) reminds us that the variety within these sport-related roles is so great as to make generalizations about their status difficult. However, in broad categories, it should be possible to draw some useful comparisons with other occupations. For example, in seminar papers, analyses of the roles of teachers, coaches, sport managers and professional sports people could focus on the ways in which they reflect, create and perpetuate social class inequality. Clearly, such analyses will involve making links with broader social structures of which the roles are a part – education being one obvious example. Importantly, where students can identify and discuss realistic opportunities for resistance and change, then the task may have proved to be helpful in a very practical way.

Conclusion

This chapter has been structured around three main tasks: to identify and discuss contemporary social class concepts from the general field of sociology; to highlight the complexities of the links between sport and social class; and to suggest practical ways in which students might learn about the multilayered nature of those links. The case has been made that, despite claims to the contrary, social class is still an important factor in determining an individual's life-chances. Indeed, Rose (1998) argues persuasively that 'being working class can seriously damage your health . . . being working class can shorten your life . . . being working class increases your chances of experiencing unemployment' (p. 757). Furthermore, it has been suggested that sport, in conjunction with other social structures, is helping to create and perpetuate such inequalities, but that opportunities exist for resistance and social change. Put simply, sport, in most manifestations, is not a 'classless' activity offering equal opportunities for all.

It has also been stressed that an analysis of sport and social class which does not take into account other social characteristics, such as race and gender, can only be partial. In this respect, Bourdieu's theory of the centrality of the body in society could help to inform a more holistic understanding of sport and social class. Bourdieu uses the term 'habitus' to summarize his theory of the body/person and its relationship with society. It is a complex concept that attempts to represent the key social characteristics of individuals and seeks to explain how their actions are both determined by, and determining of, society: 'Habitus then is an embodied internalised schema that structures but does not determine actions, thoughts and feelings' (Jarvie and Maguire, 1994, p. 191). The concept of habitus also helps to explain why sociological analysis is often challenging – 'when habitus encounters a social world of which it is a product, it finds itself "as fish in water", it does not feel the weight of the water and takes the world about itself for granted' (Wacquant, 1989, p. 43). In other words, we see the social world, and the position of ourselves and others in it, as unexceptional – and so critical analysis and social change appear unnecessary. However, to reiterate Lemert's earlier point, this may be a very good example of the 'sneaky' nature of power.

This, then, is the backdrop against which we should consider our positions as sport-related professionals. There is no suggestion that resistance and social change ought to be the central goal of all those who work with or within sport. Nor that those with an interest in social issues will strive for social change all of the time. Rather, it is argued that for those who seek to be professionals, an awareness of the life-chance differentials of 'clients' is essential knowledge upon which to base any policy or practice that aims to widen access, participation and achievement in sport.

Acknowledgement

I would like to thank Juan-Miguel Fernández-Balboa (Montclair State University, New Jersey) for his comments on an earlier draft of this chapter.

References

● Adonis A. and Pollard S. (1997) *A Class Act: The Myth of Britain's Classless Society*, London: Penguin.
● Armour K.M. (1999) 'The case for a body-focus in education and physical education', *Sport, Education and Society* 4(1): 5–16.
● Blackburn R.M. (1998) 'A new system of classes: but what are they and do we need them', *Work, Employment and Society* 12(4): 735–41.
● Bourdieu P. (1978) 'Sport and social class', *Social Science Information* 17: 819–40.
● Connell R.W. (1999) 'Foreword to the 1999 edition', in R. Gruneau *Class, Sports, and Social Development*, Champaign, Ill.: Human Kinetics, pp. vii–ix.
● Crompton R. (1993) *Class and Stratification: An Introduction to Current Debates*, Cambridge: Polity Press.
● Davis L.R. (1993) 'Critical analysis of the popular media and the concept of ideal subject position: *Sports Illustrated* as case study', *Quest* 45: 165–81.
● Devine F. (1998) 'Class analysis and the stability of class relations', *Sociology* 32(1): 23–42.
● Donnelly P. (1996) 'Approaches to social inequality in the sociology of sport', *Quest* 48: 221–42.
● Duncan J. (1997) 'Focus group interviews with elite young athletes, coaches and parents', in J. Kremer, K. Trew and S. Ogle (eds) *Young People's Involvement in Sport*, London: Routledge, pp. 152–77.
● Evans J. and Davies B. (1993) 'Sociology, schooling and physical education', in J. Evans (ed.) *Physical Education, Sport and Schooling*, London: The Falmer Press, pp. 11–37.
● Fernández-Balboa J.-M. (1993) 'Sociocultural characteristics of the hidden curriculum in physical education', *Quest* 45: 230–54.
● Figler S. (1981) *Sport and Play in American Life*, Philadelphia: Saunders.

● Gerteis J. and Savage M. (1998) 'The salience of class in Britain and America: A comparative analysis', *British Journal of Sociology* 49(2): 253–74.
● Goldthorpe J.H. (1987) *Social Mobility and Class Structure in Modern Britain*, 2nd edition, Oxford: Clarendon Press.
● Goodger J.M. (1986) 'Pluralism, transmission, and change in sport', *Quest* 38: 135–47.
● Gruneau R. (1999) *Class, Sports and Social Development*, Champaign, Ill.: Human Kinetics.
● Hall M.A. (1985) 'How should we theorize sport in a capitalist patriarchy?', *International Review for the Sociology of Sport* 20(1): 109–15.
● Hall S. (1977) 'Culture, the media and the "ideological effect"', in J. Curran, M. Gurevitch and J. Woollacott (eds) *Mass Communication and Society*, London: Open University Press, pp. 315–48.
● Hargreaves J. (1986) *Sport, Power and Culture*, Oxford: Polity Press.
● Holt R. (1989) *Sport and the British. A Modern History*, Oxford: Clarendon Press.
● Jarvie G. and Maguire J. (1994) *Sport and Leisure in Social Thought*, London: Routledge.
● Jones H. (ed.) (1997) *Towards a Classless Society?*, London: Routledge.
● Jones S.G. (1988) *Sport, Politics and the Working Class*, Manchester: Manchester University Press.
● Kelley J. and Evans M.D.R. (1995) 'Class and conflict in six Western nations', *American Sociological Review* 60, April: 157–78.
● Kellner D. (1996) 'Sports, media culture, and race – some reflections on Michael Jordan', *Sociology of Sport Journal* 13: 458–67.
● Lawson H.A. (1997) 'Children in crisis, the helping professions, and the social responsibilities of universities', *Quest* 49: 8–33.
● Lawson H.A. (1999) 'Education for social responsibility: Preconditions in retrospect and in prospect', *Quest* 51: 116–49.
● Lemert C. (1997) *Social Things. An introduction to the Sociological Life*, Maryland, USA: Rowman and Littlefield.
● Mangan J.A. and Park R.J. (eds) (1987) *From 'Fair Sex' to Feminism: Sport and the Socialization of Women in the Industrial and Post-industrial Eras*, New Jersey: Frank Cass.
● Marshall G., Swift A. and Roberts S. (1997) *Against the Odds: Social Class and Social Justice in Industrial Societies*, Oxford: Clarendon Press.
● Martinek T. and Hellison D. (1997) 'Service bonded inquiry: The road less travelled', *Journal of Teaching in Physical Education* 17: 107–21.
● Mills C.W. (1959) *The Sociological Imagination*, Oxford: Oxford University Press.
● Norton C. (1998) 'Upwardly mobile Britain splits into 17 new classes', *The Sunday Times*, 13th September, Section 1.
● Novak T. (1997) 'Young people, class and poverty', in H. Jones (ed.) *Towards a Classless Society?*, London: Routledge, pp. 13–35.
● O'Reilly K. and Rose D. (1998) 'Changing employment relations: plus ça change, plus c'est la même chose? Reflections arising from the ESRC review of government social classifications', *Work, Employment and Society* 12(4): 713–33.
● Prandy K. (1998) 'Deconstructing classes: Critical comments on the revised social classification', *Work, Employment and Society* 12(4): 743–53.
● Renson R. and Careel C. (1986) 'Sporticuous consumption: An analysis of social status symbolism in sport ads', *International Review for the Sociology of Sport* 21, 2/3: 153–69.
● Rose D. (1998) 'Once more into the breach: In defence of class analysis yet again', *Work, Employment and Society* 12(4): 755–67.
● Sage G.H. (1998) *Power and Ideology in American Sport*, 2nd edition, Champaign, Ill.: Human Kinetics.

● Saunders P. (1996) *Unequal but Fair? A Study of Class Barriers in Britain*, London: The IEA Health and Welfare Unit.
● Sewert A., Prandy K. and Blackburn R.M. (1980) *Social Stratification and Occupations*, London: Macmillan.
● Sugden J. (1996) 'The exploitation of disadvantage: The occupational subculture of the boxer', in J. Horne, D. Jary and A. Tomlinson (eds) *Sport, Leisure and Social Relations*, Keele: The Sociological Review Office, pp. 187–207.
● Thomas D. (1994) 'The Americans took a working-class sport and turned it into a middle-class, summer entertainment', *The Daily Telegraph*, Saturday 16th July.
● Travers M. (1999) 'Qualitative sociology and social class', *Sociological Research Online*. Available: http://www.socresonline/4/1/travers.html.
● Wacquant L.J.D. (1989) 'Towards a reflexive sociology: A workshop with Pierre Bourdieu', *Sociological Theory* 7: 26–63.
● Walden B. (1989) 'Why a political pact would fall down the equality gap', *The Sunday Times*, 29th January.
● Whannel G. (1992) *Fields in Vision: Television Sport and Cultural Transformation*, London: Routledge.
● Woods R. and Norton C. (1999) 'Cloning the middle class', *The Sunday Times*, 17th January, Section 1.

Chapter Seven

Sport, Nationalisms and Their Futures

Irene A. Reid and Grant Jarvie

Introduction

By the middle of the twentieth century there was a belief that the ideology of nationalism was dead. However, a resurgence of nationalism during the last quarter of the twentieth century has demonstrated that this is a powerful and pervasive ideology which manifests itself in different ways (McCrone, 1998). Observations and popular accounts of recent international sport suggest that this view of nationalism is an accurate one. The rugby, soccer and cricket World Cups, the Olympic Games, European rugby championships and Davis Cup tennis competitions, are some examples of the occasions when sport provides an outlet for the display of sentiments and loyalties which are associated with national communities; many nations have their particular national sports, and particular sports clubs or individuals are the focus for national and cultural identities. International sports occasions between individuals, clubs or national teams, are marked by rituals and symbols (e.g. flags, emblems, opening ceremonies, uniforms, songs, face decoration) which make statements about attachments to competitors. The connection between sport and nationalism has also been used to construct an image of the nation, to contribute to a sense of a nation's greatness, and as the glue which transcends social and cultural divisions.

Studies of these social practices, of sport and domestic government policies, sport and international relations, or sport and political ideologies are now quite common and have contributed to our understanding of the close relationship between sport, nationalisms and society (Duke and Crolley, 1996; MacClancy, 1996). This chapter examines sociological knowledge concerning nationalisms to provide sports practitioners with certain tools to enable them to be more reflective about this dynamic relationship and its implications for the organization, practice and administration of sport.

For the sports practitioner, nationalisms may appear to have little application to the world of playing and organizing sport. Nonetheless, there are a variety of practical questions that sports practitioners might consider which an understanding of broader social, cultural and political contexts can assist in answering. For example: can sport contribute to international and cultural understanding? Does sport transcend specific social, political, cultural and economic barriers? Does sport provide opportunities for celebrating cultural diversity and difference? Why do governments invest in sport? How do governments and other agencies justify support for international events? Does sport contribute to a sense of national community and pride? Can sport be a vehicle for reconciliation and unity in divided societies?

The informed and reflexive practitioner should be able to translate abstract knowledge into the practices of their specific situations in order to respond to such challenges.

These questions posed are general but they can be answered through specific and comparative case studies using sociological concepts. The danger in looking at what the sociology of sport has had to say about the relationship between sport and nationalisms is that the general replaces the specific. In attempting to accomplish an overview of key elements of practice and thinking about sport, nationalisms and their futures, this chapter has been developed around four main sections: (1) an abstract but necessary discussion of some of the core conceptual tools sociologists have used to answer questions about nationalisms, nations and identity; (2) a reflection upon concrete themes that are evident in studies of sport, nationalisms and identities; (3) a reflection upon key issues addressed in the sociology of sport concerning nations and cultural identity; and (4) a specific comment about the issue of sport, autonomy and civil society.

Nationalisms and nations: Some definitions

The purpose of any sociological analysis is ultimately to provide an explanation and, as such, this section is necessarily conceptual. Much of the most recent literature adopts a flexible, eclectic approach to any conceptual explanation. The body of knowledge about nations, nationalisms and identities demonstrates that these are complex and ambiguous concepts (Anderson, 1991; Birch, 1989; Hall, 1996). This section maps out some key terms associated with nationalisms and nations that are used in the existing literature and which are used in specific case studies involving sport. This discussion considers four questions: (i) why is it appropriate to speak of *nationalisms*? (ii) what are the connections between the terms *nation-state*, *state* and *nation*? (iii) how can we define *nationalism* as a basis for analysis? and (iv) what are the distinctive characteristics and implications of *ethnic* nationalisms and *civic* nationalisms? Two general points should be made: first, nationalism is a powerful and persuasive global phenomenon that is not the preserve of any one political philosophy; and second, all nationalisms express aspirations of self-determination that result in some form of *autonomy*.

Why nationalisms?

It is important first to clarify why we refer to nationalisms, rather than to nationalism. As suggested in the introduction, sports are forums in which people display attachments to their nation which distinguish them from other nations. On the surface, these symbols and practices illustrate that there are many different nations each with their own nationalism, therefore, there is a case for speaking of nationalisms. But there are other reasons why it is appropriate to speak of nationalisms, which are revealed by thinking of nationalisms as multilayered phenomena. First, there are particular types of nations; for example, nation-states like the United Kingdom, Canada, Ireland or Spain, and cultural nations like Catalonia, Scotland and Wales. In the context of sport, but not exclusively, different types of nations express distinct kinds of nationalisms. At a second level, each nationalism characterizes the specific historical, social, cultural and political circumstances of the nation. These circumstances may have some broad similarities with other nations (e.g. industrialization, political democracy, influences from a global culture and economy), but these are contoured by distinctive cultures in specific national contexts. If we peel back further layers, we can reveal that a variety of sports are used to express different types of nationalism within one nation, and that during different historical periods, distinct nationalisms may be articulated within one nation. This multilayered approach poses a challenge for studies of sport, nationalisms and society: to explain all nationalisms in relation to their specific time periods, contexts and content.

Nation-states, states and nations

In spite of the different theories, one point offers a limited consensus on nationalisms: that they are contingent upon cultural formations called nations. This appears to be a straight-forward explanation but close scrutiny of the literature reveals that there are different sorts of nations and, indeed, uses of the term. The question '*what* is the nation?' elicits differ-ent responses that tend to reflect the sociological, historical or political orientations of those involved in explaining particular structures. For some, nations are natural units of human social organization which have been with us since time began, but most of the more recent contemporary literature rejects this assumption (Gellner, 1983). There are a number of weak-nesses with this assertion, one of which is that it implies nations are abstract and fixed entities. From a sociological and social historical perspective, an understanding of the nation begins from the supposition that it does not fit into 'a framework of permanence and universality' (Hobsbawm, 1992, p. 6). The sociological understanding of the term may emphasize that the 'nation' is a conceptual category connected with social praxis (Hall, 1993a), that is, it is concerned with human action and meaning. In this respect, the term nation reflects a variety of practical uses that 'structure perception . . . inform thought and experience . . . organize discourse and political action' (Brubaker, 1996, p. 10).

The connection between social praxis, structure, experience and political discourse is evident in much of the literature that considers what the nation is, but three terms stand out: nation-state, state and nation. The nation-state is defined as a sovereign political unit defined by territory in which one nation is dominant such as the United Kingdom (UK), in which the English nation has been the dominant constituent nation; the state is a legal and political concept represented by autonomous public institutions (e.g. government, legal system, armed forces) within recognized territorial boundaries, and operates in relation to other states (Tivey, 1981; Smith, 1996). There is clearly a political dimension to the nation-state and the state which is not evident in respect of the term nation, which is understood to be the people within the state who share a common culture, ethnicity and historical continuity.

Although nation-states have been the dominant organization of sovereign politics for almost 300 years, the perfect congruence of the nation-state does not exist. As Kellas (1991) explains:

> While many states share the features of nations, and can be called 'nation-states', there are also nations within states, and such states are correctly called 'multinational states' . . . today there are states consisting of more than one nation such as the United Kingdom, Switzerland, Belgium and Canada.
>
> (1991, p. 3)

To simplify these definitions, it is sufficient to refer to 'the state' to account for the political and legal units which have dominated the organization of territories since the eighteenth century. The state is different from the nation, which is explained as 'a community of people' (Birch, 1993, p. 14), rather than a sovereign political unit. The nation can be further clarified as 'a group of people who feel themselves to be a community bound together by ties of history, culture, and common ancestry' (Kellas, 1991, p. 2). This cultural con-ceptualization is endorsed by Smith (1996), who defines the nation as 'a named human population sharing an historic territory, common myths and memories, a mass, public culture, a single economy and common rights and duties for all members.' (p. 359). The significance of this emphasis on culture, is that it identifies the central content of all nationalisms, and the historic or pre-modern community as the cultural context of nations. The important point being made, is that it is the cultural formation and meaning of the nation that provides the social structure for nationalisms.

What is nationalism?

One consequence of the variety of academic contributions to understanding national-isms is that there is no universal definition of this phenomenon or of its origins (Anderson, 1996). For instance, a political-sociological perspective asserts that 'nationalism is ... about politics', and is the ideology of nation-states (Breuilly, 1982, pp. 1–2). From this definition, nationalism is not usually attributed to societies that are not states. This is also the case presented by certain sociological assessments such as that of Ernest Gellner (1983), who was unequivocal in his contention that 'nationalism does not arise for state-less societies' (p. 4). This interpretation is rejected for two main, but connected, reasons. First, it restricts nationalism to an abstract political ideology of nation-states and does not adequately explain the diversity of nationalisms that are evident in particular concrete forms throughout the world. Second, this interpretation is not appropriate in cases where cultural identities are articulated through sport and which may contradict the conventional political structure of nation-states.

In contrast to perceptions of nationalism as the political ideology of nation-states, a sociological perspective might emphasize the cultural dimension of nationalism, and describe it in terms of sentiment, aspiration and consciousness. The definition of nationalism preferred in this chapter is drawn from the work of Anthony Smith (1991) who suggests that all nationalisms are ideologies that have cultural phenomena and which may be associated with politics. One of the important strengths of this definition, is that nationalisms are understood to be meaningful expressions of collective identities that are perceived as national by those who articulate them. This idea of collective shared agency is a feature of nationalism that is often overlooked in analyses that reflect on an abstract ideology, and it recognizes that at the core of all nationalisms there is a cultural dimension which gives any nationalism its content, and contributes to its social and political context (Smith, 1991).

Ethnic and civic nationalisms

The final aspect of nations and nationalisms considered here concerns the distinction between civic and ethnic nationalisms. This is a useful analytical categorization, but in practice the distinction is rarely clear cut. In order to understand the two broad categories of ethnic and civic nationalism, it is first necessary to reflect on the idea of community. There are two relevant points to be made. First, community can refer to a specific geographical area with its particular social institutions; second, community is to do with 'a feeling of belonging, a sense of special identification with a particular grouping of people' (Lindsay, 1976, p. 100). Both are important in understanding nations and nationalisms, but it is the sense of belonging, a less tangible but apparently strong emotional sentiment, that is a vital component of shaping ethnic and civic nationalisms. All nationalisms appear, in part, to express a sense of belonging and loyalty to a particular national community and, in doing so, they implicitly articulate recognition of collective difference from other groups. In this way, all nationalisms contribute to defining the 'Other', or one who does not belong to specific national communities. There is, however, a dual emotional response invoked by nationalisms that are represented in notions of blood and belonging (Ignatieff, 1993). According to Anderson (1991), it is this strong emotional pull of belonging to a national community that has made it possible for many millions of people to engage in the bloodshed that can come with defending (or expanding) national communities.

In considering the discourses associated with ethnic and civic nationalisms, a key question to ask is 'Who is the nation?' (Smith, 1991, p. 19). The answers to this question provide evidence of the essential conceptual distinction between the two forms, but they also raise important ideas about the status and even legitimacy of certain communities and their respective nationalisms. In the case of civic nationalisms, who constitutes the nation is based on assumed acceptance of a system of political principles governing a specific territory and associated institutions, common values and patterns of social interaction (Keating, 1996). These political principles are those represented as the objectives of the French and American Revolutions, such as liberty, democracy, and equality, and we might add to these the right to individual privacy and protection under the law. In this respect, Ignatieff (1993) observes that it is law that binds the members of civic nations together, rather than perceived common ethnic roots. Civic nationalisms are, therefore, regarded as incorporative ideologies which recognize the legal rights of individual citizens irrespective of cultural or ethnic differences such as gender, religion, ethnicity or political creed.

Who constitutes the ethnic nation is encapsulated in the notion of blood, or more precisely blood ties. Membership of ethnic nations is usually restricted to those who fulfil certain conditions of ethnicity that are represented by a combination of ascriptive and inherited markers, such as common ancestry, religion, language, colour, customs, kinship or tribal attachment. Inherited markers like colour, blood and kinship are powerful but limited characteristics, and it may be difficult to claim the ethnic purity of a nation on this basis alone. Nonetheless, a number of contemporary nationalist tensions have been influenced by ethnic nationalism.

These fundamental distinctions between ethnic and civic nations are useful, but one consequence of the ways in which who belongs to the national community are decided, has been the status and perceived legitimacy of ethnic and civic nationalisms in both academic and popular discourses. A problem that often arises in thinking about nationalisms is that they are considered to be either inherently good or bad, but in an abstract sense nationalism cannot be considered to have any moral quality (Lindsay, 1976). There is a tendency to represent 'our' nationalism as the sentiment of patriots and 'yours' as irrational nationalistic fervour (McCrone, 1998), but in addressing ethnic and civic forms the problem is compounded, since it is not nationalisms *per se* that are judged in this way, but certain types of nationalisms are considered to be good or bad. More specifically, ethnic nationalisms tend to be portrayed as undemocratic and evidence of the persistence of, or the return to, primitive, pre-modern social formations and irrational human action. This is described by some theorists as representing the 'dark gods of nationalism' (Gellner, 1983; Hobsbawm, 1992). In contrast, Kellas (1991) explains that civic nationalisms are given a 'more noble status' (p. 4), although his own reference to 'official' nations and nationalisms appears to reproduce implicitly the derisive tag assigned to ethnic forms.

The terminology and meanings associated with civic and ethnic nations remain important elements for understanding contemporary nationalisms but, in concluding, an important point can be made. Ethnic nations can be exclusionary and intolerant communities supported by negative ideologies, but civic nations and nationalisms are not always positive, inclusionary and tolerant. Civic nations may also be intolerant and values may be unfairly applied (Keating, 1996), as is the case, for instance, with the experiences of Black Americans and Britain's Black and Asian citizens, yet such evidence is often hidden or ignored when nationalisms are considered. In contemporary contexts, most nationalisms can have the dual function of defining who belongs and who does not belong to the nation or cultural community.

These conceptual definitions are important in considering the relationship between sport, nationalisms and cultural identity. In specific studies of sport, nationalisms do not always cohere with states, but they are sometimes associated with nations, or with ethnic and cultural groups within states. These ideas are now considered in relation to sport.

Sport, nationalisms and identities

There are many examples of the different ways in which sport, nationalisms and identities intersect; however, most of these may be examined as either examples of nationalisms which represent an extension of the state, or as nationalisms which represent nations and identities within states (Duke and Crolley, 1996). In this section, we overview some examples of these two broad categories of sporting nationalisms, but there are many variations. No two forms of sporting nationalisms are identical and, therefore, each case must be examined in terms of specific time periods, contexts and content (Jarvie and Walker, 1994). In each case, it is important for students and researchers alike to examine the nature of the evidence in order to explain or interpret each case or incident.

There is an established literature which examines the significance of sport in society, and this has paid increasing attention to the links between sport, nationalisms, and cultural identities. As Whitson and Macintosh (1993) explain, sport is one of a number of cultural practices which have at least two important roles for nations: (i) they represent the nation to the rest of the world; and (ii) they mobilize national sentiments amongst the citizens within the nation. In short, sports 'are vehicles and embodiments of meaning, whose status and interpretation is continually open to negotiation and subject to conflict' (MacClancy, 1996, pp. 7–8).

The connection between modern sports practices, expressions of nationalism and a cultural identity has an established history. In the twentieth century, sporting contests provided tangible contexts through which a sense of belonging to a national community could be expressed. In this sense, sport may provide a unique arena for at least three reasons. First, sport, in some quarters, is still generally considered, and wrongly perceived, to be an apolitical activity, although, in reality, it cannot be isolated from the political environment in which it exists. Second, sport is thought to transcend social divisions such as class, gender, race or disability and therefore, on certain national and international sporting occasions, can bind the people of the nation in spite of other differences. Third, the inherent structure of international sporting competitions (both between nation-states, and nations-within-states) between our representatives (teams or individuals) against theirs, serves to reinforce the essential element of all nationalisms; that is, that they define what and who the nation is and is not. The interplay between these three scenarios dominates much of the research in this area.

Modern international sport was developed towards the end of the nineteenth and beginning of the twentieth centuries, during the period when the imperial capitalism of certain European nation-states was at its zenith (Jarvie and Maguire, 1994). The modern Olympic movement, which began in Athens in 1896, had an ideal objective of bringing together the peoples of the world through friendly and peaceful competition. It has been suggested by Tomlinson (1984) however, that Baron de Coubertin's motives may have been fuelled by a desire to promote French imperial superiority through a seemingly apolitical activity. There have been many occasions when success in international sports events has been used by countries to generate patriotism if not national feeling and pride. The 1936 Berlin Olympic Games were used in this way by the Nazi party, and during the cold war period, sporting competition between the United States of America (USA) and the Union of

Soviet Socialist Republics (USSR) was used to symbolize the superiority of one political-economic system over the other.

During the 1940s, George Orwell suggested that 'at the international level, sport is, frankly, mimic warfare' and that the modern cult of sport is tied up with the rise of nationalism which he described as 'the lunatic modern habit of identifying oneself with large power units and seeing everything in competitive prestige' (Orwell, 1943). The idea that international sport is 'war without weapons' is common in media commentaries of international sport, and often these draw on previous or existing conflicts between the states or nations involved. It has been suggested that this metaphoric warring nationalism has replaced patriotism, a 'milder' expression of support for the representatives of a particular country (Petrie, 1975). International sport might be a metaphor for war, but this is not an adequate theoretical analysis of either sport or nationalism. There is something that we might take from Orwell's remarks given the social and political context in which they were made. In a period when two world wars had been induced by nationalist sentiments, international sport may have, in some way, embodied and perhaps reinforced these sentiments This 'war without weapons' analogy may not be an adequate theory of sport, nationalism and cultural identity, but it perhaps did explain a dominant sporting nationalism of the 1940s.

Nationalism as the ideology of the nation-state is evident in many sports contexts, and there have been sociological and social-historical analyses of such cases. This connection between sport and nationalism can be explained as the way in which sports are seen to be an extension of the state, in that they 'come to reflect the structure of the political system' (Duke and Crolley, 1996, pp. 6–7). This relationship between state nationalism and sport is often perceived by other countries as a negative one, but this is not always the case. For example, sport as an extension of state nationalism has been used in many African countries which, as Jarvie (1993) points out, has been praised by liberal historians as a symbol of the integration of diverse social, cultural and ethnic groups. The use of sport as a vehicle for integration is common in developing countries, and was also one reason for the political control of sport in many communist countries. In these circumstances, national sport may provide a common focus in countries with diverse religious, ethnic, linguistic and class divisions (Riordan, 1986).

The sport–state nationalism alliance is not unique to sport in developing nations. Since the late 1960s, the Canadian federal government has increased its intervention in elite national sport. It has been suggested that this process was, in part, to reinforce unity in Canada, and may have been a reaction to concerns about the rise of separatist nationalism in Quebec and the subsequent political threat to the Canadian federal government (Macintosh, Bedeki and Franks, 1987). It may also have provided a focus for consolidating a Canadian identity that was distinct from the USA, presenting this to the world, and mobilizing a Canadian national identity amongst its citizens. The idea that sport provides a vehicle for integration within nations and, therefore, provides a focus for state-nationalism, is thus also evident in advanced democratic capitalist states.

National sport may provide a common focus for the diverse groups that comprise all nations, but it does not follow that the social divisions that exist in all societies will disappear because of sport (Jarvie, 1993). This is exemplified by the case of South Africa. The idea that sport has the potential to unite and integrate different ethnic and racial groups in a new nation-state has been an important element of South African policy in the post-apartheid era (Jarvie and Reid, 1999). The success of South Africa's international team in the 1995 rugby World Cup was achieved with only one non-White player in the squad, yet the Springboks' achievement was celebrated as a symbol of the reconciliation and nation-building which had been the policy of the African National Congress (ANC) majority government elected in April 1994. The success of the soccer team in winning the African

Nations Cup in 1996 and qualifying for the 1998 World Cup finals was also considered to symbolize unity in the 'Rainbow Nation'. This new South African sporting nationalism appeared to represent a superficial reconciliation and unity, as accusations of continued racial divisions in many sports emerged during 1997.

The case of sport, nationalism and identity in South Africa was an interesting one during the apartheid era. It is generally assumed that during this period, rugby union was the national sport of the Afrikaner community, but some leaders of South Africa's anti-apartheid movement have described how the game was a popular activity within many Black and coloured communities, especially in the Eastern Cape. They have also explained how international matches between the Springboks and other rugby nations had an important place in their continued resistance of apartheid during their imprisonment ('Lily-white Springboks are a thing of the past', by Mick Cleary, *The Guardian*, 21 May 1995, p. 13). Sport, therefore, provided a vehicle for different meanings and different expressions of the nation, depending on: (i) which ethnic, racial, cultural or class groups were speaking through that sport; and (ii) their relationship to the social and political conditions of power. These different nationalisms may be expressed by different groups (e.g. class, gender or ethnic) through the same sport, or through different sports. Whatever ways, they are examples of nationalisms in sport that are not only extensions of the state, but which may contradict or conflict with state-nationalism.

The sporting nationalisms of nations-within-states have also been considered using sociological knowledge about nationalisms and nations. For instance, sport is a vital cultural practice through which many Celtic nations-within-states like Brittany, Scotland and Wales celebrate their distinct and usually historic cultures (Jarvie, 1999). These Celtic nations are usually part of larger states which do not have a Celtic cultural core, and usually it is the non-Celtic culture which is perceived to be dominant in the nation-state, while the history of Irish nationalism and Irish sports are closely connected. The case of the Gaelic Athletic Association (GAA) in Scotland is particularly interesting, because it illustrates how specific elements of cultural identity, like religion, are incorporated into the construction of nationalisms which are meaningful to those who express them in sporting contexts (Bradley, 1998, 1999).

The national-cultural divisions in Spain, particularly in the Basque nation and in Catalonia, have been considered in relation to the soccer clubs Athletic de Bilbao and Barcelona (MacClancy, 1996; Duke and Crolley, 1996). It may not be just football that offers stateless nations an outlet for national sentiment, as other sports and cultural practices may also serve as a focus to celebrate 'actual' or 'latent' nations. This was illustrated through representations of the national and cultural divisions in Spain associated with the 1992 Olympic Games (Hargreaves, 1992; Hargreaves and Ferrando, 1997). The 1992 Olympics were held in Barcelona the capital of Catalonia, a region of Spain with a strong cultural identity which is distinct from the Castillian dominated central Spanish State. Although the Olympic Games provided a focus for Spanish nationalism, and appeared as such to other countries, it has been argued that the Catalans used them to celebrate their Catalan national identity through an international sports event. The use of the Catalan flag as well as the Spanish flag was, Hargreaves argued (1992), an important symbolic gesture in both Catalonia and in Spain. Both flags are coloured red and gold, with different striped designs and the significance of this gesture of Catalan nationalism may have gone unnoticed except to the most informed observer from outside Spain. The point is, that global sports events may be used to articulate what are often complex relationships between particular national groups and the political states within whose boundaries they are considered to live. It is suggested that the Barcelona Olympics provided a forum in which the dual identity of Catalans, loyal to the Spanish state and to the cultural nation, was articulated; at the same time, they accommodated the antagonisms between these communities (Hargreaves and Ferrando, 1997).

The politics of cricket in the colonial West Indies has also been used to explain the relationship between cricket and the colonial experience. Sport may have appeared to be a level playing field but, through their sports, Englishmen in the colonies used this moral code 'as a mark of differentiation' (James, 1963, p. 40) which helped to sustain power and status in a colonial society. For instance, in Trinidad, where James was from, the structure and membership of first-class clubs mirrored the hierarchical boundaries and social strata of the island. The relationship between cricket, nationalism and cultural identity however, is best represented by the coincidence of the campaigns for a Black player to captain the West Indies cricket team and the rising tide of nationalist independence movements during the late 1950s and early 1960s. Returning to Trinidad in 1958 after 26 years abroad, James became the secretary of the West Indian Labour Party and editor of the *Nation*, a political paper that represented the People's National Movement. Through the pages of the *Nation* in 1960, James campaigned for the appointment of Frank Worrell as the first Black man to captain the West Indian side, not on the basis of colour but on that of ability, experience and leadership qualities. The matter had become a final symbol of colonial rule, and one that James and others during the 1950s considered to be discrimination against Black men by the West Indian Cricket Board and a matter of international scandal. As James (1963) explained:

> An individual easily gets over the fact that he is disappointed in his desire to be captain. It is the constant, vigilant, bold and shameless manipulation of players to exclude Black captains that has so demoralized West Indian teams and exasperated the people – a people, it is to be remembered, in the full tide of the transition from colonialism to independence.
>
> (1963, p. 232)

More recent studies have demonstrated that cricket retains its place in the popular discourses which seek to establish nationalist and cultural identities in independent nations such as the West Indies, India and Pakistan which were former British colonies. There are also studies that illustrate that within the British State, the established communities of peoples whose familial origins may have been former colonies often use cricket as the terrain on which specific cultural identities are secured. One suggestion for this is that cricket provides the cultural terrain on which the former colonial power can be beaten at its own game and although this is a persuasive argument, it obscures the complex social, cultural and political realities of all peoples living in contemporary nation-states. This point is made by Edward Said (1994), who argued that the contemporary societies of former imperial nations like Britain are dramatically different from what they were at their imperial zenith, most notable of which is that these states now have 'large non-white immigrant populations' which seek ways 'for their narratives to be heard' (pp. xxvii–xxviii). This is a powerful and legitimate argument. The discourses of national independence movements and of imperialism cannot contribute fully to an analysis of contemporary societies that are now much more multicultural in composition and experience. These hybrid cultures and identities that constitute experiences of people in contemporary nation-states have replaced monolithic, rationalist and distinctively separate cultures and not just because of population migration from former colonies, although that is important. The global mass media plays an important role in the formation of hybrid cultures, albeit that it tends to favour particular realities and cultural forms (Said, 1994). The emphasis now must be on overlapping territories, histories and identities within a world order that retains the nation-state as its primary organizational form.

It is not possible, nor necessary, in the context of this chapter to examine all of the many ways in which sport, nationalisms and identities intersect. The examples used in this section have been selected to illustrate three themes evident in research connecting sport, nationalism and cultural identity: (i) sport as an extension of state-nationalism; (ii) sport as arena through which identities of nations within states are expressed; and (iii) sport as a focus for nationalisms which draw on specific ethnic or race identities within states.

Nations, cultural identity and the sociology of sport

A variety of theoretical positions have been used to examine the connections between sport, nationalism and cultural identity. Within the area of sociology of sport, functionalist theories, Marxist theories, figurational theory, cultural studies and postmodern theory have been most prominent. Two general principles dominate the sociological and historical explanations of nationalism: first, that nations are constructed entities; and second, that nationalisms form under a combination of necessary and sufficient conditions (Kellas, 1991). Yet it is important to realize that nations are never 'completed' entities and that nationalisms can only be understood as selective, time-bound expressions of the nation, not as predicted inevitable consequences of internal and external conditions.

Much of the literature on nations and nationalisms attempts to connect the origins of nations and the processes by which nationalisms are made. Two crucial points can be made here. First, that nations are imagined communities (Anderson, 1991) in the sense that it is not possible for the members of a nation to know all its other members. Second, nations and their nationalisms are not fixed entities and abstract ideologies, but are dynamic processes which constantly change and adjust in order that imagined communities have relevance in the present while reinforcing the continuity of the past. In short, the formation of nations can never be completed but must look to find new ways of mapping its territory, both actual and imaginary. Furthermore modern sport does not exist in some social and political vacuum and, therefore, either in an intended or unintended way, contributes to these processes.

In an analysis of sport, nationalism and cultural identity, Jarvie (1993) explained that his concern was with the ways that sport can assist in the search for identity. Adopting a similar position to Whitson and Macintosh (1993), Jarvie argued that nationality is only one of a number identities that sport contributes to and which draws on shared cultural characteristics. In this section, attention is focused on two related concepts arising out of this work: culture as the material content of nationalism; and identity as the collective subjective feeling of nationalism objectified as culture. It is argued that as well as being a cultural practice, sport also provides certain institutional structures through which shared cultural identity can be expressed.

The concept of cultural identity has been the subject of much consideration in sociological research. A common starting point in the literature appears to be a consideration of culture, a much used but ambiguous and complex term (Williams, 1976; Palmer, 1982; Jenks, 1993). To explain this concept and its ambiguous meanings, the work of Raymond Williams (1961, 1962, 1977) is often used. Williams identified culture as one of five words that either came into common use, or took on new meanings, during the last decade of the eighteenth century and the first decades of the nineteenth century. He suggested that culture itself has had five meanings associated with it: (i) the cultivation of natural growth prior to the eighteenth century, which subsequently came to represent: (ii) 'a general state or habit of the mind', invoking a notion of human perfection; (iii) 'the general state of intellectual development in society as a whole'; (iv) 'the general body of the arts' such as certain forms of literature, music and art; and (v) 'a whole way of life, material, intellectual and spiritual' (Williams, 1962, p. 16). In sociology and cultural studies, this last meaning has informed the assertion that, as a way of life, culture includes 'the development of literacy, holidays, sport [and] religious festivals', as well as intellectual and aesthetic activities (Storey, 1993, p. 2). This is only a summary of what constitutes the content of culture which might also include language, ways of dressing, arts, crafts, religious practices, legal procedures, educational processes, customs, heroes and heroines, poetry, literature, folk tales, architecture, ways of acting and feeling (Smith, 1991). The selection by groups of people of a certain mix of cultural content contributes to the social construction of nationalism, which represents 'the element of artefact, invention and social engineering' involved in the making of nations (Hobsbawm, 1992, p. 10).

The figurational approach to the sociology of sport however, utilizes a different interpretation of culture that incorporates the Elisian notion of 'civilizing processes' (Elias, 1978) as a central tenet. In this respect, there is something in Elias' approach to culture that draws on those meanings of the term that emphasize certain activities as indicative that a community has achieved the state of a civilized society. Unlike earlier interpretations, figurational sociology asserts that modern sports practices are symbols of a civilized society, and can, therefore, be usefully incorporated into the processes. It is also important to note that in figurational sociology, culture and cultural identity cannot be understood without the people who practise it being aware of it. Sport is a specific cultural activity, but more importantly, it is a carrier of cultural values and structures (Maguire, 1994); sport is, therefore, one of a number of structures on which specific ideas and meanings which are part of distinctive ways of life (i.e. of cultures) can be constructed, developed and articulated. This deeper role for sport in society, as a signifying practice and symbol of a particular way of life, provides what might be described as a tangible context through which ethereal ideas associated with nations, nationalisms and aspects of cultures may be given meaning.

At the core of analyses of sport and identities, figurational sociology utilizes Elias' concept of interdependence to explain the multiple bonds that individuals and groups form, and, in doing so, establish an infinite variety of social networks (Jarvie, 1988, pp. 92–3). An important dimension to figurational sociology is that these interdependencies are formed in relation to emotional, political and economic spheres of activity, and at different levels. For instance, the emotional bonds that may attach to national symbols such as flags, emblems or songs, provide one level of interdependence and awareness of collective identity among individuals. At another level, these bonds may form between larger units such as villages or towns, but never independently of the political and economic spheres of activity within the social formation.

In relation to the sociological study of sport, nationalism and cultural identity, the definition of culture as the symbols and practices of a whole way of life has tended to be the most dominant one. The idea that sport is one of a number of practices that are part of a distinctive culture is a useful basis from which to understand the connection between sport and cultural identity. In this context however, identity is not superficial or uniform but is 'something deep-rooted' and concerned with 'subjective feelings and valuations' of individuals and groups (Jarvie, 1993, p. 61). Cultural identity knits together individuals, classes, genders, religious groups and ethnicities, helping them to make sense of their common experiences and often enabling them to imagine themselves as a nation.

The concept of identity resonates with both individual and collective meanings but, from a sociological perspective, it is the latter forms of identity which are often most pertinent. It may be argued that, as individuals, we develop multiple identities which are based on a number of categories the most important of which are gender, space and territory, socioeconomic status, religion and ethnicity (Smith, 1991). Following this principle, Smout (1994) maps a more comprehensive framework of multiple identities which combines a range of territorial identities including family, clan, locality, nation, state and supranational loyalty, and a range of social identities such as gender, class, occupation, colour, language, religion and sport. What is evident from the two explanations is that no single category of identity is sufficient to explain cultural identity. Hall (1996), who prefers to speak of identification rather than identity, reiterates this point, or more accurately argues that cultural identity concerns a process that has more than one category at its core. An understanding of sport and identity must, therefore, reflect on this impression of multiple identities which inter-weave individuals and groups into a dynamic framework of local, national and in the late twentieth century, transnational contexts (Maguire, 1994).

No single definition or explanation of these multiple identities is satisfactory, but two important assertions arise from the analysis of collective forms of identity. First is the idea that collective identities are constructed on an assumption of sameness (Smith, 1991). The idea of collective identity is based on shared cultural artefacts such as language, customs, common experiences, religion, and significant practices which mark the boundaries of sim-ilarity. Second, and by extension, collective identities that draw on shared and common meanings and practices also define difference from other collective identities that are recognized by other sets of cultural characteristics and practices (Hall, 1996). Stuart Hall has suggested that the cultural practices and symbols used to define 'sameness' may change in the process of constructing collective identity, but that the condition of defining differ-ence remains (Hall, 1996). A similar point is made by Maguire (1994) who emphasizes that definitions of 'sameness' and 'otherness' coexist through cultural identities which change 'over the life of an individual [and] the *longue durée* of a nation' (p. 402).

The role of sport in helping to define distinctive cultural identities is identified in much of the literature on sport. As such, identities are important factors because they give concrete frameworks on which to build amorphous identities. Nations are centralized, symbolic formations that incorporate cultures and national identities, 'which claim to subsume all differences into their imagined unity' (Hall, 1993b, p. 351). Socially constructed cultural identities then are selectively adopted to represent the common experiences and shared characteristics of a nation, an imagined community, which is contextualized for most people through cultural practices and institutions. Sport, in all its different forms, contributes to these processes.

Sport, autonomy and civil society

A key argument in the literature which examines sport, nationalism and cultural identity appears to be that sport is an activity through which common experiences and otherwise subjective, intangible feelings can be expressed. When one explains national or cultural identity from sociological perspectives, it is essential that two points are addressed: (i) a satisfactory explanation of how the structures of sport, for example clubs and national governing bodies, are related to other structures of nations and states; and (ii) how sport, its organizations and associated expressions of collective identities are to be understood in relation to power. Some of this ground has been covered in analyses of sport and gender and sport, race and ethnicity, but this has not always been examined effectively in studies of sport, nationalism and other aspects of cultural identity. In terms of moving towards future concepts which might inform studies in this area, the notions of civil society and autonomy are worthy of a mention.

A number of theorists have used the idea of civil society as an institutional network which mediates the set of practices, values, and attitudes that constitute culture. Kumar (1993, pp. 382–3) contends that 'civil society is the sphere of culture in the broadest sense', which appears to be consistent with other interpretations of this concept. This is perhaps too broad a definition, or at least it is too similar to one of the meanings of culture considered in the previous section. A more helpful definition is that civil society is 'the space or arena between the household and the state . . . which affords possibilities of concerted action and social self-organisation' (Bryant, 1993, p. 399). This proposition suggests that civil society is represented by the institutional terrain of culture and, specifically, of areas of self-organization not regulated by the state. Civil society must, however, be understood in relation to the political apparatus of the state, like government, and forces of internal and external law and order.

It is argued here that as part of a self-regulated civil society, sport has been, since the latter part of the nineteenth century, a real day-to-day space, through which both collective official (political) identities (like state-nationalism) and distinctive contrasting but locally meaningful identities (like nationalisms and cultural identities of nations-within-states) could be expressed. In presenting their distinctive cultural identities, groups of people who perceive themselves as the same look back to the range of historical experiences, symbols, customs, attitudes and so on in order to selectively reconstruct and redefine themselves for the historical period in which they move. An established network of self-regulating civil society related to, yet separate from, the state, represents the structural framework within which distinctive cultural groups can express the characteristics of their own cultural identity without disrupting the apparent unity of the state. It must be noted that, from a sociological perspective, since nationalism is a cultural phenomenon and political ideology, the concept of civil society provides a pertinent institutional context even in nation-states. Even as a political ideology, nationalism tends to be constructed as the non-politically partisan expression of a nation or state. The apparently autonomous institutions of civil society like sport, therefore, serve as the ideal arenas for state nationalism and cultural nationalism, because these are not considered to serve the interests of particular agents of the state apparatus. Morton (1996) suggests that one of the strengths of the relationship between the state and civil society is that it is a reciprocal one. While civil society may legitimate the state, it has the potential to 'produce and sustain its own ideology, its own nationalism' (Morton, 1996, p. 262). In a state such as the UK, the self-regulating clubs, societies and associations of sport which are part of civil society, rather than the political apparatus of the state, have often provided the institutional framework in which social and cultural identities can be constructed, and where the nationalisms of nations-within-the state (e.g. Scotland and Wales) can be expressed.

The notion of autonomy, is concerned with the search and arrangements for the administration of power in cultural, national and state territories. In a recent consideration of the term nationalism, Smith (1996) explained that he took it to be 'an ideological movement for the attainment and maintenance of autonomy, unity and identity of a human population, some of whose members conceive it to constitute an actual or potential "nation"' (p. 359). This follows his earlier assertion that nationalism is concerned with arrangements for attaining and maintaining the autonomy, unity and identity of a nation, and is the goal of every nationalist (Smith, 1991). In explaining his conception of autonomy, Smith reveals that it is concerned with self-determination. For exponents of the 'nationalism as the ideology of the nation-state' theory, the objective of all nationalist movements is to establish control of its own independent state determined by its own government. The term autonomy is not used extensively in such literature, yet it seems that in political theories, nationalism is precisely about the right to self-determination. This would appear to support two of the three assertions about autonomy and nationalism drawn from Smith's work.

How then are we to understand autonomy in those cultural nations or regions of larger states that neither have, nor seek, political autonomy in their own state? The answer may be revealed, in part, by broadening the potential spheres of social and political life in which autonomy might be experienced and the extent to which aspirations of self-determination, power and authority have already been fulfilled. Clarification of this may be found in Smith's own assertion that certain cultural nations, like Scotland and Catalonia, have, in specific circumstances, been satisfied with some form of devolved political power or with opportunities to assert cultural parity, rather than straightforward political independence (Smith, 1991). It is being suggested here that there is more than one way in which to seek or establish autonomy. As Lindsay Paterson (1994) has argued:

> Autonomy has taken many forms, and can operate in many different ways. A society can be almost wholly independent in one aspect of its existence (education, let us say), yet be almost wholly dependent in another (most usually defence policy). And that independence is perfectly consistent with freely chosen assimilation towards the norms of a larger neighbour.
>
> (p. 5)

This conception, that there are forms of autonomy has a number of benefits in theorizing sport, nationalism and cultural identity. First, it is a flexible, theoretical concept, that is relevant to both nation-states and nations-within-states which assert collective identities through cultural practices like sport. Second, there is a sense in which autonomy is neither an abstract nor permanent aspiration but is part of the process of everyday experience which can, and does, change over time and in distinct social and cultural contexts. Third, it illustrates that different spheres of social, cultural and political activity within specific societies can satisfy multiple aspirations and degrees of autonomy simultaneously. In providing the institutional structure for self-regulation and the development of specific identities, the activities that dominate civil society provide the essential spaces in which different forms of autonomy can be practised.

Conclusion: Sport, nationalisms and their futures

Despite the momentous events of this century the nation-state remains a basic unit of political currency as we enter the new millennium. It is a brave person who would predict the future make up of the World Cup, the Olympic Games or any other world sporting event. The proliferation of nationalisms and nation-states over the last 20 years confirms this point. The complex relationship between sport and nationalism shows no sign of dying and, although no single theory of sport, nationalisms and their futures is possible, the sociological, political and psychological functions of nationalism make it a particularly potent logic and force that will be with the sporting world for some time to come.

It will not be possible to reduce any nationalism automatically to one of these functions but the rapidly increasing rates of social change, in different parts of the world, make it more, rather than less, likely that in the future, the sporting world will remain a potent arena for the display of different forms of social identities and protest. The quest for new forms of autonomy lends itself to different challenges from different social groups who often feel excluded from the world in which we live. This holds true both for individuals and collective national formations and, as such, the relationship between sport, nationalisms and their futures is both a personal and collective one.

Sport will continue to play a part in response to the questions 'who are we?', and 'who do we wish to become?'. The distinctive modern feature of nationalism is the belief that people are capable of acting collectively, and of conferring authority on political and social institutions as an expression of this act. This will impinge upon the European Union (EU), the United Nations (UN) and North Atlantic Treaty Organization (NATO) as well as on sporting organizations like the Fédération Internationale de Football Association (FIFA) and the International Olympic Committee (IOC). One might not agree with the logic of nationalism, but as a social phenomenon it will need to be addressed by future students, scholars, and athletes who are interested in explaining what processes are affecting either sport or themselves. The often forgotten relationship between personal action and public concerns or troubles (Mills, 1959) may take on different forms, but it remains a valuable guideline to understanding practice in sport.

References

- Anderson B. (1991) *Imagined Communities*, 2nd edition, London: Verso.
- Anderson, B. (1996) 'Introduction', in G. Balakrishnan (ed.) *Mapping the Nation*, London: Verso, pp. 1–16.
- Birch A.H. (1989) *Nationalism and National Integration*, London: Unwin Hyman.
- Birch A.H. (1993) *The Concepts and Theories of Modern Democracy*, London: Routledge.
- Bradley J.M. (1998) *Sport, Culture, Politics and Scottish Society: Irish Immigrants and the Gaelic Athletic Association*, Edinburgh: John Donald.
- Bradley J.M. (1999) 'Heritage, culture and identity: The Gaelic Athletic Association in Scotland', in G. Jarvie (ed.) *Sport in the Making of Celtic Cultures*, London: Cassell Academic, pp. 166–77.
- Breuilly J. (1982) *Nationalism and the State*, Manchester: Manchester University Press.
- Brubaker R. (1996) *Nationalism Reframed: Nationhood and the National Question in the New Europe*, Cambridge: Cambridge University Press.
- Bryant C. (1993) 'Social self-organization, civility and sociology: A comment on Kumar's "civil society"', *British Journal of Sociology* 44(3): 397–407.
- Duke V. and Crolley L. (1996) *Football, Nationality and the State*, Harlow: Longman.
- Elias N. (1978) *The Civilising Process*, Oxford: Blackwell.
- Gellner E. (1983) *Nations and Nationalism*, Oxford: Blackwell.
- Hall J.A. (1993a) 'Nationalisms: Classified and explained', *Daedalus* 122(3): 1–28.
- Hall S. (1993b) 'Culture, community, nation', *Cultural Studies* 7(3): 349–63.
- Hall S. (1996) 'Who needs "identity"?', in S. Hall and P. du Gay (eds) *Questions of Cultural Identity*, London: Sage, pp. 1–17.
- Hargreaves J. (1992) 'Olympism and nationalism: Some preliminary considerations', *International Review for the Sociology of Sport* 27(2): 119–37.
- Hargreaves J. and Ferrando M.G. (1997) 'Public opinion, national integration and national identity in Spain: The case of the Barcelona Olympic Games', *Nations and Nationalism* 3(1): 65–87.
- Hobsbawm E.J. (1992) *Nations and Nationalism since 1780: Programme, Myth, Reality*, 2nd edition, Cambridge: Canto.
- Ignatieff M. (1993) *Blood and Belonging: Journeys into the New Nationalism*. London: BBC Book/Chatto and Windus.
- James C.L.R. (1963) *Beyond a Boundary*, London: Serpents Tail.
- Jarvie G. (1988) *A Sociological Analysis of the Scottish Highland Games*, a thesis presented to the University of Leicester for the Degree of Doctor of Philosophy.
- Jarvie G. (1993) 'Sport, nationalism and cultural identity', in L. Allison (ed.) *The Changing Politics of Sport*, Manchester: Manchester University Press, pp. 58–83.
- Jarvie G. (ed.) (1999) *Sport in the Making of Celtic Culture*, London: Cassell Academic.
- Jarvie G. and Maguire J. (1994) *Sport and Leisure in Social Thought*, London: Routledge.
- Jarvie G. and Reid I.A. (1999) 'Sport in South Africa', in J. Riordan and A. Kruger (eds) *International Politics of Sport*, London: E & F.N. Spon, pp. 93–102.

● Jarvie G. and Walker G. (eds) (1994) *Scottish Sport in the Making of the Nation: Ninety Minute Patriots?* Leicester: Leicester University Press.
● Jenks C. (1993) *Culture: Key Ideas*, London: Routledge.
● Keating M. (1996) *Nations Against the State: The New Politics of Nationalism in Quebec, Catalonia and Scotland*, Basingstoke: Macmillan Press.
● Kellas J.G. (1991) *The Politics of Nationalism and Ethnicity*, Basingstoke: Macmillan Press.
● Kumar K. (1993) 'Civil society: An inquiry into the usefulness of an historical term', *British Journal of Sociology* 44(3): 375–95.
● Lindsay I. (1976) 'Nationalism, community and democracy', reproduced in L. Paterson (ed.) (1998) *A Diverse Assembly: The Debate on a Scottish Parliament*, Edinburgh: Edinburgh University Press, pp. 96–101.
● MacClancy J. (ed.) (1996) *Sport, Identity and Ethnicity*, Oxford: Berg.
● Macintosh D., Bedeki T. and Franks C.E.S. (1987) *Sport and Politics in Canada: Federal Government Involvement Since 1961*, Montreal: McGill-Queen's University Press.
● Maguire J. (1994) 'Sport, identity politics and globalization: Diminishing contrasts and increasing varieties', *Sociology of Sport Journal* 11(4): 398–427.
● McCrone D. (1998) *The Sociology of Nationalism*, London: Routledge.
● Mills C.W. (1959) *The Sociological Imagination*, Harmondsworth: Penguin.
● Morton G. (1996) 'Scottish rights and "centralisation" in the mid-nineteenth century', *Nations and Nationalism* 2(2): 257–79.
● Orwell G. (1943) 'The sporting spirit', *The Tribune*, 14th December.
● Palmer B. (1982) 'Classifying culture', *Labour/Le Travailleur* 8/9: 151–83.
● Paterson L. (1994) *The Autonomy of Modern Scotland*, Edinburgh: Edinburgh University Press.
● Petrie B. (1975) 'Sport and politics', in D. Ball and J. Loy (eds) *Sport and the Social Order*, Reading, Massachusetts: Addison-Wesley, pp. 207–32.
● Riordan J. (1986) 'State and Sport in Developing Societies', *International Review for the Sociology of Sport* 21: 287–309.
● Said E.W. (1994) *Culture and Imperialism*, London: Vintage.
● Smith A.D. (1991) *National Identity*, London: Penguin.
● Smith A.D. (1996) 'Nations and their pasts', *Nations and Nationalism* 2(3): 358–65.
● Smout T.C. (1994) 'Perspectives on Scottish identity', *Scottish Affairs* 6: 101–13.
● Storey J. (1993) *An Introductory Guide to Cultural Theory and Popular Culture*, London: Harvester Wheatsheaf.
● Tivey L. (ed.) (1981) *The Nation-State: The Formation of Modern Politics*, Oxford: Martin Robertson.
● Tomlinson A. (1984) 'De Coubertin and the modern Olympics', in A. Tomlinson and G. Whannel (eds) *Five-ring Circus: Money, Power and Politics at the Olympic Games*, London: Pluto Press, pp. 84–94.
● Whitson D. and Macintosh D. (1993) *National Sports and National Identities: Cultural Travelling in an Era of Globalization*, a paper presented at the annual conference of the North American Society for the Sociology of Sport, Ottawa (November).
● Williams R. (1961) *The Long Revolution*, London: Chatto and Windus.
● Williams R. (1962) *Culture and Society 1780–1950*, London: Penguin Books.
● Williams R. (1976) *Keywords*, Glasgow: Fontana.
● Williams R. (1977) *Marxism and Literature*, Oxford: Oxford University Press.

Chapter Eight

From Athleticism to Commercialism: Engaging with the Future
Alan Tomlinson

Introduction

Many debates about the nature of contemporary sport are essentially moral debates about the meaning of sport, and relate to the values that people attribute to different sports and different ways of playing, following and consuming sport. Take, for instance, the incident which permanently marred boxer Mike Tyson's reputation as a fighter, even more so than his conviction for the rape of a young Black woman. When he bit off a chunk of Evander Holyfield's ear, moral outrage was expressed by commentators, fans and athletes through-out the world. It was legitimate to maul and punch an opponent, to disfigure, maim and sometimes kill the rival in the name of the 'noble art', but in going beyond the rules Tyson crossed over into a sphere of taboo. He was portrayed as primitive, as cannibalistic. 'What has sport come to?', morally outraged people asked in and beyond the world of sport. And how had things come to this? Too much money? Too much to lose? Where were the 'true' values of sport in a world of showbiz and spectacle relayed throughout the world on prime-time broadcasting media? The Tyson affair pricked the conscience of modern professional sport, conjuring up images of a more innocent age of sportsmanship, when respect for opponents and fair play governed sporting conduct. Yet, in some ways, Tyson's action was a normal enough form of deviance in sport. Critcher (1997, p. 34) argues that an emphasis on winning, ambiguity in rules, corruption in management, and mechanisms of socialization, combine to produce forms of behaviour in sport that are often labelled deviant, but that are hardly surprising.

The professional sportsman or woman faces a difficult task in a time of saturation media coverage. If you are dignified, supremely talented and focused, and uncontroversial – if you are tennis player, Pete Sampras, for instance – you might be labelled boring and dull. If you come close to victory but don't quite make it you will be branded a 'choker', seen as lacking bottle, psychologically defective. Such was the fate of French golfer Jean Van De Velde in the British Open championship in Carnoustie, Scotland, in 1999. He took seven strokes at the last hole of the four day tournament, when even a six (at a par four hole) would have won him the championship. His levelheaded response was truly refreshing. He had won a little under £200,000, rather than £350,000. But he'd given it his best shot, he said; and there are more important things in life than sport, he reminded the world's media. The French golfer's response suggested that commercialized, professional sport need not abandon traditional core values of sport. As we debate sport, contest its meanings and significance and its extraordinarily high profile in contemporary life, it is important to consider what these values are, where they came from, and what currency they might retain today and into the future. Such a consideration is a concern with morality, with the values or beliefs on the basis of which we should act and live: morality being '[i]n its prescriptive sense, . . . that consideration, or set of considerations, providing the strongest reasons for living in some specified way; in its descriptive sense, such a consideration, or set of such considerations, adhered to, or avowed by, some person or group' (Crisp, 1993, p. 399).

To grasp this moral dimension of sporting practice, it is necessary to understand the fundamental features of athleticism, the set of values in a predominantly amateur context that shaped such a dominant form of Western sports in the nineteenth century. This chapter concentrates on the historical legacy of athleticism, and its relation to emerging forces of commercialism in some selected team and individual sports. By drawing in informed fashion upon the past, it offers an agenda for engaging with the future. Such an agenda should be illuminated by sociohistorical knowledge and critical social scientific analysis of the meaning of sport. If arguments are made about the corruption of sport, the values that are alleged to have been corrupted should be closely scrutinized. Sport is, and always has been, more than a mere diversion from the more serious matters of life, and to leave its future to, for instance, market forces is to forsake some of the moral force that has been widely attributed to it; and to abandon the space that sport can occupy in public life and civic society. All practitioners, therefore, in forging the future of sport, should be aware of the moral stakes and implications of their actions and beliefs.

Athleticism

Many of the core characteristics of modern sports were shaped in the British public schools of the nineteenth century (Holt, 1989; Hargreaves, 1986). The primary source for an understanding of the nature and impact of the public schools' approach to games, sport and physical activity is the work of Mangan (1981) on the public schools of the nineteenth and early twentieth century, a substantial empirical study of the genesis and impact of the 'ideology of athleticism'. Four educational goals were stressed by physical educators in the public schools. Physical education, it was believed, would cultivate desirable moral values: physical and moral courage; loyalty and cooperation; the capacity to act fairly and take defeat well; and the ability to command and obey (Mangan, 1981). With such an agenda, the public school educators attributed to sports a capacity for character building. As Mangan shows so vividly, riotous and brutal forms of activity by the undisciplined public school youth – such as 'a brutal frog hunt in the school grounds' in the early 1840s at Marlborough, in which the frogs were beaten to death and the bodies piled high (Mangan, 1981, p. 18) – were replaced by formalized disciplined activity. From around 1870, Bamford notes, 'there was a subtle but organized drive by authority to sublimate the boy's self to a team' (Bamford, 1967, p. 83). The particular achievement of the public schools in sport was the development of a vehicle for the transmission of moral values to newly-educated generations of upper-class and upper-middle class males. In his 1904 book *Let's Play the Game: The Anglo-Saxon Sporting Spirit*, Eustace Miles wrote that cricket could illustrate:

> such valuable ideas as cooperation, division of labour, specialization, obedience to a single organizer (perhaps with a council to advise him), national character, geography and its influences, arts and artistic anatomy, physiology and hygiene; ethics and even – if the play can be learnt rightly – general educational methods.
>
> (cited in Dobbs, 1973, p. 28)

There is a clear manifesto here for the production of the disciplined individual with a set of socially acceptable moral values. It would be difficult to overestimate the importance of what Peter McIntosh (1979) has noted as the equation of physical education with moral education. McIntosh notes too that the recognition that physical education can contribute to moral education emerged in the late eighteenth century, out of the ideas of French philosopher and educationalist Rousseau concerning the body–mind relationship, and out of pioneering developments in gymnastics on the European mainland. But the public schools were to institutionalize such ideas into powerful sets of principles and a coherent working ideology. As McIntosh puts it:

> It was in the public schools during the second half of the (nineteenth) century that two basic new theories were developed. The first was that competitive sport, especially team games, had an ethical basis, and the second was that training in moral behaviour on the playing field was transferable to the world beyond.
>
> (McIntosh, 1979, p. 27)

Lest one might think that such views have been long discredited, consider how much they have in common with the declarations of former Conservative Prime Minister John Major, in his introduction to the government's policy document *Sport – Raising the Game* (DNH, 1995). Framed as 'ideas to rebuild the strength of every level of British sport', and claimed as 'the most important set of proposals ever published for the encouragement and promotion of sport' (p. 1), the policy document was rooted in the founding principles of the morality of athleticism. *Sport – Raising the Game* argued that sport should be cherished for its capacity to bond and bind people together across ages and national borders; and, 'by a miraculous paradox', to also represent 'nationhood' and 'local pride'. In doing this, sport is claimed to (DNH, 1995, p. 2):

- through competition, teach lessons which last for life;
- be a means of learning how to be both a winner and a loser;
- thrive only if 'both parties play by the rules', and accept the outcome 'with good grace';
- teach how to live with others as part of a team;
- improve health;
- create friendships.

The vehicles for the inculcation of these values were 'our great traditional sports – cricket, hockey, swimming, athletics, football, netball, rugby, tennis and the like' (DNH, 1995, p. 3) – an explicit acknowledgement of the moral values long attributed to the playing field and above all to team games.

Compare the Major eulogy for sports with celebrations of the values of games from a century earlier. Mangan reported the beliefs of an early apologist for public school games who believed that these games could help produce 'a manly straightforward character, a scorn of lying and meanness, habits of obedience and command, and fearless courage. Thus equipped, he goes out into the world, and bears a man's part in subduing the earth, ruling its wild folk, and building up the Empire' (cited in Mangan, 1981, p. 9); well prepared by his grounding in the 'institutional wars on the playing field . . . The alliance between character-building and games promoted self-restraint and cooperation without wholly destroying a competitive sense of struggle' (Wilkinson, 1964, p. 30). In 1909, the captain of the Cambridge University cricket team of 25 years before could still write, in the *Empire Annual for Boys*, that to play the game was to exhibit a 'supreme standard of excellence' (Studd, 1909). From such a perspective, three main sporting values were worthy of cultivation: 'to aim high, to never lose heart, and to help your neighbour' (Kanitkar, 1994, p. 187). Cricket, rugby and football were the sports which featured most in this kind of rhetoric. Arthur Mee, too, famous in mid-century as the author of *The Children's Encyclopaedia*, stressed the importance of the playing field for the laying down of the 'laws of honour'. Belief in the importance of games and sport was deeply rooted in the schools, and practice matched rhetoric throughout the twentieth century. In the mid-1960s, most (boarding) public schools still allocated three or more half-days per week to organized games (Kalton, 1966, p. 110); in 1963 sporting activities could still serve as a primary form of 'ritualistic symbolization of the social values on which . . . the public school system rests' (Wakeford, 1969, p. 124); in the academic year 1993/4, 83 per cent of 11-year-old pupils in independent secondary schools had more than two hours of physical education per week, compared to 48 per cent in state schools, with weekend, lunch time and after-school sport reported to have further decreased in the state sector (Secondary Heads Association, 1994, p. 8). The legacy of athleticism was still being widely preached in the pedagogy of the privileged close to a century and a half on from its inception.

Core principles of amateurism – fair play, working for others in teams with character-building benefits – have in many respects been admirable, and certainly long-lasting. Fabled star of the 1981 movie *Chariots of Fire*, the 1924 Olympic gold medallist and athletics writer Harold M. Abrahams could write, in 1948, of the forthcoming London Olympic Games: 'First and foremost we must really get away from the point of view of regarding only the *winners* of Olympic events as those who are worthy of praise. It is this very narrow point of view which is so wrong and unfair . . . I was lucky enough in 1924 to win an Olympic title, and I realize to the full that the praise showered upon me was out of all proportion to the occasion. I am not going to pretend that I did not train extremely hard, but I realize to the full that luck played an enormous part' (Rivers, 1948, p. 14). Here, immediately post-World War II, the amateur-based spirit of athleticism still prevailed. And into the last decade of the century, a prominent figure in sports broadcasting, cricket commentator Brian Johnston, could call upon the central themes of athleticism as a driving force, offering lessons for life more generally, and not just sport. From his background at Eastbourne College, Eton, and Oxford University, and then the BBC establishment, Johnston could comment:

> All that time spent on just a game! Or is it something more than that? Many of us believe that it is. More than anything else in my life it taught me to try and work and play with others, and to be a member of a team. I was taught the importance of improving my own performance by practice, dedication and discipline; and to accept the umpire's decision, to win or lose gracefully and to take the inevitable disappointments with a smile. These are the ideals and I am not boasting or pretending that I have ever lived up to them, but they do explain the phrase 'it's not cricket'.
>
> (Johnston, 1990, p. 1)

Generations schooled in such an ethos sought to offset the rising influences of professionalism and commercialism in sport (whilst, ironically, in the cases of both Abrahams and Johnston, gaining a good living from the rising cultural profile of sport), acting in their own way as latter-day rational recreationists. Yet veiled in hypocritical notions such as effortless excellence, the values of athleticism became tarnished and, in the British example, came to operate as a conservative and discriminatory force, effecting the marginalization of much talent. However, the legacy of athleticism has resurfaced in some surprising spheres. American social scientist Amitai Etzioni – with a far from negligible influence upon the

British Prime Minister Tony Blair – in his book *The Spirit of Community* (1994), has argued for a new moral, social, public order – without puritanism or oppression, based upon shared values, the renewal of social bonds and the reform of public life. It was to extracurricular activities, in the form of school games and team sports, to which Etzioni turned when seeking an example of how the values necessary to such an order might be cultivated. Sports, he recognized, could be abused, if coaches focused upon winning as the sole object of the activity, and neglected:

> to instil learning to play by the rules, teamwork and camaraderie. 'Graduates' of such activities will tend to be people who are aggressive, maladjusted members of the community . . . If parents see the importance of using sports to educate rather than to win, sports can be a most effective way to enhance values education . . . they generate activities that are powerful educational tools. Thus, if one team plays as a bunch of individuals and loses because its adversary plays as a well-functioning team, the losing players learn – in a way that no pep talk or slide show can – the merit of playing as a team.
>
> (Etzioni, 1994, p. 103)

From the playing fields of Rugby, and elsewhere, to the policy chambers of the White House and 10 Downing Street – athleticism and its related ideologies, seeing moral education in physical activity, will go down as more than a mere footnote in the history of Britain; the struggles over the meaning of different conceptions of sport as more than a sideshow to mainstream political and cultural life. These core values of nineteenth-century athleticism can be seen to have been eroded as both individual and team sports have become more influenced by the forces of professionalism and commercialism. In their nineteenth-century form they were based upon class privilege, and patriarchal power. They were also tools of imperial domination across the British Empire, used to reconstruct cultures according to a British-based and racist conception of the colonial 'Other'.

Yet such sports were undeniably powerful moral and ideological forces, with long-lasting impact. The following discussion gives most attention to athletics, but gives brief consideration to the case of football. The cases concentrate on the rise of commercialism and consumerism in sport – the conditions whereby the commodification of sport (the intensifying production of sport and sport-related goods for the market, for sale and for profit) has been established and promoted.

Athletics

Whannel has summarized the pre-modern form of athletics in Britain, which had existed for centuries:

> The rural festivities of the sixteenth and seventeenth centuries featured running races. A tradition of rural athletic meetings in the eighteenth century became particularly strong in the North of England and Scotland with events like the Highland Games and the Border Games. Pedestrianism and the running of head-to-head matches for gambling was well-established before the nineteenth century. In the nineteenth century it is known that there were both open professional athletic events, with prizes, and open meetings that were mainly middle-class affairs, with low-value prizes.
>
> (Whannel, 1983, pp. 43–44)

The amateur form of athletics superseded these established practices, in the context of class disputes and tensions, as upper-class, middle-class and working-class enthusiasts struggled to gain control of the emerging institutional base of the sport. If the traditional forms can be seen as the first phase in any periodization of the historical development of the sport, then the succeeding phases were: the formation of clubs and the struggle to lead the sport, rooted in class-specific tensions over the amateurism issue; the dominance of the amateur ethos, during which there also developed women's athletics; a period of athlete power in which the premises of athleticism were questioned, disputed and opposed, and which also coincided with the high point of 'shamateurism'; the impact of commercialism and of open professionalism, in intensifying forms as media interests and sponsors effected a commodification of the athletic event and its champions and stars, with the production of the athletic event and the construction of the athletic celebrity (and associated goods and products) in increasingly uncompromising market terms.

Definitions of amateur status were commonly based upon forms of privilege and power rooted in class position and relations. The AAC (Amateur Athletic Club, formed in 1866, later to become the three As, when 'Club' was changed to 'Association') formulated an influential definition of the 'amateur' (Bailey, 1978, p. 131) which affected a range of sports in their deliberations on the issue. The Club was formed to enable gentlemen amateurs to practise and compete among themselves 'without being compelled to mix with professional runners'. The AAC offered an elitist and excluding definition of 'amateur':

> Any person who has never competed in an open competition, or for public money, or for admission money, or with professionals for a prize, public money or admission money, and who has never, at any period of his life, taught or assisted in the pursuit of athletic exercises as a means of livelihood, or is a mechanic, artisan or labourer.
>
> (Bailey, 1978, p. 131)

So, just in case any non-elitist athlete might qualify for membership, the AAC came clean in its last clause, and expressed the class basis of its constitution.

The Amateur Rowing Association and the Bicycling Union also barred such workers from membership, on the rationale that workers who worked 'physically' would enjoy an unfair advantage in competition with the more sedentary professional, and was really in need of more mental exercises away from work. In golf, too, similar emphases were articulated concerning the material gains that might accrue from playing or providing services for sport (Cousins, 1975, p. 39), though the English Amateur Athletic Club's definition did not explicitly exclude on the basis of social class or type of work. But generally, professionals were defined as an unacceptable other, on the basis of criteria of exclusion – if you were characterized by X, then you could not be included in category Y. The organization and administration of athletics was shaped by such excluding principles.

The modern form of athletics was modelled on the Amateur Athletic Club's first championship, held in the mid-1860s. Clubs were formed within the networks of the public schools, the universities, the professions and business (Crump, 1989). The notion of the club was critical, providing 'an element of collective endeavour' (Crump, 1989, p. 44) which fuelled the team spirit characteristic of organized games, and marked the new sport off from the competitive individualism of pedestrianism, the established form of running races. The Amateur Athletic Association (AAA), formed in 1880, was the initiative of three former Oxford University athletes, and successfully united amateur athletics in England, at least until the British Olympic Association was established to organize the 1908 Olympic Games in London, and the Women's Athletic Association was established in 1922. The AAA campaigned against professionalism and illegal payments to athletes, defending the purity of the amateur ideal and was bolstered in the 1890s by the formation of the Olympic movement by the French aristocrat Baron Pierre de Coubertin. We have seen that the Amateur Athletic Club's 1866/7 definition of amateur ruled that no mechanic, artisan or labourer could be accepted as an amateur, reasoning that manual labour would give such people an unfair advantage in athletic competition. This definition was loosened in 1868 but still stated that 'An amateur is a gentleman who has never competed' (Crump, 1989, p. 51). The AAA revoked this 'gentleman' clause, but fought a long-term offensive against professionalism.

Professional athletics continued to flourish nevertheless, especially in regions such as the North of England and in the Scottish Highlands. The AAA excluded professionals from other sports, such as cricket and football, in 1883 and 1899 respectively, and funded the prosecution, for fraud, of those breaching the ban, some even receiving prison sentences. In 1899, the AAA authorized payment of travel expenses to athletes, and it appeared that the leadership and shape of the sport were by then well-established, in class-based and amateur form; so much so, that in the 1920s the gentleman amateur dominated British athletics, with the national team being made up in most part by members of the Achilles Club, which had been established by, and for, Oxbridge graduates.

Women's athletics developed separately from the men's. The first women's athletics club to be formed in England was the London Olympiads Athletic Club, formed by women returning from the Women's Olympiads in Monte Carlo in 1921 and Paris in 1922 (Hargreaves, 1994, p. 130). Most of these women were from the Regent Street Polytechnic, and with others who ran and played netball for England, they provided the basis for the formation of the Women's Athletic Association (WAA). Women's athletics, Hargreaves argues (1994, p. 131), was less exclusively middle-class than many other female sports, as it was considered to be unladylike. Indeed, the administrators of the WAA commissioned a medical report in 1925 which argued that 'even if one does not see any ill results at the time from too strenuous devotion to athletics, the final result may be very deleterious to the girls' health and natural functions' (Hargreaves, 1994, p. 133). The report claimed that child-bearing could be adversely affected by participation in athletics, and the WAA accepted the report without question. Although some women may have challenged class dominance in developing women's athletics, prejudices about the female body continued to inhibit the sport's development. Fragmentation in the organization of British athletics was such that, when the Scottish Amateur Athletic Association complained to the International Amateur Athletic Federation about the power and nature of the AAA, the British Amateur Athletics Board (BAAB) was set up in 1932. In 1981, the Minister of Sport Neil MacFarlane was shocked to find that 19 organizations could claim to control some aspect or other of British athletics (Crump, 1989, p. 49).

The final phase in the growth of athletics saw it break free from the stranglehold of the amateur ideal, and open the door more widely to the forces of commercialism, and to open professionalism. In this, a form of athlete-power was important when the International Athletes Club was formed in 1958, developing out of the dissatisfaction felt by non-university athletes during, and after, the 1956 Olympics in Australia, and disputes concerning the payment of pocket money to athletes. A confusing period of 'shamateurism' – with underhand payment to so-called amateurs, hand-in-hand with manufacturers such as Adidas – was followed by the introduction of the trust fund in 1982. This fund enabled athletes to keep all appearance, sponsorship and advertising income for the purposes of subsistence, training and retirement, whilst retaining the status of amateur. The BAAB retained the right to authorize arrangements for any trust funds.

Reports and committees in the 1960s and the 1980s were to warn that unless British athletics united, increasing sponsorship income could be misdirected. These reports were shown to be timely when the boom years of athletics in the 1980s were followed by the bust years of the 1990s and, ignominiously, the BAAB plunged into financial crisis with little explanation as to what had happened to the huge income flowing into the sport during its prosperous years. Emblematic of such mismanagement was the famous race between Zola Budd and Mary Decker-Slaney, in 1985 (Crump, 1989, p. 56; Channel 4, 1986).

Decker-Slaney had raced against Budd in the final of the 3,000 metres at the 1984 Los Angeles Olympics, blaming Budd for a collision and a fall which she claimed lost her the race. The rematch, at Crystal Palace in July 1985, attracted £200,000 sponsorship from a US television company. Budd, a South African running at the Olympics by claiming British citizenship, was paid £90,000; Decker-Slaney received £54,000. It was widely perceived that Decker-Slaney was the superior athlete, with a personal best eight seconds faster than Budd's. Budd herself commented at a pre-race press conference that 'I certainly don't think I can win', but that 'anything can happen in a race'. The stadium was far from full, as the meeting had been stretched into a second day in order to accommodate Saturday coast-to-coast coverage of the race in the USA. Many spectators at the first day were, there-fore, disgruntled at the changed schedule, and the unpredictability of the line-up in other races, as Sebastian Coe, Steve Cram and the Brazilian athlete Cruz were announced as running in separate races rather than against each other, or not at all.

Meanwhile, behind the scenes, the sponsor of the event, Peugeot Talbot, entertained its 900 key customers in its hospitality suite, with the company's director Tod Evans wel-coming these clients as family and friends. Peugeot was also taking advantage of a new regulation which permitted sponsors to advertise during the programme breaks in those programmes which they were themselves sponsoring. Cavalcades of Peugeot's new model were filmed on the track, and a special advertisement had been made for broad-casting over the two days of the meeting. Peugeot's John Russell could draw analogies between his own company's values and those of athletics, the latter described as clean, lively, full of integrity, dynamic. Professional commentators were less fulsome in their praise. In a documentary made for Channel 4 entitled *Take the Money and Run* (Channel 4, 1986), Steve Goldstein, a print journalist from Philadelphia, commented that 'this is one of the biggest showbiz extravaganzas that's ever taken place in sport', comparing it to soap opera and the television audience expectations for a mix of drama and celebrity. Sports journalist Colin Hart (of the *Sun*) described the contest as 'an event not a race, no contest, a mismatch . . . they're selling advertising, it's money' (ibid.). Alan Pascoe, of Alan Pascoe Associates, the man responsible for guaranteeing British athletics a sponsor-ship income of £3 million over five years, labelled the event as 'one of the big personality races of the century' (ibid.). Created for television, this 'head-to-head that had to happen' was a complete mismatch, heralding an era of event-management in the sport, in which entertainment and celebrity could become as important as competitive realities. New alliances between the sport, sponsors and television – brokered in important ways by marketing figures such as Pascoe – established a financial bonanza for British athletics. But as Decker-Slaney strolled to her victory at Crystal Palace, British athletics proceeded down the road to its eventual insolvency. Individual athletes such as Daley Thompson, Linford Christie and Sally Gunnell would benefit greatly from this, but athletics itself failed to disseminate its new-found riches, with entrepreneurial opportunists doing little for the wider development of the sport (Downes and Mackay, 1996). In this process, too, the *esprit de corps* of the amateur ideal and national pride has given way to a more individualistic ideal: 'the athlete's effort and dedication are directed at least as much to self-realization and to the peer group of athletes as to the national team and the wider public' (Crump, 1989, p. 59).

Such self-realization has been driven as much by financial motives as by performance aspiration. Downes and Mackay see the Budd versus Decker-Slaney event as pivotal in the transformation of athletics, a process which they label as a 'loss of innocence' based upon the perceived market value of individuals:

In athletics' first ten years of professionalism, a strange, arcane system of 'subventions' had grown up, mainly about the sport's continuing coyness about paying large sums of money to its leading performers. Under this subvention system, star quality was recorded, but not actual performance. The meeting promoters would decide on an athlete's worth, and agree a fee with the competitor or their agent in advance of the meeting. Athletes were being paid to appear, not to compete. The sport's values soon began to warp.

(Downes and Mackay, 1996, p. 18)

Such warping or distortions would include not just made-for-TV fiascos such as Budd versus Decker-Slaney, but a range of examples corrupting the values of fair competition. British athletics promoter Andy Norman, for instance, ensured that top stars were not present, and allegedly offered payment to a runner not to win in the 'carefully orchestrated event' that was Alan Pascoe's last race, in front of a capacity crowd at Crystal Palace in 1979 (Downs and Mackay, 1996, p. 91). In 1995, Kenyan athlete Moses Kiptanui, running in Sweden, deliberately avoided breaking his own world record in the 3,000 metres steeplechase World Championships final, so that he could reap all the benefits on offer at the meeting in Zurich later in the week – where, being the first man to run under eight minutes, the Kenyan's bonuses and fees amounted to around £130,000 (Downs and Mackay, 1996). Corrupt officials would contribute to fixed outcomes. International Amateur Athletics Federation president, Italian Primo Nebiolo, built an extra lane and bent the rules to get the host nation into the final at the Rome World Cup in 1981; and was implicated, in the cover-up at least, when long jump measurements were fixed in the computer at the 1987 World Championships in Rome, so guaranteeing an Italian competitor a medal (Downs and Mackay, 1996). Nebiolo is also reported to have rigged the voting in the poll for World Athlete of the Year in 1995, so robbing English hurdler Sally Gunnell of a second successive such honour (ibid.); and to have covered up a positive drug test on an Italian hammer thrower at the 1984 Los Angeles Olympics (ibid.). The systematic use of drugs has also distorted the record books, especially up to the point at which Canadian Ben Johnson set his steroid-aided all-time 100 metres record at the Seoul Olympics: 'in the doping control clampdown that followed the Johnson scandal, there was not one world record set in a women's Olympic event for five years' (ibid., p. 158). Not just state-centred regimes such as East Germany and Bulgaria were prominent in the administration of performance-enhancing substances. A sudden emergence to prominence of Italian distance runners in the mid-1980s has been attributed to doping by steroids, and blood transfusions (ibid.).

Athletics – in its basic form, the glorious epitome of sporting competition – has emerged as a celebration not merely of individual athletic talent, but as a sport increasingly vulnerable to exploitation by individual performers, administrators, and political and market forces. The riches which poured into British athletics in the boom years of the 1980s and the early 1990s – redistributed at times 'in a brown paper bag' and 'a stack of used notes' (Downes and Mackay, 1996, p. 108) by Andy Norman – did little to secure the longer term prosperity of the sport. The case of the Chafford Hundred Athletics Club is a revealing one, related by Downes and Mackay. This club was created in 1991, and became, overnight, the richest athletics club in Britain, though entering and competing in no conventional club or team competitions: 'Chafford Hundred AC was established purely as a marketing ploy, a one-stop shop for sponsors wanting to become involved in one of Britain's most successful sports' (Downes and Mackay, 1996, p. 104). Top British athletes – including Christie, Gunnell, and John Regis – could wear the vest of this fictional club on the international Grand Prix circuit, plastered with whatever logo the elite group agreed to display from the favoured sponsor. Income into the sport would thus, flow into the individual accounts of a few stars, bypassing the development programmes of the grass roots of the sport. The Chafford Hundred club – named after an Essex housing development close to Andy Norman's home, and managed by Fatima Whitbread, former javelin world champion and Norman's fiancée – diverted potential income away from the sport's federation, and real conventional clubs, and was 'just the latest manifestation of the greed and money motive that threatens to corrupt athletics forever' (Downes and Mackay, 1996, p. 104). In the light of marketing initiatives such as this, and the collapse of the financial infrastructure of British athletics, it is no surprise that Peter Radford, former Olympic sprinter and erstwhile head of the British Athletics Federation, has argued that sport is too important to be left to the sports organizations and other agencies, and that a degree of state involvement and direction is now necessary if sport is to fulfil its true potential (BBC Radio 4, 1998). In August 1999, when the news broke that Linford Christie had tested positive for a banned drug earlier in the year, overdue questions began to be asked about the nature of the administration of British athletics. One prevailing view attributed the reformed federation's debt of more than £5 million pounds to a false sense of priorities – the organization had been 'administration-led', rather than 'athlete-led'. A closer sociological scrutiny might reverse this analysis. Whilst athletes were pocketing vast fees in the boom years, scarcely any were worrying about the sport's administration or its grass roots development.

Association football

The social history of the game of association football in England can be divided into seven distinct phases: the folk game; the formalization of the athleticist-amateurist codes in the public schools; the split between association football and rugby football, and then later within rugby football itself – bound up with the emergence of the professional game; the insularity of the British game in the interwar years of the twentieth century; the postwar years of austerity; the years of further commercialization of the game in the 1960s, 1970s and 1980s; and the more recent phase based upon the creation of a breakaway elite Premier League and sponsorship and media influences upon the game.

Responses to commercialism from traditionalists were widely critical of professional sport. One writer in the *Birmingham Daily Mail* (November 4, 1881) observed that the 'creeping' development of 'gate money exhibitions' would be accompanied by the 'inevitable tendency' towards the lowering of the game's character. The intrusion of money into the game was, for this writer, anathema to the spirit of the amateur code, 'giving a sordid aspect to the contests which, if carried on at all, should be for the honour of victory alone without any ulterior thought as to how much the "gate" is worth' (cited in Tischler, 1981, p. 41).

Mason has documented the nature of this debate, and shown more fully the respective arguments used by the opponents of professionalism. The two main ones were premised on a view of the nature of leisure itself, and an opposition to the potential scale and scope of commercialized sport. First, it was said that the nature of a 'voluntary leisure activity' would be corrupted by turning it into a business. Second, it was alleged that professionalism would undermine the survival of all but larger, wealthier clubs and so threaten 'essentially local rivalries' (Mason, 1980, p. 72). Three further arguments were used in this debate. It was believed that professionalism would destroy amateurism because the latter would not be able to compete on equal terms with the former; that professionalism would produce an overemphasis on winning, at any cost; and that the football professional was no true 'professor' anyway, for he had no teaching responsibilities (Mason, 1980). Against this trend of professionalism, the middle classes believed that the amateur code of the game 'was good for the physique, it helped to build character, it perhaps led to diminution in drinking, it brought the classes together' (Mason, 1980, p. 229).

The defendants of amateur values would have seen the modern professional footballer as the epitome of the threat of professionalism. Mason sees in Kevin Keegan 'the arrival of the modern footballer-businessman'. Keegan – player for Scunthorpe, Liverpool, Hamburg, Southampton and Newcastle United:

> signed contracts to promote Faberge Toiletries, Harry Fento suits, Mitre Sports Goods, Patrick (UK) Ltd. Boots, Nabisco Shredded Wheat and Heinz Baked Beans. He formed companies registered in tax havens such as the Isle of Man: Kevin Keegan Investments Ltd., Kevin Keegan Enterprises Ltd., and Kevin Keegan Sport and Leisure Ltd. He also had a four-year contract with BBC Television worth, it was reported, £20,000 . . . more players were participating in soccer than ever before and they were buying £23 million worth of football boots each year. *Sports Trader* has charac- terized the 1980s as a 'veritable soccer boom'. It was a boom which enabled Bryan Robson to sign a contract for £25,000 a year to wear Balance Boots and Gary Lineker to endorse a boot for a 3 per cent royalty on sales which, his accountant hopes, will net one million pounds. In 1951 Stanley Matthews received £20 per week for endorsing football boots made by the CWS.
>
> (Mason, 1989, p. 163)

By the middle of the 1990s football embodied the central features of a modern high-profile sport, as much a mediated spectacle and vehicle for insatiable consumerism as a forum for physical pleasures, cultural affiliation and playful creativity. New breeds of entrepreneur had moved into the game, making fortunes in share and property deals as top clubs became public limited companies, and the football business expanded to meet the needs of share-holders and accountants rather than members and administrators (Conn, 1997). At the end of the 1997–98 season, Premier League chairmen (for they were still all men) voted against the introduction of pay-per-view coverage on Rupert Murdoch's Sky Sports operation. Their motives were less likely to do with issues of universal access than with bargaining strat-egies for clinching the best economic package. The people's game had become a lucrative global commodity (Sugden and Tomlinson, 1998), and the Premier League chairmen were clearly not prepared to sell themselves short in the global marketplace.

Moral concern over the commercializing trend of professionalism had been expressed at the end of the nineteenth century in the most extreme forms. One commentator in the *Contemporary Review* recognized the 'mighty influence' of football, and saw the pro-fessional game and associated competitive forms as 'thoroughly evil', the 'sordid nature' of the professional game, particularly in its recruiting processes, savouring of 'bribery and corruption' (Ensor, 1898, p. 752). In such discussions, it was taken for granted that debate about the nature of the game was a moral debate. H.H. Almond claimed that the 'accursed money element' threatened the benefits of sport, in this case rugby football. 'The football scrummage is a great educator', he wrote, and could 'foster that virtue which is most closely allied to purity, and without which no nation can be either great or truly prosperous, viz. the virtue of courage'. Players were in fact moral agents in Almond's view, condemning 'foul play and the infliction of wilful injuries as criminal and odious' (Almond, 1893, pp. 911, 903 and 902). In a time when the state as regulatory agent can bar the purchase of Manchester United PLC by Rupert Murdoch's BskyB, in the name of some fairly amorphous 'best interests' of the English game, such moral interventionism may not be as redundant as it might have once seemed.

Conclusion

Sociohistorical case studies are not coffee table indulgences. As sport policy is debated, and sport's value and role in the future variously disputed and justified, knowledge of its resilient forms and contested meanings is essential. Without such knowledge, old idealism will clash with new forces and simplify and distort the issue of what sport should be for, and in whose interests it is worth developing.

Professional forms of competitive activity had well established and deep cultural foundations by the middle of the twentieth century. Yet fans of top professional football could still, in the late 1950s and early 1960s, receive a set of rules on becoming a life-member of Charles Buchan's Boys' Club which echoed the mission of the public schools and the philosophy of amateurism. The 'Rules' for membership of this club were:

1. To improve your skill to the best of your ability.

2. To support your team in good times and bad.

3. To play the game as a true sportsman.

4. To be modest in victory and cheerful in defeat.

In a time more than a third of a century on, when the basis of affiliation is television sport and Premier League merchandise, this set of rules seemed quaint and rather innocent. Yet, it also represented a central paradox that has run through the social history of sport in the modern period – the tension between, on the one hand, the amateurist model of participation based, at its peak, in apparently effortless excellence, and, on the other, the professional model of hard work, professionalism, winnning at all costs and personal financial reward. There were positions between such extremes, of course. The first man to run the mile under four minutes, Sir Roger Bannister, comments supportively upon the 'fundamental belief that sport can and should be a civilizing force of beauty and moral power' (McIntosh, 1979, foreword). Yet, he certainly did not achieve this without hard work, a professional-style application and sound tactical planning and support. But these were balanced by his prevailing amateur morality, which spurned monetary reward or the commercialization of his achievement.

There are no Bannisters at the top at the beginning of 2000. Sports in which top-level participants can hold out for £40,000 a week have produced the sports celebrity on unprecedented scale. Greg Williams, author of *Football Crazy* (1999a), comments on how sports or entertainment are now in themselves news: 'Footballers are the peacocks, cads and lotharios of our age, dovetailing perfectly within the soap of beautifully boring celebrity that self-consciously plays itself out in the public domain' (Williams, 1999b, p. 39). Eric Dunning (1999) describes such highly commodified and commercialized professional sports as symptomatic of a situation, in the Durkheimian sense, of 'classic anomie': 'Given the amounts of money flooding into the game and the accelerating pace of European and global change, the standards by means of which individual greed used to be kept reasonably in check have broken down' (pp. 128–9). Anomie is a term derived from the Greek *anomia*, meaning without law. In Western philosophy and social science it came to mean the absence of rules. Unbridled commercialization and an unregulated market in football, therefore, produce an individualistic morality of personal gain and a crude economic morality of elite dominance and profit.

The former Sports Council (UK) identified different levels of sport involvement, beyond just the elite level. In its sport participation continuum, a foundation in sport might be followed by different levels of involvement and accomplishment: participation, performance, and excellence. This is a reminder that sports are played in the local park, the neighbourhood or school team, the local and regional club. At these varying levels, people practically involved in sport – from teachers to parents to coaches to volunteer administrators – need to work out what sport should mean. Sometimes such practitioners are the main offenders – parents on the touchline, for instance (Embrey, 1986), acting as if they were professional managers; coaches turning a blind eye to drug use – and means must be found to combat and change this. The intensified commercialism of top-level sport, and the direction of cash flowing to the sphere of excellence rather than across the different levels of the continuum, will create boom and bust sport cultures in which – if practitioners simply follow the tide, drop debate and make no interventions – the more positive side of the athleticist legacy will be increasingly undernourished and undermined. At its peak, the amateur athleticist ideology represented the interests of a dominant and privileged elite. But that is not to say that all of its values should be scorned and jettisoned. As sport negotiates its future, the moral claims of athleticism call out for reevaluation, for informed consideration by those practitioners who engage with the present and the future of contemporary sport. In such a consideration, the concern of the apologists of amateurism and athleticism for the survival of their moral codes in the wake of the impact of professionalism may be more than a mere footnote to the social history and sociology of sport. Rather, it may be a valuable reminder of sport's capacity to champion other values than those central to the commercialized, commodified professional sports so prevalent today. If contemporary sport cultures aspire to moral worth, then a critical appropriation of some of the more positive side of athleticist morality – minus its elitist and paternalistic assumptions – can contribute towards a resolution of sport's current anomic state.

Acknowledgements

This chapter draws its case studies of athleticism, athletics and association football from excerpts from my Chapters 1 and 2 in J. Horne, A. Tomlinson and G. Whannel (eds) *Understanding Sport: An Introduction to the Sociological and Cultural Analysis of Sport*, London: E & FN Spon/Routledge, 1999.

I am grateful to the editors of this volume for their patience in awaiting delivery of this chapter; and to Dr Ben Carrington of Sport and Leisure Cultures, Chelsea School Research Centre, The University of Brighton, for his close reading of a draft of the chapter, and for valuable suggestions on emphasis and content.

References

● Almond H.H. (1893) 'Football as a moral agent', *Nineteenth Century* 34, December, pp. 899–911.
● Bailey P. (1978) *Leisure and Class in Victorian England: Rational Recreation and the Contest for Control 1830–1885*, London: Routledge and Kegan Paul.
● Bamford T.W. (1967) *Rise of the Public Schools: A Study of Boys' Public Boarding Schools in England and Wales from 1837 to the Present Day*, London: Nelson.
● BBC Radio 4 (1998) *Current Affairs*, Autumn.
● Channel 4 (1986) *Take the Money and Run*, in Open the Box series, Programme Researcher Garry Whannel, Producer Michael Jackson, Director Mike Dibb, Beat Productions and BFI Education for Channel 4, Channel 4 Television Co. Ltd., broadcast 2 June.
● *Chariots of Fire*, film, directed by Hugh Hudson. UK: 20th Century Fox/The Ladd Company, 1981.
● Conn D. (1997) *The Football Business: Fair Game in the 90s*, Edinburgh: Mainstream Publishing.

● Cousins G. (1975) *Golf in Britain: A Social History from the Beginnings to the Present Day*, London: Routledge and Kegan Paul.
● Crisp R. (1993) 'Morality', in W. Outhwaite and T. Bottomore (eds) *The Blackwell Dictionary of Twentieth-century Social Thought*, Oxford: Blackwell, pp. 398–9.
● Critcher C. (1997) 'Running the rule over sport: A sociologist's view of ethics', in A. Tomlinson and S. Fleming (eds) *Ethics, Sport and Leisure: Crises and Critiques*, Aachen: Meyer and Meyer, pp. 25–35.
● Crump J. (1989) 'Athletics', in T. Mason (ed.) *Sport in Britain: A Social History*, Cambridge: Cambridge University Press, pp. 44–77.
● DNH (1995) *Sport – Raising the Game*, London: Department of National Heritage, DNHJ0096NJ.July 1995.70M.
● Dobbs B. (1973) *Edwardians at Play: Sport 1890–1914*, London: Pelham Books.
● Downes S. and Mackay D. (1996) *Running Scared: How Athletics Lost Its Innocence*, Edinburgh: Mainstream Publishing.
● Dunning E. (1999) *Sport Matters: Sociological Studies of Sport, Violence and Civilization*, London: Routledge.
● Embrey C. (1986) 'The nature of dissent: A study of school and junior club soccer', in J. Evans (ed.) *Physical Education, Sport and Schooling: Studies in the Sociology of Physical Education*, London: The Falmer Press, pp. 133–51.
● Ensor E. (1898) 'The football madness', *Contemporary Review* November, pp. 753–60.
● Etzioni A. (1994) *The Spirit of Community: The Reinvention of American Society*, New York: Simon Schuster/Touchstone.
● Hargreaves Jennifer (1994) *Sporting Females: Critical Issues in the History and Sociology of Women's Sports*, London and New York: Routledge.
● Hargreaves John (1986) *Sport, Power and Culture: A Social and Historical Analysis of Popular Sports in Britain*, Cambridge: Polity Press.
● Holt R. (1989) *Sport and the British: A Modern History*, Oxford: Oxford University Press.
● Johnston B. (1990) *It's Been a Piece of Cake: A Tribute to My Favourite Test Cricketers*, London: Mandarin.
● Kalton G. (1966) *The Public Schools: A Factual Survey of Headmasters' Conference Schools in England and Wales*, London: Longman.
● Kanitkar H. (1994) ' "Real true boys": Moulding the cadets of imperialism', in A. Cornwall and N. Lindisfarne (eds) *Dislocating Masculinity: Comparative Ethnographies*, London: Routledge, pp. 184–96.
● Mangan J.A. (1981) *Athleticism in the Victorian and Edwardian public school: The Emergence and Consolidation of an Educational Ideology*, Cambridge: Cambridge University Press.
● Mason T. (1980) *Association Football and English Society 1863–1915*, Sussex: The Harvester Press.
● Mason T. (ed.) (1989) *Sport in Britain: A Social History*, Cambridge: Cambridge University Press.
● Mee A. (ed.) (1913) 'Letters to boys of the future: The boy who loves a game', *The New Children's Encyclopaedia*, The Amalgamated Press, p. 6.
● McIntosh P. (1979) *Fair Play: Ethics in Sport and Education*, London: Heinemann.
● Rivers J. (ed.) (1948) *The Sports Book 2: Britain's Prospects in the Olympic Games and in Sport Generally*, London: Macdonald and Co. Ltd.
● Secondary Heads Association (1994) *Enquiry into the Provision of Physical Education in Schools 1994*, Secondary Heads Association.
● Studd J.E.K. (1909) 'Foreword', *Empire Annual for Boys*, pp. 7–9.

- Sugden J. and Tomlinson A. (1998) *FIFA and the Contest for World Football: Who Rules the Peoples' Game?*, Cambridge: Polity Press.
- Tischler S. (1981) *Footballers and Businessmen: The Origins of Professional Soccer in England*, New York: Holmes and Meier Publishers, Inc.
- Wakeford J. (1969) *The Cloistered Elite: A Sociological Analysis of the English Public Boarding School*, London: Macmillan.
- Whannel G. (1983) *Blowing the Whistle: The Politics of Sport*, London: Pluto Press.
- Wilkinson R. (1964) *The Prefects: British Leadership and the Public School Tradition: A Comparative Study in the Making of Rulers*, London: Oxford University Press.
- Williams G. (1999a) *Football Crazy*, London: Fourth Estate.
- Williams G. (1999b) 'Hold the back page: How football became soap opera', *Arena*, September, p. 39.

Chapter Nine

From Theory to Application in the Sociology of Sport
Andrew Yiannakis

Introduction

It was nearly 40 years ago that sociologists (e.g., Stone, Lueschen, Page, Dunning, Schafer, among others) first drew our attention to the sociological study of sport, a phenomenon which, until the early 1960s, the academic community had not found worthy of scholarly investigation. It took much courage for these early pioneers, some of whom put their academic reputations on the line, to invest their intellectual energies in a phenomenon which, at the time, was seen mostly as a frivolous and non-serious activity. Operating in such a climate was problematic for early sociologists of sport because they were constantly challenged by colleagues, both within their own disciplines as well as from the wider academic community, to demonstrate both the scholarly rigour and worth of such activity. Thus, early efforts to establish academic legitimacy for the newly emerging field of sport sociology focused on conceptual and methodological issues and the need for theory building and testing. After all, this is how one goes about gaining academic legitimacy, and such legitimacy was what was needed in order to establish sport sociology in universities and colleges at the time. Given such a climate, concerns with relevance and application were given short shrift and often the mere mention of doing applied work would relegate the culprit to the lower echelons of the academic totem pole.

Today, applied work is still approached with mixed feelings with most social scientists believing it not really worthy of their best efforts. This is just as true of sport sociologists, many of whom still feel that the road to academic recognition and legitimacy does not lie with applied work. We are now beginning the second millennium, conditions are very different from those early and often turbulent days from which sport sociology emerged, and the need for applied work has increased. Today, we live in a world of diminishing resources, where we are told that, as academics, we need to produce more and make do with less, and securing funding from external sources (e.g., foundations and the private sector) has become a necessity of everyday academic life. This shift in funding, from internal institutional support to external sources, has placed a greater emphasis on the production of research with applied consequences, thus giving greater legitimacy to applied research, and applied work in general (note that not all applied work involves research). This trend has also created, especially for universities and higher education in general, a need for greater accountability and the necessity for making education more relevant to the needs of students and society at large. The response from academics has been mixed. Among sport sociologists in the United States the response has been slow in coming. In fact, American sport sociologists, primarily because of their concern with academic legitimacy and the adoption of primarily conflict/critical paradigms, have not only failed to demonstrate the relevance and uses of their field, but have also managed to alienate sport sociology from much of the world of sport. While there is much to criticize about American sport, from the commercialization of college athletics to homophobia, racism and sexism, to name but a few issues, American sport sociologists appear to have devoted most of their intellectual energy on social criticism without offering much by way of solutions to the very problems they have been addressing. As a consequence, sport sociology in the United States has been on the decline on many fronts. Ph.D. programmes in universities are being phased out, jobs in the field are scarce, and fewer courses in sport sociology are included either as required offerings or as electives. And, of course, fewer students are now choosing to specialize in sport sociology, at either the undergraduate or graduate level.

While Britain initially experienced somewhat similar problems, the field acquired academic legitimacy much more quickly, both in departments of sociology and physical education, and became integrated in the curricula of such programmes. Further, such theoretical perspectives as cultural studies and feminist critique gained much wider acceptance in higher education, and their relevance in clarifying issues pertaining to sport and physical education was more effectively demonstrated by British academics. And the adoption of the sociology of sport as an integral part of professional preparation for physical education, sport management and other related applied fields, especially by leading institutions such as Loughborough, among others, further served to institutionalize and legitimate the field within higher education and, by extension, society at large.

Finally, British sport sociologists appear to have cultivated links with the British media to a much greater degree than their American counterparts. This has had significant positive consequences for the field because it served to introduce and promote sport sociology to the lay public, to business and industry, and of course, to the world of both professional and amateur sport. By shedding light on topics of importance and significance in sport, by clarifying issues, by suggesting solutions and by providing reasoned arguments on a variety of topics from doping in sport to amateurism and sportsmanship among others, British sport sociologists have been able to demonstrate both the academic and practical value of the field.

Thus, while the field in the USA appears to be in a slow decline, it is clear that sport sociology in Britain is in a growth state: a growth state that is attributable, in large measure, to the efforts of British sport sociologists to demonstrate both the academic viability, as well as the relevance and application of the field beyond the boundaries of academe. It is the purpose of this chapter, therefore, to pull together, update and integrate my prior work in the area with current trends and developments. Further, I wish to discuss some key issues and challenges facing sport sociology in the twenty-first century and offer some possible solutions and courses of action.

Lessons from sociology

The issue of application in sociology of sport surfaced in the literature over 20 years ago. Since those early works by Schafer (1971), Lenk (1973), and Voight (1974), the need for an applied sociology of sport has been the subject of considerable debate in published works and presentations (Greendorfer, 1977, 1985; Heinemann, 1983; Hellison, 1986; Krawczyk, 1977; Lueschen, 1985; Massengale, 1985; McPherson, 1986; Melnick, 1975, 1980; Rees, 1984; Sack, 1986; Sage, 1977, 1985; Widmer, 1977; Ulrich, 1979; Yiannakis, 1986, 1988, 1989a, 1989b, 1990; Yiannakis and Greendorfer, 1992; Kjeldsen, 1988; Santomier, 1988, among others), and has been the focus of deliberation at three major national conferences (North American Society for the Sociology of Sport [NASSS], Boston, 1985; American Alliance for Health, Physical Education, Recreation and Dance [AAHPERD], Cincinnati, 1986; NASSS, Cincinnati, 1988). Yet, despite an increasing interest in the field today, little has been done to further, either conceptually or methodologically, the work of the early pioneers.

Among sociologists, the issue of relevance and application has been the subject of discussion for a number of years as evidenced by a variety of published works (Coller, 1955; Yonebayashi, 1960; Veidemanis, 1964; Jalowiecki, 1967; Gelfand, 1975; Street and Weinstein, 1975; DeMartini, 1979; Rossi, 1980; Berk, 1981; Boros and Adamek, 1981; Kalmuss, 1981; Murphy, 1981; Watts, Short and Schultz, 1983; Sherohman, 1984; Lyson and Squires, 1984; Klein, 1984; Bulmer, 1985; Foote, 1985, among others), conferences on the topic, job advertisements, and new course and programme developments. Several journals are also in existence, which are devoted exclusively to works in applied sociology (e.g., *Applied Sociology; Sociological Practice; Journal of Applied Sociology; Journal of Sociology and Social Welfare;* and, *The Journal of Applied Behavioural Science,* among others).

In developing an applied sociology of sport, therefore, what might we learn from sociology? What issues and problems did sociologists encounter? What efforts were made to address them? Were these successful? How is applied sociology conceptualized today? How does it differ from basic work? And, how were ethical issues addressed and resolved by the parent discipline?

The discussion which follows presents those key issues which preoccupied many sociologists in the 1960s and 1970s in their efforts to develop applied sociology. The various perspectives which such an approach yields are essential in the present debate; for what appears to be hindering the growth of applied sport sociology today is the absence of a broad theoretical context in which the current thinking may be grounded. The lessons from sociology are, therefore, instructive since they provide essential insights and understandings. A careful scrutiny of the pitfalls, challenges, and lessons learned by earlier sociologists is, thus, a necessary exercise.

Street and Weinstein (1975) provide a broad historical perspective of the issues and problems which confronted applied sociology up to 1975. What is especially noteworthy about their analysis of the sociocultural changes of the 1960s and early 1970s is their upbeat perspective and optimism regarding the growth of the field and the demand for applied work. It will be remembered that during this period, the United States was experiencing major social upheavals which included opposition to the Vietnam War, student demonstrations, race riots, and a general questioning of the basic values of society. No institution was immune from scrutiny or challenge, including sport. It was a period that spawned much of the early critical sport literature, and works such as Jack Scott's *The Athletic Revolution* (1971), Dave Meggyesy's *Out of Their League* (1970), and Paul Hoch's *Rip Off The Big Game* (1972) became cause for much heated argumentation and debate.

For sociologists interested in the study of conflict and social change, this period must be considered one of the most challenging in recent history. For, where else could one find a field setting as rich and as stimulating; a sociological laboratory on one's front doorstep? It was not surprising, therefore, that opinion leaders and others looked to sociology for solutions during these troubled times. And it was not surprising that interest in sociology grew dramatically in the 1960s. Street and Weinstein point out that the demand for sociology during this period took many forms: in universities, sociology faculties and enrolments grew rapidly; there was talk of introducing sociology at the high school level; federal spending on applied social research increased; sociological analyses and columns were introduced in various popular magazines and the inclusion of sociological jargon such as 'power structure', 'social class', 'role', and 'norm' became commonplace (Street and Weinstein, 1975) in everyday parlance. Clearly, society was in need of answers – answers whose practical importance and significance could provide effective solutions to the problems which, to a greater or lesser degree, touched almost everyone. Society's call, which went mostly unheeded, was one for relevance and application; the plea was for an applied form of sociology. Unfortunately, we believe that sociologists failed to fully meet this challenge; that is, they failed to provide society with the short-term remedies it wanted, and the long-term solutions it needed. Instead, sociologists (certainly in the United States) mostly debated the theoretical, ethical and political ramifications of engaging in applied work and, ultimately, failed to provide adequate and relevant explanations and solutions. Sociology as a relevant and 'useful' social science had failed to deliver. In the public arena, this was a major setback from which the field has never fully recovered.

Today, as Rossi (1980) pointed out two decades ago, applied work is still approached with mixed feelings by sociologists who, on the one hand, see it as an important reason for sociology's existence while, at the same time, believe that applied work is not really worthy of their best efforts. Thus, because applied social research does not rate highly on 'the academic totem pole of prestige', universities and social science departments have not participated to any great degree in 'the burgeoning market for applied social research' (Rossi, 1980, p. 902). This, Rossi laments, has caused sociologists to miss out on some important opportunities with the result that the intellectual health of the discipline may have suffered as well. For, applied work 'provides important opportunities to learn more about how society works, for building theory and for strengthening our base of empirical knowledge' (p. 902). But, there are also some important organizational reasons for participation in applied work. Academic employment opportunities for sociologists are limited; undergraduate curricula that fail to provide students with some viable occupational skills are shrinking, and junior level research opportunities in the private sector are simply missed due to lack of training in applied research skills. Therefore, Rossi suggests closer links need to be established between academic sociology and applied social research, and graduate students should be trained in applied research methods so as to compete successfully for available funds. Finally, Rossi recommends that universities themselves should consider building their own research centres where applied research may be carried out.

It would be inaccurate, however, to suggest that sociologists were totally unresponsive during this rather volatile period in American history; nor was the field totally to blame. On the contrary, much good work emerged during this period (Cloward and Ohlin, 1960; Coleman, Campbell, Hobson, McPartland, Mood, Weinfeld and York, 1966; Schur, 1965; Moynihan, 1965; Sewell, Hauser and Featherman, 1976; Wright, Rossi, Wright and Weber-Burdin, 1979), reports were published, and efforts to communicate 'the message' were made. A combination of factors conspired to undermine the impact of sociologists' efforts however, and a brief discussion at this point would be instructive for the emerging field of applied sociology of sport. These may be summarized thus:

1. Much applied research by sociologists failed to incorporate a practitioner's definition of what application really entails. In fact, to many sociologists even today, the application of sociological theory and methods to the study of any issue or problem automatically defines the end product as 'applied research'. While the producers of such knowledge may continue to claim that such an approach is 'applied research', clearly those for whom such work is intended do not think it so (Lyson and Squires, 1984). Yet, sociologists, for the most part, have failed to grasp this point, or they have been unwilling to engage in applied work that is of practical value to those who need it.

2. Published works in applied sociology often failed to reach consumers, government agencies and the private sector since most such works appeared in scholarly journals. Additionally, scant efforts were made to communicate the findings in language that the consumer could understand, or in media that were readily accessible to the public.

3. Most sociologists generally shied away, not only from applied research (Rossi, 1980), but also from knowledge transfer (the process of simplification and dissemination).

4. Sociologists also appeared to shun actual implementation. That is, they shied away from the process of actually installing, carrying out and evaluating the effectiveness of particular solutions or courses of action.

5. There was little organized and coordinated activity by sociology organizations and societies to penetrate societal institutions, government agencies, and local communities and promote/publicize the potential contributions of applied sociology. Sadly, even academe must be marketed if it is to compete effectively in the arena of diminishing funds and public opinion.

6. Discussions, and at times heated debates over the ethical and political issues arising out of a commitment to applied work mired the field in intellectual battles; battles which, in the long run, diverted much attention from the social issues and more immediate social problems of society. While such debates and occasional conflict are needed to keep a field alive and vibrant, these, unfortunately, were conducted at a time when society required solutions to more immediate problems and concerns. Thus, while such intellectual debates went on, the 'patient' either sought help elsewhere, or simply perished.

7. And finally, we cannot ignore the fact that the lowly status of applied work in universities contributed in some measure to the general lack of interest and expertise in applied work. Sociologists were simply not trained to successfully apply their skills and knowledge to the solution of real problems and concerns beyond the boundaries of academe.

Ironically however, despite the stigma associated with applied work, Rossi points out that many of the most prominent sociologists in the world such as Durkheim, Stouffer, Park, Lazarsfeld, Duncan and Coleman, among others, were known in their day for conducting some significant applied work. Yet, many are not remembered for their applied work because, over time, much of their significant contribution has been redefined as basic work (Rossi, 1980).

The demand for applied researchers, particularly in the private sector, appears to be quite high. According to estimates (Abt, 1980), federal spending on applied social research in the United States has varied from about $1 billion to possibly $2 billion dollars, thus making applied social research a significant growth sector of the economy. Interestingly, a substantial amount of this figure does not go to universities but to private research organizations employing mostly social science Ph.Ds. Clearly, a need for applied social research exists and because universities have been slow to respond, particularly sociology departments, private organizations have expanded to meet this demand. This should be an important lesson for sport sociologists, who continue to ignore the potential for applied research in both the private sector (e.g., the huge sport and leisure industry) and the public sector.

What are the issues?

Progress in applied sociology of sport appears to have been hindered by a failure to adequately address, and resolve, many of the very same issues which confronted sociology in the 1960s and 1970s. For sport sociology, these include:

1. The relationship of theory to application and, more specifically, the relationship between basic and applied forms of research.

2. The need to evaluate models from sociology and determine what might be learned from the field's early attempts to develop an applied sociology.

3. Problems of precise definition with the term 'application' which appears to have a variety of meanings; some include such interpretations as the 'application' of theory/methodology to the study of a particular phenomenon. Others refer explicitly to usage in practical settings; while others use the term to refer to efforts to provide solutions or to effect change. Clearly, a precise definition is required if we are to escape the morass of conceptual confusion which has thus far plagued the field.

4. The need to clarify how different levels of theoretical abstraction relate to, and give rise to, different forms of applied activity; and to map out the boundaries which these levels of abstraction are associated with.

5. A clarification of the role(s) of the applied sport sociologist and the ethical and political issues applied activities often raise.

A satisfactory resolution of the above issues is clearly essential, therefore, if we are to develop a conceptual basis for guiding future developments in applied sociology of sport.

The relationship of theory to application

The distinction that is often made between theory and application, or more specifically, between basic and applied forms of research and other activity, suggests an inadequate understanding of the relationship between two essentially interdependent tasks; the process of conceptualizing (or formulating) ideas and the process of carrying them out (implementing them). For, it is through experience that we observe, learn, and formulate explanations (theories) about the world around us (the inductive process), and it is through the implementation (or testing) of aspects of such theories that we attempt to verify or refute their validity/applicability (the deductive process). We recognize, of course, that when a social scientist engages in inductive-deductive operations, the primary goal is the development and testing of theory and its contributions to the larger body of knowledge. Thus, providing solutions to immediate practical problems, contributing to change, and ameliorating the human condition are not often of primary concern in basic research, although spin-offs from basic discoveries often do have implications for practice. However, even in basic research, the ultimate test of a theory is the extent to which it explains and predicts social reality. Thus, if social scientists are truly interested in the 'worth' of their research, logic dictates that their findings be put to the test in the world beyond the boundaries of academe. Thus, engaging in applied research, knowledge transfer activity or implementation, should not be seen as unworthy of our best efforts but rather, as a necessary process in both the inductive and deductive phases of the research enterprise. Of course, there is good and bad applied work. For example, research which is not theoretically informed, which is not grounded in the existing body of knowledge, of the 'shot-gun' variety, which fails to raise and investigate conceptually grounded questions, is likely to generate findings of a narrow and ungeneralizable value. This is often the case in market research, where researchers attack a problem as though it were a unique phenomenon rather than a specific manifestation of a broader pattern of events.

In contrast to applied research, basic research focuses on the analysis, description, and explanation of particular phenomena, for the purpose of discovering the possible existence of stable broader patterns and trends. Such discoveries enable social scientists to make generalizations about human behaviour whose applicability transcends the phenomenon under scrutiny. For, the ultimate goal of all social science which adheres to a 'normal science paradigm' is the development of explanations (theories) about human social behaviour. Thus, the particular phenomenon under study is often relatively unimportant, in and of itself, except for what it can contribute to our understanding of a broader set of explanations about such phenomena. That is, the phenomenon under study serves as a *means* to the development of broader forms of understanding. For applied research, however, the phenomenon under investigation is the focus of inquiry and, as such, it is important in, and of, itself (Berk, 1981). The applied researcher wishes to know, for example, why certain countries win more Olympic medals than others (Levine, 1974); why certain individuals persist in fitness programmes and others drop out (Snyder and Spreitzer, 1984); and whether winning in collegiate sports increases alumni contributions to the university (Sigelman and Bookheimer, 1984). Such information (which reflects research in the explanatory phase, a phase which helps illuminate issues and problems and creates the intellectual conditions for problem solving) is essential, since it provides the knowledge base upon which work seeking more narrow technical solutions (research in the operational phase) may be based.

Given the logical interdependence of different levels (levels of theoretical abstraction) of research activity, it also follows that a good applied social scientist must be sensitive to the fact that even narrow technical problems are grounded in broader social structures. For example, achieving success in international competition is a process that is intimately tied to many other micro and macro social processes (e.g., gross national product), as Levine (1974) points out. Thus, in order to appreciate the true ramifications and depth of a problem requiring a solution, it is essential to be able to see the larger picture. Such a vista affords a wider set of solutions to select from than the narrow focus of an untheoretically guided practitioner. Thus, effective application must be grounded in good social science; and good social science, by definition, demands that all research (applied or otherwise) be tied or linked to a larger body of knowledge, or theory.

In summary, therefore, good applied research is a major dimension of the inductive-deductive phase of the research enterprise; and the primary goal of applied research is not the development of theory (although good theory can come of it) or 'to advance the current level of discourse within the discipline' (Berk, 1981, p. 205), but the solution of current human problems and concerns and, ultimately, the amelioration of the human condition. Thus, I view the role of the social sciences as one of advancing the body of knowledge in the field through discovery, description, explanation and prediction, and that of applied work as one of contributing to:

- *timely solutions* to problems of practical importance or significance;
- bringing about *social change*; and,
- the *amelioration* of the human condition.

What is application?

Applied work is work that has practical value. In the context of this chapter 'application' pertains to the business of: providing timely solutions to problems of practical importance or significance; assisting in bringing about social change, and contributing to the amelioration of the human condition. Thus, applied work concerns itself with what 'ought to be' rather than with the discovery, explanation and prediction of 'what is'; the latter clearly being the business of all science.

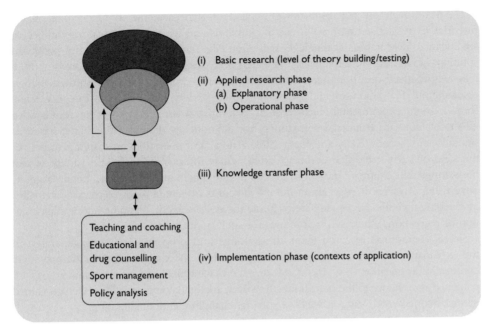

Figure 9.1
Relationships
among levels of
abstraction in
sociology of sport.
Basic and applied
forms of research,
knowledge transfer
and implementation.
(Arrows indicate
direction and
exchange of
information.)

The phases of application

Application is characterized by several levels of abstraction which I call 'phases of application' (see Figure 9.1). These are:

- The applied research phase. This phase is further subdivided into the following:
  - the explanatory phase
  - the operational phase
- The knowledge transfer phase
- The implementation phase

The applied research phase

The applied research phase consists of two levels of abstraction (see Figure 9.1). The higher level, which is called the '(a) Explanatory phase', provides the foundation upon which more narrowly focused research may be based. Explanatory research therefore:

- addresses questions of practical importance or significance;
- helps explain those underlying causes or influential factors contributing to the existence of the problem; and,
- provides explanations of relatively narrower theoretical scope than basic forms of research.

Thus, explanatory research serves to illuminate issues and problems and creates the intellectual conditions for problem solving, decision making, and more focused applied research.

The next (lower) level of abstraction in applied research, called the '(b) Operational phase', provides narrower technical solutions to problems and issues of practical importance or significance. Researchers at this level will often take the findings, insights, and proposed solutions advanced by explanatory research and design research that addresses more narrowly focused questions of practical consequence. Voting behaviour studies, market research, public opinion research, feasibility studies and the like, fall in this category. Some forms of field experimental research such as Kelly and Baer's work on the comparative effects of Outward Bound as a treatment for delinquency may also be characterized as operational research (Kelly and Baer, 1971). The aim of operational research is to deliver the kind of knowledge that is most readily 'usable' by professionals in a variety of real life settings. For example, data from market research help an organization better target its advertising. And knowledge about the effectiveness of certain types of physical activities in reaching juvenile delinquents helps guide the development, planning and implementation of recreational/therapy programmes for such populations.

Good operational research takes the findings and proposed solutions generated in the explanatory research phase and investigates their effectiveness and utility in specific contexts of application (e.g., the classroom, the playing field, the international arena). Of particular importance to the practitioner, however, are the recommendations often contained in such works which suggest ways of solving, changing, and ameliorating.

The knowledge transfer phase

However, effective contextual application requires one final step. One professional articulated the knowledge transfer phase thus: 'It explains the means by which your supplies are delivered to the fort'. That is, it bridges the gap between knowledge and practical action. There is a clear need for systematic efforts to translate the findings and solutions provided by applied research into usable knowledge pertinent to specific contexts of application. Knowledge which speaks to objectives, deficits, and recommendations for action by practitioners. Knowledge free of jargon and technical information which the practitioner can use. This step, which I call the knowledge transfer phase (see Figure 9.1), requires that a *synthesis* be made of what is known about a specific problem area, or issue, together with a specification of the steps or strategies for solving, changing, and hopefully ameliorating the situation.

The knowledge transfer phase encompasses the following steps:

1. The applied scientist identifies and defines the problem; reviews and produces a synthesis of what is known about the problem by examining the findings of pertinent works from explanatory and operational research;

2. reviews and assesses solutions for given contexts of application and recommends courses of action; also provides rationale for suggested courses of action;

3. specifies steps and makes recommendations for implementing solutions in specific professional settings or contexts (e.g., in physical education, athletics and the like).

Knowledge transfer activity can take many forms. Teaching is one such form. So is the act of writing for popular magazines, writing books for the lay public, public speaking to professional groups of practitioners (e.g., coaches), media appearances and the like. All such activities have in common the act of taking knowledge generated by applied research, interpreting it, 'translating it', repackaging it and delivering it to diverse audiences in a form that is both easily understandable and usable.

The implementation phase

Implementation herein is defined as the process by which programme or policy recommendations are converted into programmes of action, installed in specific contexts, and are actually carried out. Implementation is the final stage in the chain of activities which characterize applied work (see Figure 9.1). Implementation may take place in a variety of contexts of application (e.g., in physical education, coaching, and the like).

In this phase of application, the applied academic becomes totally immersed in the process by becoming the actual change agent. This process involves the application of a model, programme, or method to the solution of a problem, for the purpose of changing behaviour and achieving specific desired objectives.

Becoming a change agent sometimes poses a variety of problems for sport sociologists and this issue has not been adequately addressed in the literature (Yiannakis, 1989a; Ingham and Donnelly, 1990). It should be clear, however, that when a social scientist assumes the role of a change agent, that is to say he or she becomes an activist in the pursuit of social change, he or she is no longer acting (but perhaps should be expected to act) as a scientist in the 'dispassionate' pursuit of truth. In this context, the change agent is in possession of an agenda that he or she is attempting to implement. If these agendas have political ramifications, as when attempting to combat sexism or homophobia in sport, then change agency may generate considerable conflict and opposition. Of course, if we believe in the rightness of our position, conflict and opposition should not deter us from working to bring about positive social change. However, it should be made clear that when a scientist assumes the role of a change agent, he or she is no longer acting as a dispassionate searcher of the 'truth'. For, change agency assumes that one is already in possession of that 'truth' (however defined), and is committed to using it to bring about social change.

Not all forms of change generate opposition, of course, and not all forms of change agency acquire political overtones. However, change agency is a process that suggests commitment to a course of action for the purpose of bringing about some form of change. Therefore, change agency is clearly not about the dispassionate search for truth, even though such commitment on the part of the change agent may be grounded in scientific knowledge, even knowledge that the change agent may have produced in his or her role as a social scientist. It should be remembered that science stresses the discovery, explanation and prediction of human behaviour in as objective a manner as is humanly possible (the study of *what is*), while change agency involves the unabashed commitment to change for the purpose of constructing a social reality in our vision of how we think things *ought to be*.

The preceding discussion may leave the reader with the impression that good social scientists should not engage in change agency. This could not be further from the truth. For, if this were the case, social scientists would then go though life merely as detached observers of the human condition. While for some, this may be a satisfactory way of living, never having to grapple with moral dilemmas and attacks of conscience, for most social scientists, it is often impossible to remain bystanders in the face of inequality, exploitation, abuse and discrimination in life, or sport. So, many of us are compelled to engage in change agency from time to time to help 'ameliorate the human condition'. However, it should be clear to all who are contemplating engaging in change agency, especially of the kind that has political ramifications, that, as change agents, we no longer behave, nor are we viewed as social scientists/academics, but rather as activists with a cause. This type of involvement may diminish the change agent's reputation in the eyes of his or her colleagues and may even undermine his or her credibility in the eyes of some sectors of society. Unfortunately, there is a price to pay for engaging in this type of applied work.

Given this apparent conflict in roles (being scientists and acting as change agents), is there a reasonable course of action that the applied academic may pursue? At one extreme, we can retain our pristine 'scientific purity' by remaining 'huddled behind self barricaded intellectual ghettos' as Gouldner (1963, p. 43) aptly stated over a quarter of a century ago, or, we may opt to participate in the business of life and take both the criticism when deserved, and the rewards when earned. It is clear that good judgement must be employed if the interests of science and the problems of society are to be effectively addressed. It is important to note and distinguish, however, among the different roles available to the applied academic which differentiate academic from professional/activist involvement. As a change agent, for example, it is clear that one is no longer a scientist in the dispassionate pursuit of truth (to the degree that this is possible), but rather, as someone whose efforts and activities seek to solve, change, and ameliorate (hopefully) the human condition. Thus, an applied academic in the role of change agent must, of necessity, be concerned with what 'ought to be' rather than with 'what is'. This inevitably requires that value judgements be made about what is good, desirable and worthwhile. Therefore, so long as the individual recognizes that such an unabashed and committed declaration of what 'ought to be' is incompatible with the more dispassionate stance expected of a social scientist, many pitfalls and potential role conflict situations may be avoided. However, when the role of social scientist is confused with the role of change agent, the dispassionate and objective search for truth, to the degree that this is possible (Gouldner, 1963; Friedricks, 1970; Polsky, 1972), can be easily contaminated and compromised.

Phases of application, work roles and contexts of application

In my discussion so far, I have identified at least three clusters of activities which can be subsumed under the general rubric of applied work. Thus, we can state that a social scientist is said to be engaging in applied work when he or she:

- Engages in explanatory or operational research and disseminates findings to client groups; that is, he or she becomes an *applied researcher*;
- Becomes a *knowledge broker*, translating and delivering explanatory and operational knowledge to sport professionals (engaging in the process of knowledge transfer) through teaching, workshops, books, newsletters, and the like;
- Becomes the actual *change agent* and personally implements findings from applied research for the purpose of solving, changing, and ameliorating.

In order to link effectively the different types of applied work with the various contexts of application (e.g., teaching physical education, coaching, counselling) applied scientists must be trained in the work roles of applied researcher, knowledge broker, and change agent. What does such work entail and how is it related to the explanatory, operational, knowledge transfer, and implementation phases? Figure 9.2 and the following sections address these questions.

The applied researcher

Work in the explanatory phase requires of the researcher a commitment to addressing questions of practical importance, or significance, and tends to be of a higher theoretical abstraction than activity in the operational phase. Answers to such questions create the

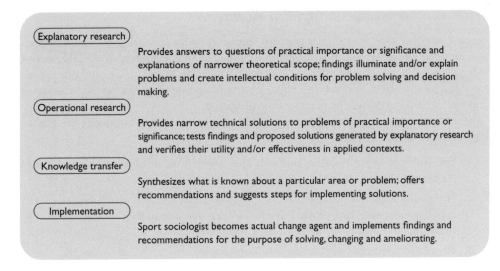

Figure 9.2
Phases of
application in
applied sociology
of sport.

Explanatory research

Provides answers to questions of practical importance or significance and explanations of narrower theoretical scope; findings illuminate and/or explain problems and create intellectual conditions for problem solving and decision making.

Operational research

Provides narrow technical solutions to problems of practical importance or significance; tests findings and proposed solutions generated by explanatory research and verifies their utility and/or effectiveness in applied contexts.

Knowledge transfer

Synthesizes what is known about a particular area or problem; offers recommendations and suggests steps for implementing solutions.

Implementation

Sport sociologist becomes actual change agent and implements findings and recommendations for the purpose of solving, changing and ameliorating.

intellectual conditions for subsequent problem solving and decision making. Work in the operational phase emphasizes activities of a lower level of abstraction that seek to provide more narrow technical solutions, to test findings, and to provide information that serves the needs of professionals in the field. In either case, the social scientist must assume the role of 'applied researcher'.

The knowledge broker

An area that receives even less training, or emphasis in graduate schools is the knowledge transfer phase. This phase stresses the transfer and delivery of knowledge generated by explanatory and operational research to the lay public and to practising professionals in different contexts of application. This phase requires a variety of diverse skills, including the ability to 'translate' epistemological jargon and complex research findings into language that non-academics can understand and use. It also requires an ability and a willingness to disseminate findings and other relevant bodies of knowledge through presentations and workshops, and by publishing material in periodicals read by professionals and the public. Additionally, or alternatively, a knowledge broker must be willing to popularize applied research knowledge by writing books with the practitioner specifically in mind, making media appearances, and addressing parent and other community groups.

The change agent

Social scientists who choose to work in the implementation phase assume the role of change agent. This role is one that is most difficult to enact because it is often fraught with conflicting demands and expectations. In this phase, the change agent is responsible for converting findings and policy recommendations into programmes of action, installing them in specific contexts, and actually carrying them out.

What do these roles actually entail, and how might we prepare sport sociologists to engage effectively in applied work?

Skills and knowledge for applied researchers

Because applied sport sociologists concern themselves with answering questions of practical importance and significance, problems for possible investigation must lend themselves to solutions of practical consequence. Such solutions enable the researcher and practitioner to clarify issues, select options or courses of action, and develop both policy statements and strategies for solving, changing, and ameliorating.

In summary, it seems reasonable to suggest that applied research requires the following skills and competencies:

1. The ability to *reformulate* a problem at a lower level of abstraction and tie it to concerns about utility and application.

2. The ability to define the purpose of the project and frame research questions and hypotheses in ways that provide *timely* solutions that inform the processes of solving, changing, and ameliorating in the *here and now*.

3. The ability to apply appropriate (*problem-centred*) research methodology.

4. The ability to develop discussion and recommendations that focus on the *applied consequences* of the findings.

Skills for knowledge brokers

Knowledge brokers tend to be central and, therefore, highly visible figures in applied work. The role thus assumes great significance because it serves to link academe with the public, and with professionals in the field. To be effective as knowledge brokers, social scientists need many and diverse skills. First, they must be well-versed in the accumulated body of knowledge in the explanatory and operational domains. Second, they must be able to 'translate' and communicate this information to different publics. Third, knowledge brokers must have a good understanding of the needs of their clients and be able to advise professionals on how the accumulated body of knowledge can help them in their work. Further, because a knowledge broker's activities can take many forms (books and articles, speeches, workshops, media interviews and the like), knowledge brokers need superior skills in written and verbal communication, and in working with people. These are essential, since they facilitate interaction, help establish rapport, and can help promote more effectively the utility and worth of applied sociology of sport.

Social scientists who wish to specialize as knowledge brokers should include coursework in communications and marketing in their training. They must possess superior writing skills and should be effective speakers and teachers. Finally, to reach appropriate publics and professional groups more efficiently, it is highly desirable to have a working familiarity with various communications outlets, especially the media.

Skills and knowledge for change agents

Change agents are persons who choose to actively involve themselves in the process of implementation. This phase incorporates diverse activities and includes the following examples:

1. Using sport in a correctional facility to bring about changes in racial attitudes among inmates.

2. Offering organizational assistance to a sport group pursuing a grievance, or fighting for reform (e.g., gender inequality in sport).

3. Building and directing a sport programme for meeting community needs.

4. Using applied research findings in the design of positive learning environments in physical education and coaching.

5. Implementing a recreational programme of activities to improve an organization's employee morale.

Although the specific skills and knowledge required may differ with the activity, a variety of academic, technical and social skills are again called for and, certain types of work may necessitate even additional skills. For example, programmes with a political agenda, or which stress educational reform, may depend for their survival on effective public relations, marketing, fund-raising, proposal writing, and considerable political 'savvy'.

Clearly, not all forms of change activity require such a complex arsenal of skills. However, to be effective change agents academics need to have more than a desire to do good. Interfacing with other sectors of society requires specialized skills that often differ greatly from those required to function and survive in academe. Who is a change agent therefore? Change agents are individuals who take knowledge developed at the explanatory phase and operational phase and apply it through involvement in programmes and activities for the purpose of achieving change. As such, and unlike knowledge brokers who simply disseminate and share knowledge, change agents engage, either singly or in organized groups, in activities whose purpose goes beyond the mere sharing of knowledge, (although some activities include this aspect of the process). Thus, some change agents may be seen marching in the streets, engaging in demonstrations, running for political office, implementing programmes and activities in schools, prisons, hospitals and, of course, in sport. These are the individuals who are often most vocal in their efforts to combat homophobia, gender inequality, racism and the like. They may be described as the front line troopers who confront these issues head–on and whose activities sometimes generate media attention because of their controversial nature.

Not all change agency deals with controversy, however. Teachers and coaches may also be viewed as change agents (depending on degree of involvement in the implementation phase) as are physicians, psychotherapists and other professionals in the helping professions who engage in change agency on a daily basis. Change agency may be seen, therefore, as the process of applying knowledge and skills, and often considerable energy and commitment to changing behaviours, values, attitudes and practices.

Some concluding remarks

The goal of all applied work is to serve humanity by producing knowledge that helps solve problems and contributes to meaningful social change. The ultimate goal, of course, is the amelioration of the human condition. If these criteria are indeed the yardstick by which societies judge the worth and practical value of a profession, it behoves all of us in academe to consider carefully what we would like our contributions to society to be. For, alternative viewpoints argue, especially in sociology of sport, that we are already engaging in applied work by virtue of taking theory and applying it to the study of problems in sport. While this type of work does indeed come under the rubric of explanatory research, it is rarely taken beyond the explanatory phase in which connections are established between work roles and contexts of application. It is rare for sport sociologists to assume the roles of knowledge brokers (or change agents) and to 'translate' their findings (and the work of others) into information or into strategies that practitioners can understand and use. Sadly, for many academics, especially in the social sciences, the mere suggestion of establishing links with the public and private sectors is viewed with disdain.

Recommendations

1. First, applied sport sociology (and sport sociology) must gain a greater degree of acceptance and academic legitimacy in universities. Therefore, a number of structures need to be installed that will create favourable conditions for such legitimation. For this to occur, leaders in sport sociology societies and other related organizations must embrace the need for a concerted effort to develop a comprehensive strategic plan. Such a plan must speak to goals and objectives, funding sources, graduate training, rewards and incentives, marketing, and relations with the public and private sectors.

2. Second, applied sport sociology needs to develop a high degree of visibility and recognition, especially with the media. Sport sociologists must be seen to be addressing social issues and problems in sport, and their work must reach those organizations and practitioners who need it most. Clearly, the knowledge transfer phase is an important link in this process. Furthermore, applied work must be published and disseminated in ways that will inform agencies and organizations that sport sociology has something of practical value to offer. And, most importantly, key journalists and media spokespersons must be targeted for cultivation. In the United States, for example, the media hardly know that sport sociology even exists. This is quite evident by the fact that sport sociologists are invariably overlooked as consultants, discussants and panelists in both print and broadcast features on sport-related topics. Instead, coaches, star athletes, sports journalists, and physicians are invited to offer 'expert' commentary on a host of sport-related issues that are clearly the domain of sport sociologists. But for a handful of exceptions, sport sociologists are conspicuous mostly by their absence from such forums!

3. Third, it should be clear by now that applied work can take many form and, to contribute effectively, the sport sociologist must, of necessity, assume roles appropriate to the task. These roles, which include the applied researcher, the knowledge broker and the change agent (and the consultant[1]) are not taught in universities, little if any emphasis is placed in academe on the provision of applied research skills, and graduate schools do not generally equip students with the necessary skills for defining problems in applied terms. That is, in terms whose findings may contribute to the essential life tasks of solving, changing, and ameliorating.

A plea for action

As indicated elsewhere in this chapter, society in general and academe in particular are undergoing profound political, economic and cultural transformations that are gradually manifesting themselves in higher education in terms of both threats and opportunities. On a personal level, these are experienced in terms of being asked to do more with less, with funding cutbacks, with a greater emphasis placed on securing external funding and entrepreneurship, and with transformations in the role of being an academic. What is being threatened here is the genteel pursuit of scholarship and the search for knowledge for its own sake. On the upside, the increasing emphasis on academic accountability, coupled with the emphasis on securing external funding, have created a need for more applied research and applied work in general (including knowledge transfer and implementation). If this is indeed the case, this is a good time for sport sociologists to attempt to establish sport sociology as a viable applied field that has something of value to offer society and the world of sport.

I, therefore, urge all sport sociologists who care about the future of the field to employ all their skills and knowledge to make a difference by solving, changing, and ameliorating.

How so? By demonstrating the relevance of their work (regardless of ideological persuasion) in, for example, assisting a sport organization improve employee morale, by demonstrating how inequitable practices can be bad for business, by helping professional athletes deal more effectively with owners, and by helping sporting goods companies more accurately (and ethically) reach their target markets. It is time to engage in research as *applied researchers*, in knowledge transfer as *knowledge brokers*, and in implementation as *change agents*. And it is time to begin engaging in various forms of consulting as researchers, knowledge transfer agents and implementers/change agents. By contracting with the public and private sectors to provide services for fees, or as a form of public service, sport sociologists will begin to demonstrate their value to society and the world of sport as well. This is clearly an important dimension because it reflects directly on the 'worth' of the field as perceived by the practitioner.

It is vitally important for sport sociologists to promote their knowledge, skills and findings through print and broadcast media, by writing books for the public, and through public speaking to community and social organizations. Let the private and public sectors, including government at all levels, know that our work counts and our contributions have value.

Finally, sport sociologists should not be satisfied with simply exposing social ills. Rather, they should ask themselves how they might work to solve such ills, contribute to positive change and ultimately to the amelioration of the human condition.

Problems and challenges for sport sociologists in the twenty-first century

While the future holds both threats and opportunities for applied sport sociology in the twenty-first century, opportunities are of little value if sport sociologists are not prepared to both recognize them as such, and to take advantage of them. Similarly, threats can be managed more effectively when the source of the threat is better understood and an organizational structure is in place (such as a strong sociology of sport society) that can mobilize sport sociologists into collective action. Therefore, before understanding, planning and action can be brought into play, it is imperative that we define and map out the kinds of problems, changes and challenges that the field is likely to face in the twenty-first century. The following appear to me to pose some of the more major threats and challenges:

1. The current state of intellectual disarray, especially the conflict among persons representing different theoretical perspectives or schools of thought (e.g., cultural studies, feminist critique, positivism, functionalism, conflict theory and the like), has created a divisiveness that has served to undermine our political base. Further, if this conflict continues into the twenty-first century, it may well drain our intellectual energy and divert attention from more important and pressing issues.

2. The lack of cohesion I alluded to above, partly underlies the fact that sport sociology lacks a clear and strong identity as an area of study. This lack of identity, which is further exacerbated by uncertainty as to where the area belongs, has now opened up the field to various forms of intellectual and territorial cannibalization. This is now in the process of taking two forms. These are as follows:

    (i) As graduate and undergraduate sport science/sport studies programmes increasingly abandon sport sociology as a major area of study, it appears that the emerging field of sport management is adopting the subject matter, but under a different label. If this continues unchecked, the result is likely to be an even greater loss of identity for sport sociology since, under sport management, the term sport sociology will no longer be employed. In fact, the current trend in the United

States is for sport management programmes to teach our subject matter under such labels as 'issues in sport' or 'issues for sport managers', among others. In reality, what is taught in such courses is subject matter and topic areas that properly belong in sport sociology.

Ironically, what we are in fact seeing is the transformation of sport sociology into an applied area that helps inform a variety of subspecialties in the rapidly growing field of sport management. So, while the applied orientation that we, as sport sociologists are endeavoring to develop and maintain may not survive under the banner of sport sociology, it may well live on in a reinvented form in sport management programmes. Such loss of identity will be a great price to pay to keep the field alive. I see this as one of the major challenges for sport sociologists in the twenty-first century.

(ii) Another trend that appears to be emerging in the United States, especially as a result of the failure to acquire academic legitimacy for the field as a separate and independent entity, is its gradual absorption by departments of sociology. If this process is successful, then sport sociology will take its place as just another area of study along side the sociology of religion, stratification and deviancy, among others. This will undoubtedly enhance the academic credibility of the sociological study of sport, but it is unlikely to contribute to the development of its applied dimensions. While this may eventually come about, sociologists who study sport must first develop the academic and intellectual self-confidence to engage in applied work without feeling that they are perceived by their peers to be engaging in intellectually inferior work. Until progress is made in this area, the development of an applied sociology of sport in sociology departments is likely to be held back. This is the second major challenge that I envision for sociologists studying sport in the twenty-first century.

I don't believe the sociological study of sport will die out. However, the field as we know it today will undergo significant transformation before it resolves its intellectual and territorial tensions. A handful of the original sport studies/kinesiology departments that contributed to the early growth of the field may succeed in hanging on to their programmes and, in the United States, four or five institutions may continue to offer Ph.D. degrees in sociology of sport. Sport sociologists have a choice at this juncture. They can continue to remain uninvolved while these changes are taking place, or they can become active change agents and influence the course of events in ways that are likely to enhance the development of a viable applied sociology of sport. In the United States, the biggest losers in all this are likely to be the original physical education, sport studies, kinesiology and human kinetics departments which facilitated the growth of the field in its early years and which developed courses, created major fields of study, and offered MA and Ph.D. degrees in the area. Retaining such doctoral programmes will be another major challenge for sport sociologists in the twenty-first century, especially in the United States. In Britain, the field appears to have established a more secure foothold, and I predict that Britain could become, if British sport sociologists hold their course, the preeminent place for studies in sociology of sport in the twenty-first century.

Note

1. Herein defined as an academic who is hired by agencies or corporations in the public or private sector to engage in applied research, knowledge transfer or implementation as an applied researcher, knowledge broker or change agent.

References

- Abt C.C. (1980) 'What's wrong with social policy research?', in C.C. Abt (ed.) *Problems in American Social Policy Research*, Cambridge, Mass.: Abt Books.
- Berk R.A.(1981) 'On the compatibility of applied and basic sociological research: an effort in marriage counseling', *The American Sociologist* 16: 204–11.
- Boros A. and Adamek R. (1981) 'Developing applied sociology programs: Some results', *Teaching Sociology* 8(4): 387–99.
- Bulmer M. (1985) 'Applied sociology: There are more strings to your bow than this', *Contemporary Sociology* 4(3): 304–6.
- Cloward R.A. and Ohlin L.E. (1960) *Delinquency and Opportunity: A Theory of Gangs*, New York, N.Y.: Free Press.
- Coleman J.S., Campbell E.Q., Hobson C., McPartland J., Mood A., Weinfeld F. and York R.L. (1966) *Equality of Educational Opportunity*, Washington, DC: US Government Printing Office.
- Coller R. (1955) 'Notes on applied sociology', *Philippine Sociological Review* 3(2): 11–14.
- DeMartini J. (1979) 'Applied sociology: An attempt at clarification and assessment', *Teaching Sociology* 6(4): 331–54.
- Foote N. (1985) 'Challenge to apply sociology in business', *Sociological Practice* 5(2): 165–74.
- Friedricks R. (1970) *A Sociology of Sociology*, New York, N.Y.: Free Press.
- Gelfand D. (1975) 'The challenge of applied sociology', *The American Sociologist* 10(1): 13–18.
- Gouldner A. (1963) 'Anti-minotaur. The myth of a value-free sociology', in M. Stein and A. Vidich (eds) *Sociology on Trial*, Englewood Cliffs, N.J.: Prentice-Hall, pp. 35–52.
- Greendorfer S. (1977) 'Sociology of sport: Knowledge of what?', *Quest* 28: 58–65.
- Greendorfer S. (1985) *Sociology of Sport and the Issue of Relevance*, paper presented at sixth annual conference of the North American Society for the Sociology of Sport, Boston, Mass., November.
- Heinemann K. (1983) 'Practical orientation and function of sport sociology', *International Review of Sport Sociology* 18(1): 21–34.
- Hellison D. (1986) *The Relevance of Sport Sociology for Teachers and Coaches*, paper presented at the annual convention of the American Alliance for Health, Physical Education, Recreation and Dance, Cincinnati, Ohio, April.
- Hoch P. (1972) *Rip Off the Big Game*, Garden City, N.Y.: Doubleday and Co.
- Ingham A. and Donnelly P. (1990) 'Whose knowledge counts? The production of knowledge and issues of application in the sociology of sport', *Sociology of Sport Journal* 7: 58–65.
- Jalowiecki B. (1967) 'Applied sociology as an instrument of area planning', *The Polish Sociological Bulletin* 15: 69–77.
- Kalmuss D. (1981) 'Scholars in the classroom: Two models of applied social science', *The American Sociologist* 16: 212–23.
- Kelly F.L. and Baer D.J. (1971) 'Physical challenge as a treatment for delinquency', *Crime and Delinquency* 17: 437–45.
- Kjeldsen E. (1988) *The Utility of the Sport Sociological Perspective in the Preparation of Sport Practitioners*, paper presented at annual conference of the North American Society for the Sociology of Sport, Cincinnati, Ohio, November.
- Klein G. (1984) 'Applied sociology and social policy: Are we reformers, oppressors, social engineers, or marginal men? A review of the literature', *Sociological Practice* 5(1): 85–160.
- Krawczyk Z. (1977) 'Theory and empiricism in the social sciences regarding physical culture', *International Review of Sport Sociology* 12: 71–92.
- Lenk H. (1973) 'The pedagogical significance of sport sociology', *International Journal of Physical Education* 10: 16–20.

● Levine N. (1974) 'Why do countries win Olympic medals? Some structural correlates of Olympic Games success: 1972', *Sociology and Social Research* 58(4): 353–60.

● Lueschen G. (1985) 'The practical uses of sociology of sport: Some methodological issues', in R. Rees and A. Miracle (eds) *Sport and Social Theory*, Champaign, Ill.: Human Kinetics, pp. 245–54.

● Lyson T. and Squires G. (1984) 'The promise and perils of applied sociology: A survey of nonacademic employers', *Sociological Enquiry* 54(1): 1–15.

● Massengale J. (1985) *Applications of Sport Sociology to the Teaching Profession*, paper presented at the sixth annual conference of the North American Society for the Sociology of Sport, Boston, MA., November.

● McPherson B. (1986) 'Policy-oriented research in youth sport: An analysis of the process and product', in R. Rees and A. Miracle (eds) *Sport and Social Theory*, Champaign, Ill.: Human Kinetics, pp. 255–87.

● Meggyesy D. (1970) *Out of Their League*, Berkeley, Calif.: Ramparts.

● Melnick M. (1975) 'A critical look at sociology of sport', *Quest* 24: 34–47.

● Melnick M. (1980) 'Toward an applied sociology of sport', *Journal of Sport and Social Issues* 4(2): 1–12.

● Moynihan D.P. (1965) *The Negro Family: The Case for National Action*, Washington, D.C.: US Government Printing Office.

● Murphy J. (1981) 'Applied sociology, social engineering, and human rationality', *Journal of Sociology and Social Welfare* 8(1): 10–18.

● Rees R. (1984) 'Applying sociology to physical education. Who needs it?', in N. Struna (ed.) *Proceedings of The National Association For Physical Education In Higher Education* 5: 54–9.

● Rossi P.H. (1980) 'The presidential address: The challenge and opportunities of applied research', *American Sociological Review* 45: 889–904.

● Sack A. (1986) *Applications of Sport Sociology to Sport Management*, paper presented at the annual convention of the American Alliance for Health, Physical Education, Recreation and Dance, Cincinnati, Ohio, April.

● Sage G. (1977) 'Sport sociology: The state of the art and implications for physical education', *National Association for Physical Education for College Women/National Collegiate Physical Education Association for Men (NAPECW/NCPEAM Proceedings)*, 310–18.

● Sage G. (1985) *The role of sport studies in sport pedagogy*, paper presented at Association Internationale des Ecoles Supérieures D'Education Physique (AIESEP) World Conference, Adelphi University, New York, NY.

● Santomier J. (1988) *Marketing and Promoting the Sport Sociologist*, paper presented at annual conference of the North American Society for the Sociology of Sport, Cincinnati, Ohio.

● Schafer W. (1971) *Sport, Socialization and the School: Toward Maturity or Enculturation?*, paper presented at third international symposium on the sociology of sport, Waterloo, Canada.

● Schur E.M. (1965) *Crimes Without Victims*, Englewood Cliffs, NJ: Prentice-Hall.

● Scott J. (1971) *The Athletic Revolution*, New York: NY: The Free Press.

● Sewell W.H., Hauser R.M. and Featherman D. (1976) *Schooling and Achievement in American society*, New York, N.Y.: Academic Press.

● Sherohman J. (1984) 'Applied sociology and social work', *The Wisconsin Sociologist* 21(1): 37–44.

● Sigelman L. and Bookheimer S. (1984) 'Is it whether you win or lose? Monetary contributions to big-time college athletic programs', *Social Science Quarterly* 64: 347–59.

● Snyder E. and Spreitzer E. (1984) 'Patterns of adherence to a physical conditioning program', *Sociology of Sport Journal* 1: 103–16.

● Street D. and Weinstein E. (1975) 'Problems and prospects of applied sociology', *The American Sociologist* 10: 65–72.
● Ulrich C. (1979) 'The significance of sport sociology to the profession', in M. Krotee (ed.) *The Dimensions of Sport Sociology*, West Point, N.Y.: Leisure Press, pp. 11–19.
● Veidemanis J. (1964) 'Applied sociology and the refugee problem', *Indian Journal of Social Research* 5(1): 74–82.
● Voight D. (1974) 'Sociology in the training of the sport teacher and of the teacher in general', *International Journal of Physical Education* 10: 26–40.
● Watts D., Short A. and Schultz C. (1983) 'Applied sociology and the current crisis', *Teaching Sociology* 11(1): 47–61.
● Widmer K. (1977) 'Social sciences of sport and sport pedagogy as part aspect of sport science', *International Journal of Physical Education* 14: 21–35.
● Wright J.D., Rossi P.H., Wright S.R. and Weber-Burdin E. (1979) *After the clean-up: Long range effects of natural disasters*, Beverly Hills, Calif.: Sage Publications.
● Yiannakis A. (1986) *Applications of Sport Sociology to Sport and Leisure Marketing*, paper presented at the annual convention of the American Alliance for Health, Physical Education, Recreation and Dance, Cincinnati, Ohio, April.
● Yiannakis A. (1988) *A Conceptual Framework for Applied Sociology of Sport*, paper presented at annual conference of the North American Society for the Sociology of Sport, Cincinnati, Ohio, November.
● Yiannakis A. (1989a) 'Toward an applied sociology of sport: The next generation', *Sociology of Sport Journal* 6: 1–16.
● Yiannakis A. (1989b) 'Some contributions of sport sociology to the marketing of sport and leisure organizations', *Journal of Sport Management* 3(2): 103–15.
● Yiannakis A. (1990) 'Some additional thoughts on developing an applied sociology of sport', *Sociology of Sport Journal* 7: 66–71.
● Yiannakis A. and Greendorfer S. (1992) *Applied Sociology of Sport*, Champaign, Ill.: Human Kinetics Publishers.
● Yonebayashi T. (1960) 'Application of sociology and applied sociology', *Japanese Sociological Review* 10(3–4): 33–50.

Chapter Ten

Discrimination: What Do We Know, and What Can We Do About It?
Juan-Miguel Fernández-Balboa

Introduction

The purpose of this chapter is to bring awareness about discrimination. Simply stated, discrimination is the ability to identify differences. This, no doubt, is necessary for our own survival and practical living. Knowing the difference of the colours of a traffic light and being able to recognize their different meanings, for instance, is crucial for orderly circulation and safety. So, obviously, there is a valid instrumental reason for differentiating among things. Yet, when it comes to human beings, the issue of differentiation becomes much trickier given that the line between *differentiating among* people and *discriminating against* people is often blurred and easily crossed. In this vein, discrimination is both cause and means of the degradation, destruction, and death of the human spirit. This is what I want to discuss in this chapter, in particular as it refers to the human movement profession.

The American Heritage College Dictionary (1993) defines discrimination as: 'Treatment or consideration based on class or category rather than individual merit; partiality or prejudice' (p. 397). This type of discrimination permeates most of the facets of our lives. It exists here, there, and everywhere. It lives in the home, in the work place, in the playground, in the classroom, etc.; be it Calcutta, Chicago, or Chile's Santiago.

Much has been written about discrimination in physical education and sport (e.g., Churchill, 1996; Eitzen, 1993, 1996; Evans, 1993; Griffin, 1993; Pronger, 1996; Sage, 1998; Simpson, 1993; Watson, 1993). Still, most teacher education and coaching programmes devote minimal attention to this issue. As a result, graduates of these programmes possess little awareness not only about the existence of discrimination, but also about how to deal with its many faces. A common rationale in this regard would go more or less like so: 'Discrimination issues do not apply to me. You see, I am (or going to be) a PE teacher or a coach, and my role is to teach physical skills and health concepts. I know I will help many people this way, and that is a good thing, isn't it? Besides, I am a pretty good person. I like people, and some of my friends are folks of different ethnic backgrounds than me'.

This line of argumentation denotes a great deal of naivety regarding discrimination and its widespread damaging consequences. Sure, I say, you may be a very good person, and your teaching could indeed enhance many people's lives. Notwithstanding, without critically examining your beliefs and actions, there is also a chance that you may practice and teach discrimination and not be aware of it (Dodds, 1993).

The reason for my statement lies in the fact that neither physical education nor sport exist in a vacuum. By all means and purposes, these are part of a major sociocultural system. This system has inherent discriminatory values that, in one way or another, affect us all. These values are learned through a process of daily socialization in the contexts in which we grow up and inhabit, and are transmitted and legitimized through the messages and actions of parents, teachers, neighbours, peers, authority figures, the media, and so on. We find, then, that the way we see and act upon the world is strongly influenced and mediated by these socializing forces. Hence, insofar as we take things for granted, nothing can really change. This is why I believe it is crucial for teachers and coaches to critically question the origins of our beliefs and the implications of our practices. Without critical reflection, and despite our good intentions to be helpful, we run the risk of perpetuating that which is damaging and degrading.

How does discrimination develop and function?

Discrimination is a very complex matter whose roots run deep in the social fabric of society, and it starts with the necessary act of *distinguishing* among people. As babies, we know instinctively how to differentiate our mother from other adults. Growing up, we learn to recognize the members of our family and come to understand that we live in a particular community where certain groups of people are more familiar than others. As such, we acquire certain beliefs and feelings regarding 'self' and 'otherness' and gain a sense of identity and belonging.

Allow me to bring a couple of examples to the fore so as to show how arbitrary and unconscious most of what we think and do is. The first example relates to sports fans. I think it is not outrageous to say that most sport aficionados seldom question the origins of their liking one team over another. More often than not, they follow a particular team on the basis of geographical proximity. If I happen to like baseball and live in New York, the chances are that I will follow the Mets; similarly, if I reside in Manchester, England, and football is 'my' sport, then Manchester United will most likely be 'my' team. A similar logic can be applied to the second example, regarding religious beliefs. Scientifically speaking, no one is born with a particular religion in his or her genes. Being Catholic, Muslim, Jewish, etc., is the result of family ancestry and the influence of the cultural setting in which one was born. Granted, some individuals make informed and conscious decisions about what type of spirituality to profess; but, as a norm, people just go along with tradition.

This socialization process, however, quickly turns into learning concepts such as 'friend' or 'foe', 'team' and 'country', 'us' and 'them', which, in turn, end up manifesting themselves in actions of affection and rejection (i.e., we are accepted or denied by others; and we, too, show our preferences in this regard). Hence, discrimination emerges with all its moral and political implications (Coles, 1986a, 1986b). In other words, from a very early age, we learn to 'read' and act upon the world according to a complex array of messages and relationships which we internalize as a set of beliefs and externalize through our actions. These are not always life-enhancing and fair; on the contrary, by being based on perceived inequities, they serve to stigmatize, humiliate, and eliminate human beings.

In sum, discrimination is due, among other things, to the combination of a prevalent, dichotomous (i.e., either/or) way of thinking coupled with a dominant sociocultural structure (e.g., institutions, traditions), that is mainly stratified and hierarchical. These two factors contribute to the complexity and depth of the roots of the problem of discrimination and lead to the false assumption that discrimination is 'human nature'. Notwithstanding its appearance, discrimination is not natural; instead, it results from ignorance and fear.

Discrimination has at least two facets. The first is *prejudice*, an unjustified negative attitude toward others simply because they are members of a different ethnic group, gender, religion or team. The second facet is *stereotyping*, the false belief that every person belonging to a group (and let us remember that the concept of 'group' is itself socially constructed) encompasses all the characteristics attributed to that group. As such, stereotyping 'bangs people into shape with a cultural sledgehammer' (Pogrebin, 1980, p. 29). Both prejudice and stereotyping result from establishing erroneous connections between people, on the one hand, and negative conditions and connotations on the other. Once the connection has been established, it is easy for people to discriminate against those unfairly labelled. Sadly, this is very difficult to reverse, because, rather than looking at this suspiciously, we tend to seek its confirmation. To illustrate this point, let us say that we have been told and accepted that poor people are lazy. Operating under this false premise, every time we see a beggar on the street, we tend to think that the cause of his or her condition is laziness – 'if only he got off his butt and looked for a job!'. Oddly enough, we also tend to think that everyone else shares our view; which, in turn, somehow makes the pattern even more difficult to break.

Discrimination has its paradoxes. Imagine, for example, how bizarre it is that we can be victims and victimizers at the same time. In this regard, it is very possible to find a man who, after enduring racial discrimination at work, may go home and act in sexist ways toward his wife and daughter. By the same token, we could consider the instance of a woman who being constantly demeaned by her partner, does not think twice about putting down her own employees.

And there are more odd things to discover about discrimination. In his book *How the Mind Works*, Steven Pinker (1997) points this out the following:

> In numerous experiments by Henri Tajfel and other social psychologists, people are divided into two groups, actually at random but ostensibly by some trivial criterion such as whether they underestimate or overestimate the number of dots on a screen or whether they prefer the paintings of Klee or Kandinsky. The people in each group instantly dislike or think worse of the people in the other group, and act to withhold rewards from them, even if doing so is costly to their own group. This instant ethnocentrism can be evoked even if the experimenter drops the charade with the dots or paintings and divides people into groups by flipping a coin before their eyes. The behavioural consequences are by no means minor. In a classic experiment, the social psychologist Muzager Sherif carefully selected a group of well-adjusted, middle-class American boys for a summer camp, and randomly divided them into two groups which then competed in sports and skits. Within days, the groups were brutalizing and raiding each other with sticks, bats, and rocks in socks, forcing the experimenters to intervene for the boys' safety.
>
> (pp. 513–14)

In reading about these experiments, one could easily jump to the premature conclusion that discrimination is, indeed, natural; but that would be a big mistake. If we examine these experiments carefully and critically, we will realize that in neither case was discrimination the cause of antagonism. In fact, what caused it was the experimental design itself. We should not be fooled by the apparent methodological objectivity and the random distribution of the 'subjects'. The reasons for the rejection and violence stem from the fact that the experiments created two artificial spaces and divided people to begin with. They did not give 'subjects' any other alternatives. What happened here was that the individuals in both experiments were tricked into a dichotomous trap (Eckert, 1989; Fernández-Balboa, 1995) where made-up pairs of opposites determined the quality of their experiences while creating a sense of scarcity of resources and rewards. Thus, in fact, the antagonism and violence that ensued was sparked and prompted by the artificial division created by the experimenters; not by the assumed discriminatory tendencies of the participants. The old adage 'divide and conquer' becomes obvious here.

What is amazing is that this same crazy, competitive, and dividing rationale is applied in many areas of our lives (even in schooling and sport), and it affects, and is reflected in, most of our beliefs and actions. Under the dichotomous, competitive mind set, we are quick to establish boundaries to protect ourselves and get a piece of what we think is in limited supply; and, at the same time, we try to deny access to others. The cost of all this is clear; as we have seen in the experiments, apprehension, hatred, and madness quickly follow.

Discrimination in physical education and sport

Despite ample evidence that the aforesaid dynamics rule physical education and sport, teacher preparation and coaching education programmes do not usually place a substantial emphasis on the human experience from an ethico-political perspective. Far from that, physical education and sport programmes encourage students to think of life as normative by placing a disproportionate emphasis on physical development *vis-à-vis* the development of other aspects of the person (Rogers, 1989). Under this view, skills and balls become far more important than matters of bigotry. This concerns me a great deal.

The ideology of discrimination in physical education and sport is reinforced by many myths. Two of the prevalent myths are reflected in the following slogans: 'sport builds character' and 'we are a team'. Let us examine these slogans separately.

The notion that sport builds character is commonly accepted by parents, educators, and coaches alike (Chandler, 1988; Shields and Bredemeier, 1995). Yet, the term *character* is vague and must be carefully defined in relation to moral reasoning and social responsibility. Incidentally, the development of certain 'character traits' inherent in competitive sport (e.g., prowess, dominance, aggressiveness) go against moral reasoning and social responsibility by fostering discrimination in many ways. In competition, the weak, the less capable, and the ones with less resources are consistently demeaned and eliminated. Furthermore, the division between winners and losers is made even more evident by the aura of heroism and superiority the former are afforded. In the final analysis, the drive for competition forces one to think of winning as an end, regardless of the means. Under these circumstances, people (victors as much as vanquished) are turned into convenient commodities that can be easily disposed of once they no longer fulfil their purpose (Fitzclarence, 1990). This is utterly dehumanizing.

Another popular notion in physical education and sport is the concept of 'team'. Under normal circumstances, this concept is seen as positive, and, needless to say, there are some positive aspects inherent in it (e.g., collaboration, friendship, unity, belonging, community). Teams are necessary to accomplish goals that otherwise would be practically impossible for people to achieve alone. Nevertheless, educators and coaches must also consider that there are drawbacks and potential dangers inherent in this concept. For one, sports teams are built for the purposes of competition, and I have just highlighted what stems from that. Furthermore, when teams are constituted, chances are that some people will be rejected. Once again, a dichotomous way of thinking provides the grounds for discriminatory decisions regarding who gets in and who stays out, who is superior and who is inferior, and who is better and who is worse.

In addition, we must consider that discrimination also exists within teams. Most teams are not egalitarian entities; on the contrary, their dynamics are elitist, stratified, hierarchical, and eliminatory (Fernández-Balboa, 1993). In this vein, the stars and the starters (while they last) get privileges that the 'mediocre' players and the 'bench-warmers' do not. More-over, it is important to realize that in order to belong to a team, people must show their loyalty, sometimes even in ways that can hurt and humiliate others. Examples of this *modus operandi* can be seen in the initiation rituals of gangs, fraternities, secret societies, and armies. Occasionally, team rituals in sports reflect similar dynamics of abuse and violation of human rights (Neimark, 1993).

And one final point about sport teams specifically, to further expand on the whimsical nature of sports 'followership'. If we are sports fans, it is easy for us to identify those players who belong to 'our team' and those who belong to opposite teams. The dynamics of 'us' versus 'them' translate into . . . we love 'our' guys (or gals) and we do not like 'theirs' very much; in fact, we sometimes even hate their guts. But why? Often, the only reason we like 'our' players has to do with the mere coincidence that they belong to 'our team'. Further, what makes 'our' team 'ours' is also the pure chance that *that* particular team happens to play in the town where we live. If that weren't odd enough, a new problem arises when, say, the Olympics or the World Cup comes, and 'our' national team (that which 'represents' the country to which we belong) is composed of some members of our rival team. Under these circumstances, we are forced to reshuffle our reasoning and create a new rationale so as to accept those ('their') players as members of 'our' national team. As such, now we like them and cheer them on. Needless to say, once the World Cup or Olympics is over, we go back to the initial categories and feel free to 'boohoo!' them once again. Go figure! All this may seem too anecdotal to be taken into account as transcendental. One should not rush to do so, however, without mulling over the striking parallelisms that exist between this (ill)logic of 'fanhood' and that of discrimination against people of other ethnic backgrounds, religious orientation, etc.

Educators, parents, and coaches must be aware of the fact that, by instilling notions of competition and team membership unproblematically, without balancing their lessons with words of caution and tolerance, they may be planting the seeds of human suffering, hatred, and prejudice in the minds of children. Robert Coles (1986b) comments on this latter point:

> Haters, or those caught in a social network of prejudice and hate . . . are perhaps the easiest to understand, if one is trying to study how children of adults indulge in moral attribution of the Other. It is sad, and sometimes startling, to hear school-children make strong statements about people different from themselves – statements saturated with imputation, accusation, denunciation. That adults – parents and others [including teachers] – are the original authors of such remarks, have handed them down as a birthright, doesn't really help the listener as he [or she] hears the familiar stereotypes being trotted out by a boy or girl of ten or twelve who, at other moments, seems so amiably innocent. Skin colour, ethnic background, 'foreignness', social status – these are common sources of unfriendly characterizations.
>
> (pp. 225–6)

This analysis makes obvious how illogical our logic can be. Even when well intentioned and coded in the language of possibility, uncritical teaching has dangerous discriminatory implications; and it tends to reproduce a poisonous pedagogical cycle (Fernández-Balboa, 1998; Miller, 1990). This is why it is important that we remain vigilant about our sentiments and practices and ask ourselves continuously whether what we do restricts and/or denies in any way the rights and choices of others (Dodds, 1993). We must realize that as fixed and natural as these preconditions, decisions, and dynamics may seem, they are undeni-ably artificial and unstable; and, therefore, they can be transcended and transformed. This, I know, is easier said than done. But that should not stop us from trying.

Fighting the illusion, fighting discrimination

If discrimination is so embedded in our minds and our culture, what can we do to fight against it? Here are several options. The first one is to follow Johnson's (1996) steps:

1. Admit the possibility that we have prejudices (everyone, in one way or another, has them).

2. Make honest attempts to identify what those prejudices are.

3. Identify specific actions that reflect those prejudices.

4. Seek support and feedback from others who may be able and willing to help us become aware of, and overcome, our prejudices.

Burbules (1995), on his part, suggests that we exercise 'reasonableness'. This means that we must avoid both 'distorting tendencies of affect' (p. 83) and destructive dichotomies, by learning to deconstruct socially-imposed patterns and allowing reason to take the place of rage and rejection. This, in turn, may result in our willingness to accept others and be fair to their alternative circumstances and points of view. Also, it may help us develop new relations and subjectivities based on justice and tolerance. Prudence of judgement and action is fundamental here. Burbules also proposes that we think of the possibility of our own fallibility. Fallibilism 'requires more than simply making a mistake and admitting one's error. It suggests a specific form of learning in which individuals actively reconstruct understanding. This occurs as we encounter different viewpoints and interact with individuals from different . . . backgrounds. Hence, we must seek out contexts [and people] that support and encourage difference' (Ennis, 1998, p. 216).

Another important concept associated with reasonableness is pragmatism. This concept is different from practicality. In fact, practicality often contributes to discrimination (i.e., under the guise of practicality, we tend to choose the easier, more comfortable path instead of undertaking the difficult task of confronting our biases and preconceptions). Conversely, pragmatism in the way Burbules intends it, forces us to be sensitive, to deal with uncertainty and imperfection, to acknowledge our limitations and 'incompleteness', and to be flexible. This, no doubt, is very hard to do on a consistent basis. The final aspect of reasonableness discussed by Burbules is that of judiciousness, meaning 'the capacity for prudence and moderation, even in the exercise of reasonableness itself' (p. 96). This latter aspect is crucial, because it brings balance to the previous ones. As such, judiciousness enables us to distinguish between right and wrong; to deal with paradoxes, contradictions, and barriers; to remain morally principled; and, to reject that which, after thoughtful and fair consideration, we conclude is damaging and dangerous to the human spirit (Freire, 1988). In other words, through judiciousness we can make 'judgements about whether a given state of affairs is just [and equitable] . . . the heart of equity lies in our ability to acknowledge that even though our actions may be in accord to a set of rules and laws, their results may be unjust' (Evans and Davies, 1993, p. 23).

We can find another way of examining discrimination in what Paul *et al.* (1989) and Paul (1993) call the 'traits of the mind'. These are: (a) *Intellectual humility* to accept our limitations in thought. Here we can ask ourselves: Do I really understand why I act in certain ways, why I teach certain values and 'facts', why I espouse certain ideas and reject others? Do I have a holistic perspective about what I teach? Could it be that my views are partisan and limited? (b) *Intellectual courage* to confront concepts that make us uncomfortable and fearful. In this regard, we may want to wonder: Can I explore ideas with which I do not usually conform? Can I be more open-minded? If I am confronted with opposite points of view, do I get anxious and fearful? In what ways do I react while facing those instances?

(c) *Intellectual integrity* to be congruent and coherent with our fundamental moral principles. This is crucial to compensate for the emphasis placed on method by teacher and coach education programmes. Concerning this trait, we may want to ponder: Do I know what my principles are? Are my methods and teachings congruent with those principles? Is there a possibility that my principles are warped and, as a result, I may be teaching in discriminatory ways? (d) *Intellectual empathy* to be able to see things and situations from other people's point of view. In this regard, we may want to think about the following: Do I usually put myself in other people's shoes? Do I try to understand them and their circumstances? (e) *Intellectual perseverance* to be able to endure a long process of critical inquiry in order to clarify our values and principles; learn to see things from alternative perspectives; understand our motivations, interests, and circumstances; be able to separate fact from fiction, etc. With this in mind, let us ask: How much time do I devote to this? Once I discover a potential danger, do I follow through? (f) *Intellectual caution* to be able to discern false paths, premises, and promises. We all know that we must not believe everything we are told. Yet, we often do just so, thus legitimizing and reproducing something which may not be true. The same can be said with our actions. That is why it is important to ask: Do I really know why I teach the way I do? Are my methods the result of habit or the reflection of principle? Can I devise alternative pedagogies which may be more empowering and educative? What questions do I need to ask of the powers-that-be regarding their mandates, curricula, standards, tests? Finally, (g) *A sense of justice* to defend our moral principles and treat others as we would like to be treated. I can think of at least two questions here: Do I treat my students or players with equity? Do I defend and speak on behalf of the less powerful and the disenfranchised? Answering all these questions can be very illuminating.

Still another way of fighting against discrimination is by realizing the role *privilege* plays in our lives (McIntosh, 1998). Thinking about our privileges (e.g., illiteracy is used as a justification for discrimination – Freire and Horton, 1990), may help us see the other face of discrimination while forcing us to think twice before blaming the disenfranchised for their condition. Let us consider, for instance, the following questions (meanwhile, keep in mind that answering 'yes' to any of them implies some kind of privilege):

1. Do others usually do what I say?
2. Can I refuse to follow others' suggestions without being afraid of reprisal?
3. Can I choose to enter and remain in public spaces without being embarrassed or endangered?
4. Do I have reasons to believe that I live in a safe environment?
5. Do I have choices that are agreeable to me?
6. Do I feel that people around me are usually on my side?
7. Are 'my people' referred to as good, important, and powerful?
8. Do I have more than I really need?
9. Are my judgements, comments, and actions often welcomed by other people?
10. Can I assume that my voice will be heard and respected?
11. Can I choose where to live?
12. Can I freely gain access to information?
13. Do I have a full time job which includes basic benefits?
14. Can I say with a certain degree of confidence that my boss or superior respects me as a person?

15. Can I make a mistake and not fear that it will be attributed to my skin colour, religion, gender, etc.?

16. Can I participate in any cultural activities of my choosing?

17. Am I more highly educated than the majority of the population in my area?

18. Do I feel connected to, and accepted by, others on a regular basis?

19. Do I feel that my civil and human rights will be respected and honoured?

20. Am I secure in my job to the point that I can freely express my opinions?

21. Can I ask questions without being afraid?

22. Is what I eat normally satisfying and plentiful?

23. Am I often included in decision-making processes?

24. Do I frequently find myself being served by others?

25. If I were to be 'pulled over' by the police, would I feel confident that I will be treated fairly?

26. Can I speak without fear that my 'accent' or my tongue will turn people off or generate animosity against me?

27. Is the language I speak considered 'proper'?

28. Is my job a source of meaning and satisfaction in my life?

29. Do I have some control over my time?

30. Am I free to ignore or refuse to learn the perspectives, history, culture, etc., of others?

31. Do I have the means and resources to access higher education?

32. Can I freely gather with others without fearing harassment or reprisal?

33. Do I feel protected by the law?

34. Do I have institutional power over others?

35. Do I feel free to do certain things, read certain texts, teach certain concepts?

36. Does my physical presence confer dominance?

37. Is the type of knowledge that I possess reinforced and rewarded in society?

38. Can I decide when to leave a space and have the freedom to choose where to go next?

39. Is my life practically void of violence and fear?

40. Can I express my religious beliefs without chancing discrimination?

41. Does my home have, at least, the basic standards of comfort?

42. Does what I see around me reflect my values?

43. Can I afford, at least, basic medical supplies and treatment by a qualified physician?

44. Do I have private means of transportation?

45. Am I seen as an asset instead of as a liability or a problem?

Needless to say, this list is far from being exhaustive; however, I think it serves its purposes by unveiling some normally-accepted aspects of privilege. Physical educators and coaches could expand on this list in ways they deem appropriate to their context and circumstances.

A final method I want to introduce here which may be very helpful to gain an understanding of the venomous implications of discrimination is autobiographical narrative. Our own biography can be very revealing (Jackson, 1995). Here is an example of my own:

I was born with what some would consider 'funny-looking' ears (i.e., much larger than the average). When I was a child, the shape of my ears became a constant source of shame and frustration for me, especially at school where, due to my looks, I was constantly made fun of and rejected by many of my peers. At recess, they would gang up against me shouting insidious remarks such as 'Dumbo' (Disney's baby elephant with giant ears) and 'orejon!' (i.e., Spanish for 'big ear') and would not let me play with them. I, much as any kid, wanted to belong and be liked, but that was not often the case. At first, I tried to verbally confront the injurious remarks of my peers; but, over time, I began to physically fight with my peers. They, of course, were usually older and more numerous; so I often lost. To add insult to injury, my teachers often penalized me (grounding and, yes, beating me) for 'picking up fights'! I guess it was easier for them to punish me than to try to get at the heart of the problem. Being troubled, and not knowing how to deal with unjust punishment and miseries in positive ways, I eventually turned my frustration into anger and vindictiveness; that is, as I grew older and stronger, I became a bully. My guess is that I may have rationalized that hurting others would make my own hurt go away. The opposite was true. Bullying did not heal me; it only made matters worse, to the point that I found myself caught in a poisonous loop of rage and despair (Miller, 1990) from which I did not know how to get out. The cycle was broken by a PE teacher who was able to see my positive qualities and gave me his unconditional support. I latched on to him as if my life depended on it (and, in a sense, it may have). He helped me see that I had options and that I could channel my frustrations in constructive ways through sport. In due time, perhaps as a tribute to him, I became a PE teacher myself, and I made it my mission to fight against discrimination.

Needless to say, my mission will never be over, not because there is so much discrimination to fight against in the outside world, but because there is still a lot of discrimination embedded and embodied in myself. Somehow, writing this chapter, typing my tacit ideas on the screen, is not only an exercise of private self-reflection to grapple with these disturbing issues, it is also a public statement that if we are willing to delve deep into our past, we may be able to find hope and to heal.

Do you remember the first time you wanted to play a game with other children and were not allowed to join in? What did that experience tell you about them or yourself? And how about the first time you may have denied someone else his or her participation in 'your' activity? What motivations, fears, conditionings played into that denial? Do you understand what was behind those dynamics – how they got started? Can you be sure, that now, as an adult, you are not perpetuating the cycle? (Miller, 1990).

Concluding remarks

Throughout this chapter, I have tried to show: (a) that, although we seldom understand the roots and ramifications of discrimination, it is not natural but learned; (b) that discrimination can take many forms and permeate many areas of our lives; (c) that children, as well as adults, can cruelly discriminate and be discriminated against; (d) that discrimination dynamics are venomous and cyclical; and (e) that there are ways of being critically vigilant and attempting to break this endemic cycle.

As persons in general and as human movement professionals in particular, we have numerous opportunities to deal with discrimination on a daily basis. In so doing, it is important that we learn to recognize not only its signs in others but also its marks within ourselves. At the risk of being repetitive, I will state again that our roles as educators demand constant vigilance against the tricks and traps of our own reasoning and conditioning. Critically and willingly scrutinizing our thoughts and actions can help us uncover, anticipate, and deal with some of the potential dangers and the denigrating consequences of discrimination. On my part, I want to assert my willingness and commitment to practise what I preach regarding this damaging social phenomenon. I know that the more I unravel its inner workings, the better chances I will have to develop an empowering pedagogy and a politics to fight against it and to free myself and, maybe, others from its trappings.

References

- *The American Heritage College Dictionary* (1993), 3rd edition, Boston, Mass.: Houghton Mifflin Co.
- Burbules N.C. (1995) 'Reasonable doubt: Toward a postmodern defence of reason as an educational aim', in W. Kohli (ed.) *Critical conversations in philosophy of education*, New York: Routledge, pp. 82–102.
- Chandler T.J.L. (1988) 'Sports, winning and character building: What can we learn from Goffman's notion of self-formulation?', *Physical Education Review* 11(1): 3–10.
- Churchill W. (1996) 'Crimes against humanity', in S.D. Eitzen (ed.) *Sport in Contemporary Society*, New York: St. Martin's Press, pp. 134–41.
- Coles R. (1986a) *The Political Life of Children*, Boston: Houghton Mifflin Co.
- Coles R. (1986b) *The Moral Life of Children*, Boston: Houghton Mifflin Co.
- Dodds P. (1993) 'Removing the ugly "isms" in your gym: Thoughts for teachers on equity', in J. Evans (ed.) *Equality, Education, and Physical Education*, London: The Falmer Press, pp. 28–42.
- Eckert P. (1989) *Jocks and Burnouts: Social Categories and Identity in the High School*, New York: Teachers College Press.
- Eitzen S.D. (1993) *Sport in Contemporary Society*, 4th edition, New York: St. Martin's Press.
- Eitzen S.D. (1996) *Sport in Contemporary Society*, 5th edition, New York: St. Martin's Press.
- Ennis C. (1998) 'Defining the dreaded curriculum: Tensions between the modern and the postmodern', in J.M. Fernández-Balboa (ed.) *Critical Postmodernism in Human Movement, Physical Education, and Sport*, Albany, N.Y.: Suny Press, pp. 207–20.
- Evans (1993) (ed.) *Equality, Education, and Physical Education*, London: The Falmer Press.
- Evans J. and Davies B. (1993) 'Equality, equity, and physical education', in J. Evans (ed.) *Equality, Education, and Physical Education*, London: The Falmer Press, pp. 11–27.
- Fernández-Balboa J.-M. (1993) 'Sociocultural characteristics of the hidden curriculum in physical education', *Quest* 45(2): 230–54.
- Fernández-Balboa J.-M. (1995) 'Reclaiming physical education in higher education through critical pedagogy', *Quest* 47(1): 91–114.
- Fernández-Balboa J.-M. (1998) 'Poisonous pedagogy in physical education', Proceedings of the AIESEP World Sport Science Congress, Adelphi University, New York, pp. 83–7.
- Fitzclarence L. (1990) 'The body as a commodity', in D. Rowe and G. Lawrence (eds) *Sport and Leisure in Australian Popular Culture*, Sydney: Harcourt Brace Jovanovich, pp. 96–108.
- Freire P. (1988) *The Pedagogy of Freedom*, Lanham: Rowman and Littlefield Publishers, Inc.
- Freire P. and Horton M. (1990) *We Make the Road by Walking*, Philadelphia: Temple University Press.
- Griffin P. (1993) 'Homophobia in women's sports: The fear that divides us', in G.L. Cohen (ed.) *Women in Sport*, Newbury, Calif.: Sage, pp. 193–203.
- Jackson S. (1995) 'Autobiography: Pivot points for engaging lives in multicultural contexts', in J.M. Larkin and C.E. Sleeter (eds) *Developing Multicultural Teacher Education Curricula*, Albany, N.Y.: Suny Press, pp. 31–40.

- Johnson D.W. (1996) *Reaching Out: Interpersonal Effectiveness and Self-actualization*, 6th edition, Needham Heights, Mass.: Allyn and Bacon.
- McIntosh P. (1998) 'White privilege and male privilege: a personal account of coming to see correspondences through work in women's studies', working paper No. 189, Wellesley College, Mass.: Center for Research on Women.
- Miller A. (1990) *For Your Own Good: Hidden Cruelty in Child-rearing and the Roots of Violence*, New York: The Noonday Press.
- Neimark J. (1993) 'Out of bounds: The truth about athletes and rape', in S.D. Eitzen (ed.) *Sport in Contemporary Society*, New York: St. Martin's Press, pp. 130–6.
- Paul R.W. (1993) 'Critical thinking and the way we construct the meaning of things', *General Semantics Bulletin* 55: 24–37.
- Paul R.W., Binker A.J.A., Martin D. and Adamson K. (1989) *Critical Thinking Handbook: High School*, Rohnert Park, Calif.: Center for Critical Thinking and Moral Critique, Sonoma Sate University.
- Pinker S. (1997) *How the Mind Works*, New York: W.W. Norton and Company.
- Pogrebin L. (1980) *Growing up Free: Raising Your Child in the 80s*, New York: McGraw-Hill.
- Pronger B. (1996) 'Sport and masculinity: The strangement of gay men', in S.D. Eitzen (ed.) *Sport in Contemporary Society*, New York: St. Martin's Press, pp. 410–23.
- Rogers C.R. (1989) *On Becoming a Person*, Boston, Mass.: Houghton Mifflin Co.
- Sage G.H. (1998) *Power and Ideology in American sport: A Critical Perspective*, Champaign, Ill.: Human Kinetics.
- Shields D. and Bredemeier B. (1995) *Character Development in Physical Activity*, Champaign, Ill.: Human Kinetics.
- Simpson K. (1993) 'Sporting dreams on the "rez"', in S.D. Eitzen (ed.) *Sport in Contemporary Society*, New York: St. Martin's Press, pp. 318–25.
- Watson S.B. (1993) 'Discrimination against women as a subtext of excellence', *Quest* 45: 510–22.

Chapter Eleven

Issues of Equity and Understanding in Sport and Physical Education: A North American Perspective

Paul G. Schempp and Kimberly L. Oliver

Introduction

The contribution of sport and physical education to humanity, particularly in the social development of youth, has been a topic of continuing discussion and debate in North America. To the degree that sport represents a social activity, the issues and values that define a society are clearly visible in sport (Coakley, 1998; Eitzen, 1996). For example, North America can be characterized as a highly competitive, capitalistic, authoritarian, patriarchal, product-orientated culture where winning is everything. One need not look too hard or long to find these values displayed in the North American sport experience. The social values, beliefs, and biases that players, coaches and teachers hold are not left on the sidelines. They permeate playing fields and gymnasiums, to be potentially and potently absorbed by those who engage in sport.

As long as sport reflects and contributes to social injustice, it is important that those responsible for organizing, conducting, or participating in sport programmes recognize the role they play in perpetuating injustice through their sporting beliefs and practices. Those committed to promoting the positive values possible through sport, must learn to deconstruct commonly held social beliefs, values, attitudes, and taken-for-granted assumptions influencing physical activity opportunities. By deconstructing stereotypical beliefs, sport practitioners can gain greater awareness of the debilitating effects of prejudice on sport participation. Awareness is a crucial precursor to challenging and changing the stereotypes that limit people's sporting experiences.

This chapter examines particular roles that coaches, teachers, and participants/students play in perpetuating cultural stereotypes. Further, the chapter encourages participants to seek ways to deconstruct stereotypes and promote greater social justice through sport and physical education. The authors hope that by critically reflecting on some of the social concerns that affect people's ideas about, and participation in, sport and physical education, readers are better able to promote understanding, equity, and justice through sport and physical education. Given that everyone holds biases and prejudices, it would be naive to think that reading a few pages of a book might overturn deeply ingrained values and beliefs. We believe, however, that by learning to identify our biases, and through critical reflection, we can deconstruct their foundations, examine potential consequences and find alternatives.

Teachers, coaches, and sports participants can, through conscious thought and choice, discover ways that their patterns of interaction might promote a social system that treats all sport participants equitably. While not everyone can, or should, be treated the same, teachers and coaches have the responsibility and obligation for treating their students fairly. If people are to love and regularly participate in sport and physical activity, educators and coaches must create environments characterized by fairness, justice, understanding and equity. The message must be clear that all who choose to play the game are welcome to the playing field as equals.

The issues represented in this chapter are among those currently receiving attention in North America: gender, homophobia, racism, and at-risk youth. We view these issues as socially constructed. That is, they represent social categories and classifications. These issues are also dialectic. That is, an individual both defines and is defined by these issues.

While these are not the only significant social issues affecting sport or physical education, one brief chapter cannot do service to every pertinent issue. We have, therefore, selected those topics that have appeared prominent in the literature and educational programmes in North America. While these issues are presented separately in the chapter, one needs to remember that social issues are dynamic and interactive. They work together and in opposition to one another rather than independently. We begin with gender, followed by homophobia, racism, and finally we discuss a conglomeration of social conditions that result in youth termed 'at-risk'. The chapter closes with a summary and suggestions for deconstructing these stereotypes in an effort to promote greater equity and understanding in sport and physical education programmes.

Gender

Perhaps no other issue raises greater barriers to young peoples' participation in sport and physical education than gender. Gender is the social construction of male and female, whereas sex represents biological differences between males and females. Sport often divides the sexes and perpetuates distorted definitions of masculinity and femininity (Coakley, 1998). For example, in high schools and colleges there are 'boys' teams and 'girls' teams. In community recreational programmes, one often hears comments about 'girls' sports', and 'boys' sports'. The divide due to sex appears to many – both females and males – as natural and normal.

While biological differences between males and females suggest separation for the sake of fair competition in some sports, sexism appears when *social* and *cultural* gender differences are used as reasons for denying access or opportunity. There are many ways sexism manifests in sport and physical education to deny young people opportunities to participate. Sexism is embedded within the administrative structures of sport and physical education, as well as carried out by administrators, teachers, coaches, and participants/students.

Sexism within sport or physical education is at times obvious. It is all too common to hear terms like 'throwing like a girl' when in reality, the demonstrated throwing pattern is underdeveloped. Most of the differences between boys' and girls' sport skill performances are attributable to social, not physical, differences. Teach a girl to throw properly, and she is every bit as capable of performing a mature throwing pattern as a skilled boy. To deny that girl instruction in throwing because one believes 'girls can't throw' or that 'girls shouldn't throw' is where misunderstanding leads to inequity. Another example is physical education programmes that offer girls aerobics, dancing, and swimming and boys football, basketball, and soccer. These programmes not only send the message to girls and boys that certain activities are appropriate for girls but not boys and vice versa, but they also deny both girls and boys the opportunity to learn and participate in multiple forms of physical activity.

Sexism is also found in practices that are less obvious than what one finds in the names of activities or common slogans. For example, using male standards as the norm from which to compare the abilities of both males and females is not only sexist, but perpetuates gender stereotyping. Nelson (1996) claims that because sport is so pervasive in our culture, subtle and not-so-subtle symbolic messages about men, women, power, and sex often go unnoticed. She asks those interested in sport to look at the process of sport – to see those who lose as well as win.

> Who loses when a new community spends millions of dollars in tax revenue to construct a new stadium and only men get to play in it, and only men get to work there? Who loses when football and baseball so dominate the public discourse that they eclipse all mention of female volleyball players, gymnasts, basketball players, swimmers? Who loses when coaches teach boys that the worst possible insult is to be called 'pussy' or 'cunt'? Who loses when rape jokes comprise an accepted part of the game?
>
> (Nelson, 1996, p. 31)

The question we encourage teachers and coaches to ask is: 'How do my beliefs and practices help or hurt the boys and girls I teach or coach?' It is all too easy to unconsciously perpetuate the myths of masculinity and femininity that influence participation in sport and physical education (Griffin, 1984, 1985). They are the unexamined prejudices that we take into the instructional setting that often contradict our fundamental belief that sport and physical education are healthy and beneficial for all people. For sport and physical education to become more equitable it requires teachers, coaches, and participants to rethink how gender issues operate within sport and physical education to restrict or deny skill development and full participation.

Homophobia

Homophobia is as prevalent in sport as it is in other parts of society – perhaps even more so. Homophobia is more than the fear of gays or lesbians; it is a powerful political weapon of sexism (Griffin, 1996). As noted above, sport is a male dominated institution and often defined as a masculine domain. Thus, women and girls who play or work within the sporting arena, more so than men or boys, endure intense scrutiny about their sexual identity (Griffin, 1996).

Sexual identity is often questioned in sports, in part, because of sexist cultural labels placed on physical activities. In particular, contact sports and activities requiring strength are often seen as more appropriate for boys than for girls, whereas activities requiring balance, coordination, flexibility, and grace are often seen as more appropriate for girls than boys. By labelling certain physical activities, such as dancing or football as 'girls' or 'boys' sports, social problems may be created for boys who dance or girls who play football. When girls or boys participate outside their gender-labelled activities, their sexual orientation is either questioned or assumed. A male dancer may likely be called a 'fag' or 'fairy', while a girl who chooses to play football may be labeled a 'dyke' or 'butch'. This labelling process further reinforces sexism and heterosexism, because even those who do not label witness the quiet, indirect accusations whispered by others. Fear of falling prey to such accusations deters and, therefore, denies physical and sporting opportunities for both boys and girls.

The problem of labelling is particularly significant for girls, as their sexuality is commonly questioned when they participate in sport – more so than boys. Griffin (1996) recognizes that the lesbian label is applied to women in sport as a means of intimidation and control. In physical education classes, some young girls may refuse to participate when the activity is weight training because they believe weight training will make them look 'too masculine'. The fear of being called or looking masculine is, in part, a consequence of the power of the lesbian label. Until women and girls move beyond homophobic concerns by refusing to buy into the power of the lesbian label, others will control their sporting experiences (Griffin, 1996). Further, if girls and women are to ever have the opportunity to claim their athletic identities and control their physical activity choices, they must diffuse the lesbian label by combating its homophobic roots.

If sport and physical education is to be socially just, teachers and coaches must break the silence. They must speak and act out against homophobia and sexism. Until that time, patterns of participation will be founded upon fear and expectation rather than personal choice. Teachers and coaches cannot continue teaching boys and girls to participate in only 'gender appropriate' activities. The long-term health and well-being of children is, in part, reliant upon them becoming physically active for a lifetime. Teachers and coaches need to take a proactive role in stopping jokes and other practices that are homophobic. To remain silent promotes injustice. Heterosexist and sexist comments and behaviours have ways of intimidating players and students that work directly against encouraging participation.

Racism

Racism is another problem found in both society and sport. Racism is a complicated, emotionally charged process that is fraught with fear, anxiety, distrust, denial, ignorance, hate, and misunderstanding between racial groups. The seeds of racism are found in one group of people believing they are superior to another or others. The feeling of superiority leads the group to seek segregation from, and privilege over, the group or groups perceived to be inferior. These actions lead to prejudice and persecution based on racial differences.

Race is a category of people who are socially distinct due to genetic characteristics that are believed to be important in a group or society. Classification systems that are used to separate people into racial categories are often based on popular beliefs about human differences and the meanings attached to those differences, rather than based on biological factors that would allow us to categorize humans by genetic differences (Coakley, 1998). We find, therefore, that physical differences like skin and hair colour, or anatomical shapes of the eyes or nose, lead to exaggerated and inaccurate assumptions and beliefs regarding everything from intellectual and physical abilities to work ethics and morality.

Many Americans believe that sport is free of racism (Eitzen and Sage, 1993). However, because sport is a microcosm of society, it too reflects the same types of racial conflicts that exist in our culture. Some argue 'that Black visibility in collegiate and professional sports has merely served to mask the racism that pervades the entire sport establishment' (Eitzen and Sage, 1993, p. 332). Taking a closer look at the structure of sport can help us see how racism manifests itself. For example, in the assignment of playing positions in both collegiate and professional sports, minority groups are disproportionately found in certain team positions and underrepresented in others. The 'thinking' or 'leadership' positions such as quarterback or catcher are often filled with White athletes, whereas the 'non-central' positions consist mostly of minority athletes. This type of stacking reinforces racial stereotypes and promotes White supremacy (Eitzen, 1996).

Coaching is another site for racial discrimination in North America. Seldom do we see minority coaches at the collegiate and professional levels and even less seldom are there minority managers and owners. The underrepresentation of minorities in leadership positions in sport is particularly apparent in North America. For example, while African-Americans accounted for almost 60 per cent of the players in college football programmes, less than

5 per cent of college football coaches were African-Americans (Eitzen, 1999). Minority players who hope to coach have to be twice as good as their White counterparts and still, they are often hired in assistant coaching positions rather than head coaching positions (Coakley, 1998).

Within physical education programmes racism is not as structurally obvious as in collegiate or professional sports. American public schools serve a great many racial groups, including Native Americans, African-Americans, Asian-Americans, and immigrants from Central and South America, Europe, Asia, and Africa (Chepyator-Thomson, 1998). With the chemistry of race different in every school, the degree and type of racism varies. Racial background has been found, for example, to effect activity selections that perpetuate and reinforce stereotypes (Harrison, 1995). Efforts are, however, underway in North America to curb racial injustice in physical education. Sparks and Verner (1995) have advocated changes in teacher education so physical education teachers may become the change-agents and promote harmony among diverse people.

Change begins by identifying the images and perceptions our own race has for another racial group, and next, identifying our personal prejudices and biases (Adams, Bell and Griffin, 1997). This is not easy, for these may be beliefs that represent years of experience and reinforcement. Our racial biases are often unconscious, making them all the more difficult to detect. Dialoging across difference and interacting with others from different racial groups are two ways to become more aware of racist beliefs, attitudes, and behaviours. Becoming aware of racial biases is an important step in breaking down barriers between teachers and students, coaches and athletes.

While examining and understanding one's own race in relation to others is critical to building effective relationships with students, it is equally important that teachers seek to understand the racial heritage of one's students. Learning the traditions and values imbedded in students' racial background helps to understand the student in critically important ways. Standards of dress, language, personal characteristics, social interactions, celebrations, icons, and leisure activities are all keys to the values and perspectives underlying a culture (Adams, Bell and Griffin, 1997). Being able to appreciate another's culture is important for communication and understanding. In examining the cultures of students, teachers may find a common ground for more effective and socially just teaching. While the search for ways to celebrate differences and make connections across racial barriers is beginning to make an appearance in North American literature (King, 1994; Sparks, 1994), much more work is necessary for sport and physical education to serve people of all races justly.

At-risk youth

One social group that has received increasing attention in North America from scholars and practitioners in sport and physical education are children who, for one reason or another, are disadvantaged by the present social structures in our society. The difficulties and obstacles they encounter place them 'at-risk'. At-risk youth, as defined by Collingwood (1997, p. 68), are 'youth who live in a negative environment and/or lack the skills and values that help them to become responsible members of society'. In citing a Carnegie Corporation study, Collingwood noted that '50 per cent of American youth are at-risk for developing harmful behaviours' (p. 68). These harmful behaviours encompassed criminal behaviour, substance abuse, dropping out of school, violence, victimization, unwanted pregnancy, and poor health and fitness. The social structures that place these children at-risk usually consist of a combination of factors that might include economic, racial, geographic, political, cultural, physical, or social elements.

It appears that sport and physical education programmes can make a difference in the lives and futures of at-risk youth. Martinek (1997) believes that the gym can be used to teach life values and effective decision-making skills. It may also provide resources for cultural, physical, social, and educational enrichment. More importantly, he points out, the gym may provide an environment of hope. The gym can create a new sense of hope for at-risk youth by surrounding these young people with positive and constructive activities. But it takes more than a place or a programme.

Martinek and Hellison (1997) believe the key to aiding at-risk youth through sport and physical activity is to instill resiliency. 'A resilient child is one who has the ability to bounce back successfully despite exposure to severe risks' (Martinek and Hellison, 1997, p. 36). Children from underserved and working-class backgrounds are bombarded by risks of extreme severity everyday.

Promoting resiliency in troubled at-risk youth requires three key elements: *social competence, autonomy, optimism and hope* (Martinek and Hellison, 1997). Social competence is the act of being responsive to others. At-risk youth respond to skills that allow them to be flexible, caring, and create a sense of humour. When a child develops these traits, it aids in developing positive relationships with others. At-risk children need to be able to act on their own, think for themselves, and be independent. Troubled youth who can successfully adopt these traits are more able to reject negative pressures from peers and gangs. Martinek and Hellison (1997) point out that, without hope, most at-risk children fall into a sense of learned helplessness. These particular individuals will tend to give up when faced with an adverse situation. The work of Hellison (1995) and his colleagues (Hellison and Templin, 1991; Martinek and Hellison, 1997), along with the efforts of others (Gore, 1993; Lawson, 1993, 1998), give hope that physical education and sport can become effective sites for positive social change.

Summary

The purpose of this chapter was to review and highlight several of the social issues that are currently the topic of conversation and found in the physical education and sport literature in North America. Such issues cluster around a hub of equity and social justice. In particular, they represent the identification of unjust social practices and the search for improving the sport and physical education experience for all people – regardless of race, class, gender, ethnicity, ability, sexuality, or other distinctive social characteristics.

The social phenomena discussed in this chapter do not occur in singular isolation. Often race, class, and gender discrimination combine in stereotypical ways. Therefore, if one is personally committed to deconstructing biases and prejudices, the interaction needs to be understood and addressed. Social issues steeped in bias and prejudice are socially and culturally constructed. Often cultural myths attenuate the problem by providing the common, self-evidential claim that: 'Everybody knows that the youth today (or the ethnic group of your choice) are lazy'. The assumptions embedded in prejudices, therefore, go unquestioned because of culturally and socially supported truth-claims. Just enough evidence exists to make such claims appear true, and we hear them often enough to believe them, even when logic tells us otherwise.

The dangers of bias and prejudice reside in the oppressive actions that lead to a denial of opportunity, disassociation of one group of people from another, and unjustified negative perceptions and beliefs about self and others. For persons committed to the advancement of sport in society, holding oppressive beliefs and participating in socially unjust practices work directly against the promotion of sport and physical activity. Sport practitioners are, however, members of a larger society, and thus, susceptible to harbouring institutionalized stereotypes and prejudices. It is, therefore, important for sport participants, particularly teachers and coaches, to deconstruct stereotyped images and social biases.

Beginning with 'common beliefs' about any social group is a good start in deconstructing stereotypes and unjust actions. Beliefs and values need to be examined in light of their consequences for both participation in sport as well as implications for equity in the greater society. Once a teacher, coach or participant becomes aware of their beliefs regarding social groups of people, the next step is to deconstruct that belief. What is it precisely that you believe about that group of people, and why? Are those beliefs justified, and are they just? Who do they help, and who do they ignore? If those beliefs are not just, if there are no substantive bases for them, and if they manifest in harmful practices, they need to be redefined and reconstructed in ways that provide greater equity for the individuals involved.

If teachers, coaches, and participants are committed to the promotion of sport and physical education as important social and healthful activities, they must assume responsibility for, and undertake actions to tear down, the social barriers and biases that prevent full access and participation. To combat and change stereotypical myths and cultural truth-claims, teachers, coaches, and sport participants must examine and challenge both common and personal beliefs and prejudices. People in both oppressed and oppressing groups need to examine the beliefs they hold about themselves and others. As Friere (1970) noted, those in oppressed groups perpetuate their oppression by subscribing to the dominant value-set that serves to oppress them. Further, he believed a just society was not possible without all members being committed to justice. If sport is to represent a 'just' society, and contribute to justice in a larger society beyond the playing fields, it will take commitment on the part of all people in sport and physical education.

References

● Adams M., Bell L.A. and Griffin P. (1997) *Teaching for Diversity and Social Justice*, New York: Routledge.
● Chepyator-Thomson J.R. (1998) *Examination of Issues and Perspectives on Race in Mainstream Physical Education Journals*, paper presented at the National Association for Physical Education in Higher Education, New Orleans, La.
● Coakley J.J. (1998) *Sport in Society: Issues and Controversies*, 6th edition, Boston: Irwin McGraw-Hill.
● Collingwood T. (1997) 'Providing physical fitness programmes to at-risk youth', *Quest* 49: 67–84.
● Eitzen D.S. (1996) *Sport in Contemporary Society: An Anthology*, 5th edition, New York: St. Martin's Press.
● Eitzen D.S. (1999) *Fair and Foul: Beyond the Myths and Paradoxes of Sport*, Lanham, Md.: Rowman and Littlefield.
● Eitzen D.S. and Sage G. (1993) *Sociology of North American Sport*, 5th edition, Dubuque, Iowa: Brown and Benchmark.
● Freire P. (1970) *Pedagogy of the Oppressed*, New York: Seabury.
● Gore J. (1993) *The Struggle for Pedagogies: Critical and Feminists Discourses as Regimes of Truth*, New York: Routledge.
● Griffin P.S. (1984) 'Girls' participation styles in a middle school physical education team sports unit', *Journal of Teaching in Physical Education* 4: 30–38.
● Griffin P.S. (1985) 'Boys' participation styles in a middle school physical education team sports unit', *Journal of Teaching in Physical Education* 4: 100–10.

● Griffin P.S. (1996) 'Changing the game: Homophobia, sexism, and lesbians in sport', in D.S. Eitzen (ed.) *Sport in Contemporary Society: An Anthology*, 5th edition, New York: St. Martin's Press, pp. 392–409.

● Harrison L. (1995) 'African-Americans: Race as a self-schema affecting physical activity choices', *Quest* 47: 7–18.

● Hellison D. (1995) *Teaching Personal and Social Responsibility Through Physical Activity*, Champaign, Ill.: Human Kinetics.

● Hellison D. and Templin T. (1991) *A Reflective Approach to Teaching Physical Education*, Champaign, Ill.: Human Kinetics.

● King S. (1994) 'Winning the race against racism', *Journal of Physical Education, Recreation, and Dance* 61: 69–74.

● Lawson H. (1993) 'School reform, families and health in the emergent national agenda for economic and social improvement: Implications', *Quest* 45: 532–45.

● Lawson H. (1998) 'Rejuvenating, reconstituting, and transforming physical education to meet the needs of vulnerable children, youth, and families', *Journal of Teaching Physical Education* 18: 2–25.

● Martinek T. (1997) 'Serving underserved youth through physical activity', *Quest* 49: 3–7.

● Martinek T. and Hellison D. (1997) 'Fostering resiliency in underserved youth through physical activity', *Quest* 49: 34–49.

● Nelson M.B. (1996) 'We don't like football, do we?', in D.S. Eitzen (ed.) *Sport in Contemporary Society: An Anthology*, 5th edition, New York: St. Martin's Press.

● Sparks W. (1994) 'Culturally responsive pedagogy: A framework for addressing multicultural issues', *Journal of Physical Education, Recreation, and Dance* 61: 33–6.

● Sparks W. and Verner M. (1995) 'Intervention strategies in multicultural education: A comparison of pre-service models', *The Physical Educator* 52: 170–80.

Chapter Twelve

Knowing Ourselves Through the 'Other': Indigenous Peoples[1] in Sport in Canada

Victoria Paraschak

Introduction

I am a privileged member of society – White, middle-class, educated, able-bodied, heterosexual. I fit within, and oftentimes benefit from, socially accepted or legitimized ways of behaving. There is little impetus for me, or those like me, to reflect on the socially constructed nature of our reality, and the power relations which shape it. Our knowledge about the world, premised on seeing ourselves and those like us as 'the way things should be', is predominant in society. Our way of life goes largely unchallenged in societal institutions – it is valued and seen as appropriate.

Meanwhile, we view those who are different from us – the *Others* – from a distance, matching their behaviours to our stereotypes about them. We find them 'curious' or 'fascinating' or 'uncivilized' or 'dangerous', but we consistently define, and give importance to, them in relation to our ways of knowing. We attach labels to their behaviour in a unidimensional manner, focusing on how it varies from ours rather than exploring its multidimensional aspects. We fail to try and understand the world from the viewpoint of their experiences: to honour their choices as equally legitimate to ours, and to explore the ways in which we are implicated in their lives, and they in ours. In so doing, we fail to acknowledge our connectedness to them: our shared human condition. We thus, do not benefit from their experiences, which provide lessons on, and possibilities for, our own lives.

This 'us-them' style of thinking also shapes the ways we see ourselves. We continue to reify a monolithic view of ourselves as being not like the Other. We fail to see the socially constructed nature of all life – ours and theirs. We thus, continue to accept, in an unquestioned manner, the 'truth' of our way of life – a way shaped by power relations which privilege some individuals over others. We are less equipped to see clearly, challenge and change the conditions within which we live.

As you read this account about Others – the indigenous peoples of Canada – do not just set out to learn about a marginalized group in Canadian society, and the interesting ways that they are physically active. You should also be ready to reflect on your own experiences in sport. How does your experience of sport align with, or differ from, theirs? How have power relations similarly and differently shaped opportunities for sport? Why have native peoples struggled over, or accepted, particular definitions of sport? In what situations have you done the same? How have particular notions of race and gender affected their experiences in sport? How have those notions affected your own sporting lives?

As you read this account about native sport in Canada, read yourselves into it. Draw on your own experiences, and sort through the ways in which you are similar to, and different from, the native realities being discussed. In this manner, you will not only learn about indigenous peoples and their experiences in sport – both positive and negative – but you will also come to know yourself, and your naturalized assumptions about sport, more fully.

The structuring of social life

The social interconnectedness of our lives ensures that we will operate in circumstances constantly created by others as well as by ourselves. Karl Marx, in 1852, explained human behaviour this way:

> [People] make their own history, but they do not make it just as they please; they do not make it under circumstances chosen by themselves, but under circumstances directly encountered, given and transmitted from the past.

> (1963, p. 15)

Anthony Giddens (1984) provided further clarification of Marx's quote through a process he called 'duality of structure'.[2] He argues that ongoing social practices are reproduced by knowledgeable individuals. In order to attain the resources (such as funding) they require, agents have to work within socially constructed, predetermined ways of behaving (or rules). As they follow these procedures to achieve their desired outcomes, they simultaneously reproduce the legitimacy of those structures (rules and resources) for others. On the other hand, when individuals challenge the existing structures – for example, the rules which designate appropriate behaviour and/or the legitimized process for allocating resources – they undermine the unquestioned nature of the structures, providing an opportunity for change to be considered.

Individuals often act in accordance with their practical consciousness,[3] following regularized ways of behaving which they have come to adopt over time. The reproduction of select social practices becomes naturalized, as does the reproduction of assumptions which underlie them. As various parts of our lives reinforce one particular, naturalized way of doing things, we begin to adopt that way of seeing things when facing novel situations. In sport, for example, we adopt one way of viewing sport as the only way of viewing sport. We might assume that professional sport is the only legitimate model for sport behaviour. Thus, when observing – or participating in – 'traditional' native sports or games, we judge them by the criteria of professional sport, and will find them sorely lacking as 'legitimate sport'. We thus, legitimize a particular set of sport-related behaviours, and a specific way of distributing resources for sport.[4]

Giddens' way of understanding our social world is relevant to practitioners of sport for several reasons.

1. His 'duality of structure' model incorporates the *broader social context* within which sport exists. Our choices are shaped by existing possibilities – rules and resources – that others have already put in place. These possibilities benefit some individuals more than others.

2. His model also suggests that *individual actions* in sport matter. The actions people take, which are shaped by their social world, also have the possibility of shaping that world.

3. Finally, Giddens' model explains how the unconscious reproduction of 'naturalized' sporting practices, along with their underlying assumptions, follows from our *practical consciousness* and has concrete consequences – especially for those who view 'sport' in different ways.

Naturalized assumptions about sport

All of us live within bounded possibilities. We naturalize – come to accept as a given – many aspects of our social world, even though they are social constructions which could be questioned. I was confronted with one such naturalized assumption when I went to the Canadian Arctic for the first time. I was not aware that I had naturalized 'day' as lightness, meant for activity, followed by 'night' as darkness, meant for sleep. In the far North, there is 24 hour sunlight during the summer months. I thus, had no 'night' according to my naturalized assumptions. I continued to operate, for a while, as if I was still in southern Canada, going to bed in the evening despite the constant sunlight. What I discovered, however, was that many local people used the sunlight available throughout the night to play sports until 3.00 or 4.00 a.m., before retiring to sleep. Clearly, I had naturalized a particular way of living my day, which was not aligned with the way individuals operated in these conditions. Becoming aware of my assumptions helped me to appreciate the logic of a recreation programme established for Pond Inlet (a northern Inuit community) in the 1970s, which had scheduled activities throughout the early morning hours (Adams, 1978).

My naturalized assumptions have also been challenged while watching native sports. At the 1998 Arctic Sports event, during the Arctic Winter Games[5] held in Yellowknife, the final two athletes in the women's two-foot high kick had each missed once. The coach of one of the women, from Alaska, assisted the opposing athlete from the Northwest Territories by giving her some pointers on how to perform a successful jump – unheard of in mainstream sport circles! This philosophy shared by northern native competitors, which assumes that athletes do the best they can by competing against themselves rather than against the other competitors, has been naturalized as appropriate for them. This approach towards competition, however, differs greatly from the 'us versus them' mentality I grew up with playing mainstream sports.

A second sport example which challenges my naturalized assumptions concerns the dropping of an eagle feather from the outfit of a powwow[6] dancer during competition. It is the responsibility of the dancer to ensure that such an event does not occur, but if it does happen, the dance is stopped, and a cleansing of the feather is carried out through a special ceremony. No photographs are allowed. The eagle feather is considered a sacred symbol to be honoured, representing wisdom and knowledge (Crum, 1994; Roberts, 1992). Sport and sacred understandings are thus, naturalized as linked spheres in the powwow. This differs greatly from the secular way in which athlete uniforms are viewed in mainstream sports. Even if athletes are penalized for inappropriate uniforms, the penalty arises from sport-specific concerns. For example, at the 1998 Volleyball World Championships, new rules dictated that playing uniforms 'should not be loose or baggy but should follow the body line' (Fédération Internationale de Volleyball [FIVB] Website, 1998).[7] Athletes were penalized when their uniforms were not adequately revealing – a change promoted by the sport federation in order to make the sport more marketable.

Therefore, one advantage of being familiar with non-mainstream sports – the sports of Others – is having the chance to observe similarities and differences. For example, in all-native sport competitions, the rules of play usually follow those legitimized by national mainstream sport organizations. However, the method of entry (paying a substantial entry fee), requirement for participation (native heritage), prize money (often a portion of the entry fees) and context surrounding the event (which might entail a craft sale, native foods and/or traditional entertainment) differ from most mainstream sport practices. This all-native sport system highlights some cultural differences between mainstream and native sport, and also an alternative, self-sufficient approach toward competition when government funding is unavailable. The tendency among non-natives, however, is to view other styles of play and to judge them, with one's own style as the correct model from which others stray to vary-ing degrees. Rarely do individuals view alternative styles of play – the play of Others – as possibilities worthy of equal consideration. A hierarchy of appropriate sporting practices is thus created, with mainstream practices positioned at the top. This ranking system carries through into native perceptions as well, as evidenced by native awards for excellence, which honour athletes successful in mainstream, rather than in all-native, sport settings.[8]

Coaches, athletes, administrators, spectators and government officials all could learn from non-mainstream sports. They also must recognize that their usual decision – to value activ-ities which match their naturalized assumptions – has pragmatic consequences for sport. For example, coaches naturalize certain values within sport, such as aggression and com-petitiveness, while ridiculing other ways of behaving. Athletes feel bound to adopt these behaviours, because they have naturalized that coaches must always be obeyed – even if such practices put the athlete in physical or emotional danger. Administrators shape the bounds of what is acceptable in sport. They often draw direction from the spectators' preferred styles of play, which tend towards entertainment rather than skill. Finally, govern-ment officials make funding decisions about what is 'legitimate' sport – what is worthy of funding – thus, institutionalizing one particular, eurocentric[9] way of seeing sport, while discounting other interpretations which are equally valid in the eyes of others.

This eurocentric approach toward defining sport occurred in Canada during the late 1970s. The federal government had been providing funding for two sport festivals in the Northwest Territories since 1970 – the euroamerican-based Arctic Winter Games, and the Northern Games, which showcased traditional Inuit and Dene games. The Arctic Winter Games, involving primarily mainstream sports, had received consistent government fund-ing from its beginning, while the Northern Games received special grants initially, and year-by-year funding after that. In response to a federal Green Paper on Sport in 1977, Northern Games officials argued that their festival fell within the definition of 'sport':

> It seems that some outsiders view Northern Games only as a cultural organization.
> It is a cultural event of the best kind, but its focus is on games and sport. Sports in
> the south are also cultural events with a different purpose (i.e., a winning purpose
> in a win-oriented culture). Must we buy that ethic to be funded?
>
> (Northern Games Association, circa 1977, p. 3)

Although organizers thus pointed out the culturally biased definition of sport being used by the Fitness and Amateur Sport Branch, their input made no difference; government officials wrote to Northern Games organizers in 1978, informing them that funding would be curtailed because the Arctic Winter Games was better suited to the 'sport' mandate of the Branch (Paraschak, 1997, p. 12).

This example, like many others involving native sport, demonstrates the concrete con-sequences for the Other of naturalized assumptions about sport. Native peoples were not able to obtain funding for activities they considered to be 'sport', because of naturalized beliefs about sport held by government officials. Such beliefs, which are part of our prac-tical consciousness, affect the ways we see sports, the value we place on them, the resources provided to them, and the requirements we place on them, so that they may be considered 'legitimate'.

Perceptions of the Other

Putting our own experiences at the centre of knowledge results in the marginalization of individuals who are perceived to be different – the Others. Edward Said (1979) argues that knowledge about the Other is embedded in power relations which privilege the definer of that relationship, and begin from a fundamental assumption of difference between the definer and the Other. Thus, a practical consciousness is fostered which puts forth one explanation for behaviour – difference – as being legitimate while marginalizing other explanations for reality. The value placed on Others thus emerges in relation to stereotypes created about them. It is no coincidence that native peoples at the turn of the twentieth century were employed to perform their traditional native ceremonials for paying customers in Wild West Shows, rodeos and fairs. The stereotypic representations of the shows depicted ' "wild" Indians acting their savage images' (Berkhofer, 1979, p. 101), with noble savages and Indian princesses representing the best of their race, and savages and squaws providing degrading images. In either case, there was no interest or value (from an entertainment perspective) in portraying native peoples in accordance with their everyday behaviours; the focus was firmly on portraying them as the 'primitive Other'. These individuals, and their performances, were valued for their 'exotic' entertainment potential because their practices were different from those of the paying customers. Such performances reproduced stereo-typic images of native peoples in the minds of non-natives.

We also see stereotypic native images emerging in ceremonies attached to Canadian sporting competitions such as the Olympics, the Commonwealth Games and the World University Games. For example, at the closing ceremonies for the Montreal Olympics held in 1976, the March of Athletes began:

> with Amerindian folk instruments such as tom-toms, rattles, and small bells – whose rhythms evoke the chants of the American Indians . . . a group of 75 Amerindians in full dress enter the stadium . . . Moving in arrowhead formation, they escort the athletes . . . 525 Amerindians in festive costumes entered with the athletes . . . This parade produces remarkable, iridescent effects, with its Amerindian costumes, its plumes and feathered flags, and its drums and coloured wigwams, all surrounding the athletes.
>
> (Comité d'organisation des Jeux Olympiques [COJO], 1978, p. 306)

The 1988 organizers for the Calgary Olympics constructed a giant blue steel ceremonial tepee 65 metres high for the opening ceremonies, with stripes in the five Olympic colours (King, 1991). The Province of Alberta's salute to the Games began with members of five southern Alberta tribes riding in on horses and circling the stadium in traditional dress (OCO [XV Olympic Winter Games Organizing Committee], 1988). After they exited the stadium, ethnic groups from throughout the province entered to demonstrate their cultural dances, followed by chuck wagon races and trick riding. The native participants, however, were not integrated into this multicultural montage. A stereotypic conception of native peoples was thus, reinforced for the audience, as well as a static place for them in history – native peoples were the first to reside in Canada, but disappeared once they were sup-planted by non-natives.[10]

Sport mascots are another example where stereotypic native images are tied to sports. While some jurisdictions in the United States (such as Wisconsin) have recognized that the use of Indian names in public sport settings may be discriminatory (Oxendine, 1995), two very successful teams – the Cleveland Indians and the Atlanta Braves – continue to use not only stereotypic native images, but also stereotypic actions such as the use of tomahawks, the tomahawk chop, and ceremonial Indian war chants as rallying cries of support. These images reinforce stereotypic notions of Indianness, but also have a real impact on the perceptions native peoples may internalize about themselves, as they watch their ancestors being portrayed in such a derogatory manner. Claims by the management of the Cleveland Indians that their mascot was chosen to honour Louis Sockalexis, a native player at the turn of the century on the Cleveland team, have been shown by Ellen Staurowsky

(1998) to be unfounded. Her analysis of newspapers at the time the mascot was generated, reveals caricatures of Indians in degrading sketches – definitely not images which could be considered as honouring Sockalexis! The claims that native mascots honour native peoples do not hold up. If native peoples were given control over the images which represent their cultures, then groups such as the American Indian Movement would not need to continue campaigning politically to remove these mascots from sport.

Michael Kimmel (1987) identifies the cowboy as a central American cultural hero, 'the embodiment of the American spirit' (p. 238). Laurel Davis (1993) argues that this cowboy version of euroamerican masculinity is embedded in the imagery of Indian mascots, and that native mascots help perpetuate this version of masculinity. She claims that: 'Native Americans were only viewed as "positive" symbols of a proud fighting spirit after they were conquered, and only after large-scale resistance to White control was eliminated' (p. 17). In order for euroamerican masculinity to be seen as strong, they must equally see their foes (the conquered Indians) as having been strong. In this way, euroamericans once again come to know themselves through stereotypic conceptions of the Other.

Practitioners of sport have much to gain from a fuller understanding of the Other as a dynamic presence within sport. New sports teams adopt mascots; they would benefit by thinking through that process carefully. Teams already connected to native mascots need to weigh concerns over tradition – a perceived right to maintain an image that has historical relevance in their organization – with concerns over the perceptions created by such images among both native and non-native spectators. Some organizations have changed mascots completely. For example, Marquette University changed its team name and logo from the Warriors to the Golden Eagles (Oxendine, 1995). Other teams have chosen to work with First Nations groups and redesign a native image which captures a positive image of native peoples. This resulted in a satisfactory outcome, for example, between Florida State University and the Seminole Indians of Florida, concerning the costume and behaviour of Chief Osceola, the Seminole mascot (Oxendine, 1995). In the latter case, organizers, through their agency, made an intentional decision which shifted power relations between themselves and native peoples, enabling native individuals to have more control over the images which exist about them. This approach, combined with a more critical examination of representations of Others in sport festivals and images, can help reshape our practical consciousness so that we avoid naturalizing images of First Nations Peoples in a stereotypic manner which diminishes them in the process.

Unequal power relations

Our world is composed of social relations; it is important to see them as relations of power. Embedded in any social relationship are naturalized understandings which privilege some individuals, and some ways of behaving, over others. Reproduction of such relationships reaffirms unequal benefits for select individuals based on socially constructed markers of power (Birrell, 1989) such as race, class, gender, age, physical ability and sexual orientation. For example, current rules in mainstream sports privilege those who are more physically coordinated, strong, tall and aggressive. Individuals – most often men – who have these characteristics reap the benefits of sport more than less physically talented individuals. Resources for legitimate sports are provided by governments, schools and sport associations. These limited resources, often arising from public funds are not available to everyone equally, but rather privilege a select group of individuals.

This unequal access to societal resources, creating a privileged group of individuals, happens throughout sport as it does throughout life. Native peoples, in their relationship with the federal government, are more privileged when they are willing to adopt euroamerican ways of viewing the world. Government employees, who are almost exclusively non-native, have control over the shaping of policy concerned with native lives, as well as the distribution of resources for native services. Native peoples as the clients of government services are consulted occasionally, but in the end the decision-makers are government employees, not native peoples. Because the lived experiences of bureaucrats often differ greatly from those of their native clients, bureaucrats end up shaping opportunities for sport which connect to their own, rather than to native, needs. When native peoples set out to access resources under such conditions, they are more successful if they adopt government-defined understandings in their search for such resources.

A case in point is the federally created Native Sport and Recreation Programme (1972–81), established in Canada to provide segregated opportunities for native sport which would help them develop the skills needed to eventually become integrated into mainstream sport. However, the activities carried out by native peoples within this programme did not reflect solely this objective. While mainstream sports were one part of these activities, so were more 'traditional' native events such as powwows. In addition, segregated sport systems were facilitated which did not have as their goal eventual integration with mainstream sport. Bureaucrats responsible for this programme became uneasy, and eventually ended the programme in 1981 without warning or consultation with their native clients (Paraschak, 1995a).

These government decision-makers dealt with euroamerican, primarily elite, forms of sport on a daily basis. They thus had a practical consciousness which predisposed them to believe that euroamerican sport was the only legitimate form of activity worthy of funding. This orientation in practical consciousness also applies to some native groups. Paraschak (1997) outlines ways that native peoples in the north of Canada, living a lifestyle more in accordance with 'traditional' native realities,[11] develop a practical consciousness which complements a 'traditional' approach towards the structuring of physical activities. This approach differs from native peoples in southern Canada who live more closely with euroamericans; they adopt a comparably more mainstream orientation towards physical activity.

Gender relations privileging some individuals – usually males – over others are evident in sport. For example, Heine (1991) outlined the ways in which the Tlingit of Alaska privileged men over women through gambling games in the mid-nineteenth century. Women had less time to play these games because of their work obligations. They also could not gain honour through gambling games, because their material possessions were not considered appropriate as stakes for use in the games. Thus, the personal property changing hands, signifying the wealth and status of each player, was owned by men, not women. Heine concludes that men were thus differentially able to use gambling games to acquire honour and prestige in their communities through sport, because of the social context within which those physical activities were structured in the communities.

Age is another marker of power in sport. Community sport programmes – for native peoples as for others – provide services for youths more so than adults or seniors. Thus, children are privileged when it comes to accessing government-sponsored programmes. Good arguments can be made for the rationale that children's needs need to be given priority; however, that does not change the fact that differential privilege is provided, by age, within the existing system for sport.

Whether it be race, gender, age, physical ability or other markers (such as sexual orientation or ethnicity), the existing structures for sport provide resources for, and are defined in keeping with, the understandings of some individuals more so than others. This idea flies in the face of naturalized understandings of sport as a 'democratic institution'. Practitioners, once they recognize the asymmetrical nature of power relations, can work to reshape these relations by enabling Others, such as native peoples, to take control of their 'sporting' opportunities: letting them define their preferred sport practices, and providing resources necessary to achieve these practices.

Social constructions of race

People talk about 'race' as if it was solely a biological fact. For example, we use the term 'native' without clarifying who exactly is included within that catch-all category. The categories included within 'race' have been socially constructed, as are the categories within 'gender', 'class' and other markers of power used to differentiate people.[12] For example, the Canadian government has created a variety of definitions for people of Aboriginal descent, such as Status Indian, Non-status Indian, Treaty Indian, Metis and Inuit. The Indian Act of 1876 defined Indian status. A court decision in 1939 declared that Inuit had the same Aboriginal status as 'Indians'. The Metis, meanwhile, only received Aboriginal status in the 1982 Constitution Act (Dickerson, 1992).

These government-produced terms lead to material consequences. Beginning in the 1870s, Status Indians were administered within the federal Department of Indian Affairs, while the needs of Inuit and Metis were addressed within the Department of the Interior. In terms of available resources, Status Indians often qualified for government services (and resources) which were not available to Non-status Indians or Metis.

Socially constructed understandings of race also impact on individuals' perceptions about themselves and others. Some individuals justify racism – such as racial discrimination against particular individuals and racial slurs – based on their belief that natives and non-natives are identifiably different and thus, deserving of differential treatment. Perceived differences can also lead to systemic racism; procedures within an organization can be set up to favour a particular set of values, leading to unequal outcomes for some 'racial' groups.[13] Internalized racism can even be generated among native peoples, wherein they view themselves as inferior in comparison to caucasians because they lack qualities – such as 'whiteness' (along with all the positive qualities linked to 'whiteness') – which are valued by society.[14]

Government-produced definitions of Aboriginal peoples have been used in native sport. Native organizers, at times, structure 'all-Indian' competitions which are limited to participants who meet a particular definition concerning native descent (Paraschak, 1997). Participants in the 1980 Women's Fast Pitch National Championship had to 'be at least one-quarter degree of Indian blood in order to compete' (Kays, 1980). Likewise, the Little Native Hockey League, formed in the 1970s, required that athletes 'must have one parent of native birth and a federal band number. Players without these qualify by presenting a legal affidavit that proves native descent' (The Little NHL, no date). Through criteria such as the latter, the government-produced definition of 'Indian' is reproduced through its use by native organizers. Thus, any discrimination created through the definitions is reproduced by native peoples in sport. This was particularly evident prior to 1985, when native women who married non-native men lost their Indian status in accordance with the Indian Act. They, and their children, did not qualify for participation in some all-Indian competitions, even though their native descent was comparable to that of individuals who were legally allowed to compete. One woman vented her frustration when her daughter experienced this discrimination:

> When it came to Indian Summer Games, they said, 'you can't play because you're non-status. You're not an Indian'. I said, 'My God, she's got as much Indian in her as a lot of them here'. That's when I really got mad.
>
> (Silman, 1987, p. 219).

The existence of all Indian sporting competitions leads to an interesting question: What is the relative value of segregated (e.g., all Indian) versus integrated (e.g., mainstream) sport systems? This question arises especially for groups who are positioned outside the locus of power in sport: Should they aspire to be part of mainstream sport, or should they seek to develop alternative, separated areas where they can develop control over their own cultural practices? bell hooks (1990) notes the importance of spaces at the margins of mainstream societal practices, which provide people with the opportunity to be creative, and to generate practices which provide meaning to them.

> We are transformed, individually, collectively, as we make radical creative space which affirms and sustains our subjectivity, which gives us a new location from which to articulate our sense of the world.
>
> (1990, p. 153)

Native groups have been historically barred from control over the creation of their cultural practices (Paraschak, 1998). Maintaining segregated sport opportunities enables native peoples to be the creators of their own practices. Questions to consider when this happens, however, are the legitimacy which will be given to their sport endeavours – by themselves and others – and the degree to which they will reproduce the mainstream system in an unquestioned manner rather than construct a practice which suits their particular needs.

Paraschak (1996) used powwows to examine racialized spaces[15] in native sport. These spaces remain under the control of native organizers, enabling them to (re)produce cultural practices in keeping with their preferred reality. The contemporary powwow emerged from customs of warrior societies in western America, but largely died out with government suppression of traditional native practices during the late 1800s. A resurgence in their popularity occurred following the First and Second World Wars, as native veterans were honoured within these ceremonies. In the 1970s, powwows became linked to the rise in Aboriginal pride more generally, as a symbolic display of 'nativeness'. They are described by native writers as being both sport and culture, and the values connected to these events reflect those of contemporary sport as well as traditional native practices. George Horse Capture, a powwow dancer, explains that '[t]he dances of the powwow are an important competitive medium for our young people, as well as being a "sport" and a way of showing their capabilities and athletic talents' (1989, p. 50). Chief Eagle Junior also describes the Wacipi, a Lakota word for powwow dance, but demonstrates its connectedness to a native world view:

> The Wacipi . . . unites us to the earth . . . When we dance, stepping lightly with our feet on the earth, wearing our outfits of animal skins and feathers, we are calling upon the earth's magic and power to help us and heal us. The drum is the earth's heartbeat. When we dance in time to it, we are in sync with the earth and its marvellous rhythms. When we perform the Wacipi in a circle, we are honouring the ancient miraculous circle of life.
>
> (Quoted in Crum, 1994, p. 6)

The conflation of these two kinds of values demonstrates the possibilities for one activity – the powwow – to maintain native values while adopting some aspects of mainstream culture.

Images of powwow dancers are often prominent in contemporary books on native peoples.[16] These images symbolically portray a uniquely native image, which has been generated through a native-defined racialized space – a segregated sporting system. While segregated sport opportunities are not the only option which should be considered for native sport, there are definite advantages for native peoples (as for other marginalized peoples in segregated systems) in the continuation of such spaces which remain under their control. It allows native peoples to avoid the systematic bias inherent in mainstream sport systems, which privileges athletes who have greater access to resources needed for success in sport such as money, coaching expertise, mainstream sport values and ease in euroamerican life. It may appear to some that segregated systems foster a prejudice against mainstream athletes and systems. bell hooks (1992) agrees that prejudice may arise, but argues that prejudice is quite different from fostering a system of domination. Native peoples remain on the periphery of sport; for them, a segregated system will never translate into a system of domination over others in sport. The best they can hope for is to avoid participating in a system where they are disadvantaged, and to challenge the naturalized legitimacy of the mainstream system. However, a privileged group (such as White middle-class males) who generate a segregated sport system are able, through that process, to create a system of domination because what they create reinforces the unequal relations of power already existing in the larger society.

Practitioners need to be wary of socially constructed terms such as 'race', which become naturalized through our practical consciousness and form the basis for differential treatment of people. The mainstream system for sport does not provide for all individuals equally – we must work to ensure that the system becomes more inclusive, but we must also appreciate the desire which marginalized individuals have for segregated spaces where they can create their own vision of sport.

Conclusion: Knowing ourselves through the Other

Aspects about native sport covered thus far – naturalized assumptions about sport, perceptions of the Other, unequal power relations and the social constructions of race – have several ramifications for non-native Others. While a number of differences have been outlined between native and non-native sport, similarities can also be inferred from this information. Native peoples share a love of sport with those who are non-native. Sport remains an important part of the ways that they know themselves. Being an athlete is equally as important to understand in native as in non-native societies. Thus, there are many similarities between native and non-native societies when it comes to sport.

Norman Denzin (1989) provides us with an alternative approach to building our knowledge of social life on the assumption of difference. Referring to Sartre's work, Denzin argues that every individual is a universal singular: 'The person . . . is summed up and, for this reason, universalized by his epoch, he, in turn, resumes it by reproducing himself in it as a singularity' (Sartre, 1981, p. ix, cited in Denzin, 1989, p. 19). This approach points out the importance of the social context within which sport is created, as it potentially impacts on all individuals to varying degrees. It also suggests that the desire of individuals to participate in sport is not necessarily distinctive by 'race'. If each person is unique and yet of the Other, then perhaps our perceptions should shift away from an emphasis on difference. Instead, commonalities between ourselves and the Other can be explored, along with the differential (or similar) power relations which are embedded in those situations.[17] While it is important to note the similarities in affection for sport, it is also essential to draw out the differences between opportunities available to native versus non-native individuals, the resources available to native peoples for sport, and the control they have over defining the ways that sport will look.[18] As we examine these differences, it is clear that native peoples have been prevented from shaping many of their sporting practices and from receiving government funds, which are primarily targeted towards elite mainstream sports. These problems, faced by native organizers and participants in sport, align with the problems experienced by other groups who are not privileged in sport, including women, the physically challenged, the elderly and many others. Such inequalities in sport constitute conditions where power relations need to be understood and challenged by practitioners to ensure that the participants – those who will be experiencing the activity – maintain more control over that experience. When a group has historically been excluded from control over their own lives, it is particularly important that such control be returned – not only to access resources, but also to define the basis on which such activities will occur. This action, which shifts existing power relations in sport, takes a step toward a new way of perceiving the Other because it does not place mainstream experiences at the centre of the definition of what is 'legitimate' sport. It does not just provide mainstream opportunities or stereotypic activities, as defined by mainstream organizers, for Others. It instead provides native groups with the ability to define the physical activities which most suit their interests – the ways in which *they* will define legitimate sport – and enable resources to be provided accordingly.

We – practitioners of sport – move closer to a re-knowing of the Other when we acknowledge the privileged position held by non-natives, who socially construct definitions of 'race' and 'sport' and treat people in accordance with those definitions regardless of the artificial separations created by such terms. We – the privileged – also need to abdicate current privilege when it comes to sport, in light of the historical colonization of native lives, including their sporting practices. We – non-native Others – are implicated in the historical control of native sport by non-natives. Mainstream sport has largely been a radicalized space – a place where euroamericans can go and comfortably participate in practices shaped in accordance with their own values. Segregated native spaces for sport are flourishing, and remain one place where native participants can gather to share their lives as well as their sports. In a world where they remain numerically outnumbered, such spaces are hard to come by and greatly valued.

Notes

1. Indigenous peoples are the descendants of the first inhabitants of North America, often referred to as 'Indians' and 'Eskimos'. Other terms which are used include native peoples: First Nations, Status Indians, Inuit, Dene and Aboriginal peoples. Individuals included in this category are those who identify themselves, or are identified by others, as being of native descent. These terms are pluralized to indicate that, within this collectivity, there are groups of people who see themselves as distinctly different, rather than forming one homogeneous group.
2. In this process, structural properties (rules and resources) within asymmetrical power relations shape, and concomitantly are shaped by, individuals as they exercise their agency – the capability to make a difference through their actions (Giddens, 1984).
3. Giddens (1984) notes that 'Practical consciousness consists of all the things which actors know tacitly about how to "go on" in the contexts of social life without being able to give them direct discursive expression' (p. xxiii).
4. Coakley (1998, pp. 98–100) calls the form of sport dominant in many societies the 'power and performance model'. These highly organized, competitive activities emphasize strength, speed and power; hierarchical authority structures; antagonism between opponents; playing with pain; stress on records, and the use of technology to control and monitor the body. Resources are preferentially provided to athletes and sport governing bodies which exemplify these attributes, especially at the international level.
5. The Arctic Winter Games is a biennial festival of primarily mainstream sports begun in 1970, which was modelled after the Canada Games. Arctic Sports, an event in the Games since 1974, includes several 'traditional' Inuit and Dene games within it.

6. The powwow is a gathering of native peoples in which participants perform a variety of traditional dances. Powwow competitors usually wear elaborate outfits which contribute to their performance. Over 100 powwows are held in North America each year.

7. The new international rules for the FIVB competitions noted that: 'The purpose of the fashion change is to bring a new brand image to Volleyball by creating a modern specific line. Manufacturers will gradually introduce the new uniforms to the public through retail outlets' (FIVB Website, 1998; rule 4). This is clearly a marketing-based rationale for uniform style.

8. For example, Angels Chalmers received recognition in Canada for her athletic excellence in international track competitions when she won a National Aboriginal Achievement Award in 1995. Indigenous athletes recognized by the Tom Longboat Award in Canada and the American Indian Athletic Hall of Fame in the United States have all excelled at the national and/or international level in *mainstream* sport.

9. In North America, a distinction is often made analytically between peoples and euroamericans (those Europeans who 'discovered' North America and their descendants). These groups, identified by 'race', would be native and caucasian respectively. A 'eurocentric' way of seeing sport would entail the viewpoint of euroamericans, who are considered the 'privileged' in North America.

10. See 'Aboriginal inclusiveness in Canadian sport culture: An image without substance' by Paraschak (1995b) for further examples and analyses of native stereotypic images created by the organizers of multi-sport athletic competitions in Canada.

11. Michael Heine (1995) uses the term 'bush consciousness' to explain 'traditional' Gwich'in culture. This approach includes 'a general tendency to avoid overt individual comparison in any domain of social life linked to a distinct tendency emphasizing self-reliance and individual autonomy' (p. 49), paired with interpersonal relationships.

12. West and Zimmerman (1991), for example, talk about the process of 'doing gender'. Select differences between males and females are given social importance, then those differences are used 'to reinforce the "essentialness" of gender' (p. 24) in standardized social occasions such as sporting events. There is thus, an ongoing construction of gender relations through the 'doing' of cultural practices.

13. For example, Coakley (1998, p. 266) describes 'race logic' which restricts the entry of Black men into management positions in North American professional sport organizations.

14. bell hooks (1992), for example, talks about internalized racism as it relates to Blacks, and points out the degree of difficulty which both Whites and Blacks have in loving Blackness.

15. Space acts as a resource potentially available to all people, but is in reality too often defined and controlled by those in positions of privilege. Racialized spaces thus become social spaces, often defined by the Other in terms of Aboriginal access or non-access. Such spaces are constructed within the context of unequal societal race relations, and subsequently tend to reproduce those relations over time (Paraschak, 1996).

16. For example, in the section 'The pursuit of sovereignty' in *Native Americans: An Illustrated History* by Ballantine and Ballentine (eds), pictures of powwow dancers are prominent (pp. 452–7).

17. While it is important to focus on similarities, this should not mean that we ignore, or devalue the differences which are unique to others. bell hooks (1992) while arguing against the commodification of differences for the Other, also warns us to acknowledge and value difference as well as sameness.

18. Measures of power identified by Richard Gruneau (1988) apply here, including the capacity to structure and institutionalize sport in preferred ways, to establish selective sport traditions and to define the range of legitimate practices and meanings linked to dominant sport patterns.

References

● Adams D. (1978) 'Inuit recreation and cultural change: A case study of the effects of acculturative change on Tununirmiut lifestyle and recreation patterns', unpublished MA thesis, University of Alberta.

● Ballantine B. and Ballantime I. (1993) (eds) 'The pursuit of sovereignty', in *The Native Americans: An Illustrated History*, Atlanta: Turner Publishing, Inc., pp. 452–7.

● Berkhofer R. (1979) *The White Man's Indian*, New York: Vintage Books.

● Birrell S. (1989) 'Racial relations theories and sport: Suggestions for a more critical analysis', *Sociology of Sport Journal* 6(3): 212–27.

● Coakley J. (1998) *Sport in Society: Issues and Controversies*, 6th edition, Boston: McGraw-Hill.

● COJO (1978) *Games of the XXI Olympiad, Montreal 1976: Official Report*, Volume 1, Organization, Ottawa: COJO 76.

● Crum R. (1994) *Eagle Drum*, Toronto: Maxwell Macmillan Canada.

● Davis L. (1993) 'Protest against the use of Native American mascots: A challenge to traditional American identity', *Journal of Sport and Social Issues* 17: 9–22.

● Denzin N. (1989) *Interpretive Interactionism*, Newbury Park, California: Sage Publications.

● Dickerson M. (1992) *Whose North? Political Change, Political Development, and Self-government in the Northwest Territories*, Vancouver: UBC Press.

● FIVB Website (1998) Available: http://www.fivb.ch/PRArchives/WChamp98/pressre74.htm. December.

● Giddens A. (1984) *The Constitution of Society: Outline of the Theory of Structuration*, Los Angeles: University of California Press.

● Gruneau R. (1988) 'Modernization or hegemony: Two views of sport and social development', in J. Harvey and H. Cantelon (eds) *Not Just a Game: Essays in Canadian Sport Sociology*, Ottawa: University of Ottawa Press, pp. 9–32.

● Heine M. (1991) 'The symbolic capital of honour: Gambling games and the social construction of gender in Tlingit Indian culture', *Play and Culture* 4: 346–58.

● Heine M. (1995) 'Gwich'in Tsii'in: A history of Gwich'in Athapaskan games', unpublished doctoral dissertation, University of Alberta, Edmonton, Canada.

● hooks, bell (1990) 'Choosing the margin as a space of radical openness', in *Yearning: Race, Gender, and Cultural Politics*, Boston: South End Press, pp. 145–53.

● hooks, bell (1992) 'Loving Blackness as political resistance', in *Black Looks: Race and Representation*, Boston: South End Press, pp. 9–20.

● Horse Capture G. (1989) *Powwow*, Wyoming: Buffalo Bill Historical Centre.

● Kays J. (1980) 'Letter to Six Nations Band Council', Ohsweken, Ontario: Six Nations Recreation Commission Files, 4 June.

● Kimmel M. (1987) 'The cult of masculinity: American social character and the legacy of the cowboy', in M. Kaufman (ed.) *Beyond Patriarchy: Essays by Men on Pleasure, Power, and Change*, Toronto: Oxford University Press, pp. 235–49.

● King F. (1991) *It's How you Play the Game: The Inside Story of the Calgary Olympics*, Calgary: Script.

● Marx K. (1963) *The Eighteenth Brumaire of Louis Bonaparte*, New York: International Publishers [originally published in 1852].

● Northern Games Association (circa 1977) Northern Games Association Reply to Green Paper on 'Fitness and Amateur Sport'.

● OCO (1988) *XV Olympic Winter Games: Official Report*, Calgary: Calgary Olympic Development Association.

● Oxendine J. (1995) *American Indian Sports Heritage*, Lincoln: University of Nebraska Press.

- Paraschak V. (1995a) 'The native sport and recreation program, 1972–1981: Patterns of resistance, patterns of reproduction', *Canadian Journal of History of Sport* XXVI(2): 1–18.
- Paraschak V. (1995b) 'Aboriginal inclusiveness in Canadian sport culture: An image without substance', in *Sport as Symbol, Symbols in Sport*, Proceedings of the 3rd International Society for the History of Physical Education and Sport (ISHPES) Congress, Capetown, South Africa, pp. 347–56.
- Paraschak V. (1996) 'Racialized spaces: Cultural regulation, aboriginal agency and powwows', *Avante* 2: 7–18.
- Paraschak V. (1997) 'Variations in race relations: Sporting events for native peoples in Canada', *Sociology of Sport Journal* 14(1): 1–21.
- Paraschak V. (1998) 'Reasonable "amusements": Connecting the strands of physical culture in native lives', *Sport History Review* 29(1): May, 121–31.
- Roberts C. (1992) *Powwow Country*, Montana: American and World Geographic Publishing.
- Said E. (1979) *Orientalism*, New York: Vintage Books.
- Sartre J.-P. (1981) *The Family Idiot: Gustave Flaubert, 1821–1857*, Vol. 1, Chicago: The University of Chicago Press.
- Silman J. (1987) *Enough is Enough: Aboriginal Women Speak Out*, Toronto: The Women's Press.
- Staurowsky E. (1998) 'An Act of honour or exploitation? The Cleveland Indians' use of the Louis Francis Sockalexis story', *Sociology of Sport Journal* 15(4): 299–316.
- The Little NHL (no date) Regulations of the reserve Little NHL, Ohsweken, Ontario: Six Nation Recreation Files.
- West C. and Zimmerman D. (1991) 'Doing gender', in J. Lorber and S. Farrell (eds) *The Social Construction of Gender*, California: Sage Publications, pp. 13–37.

Chapter Thirteen

Youth Sport in Canada: Problems and Resolutions
Peter Donnelly

Somewhere along the way we developed a distrust of idle time. Children became an investment; it cost money to join the classes and courses and sports that are supposed to turn them into well-rounded little human beings. It took adult time to drive and wait, and, well, if you have to be there anyway, you may as well get involved. Time is money, money is time. And if the child is the investment, what, then, is to be the return on that investment? Certificates, badges, trophies – perhaps even a professional career. There is simply no time for play in such a serious undertaking.

(MacGregor, 1996, p. 11)

Introduction

This chapter is about two overlapping periods in the development of youth sport participation in Canada, the problems that emerged, and the steps that were taken to resolve them. The first is the period after the Second World War when there was a significant growth in adult-organized sport for young people. The second is the period after the Montreal Olympics (1976) when there was a major shift to the early recognition and development of talented young athletes for the high performance sport system. Those involved in recognizing, drawing attention to, and attempting to resolve the problems, were often sociologists, social psychologists, and other progressive individuals and social critics who were involved, directly or indirectly, in the Canadian sport system. Thus, the social science of sport and physical activity has a crucial place in the recognition and resolution of problems associated with youth sport development. In particular, responses to social change, and the development of social policy for sport, need to be based upon researched evidence – evidence often supplied by sport sociologists.

My focus is on adult organized sports for young people. Children's play is often considered to be one of the few universal aspects of human behaviour, and a significant site of child development. While there are clearly problems that may occur in children's informal games (see Coakley, 1998), adult involvement is often associated with a whole new set of problems. Early critics of adult organized sport, such as Devereaux (1976a), argued that informal games represent an important environment in which children learn about social interaction and appropriate social behaviour – an environment that is corrupted when taken over by adults.

The development of adult organized sport for young people in Canada has many similarities with developments in the United States, other White settler dominions of the British Commonwealth (e.g., Australia, New Zealand, South Africa), and with Britain itself. However, there are several features unique to Canada. For example, developments in Francophone and Anglophone Canada were quite different; the status of ice hockey, and particularly professional ice hockey as represented by the National Hockey League (NHL) has produced a number of specific differences; and, Canada has been among the more progressive societies in recognizing and attempting to resolve problems with youth sport.

Physical activity and games developed into 'sport' in British public (private) schools during the second quarter of the nineteenth century, and sport was related to character without any of Rousseau's (1762, 1782) enthusiasm for equality. As McIntosh has noted, 'the growth of organized games and the cult of athleticism at public schools quickly made character-training its *raison d'être* and showed how, for one section of society at least, sport could be used to accustom boys "to common action and to stir up emulation" and to promote national solidarity and patriotism' (1963, p. 56). Character training reached its peak of expression in Britain, and subsequently in the 'Empire' (see Barman, 1984) and the United States, in the tenets of 'muscular Christianity'. 'The essential elements of this gospel were that physical activity and sports (especially team games) contributed towards the development of moral character, fostered desirable patriotism and that such participation and ensuing virtues were transferable to other situations and/or later life (such as from playground to battlefield)' (Redmond, 1977, p. 16).

However, as a number of commentators have pointed out (see Hall, Slack, Smith and Whitson, 1991; Mangan, 1981), there was a striking class and gender exclusivity in the idea of character training, which was initially reserved for boys at private schools. This exclusivity began to decline in the last decade of the nineteenth century. Growing industrialization and urbanization in Canada and other countries, when combined with relatively high levels of unemployment and no mandatory secondary education, resulted in the identification of urban, male working-class youth as a social problem. Realizing that missionary work need not be confined to Africa and Asia, and that declining church attendance in inner cities needed to be tackled, protestant churches, whose ministers had been educated under the principles of 'muscular Christianity', began to address the perceived problem. Various church leagues, and the Young Men's Christian Association (YMCA), were designed to provide an attractive, and Christian, diversion for youth, under the tenets of the 'social gospel' (Howell and Lindsay, 1989), and were very successful. However, the idea of character was somewhat different for working class youth in that it:

> seldom extended to include the development of leadership qualities and skills. What it did mean was respect for authority, punctuality, and the acceptance of external discipline. The virtues of following rules were explicitly emphasized, but there were few opportunities for the self-organization and leadership that were central to what character building meant in the private schools.
>
> (Hall *et al.*, 1991, p. 197; see also, Cavallo, 1981; Hardy, 1982)

In fact, sociologists and historians often characterize this formation of teams, leagues, and youth sport organizations as a 'social control' response to 'youth as a problem'. Other organizations followed, including the Young Men's Hebrew Association, the Boy Scouts, the Catholic Youth Organization, the Police Athletic League in the USA, and ethnic clubs in immigrant societies like Canada.

These differences in character education were replicated in public education where physical education in the late nineteenth and early twentieth centuries focused on 'drill'

– physical activities that emphasized external discipline and denied individuality. However, the First World War led to a much greater emphasis on physical education in public education – to prepare youth for the military. Interschool sport for boys, and physical education for girls, began to emerge in public education in the 1920s, and by the end of the 1930s, for example, some 95 per cent of US high schools had interschool boys basketball teams, and interschool sports were well-established in Anglophone Canada.[1] By the Second World War, in addition to the urban programmes noted above, there were some early community youth sport programmes in place in the US (e.g., Little League Baseball was formed with three teams in Williamsport, Pennsylvania, in 1939; see Berryman, 1975). Canada, had also experienced a first wave of adult involvement and, in addition to school sports, urban playground leagues and junior ice hockey were well established. However, there was nothing like the massive second wave of involvement of children, parents, and other adult volunteers that was to occur in the years following the Second World War.

Post World War Two: The second wave

Various analysts have looked at reasons for the rapid growth of adult organized sports in the period following the Second World War. For example, Hall *et al.* (1991, p. 188), commenting on the general increase in adult interest in children's activity, propose that it was linked to:

- a growing belief in the value of physical fitness;
- an increasing belief in the benefits of coaching and teaching for the faster development of skill, and for safety (and as a necessity to reach high performance or professional levels of sport);
- the belief that sport promotes the development of important values, attitudes, and habits ('character').

Coakley (1998, pp. 118–19), commenting specifically on parental interest, points to changes in the family in the last 50 years, especially the:

- significant increase in the number of families with both parents working outside the home, especially since the 1960s;
- significant changes in the concept of 'good parenting';
- growing belief that children's informal games may lead to 'trouble';
- growing concerns about children's safety outside the home;
- increased awareness of organized sports as a part of culture.

Hall *et al.* (1991, pp. 198–200) have provided the most comprehensive explanation of the rapid rise of adult organized youth sport in Canada after the Second World War. They conclude that this growth was:

- 'a product of unprecedented prosperity in Canada', and the use of that prosperity in the provision of facilities;
- related to 'the rise of new ideas about childhood and parenthood', especially growing parental involvement in the lives of their children (e.g., promoting social mobility in various ways from education to sport involvement, and especially giving their own children opportunities that had not been available in their own childhoods – in Europe, or in Canada during the depression);

- supported by 'conventional wisdom in psychology, spread not only through schools but through the popular media and self-help books, [which] emphasized the benefits of an early introduction to skill development and learning';
- 'a product of the increasing postwar sophistication of high-performance [and professional] sport'.

In order to complete the analysis for this period, it is necessary to point out that the growth of involvement was primarily a growth in boys' involvement, and that the social changes noted above were closely related to demographic changes in Canada that also occurred with the end of the war. These included:

- the return of troops from the various theatres of war led to the 'baby boom', and a large population of young people in Canada from the late 1940s through the 1960s; this was complemented by a significant increase in immigration during this period;
- the housing needs of young families led to a massive growth in the development of suburbs, which, with their new sport and recreation facilities, became one of the major sites of adult-organized youth involvement;
- the return of (primarily male) troops also led a to restructuring of work, with jobs that had been carried out by women during the war being reclaimed by men; while this led to the creation of what is now thought of as the 'typical' family (working father, stay-at-home mother, 2.5 children), it was also connected with the new interest in child development (e.g., Spock, 1946), and created, for middle-class and better-off working-class families, available time for volunteer work which often involved children's (especially boys') activities.[2]

The adult-organized childrens' sports that grew in this climate quickly developed a number of problems.

Problems

The growth in organized youth sports is striking, but the statistics are generally not very reliable, and vary widely. For example, in the US in 1974, 'in a US News and World Report study, it is conservatively estimated that 4 million or more youngsters from 5–14 years of age are participating in officially recognized community-sponsored sport programmes' (Coakley, 1978, p. 95). In the same year, Ralbovsky (1974) estimated that (including high school participation) there were 9 million boys and a few thousand girls, between the ages of 9 and 19, participating in adult-organized sports. By 1978, Magill, Ash and Smoll (1982) were suggesting 'approximately 20 million American youngsters between the ages of 6 and 16 [were] participating in organized sport programmes' (p. xvi).

Using the 10 per cent rule (where the Canadian population is approximately 10 per cent of the US population), this would suggest approximately 2 million Canadian young people by 1978. Ten years later, the 1988 Campbell's Survey found that, for boys, 42 per cent of 10–14 year olds and 44 per cent of 15–19 year olds were involved weekly in 'competitive' sports (organized teams, leagues, or races); while for girls, 37 per cent of 10–14 year olds and 28 per cent of 15–19 year olds were involved (Stephens and Craig, 1990).[3] By 1991, Hall *et al.* estimated that 2.5 million Canadian youths between the ages of 6 and 18 were involved in organized sport programmes.

The US News and World Report survey is striking because it was conducted at a time when there was growing interest in, and concern about, children's sports. There had been earlier concerns about adult involvement (e.g., Bill L'Heureux at the University of Western

Ontario and John Farina at the University of Toronto in the 1960s, and even some expressions of concern in the 1920s and 1930s), but these were isolated voices. The sustained criticism was rooted in a more widespread critique of organized and professional sport that started with European academics (e.g., Brohm, 1978/1976; Rigauer, 1981/1969; Vinnai, 1973), became a more popular academic critique in North America (e.g., Edwards, 1969; Hoch, 1972; Scott, 1971), and eventually the subject of what was termed 'jock-raking' journalism (e.g., Dickey, 1974; Izenberg, 1972; Lipsyte, 1975). The critiques, starting in the late 1960s,[4] began to recognize that youth sports were being run exactly like adult professional and elite sports and, if there were problems with adult sports, those problems were of even more concern when it came to children.

Smith (1975, pp. ix–x) identified four problematic beliefs which appeared to dominate children's organized programmes in the early 1970s (and which still need to be fully resolved):

- 'children play sports to entertain adults';
- 'games and sports for kids must be organized and controlled by adults if they are to be of real value';
- 'kids are miniature adults';
- 'the real value in sport lies in learning to be a winner, . . . people can be divided into winners and losers, and . . . sport is a way to make sure you (or your kids) end up in the right group';

On this last point, some have argued that the growth in community sport, especially for younger males, occurred precisely because professional educators tended to discourage or de-emphasize competition in elementary schools, and play down the intensity of inter-school competitions in high school. By the late 1960s, Howell and Howell (1969, p. 157) noted that: 'Even provincial school championships are not a common occurrence in Canada' (although these are now widely established in a range of sports).

The literature of this period indicates that concerns were expressed about:

- stressed children;
- limitations on children's social and emotional development;
- domineering and bullying adults (coaches and parents);
- violence in contact sports – especially when there were significant size differences among children;
- an overemphasis on winning;
- limited playing time for many children;
- the fact that children were being cut from programmes for lack of size or skills (instead of teaching those skills), or that they were dropping out of programmes at a disturbing rate.

On these last points, as Orlick and Botterill noted: 'It's ridiculous to promote participation on the one hand, and then to cut interested individuals from the team, or to in any way limit their participation' (1975, p. 17).

More specific to Canadian sport, was what Kidd and Macfarlane (1972) referred to as 'child buying'. Community ice hockey programmes, rather than secondary school programmes, function as the major talent development system for professional hockey in Canada[5] and, from the late 1940s to the mid 1960s, community teams were tied directly to NHL teams. 'As a result, every [hockey playing] boy in Fredericton grew up knowing he was "Black Hawk property", every boy in Winnipeg "belonged" to the Boston Bruins' (Kidd and Macfarlane, 1972, p. 56).[6] Selection drafts replaced direct sponsorship in 1966, and 'child buying' continues, especially in the form of the 'midget' draft of the best 15 and 16 year old players to elite, pre-professional 'junior' hockey teams. The system ensures that most of the talented adolescent players will have to leave home in order to continue playing – a youth sport problem that did not occur until approximately the 1980s (and never to the same extent) in some other sports.

Formal academic recognition of these problems in Canada began in 1973, at the first national conference on 'The Child in Sport and Physical Activity' held at Queen's University, Kingston, in May. Just one year later, the 'First National Conference on Women in Sport' in Toronto included a workshop on children's attitudes towards sport. These conferences laid the groundwork for the resolutions that followed.

Resolutions

Social problems are not resolved in a social vacuum. First, they must be recognized and identified as problems. Second, there is a period of criticism, and argument, during which those who have recognized that a problem exists begin to publicly name it as a problem, and confront the counter arguments from those who have some form of vested interest in the *status quo*. Third, there is a period of negotiation during which policies are changed, although rarely to the complete satisfaction of either side in the argument. Since sociology is a critical science, with a prime mandate to question 'common sense' views of the way things are, it is ideally placed – as is the sociology of sport – to be a major player in this process.

So, solutions begin in critique; and while criticism is often thought of as a destructive act, where social problems are involved criticism very often comes from dedicated individuals who are committed to improving the situations in which they are involved. Sage (1990) makes this point by substituting 'sport' for 'country' in this quote from US Senator John Fulbright:

> To criticize [sport] is to do it a service and pay it a compliment. It is a service because it may spur [sport] to do better than it is doing, it is a compliment because it evidences a belief that [sport] can do better than it is doing.
>
> (Holt, 1984, p. 33, cited in Sage, 1990, p. 11)

Criticisms of adult organized youth sports became widespread in the early 1970s, a time of widespread criticism of institutions (e.g., education, the military) and social inequalities, and of democratizing movements (e.g., women's movement, civil and native rights movements, anti-poverty movements, etc.). As noted previously, the critique of youth sport was rooted in a more widespread criticism of organized sport, and took two basic forms:

1. A recognition, and critique, of the ultra-conservative, even fascistic, nature of organized sport;[7] an approach that effectively destroyed the joy of participation, even for children.

2. A recognition that, if there were positive aspects to participation (health, social and mental development, the pleasure of participation), then such benefits should be available to all children.

Every critic agreed that adults were the problem in youth sports – Bill L'Heureux, at the University of Western Ontario, summarized this view by noting that, 'the only problem with kids' sports is adults'. But critics were divided over the resolution to the adult problem, and tended to fall into two camps.

Adults are the problem – get rid of the adults

Devereaux's (1976a) article, and his film, *Two Ball Games* (1976b) are the most vivid representations of the 'get rid of the adults' solution. He argued that the involvement of adults, who take 'fun' out of the activities, impoverishes children's games, and also that important educational aspects of children's games are lost when adults become involved.[8] In comparing 'backyard' and Little League baseball games (in text and film), and coining the term 'Little Leaguism', Devereaux raised the issues of freedom and constraint that were an important part of the countercultural social critique at the time. However, this work is sometimes criticized as being rooted in a rather romanticized view of children and 'freedom', that is, not fully taking into account that supervision is sometimes appropriate and necessary.

Coakley, who characterizes informal, player-controlled sports as 'action centered', and formal, adult-controlled sports as 'rule centered' (1998, p. 127), has carried out the most systematic comparison between the two. He found that, when children organize their own games, they emphasize action, personal involvement, a close score, and opportunities to reaffirm friendships. When adults organize children's team games they emphasize playing positions, rules, and rule enforcement. Coakley concludes that:

> each experience makes different contributions to the lives of children, and neither is without problems. However, people have traditionally overrated the contributions of participation in organized sports, and underrated the contributions of participation in informal sports.
>
> (1998, p. 127)

It has become even more clear in the 1990s that children need to have opportunities to interact, learn and play in contexts other than those directly supervised by adults, and that such opportunities have become even more rare, at least for middle-class children, since the 1970s (see Elkind, 1981). However, it is also clear that many young people enjoy their participation in adult-organized sports, and the 'get rid of the adults' solution was, for the most part, a non-starter.

Adults are the problem – change the adults

Recognizing that the structures of organized youth sport were well and truly in place, and that reversion to a supposedly idyllic time of informal youth sport was probably impossible, academics, educators, and other policy makers set about devising ways of changing the behaviour of adults involved in youth sport programmes. The recommendations of the 1973 (Queen's University) and 1974 (Toronto) conferences, noted above, accepted that adult involvement was here to stay, and proposed the forms of that involvement (Orlick and Botterill, 1975). By 1977 the United States, which had been more polarized over the issue, reached a similar resolution:

> Two documents [Thomas, 1977; Martens and Seefeldt, 1979] summarize the content of the historic meeting between groups that formerly opposed children's sports and representatives from nonschool sports agencies. In essence, the two groups agreed to recognize that athletic competitions for children had become an enduring part of our culture. The conditions under which healthful competition should occur were described in [Martens and Seefeldt's] 'Bill of Rights for Young Athletes'.
>
> (Seefeldt, 1982, p. 18)

Once the presence of adults had been accepted, the issues at stake in youth sport, and in physical education more generally, were then 'about "education through the physical" [as in the private school legacy] or about the "production of performance", and whether demonstrably successful ways of achieving the latter (new training methods, for example, or particular game tactics) are to be tempered by philosophies of humanistic education' (Hall *et al.*, 1991, p. 200).

The ten articles from Martens and Seefeldt's 'Bill of Rights for Young Athletes' are worth citing here because they give a clear indication of the level of progressive thinking about children's participation in adult organized sports in the late 1970s. They suggest that the 'production of performance' was to be severely moderated in favour of a positive experience for the child, but only Article five clearly indicates concern for 'education through the physical':

1. the right to participate in sports;
2. the right to participate at a level commensurate with each child's maturity and ability;
3. the right to have qualified leadership;
4. the right to play as a child and not as an adult;
5. the right of children to participate in the leadership and decision-making of their sport participation;
6. the right to participate in safe and healthy conditions;
7. the right to proper preparation for participation in sports;
8. the right to an equal opportunity to strive for success;
9. the right to be treated with dignity;
10. the right to have fun in sports.

Perhaps indicative of the lack of progress we have made in 'changing adults' is that we recognize a number of these rights which are unfulfilled, even after 20 years.

However, quite significant progress has been made in the training of coaches. The Coaching Association of Canada was established in 1971. Its formation was, in part, a response to the critique of children's sport programmes; but it also coincided with a significant period of development in Canadian sport as the country geared up to host the 1976 Montreal Olympics. The mission of the Association is to: 'enhance the experience of all Canadian athletes through quality coaching' (www.coach.ca). The National Coaching Certification Programme was established in 1974, with five levels of accomplishment (from Level 1, novice, to Level 5, national) based on theoretical, technical, and practical elements. With regard to youth sport, Level 1 certification is strongly recommended, and has become mandatory for volunteer coaches in many youth sport organizations. It ensures that coaches have at least a minimal knowledge of physiological, psychological, and social issues regarding child development and participation. The achievement of certification does not mean that coaches discard all of their negative practices, but it's a step in the right direction.

Coach education has been backed up with the publication of numerous accessible books and pamphlets aimed at 'changing adults' (especially parents and coaches) in terms of their behaviour around youth sports. Initially, these emerged from the critical and 'jock-raking' literature, with books such as Ralbovsky's (1974) *Lords of the Locker Room* concluding with a chapter titled: 'A general guide for parents: What to look for in a coach (or, how to preserve your son's health and sanity)'. The following year, as a precursor to the National Coaching Certification Programme, the Coaching Association of Canada in conjunction with the Manufacturer's Life Insurance Company, published, and made widely available in Canada, a 130 page paperback titled *How to Be an Effective Coach* (Taylor, 1975), while in the same year, Orlick and Botterill produced the widely read, *Every Kid Can Win*. Additionally, the Canadian Council for Children and Youth produced an extremely popular pamphlet and poster series called *Fair Play Codes for Children in Sport* (1979), covering ethical and appropriate behaviour for parents, coaches, players, officials, and spectators.[9] Since then, numerous self-help books have been published (e.g., Spink, 1988; Thomas and Lewis, 1994), and the US magazine, *Sports Illustrated* had a long-running column, written by a sport psychologist, with advice for parents of young athletes. However, on the 'production of performance' side there have also been numerous books claiming to teach parents how to turn their children into champion athletes.

The most practical step in terms of changing adults was a change in league structure and philosophy. Youth leagues, particularly in ice hockey, were organized as 'house leagues', and the more elite 'travel leagues'. House leagues became a specific focus of criticism, and attempts to bring about changes. In a key move in the early 1970s, Dick Moriarty and Jim Duthie at the University of Windsor began to conduct 'change agent research' on the problems in youth sports. They interviewed parents and coaches about the benefits and values of youth sports, videotaped their behaviours during games, and discussed the contradictions with them in light of the video evidence. They also began to identify what are now termed 'best practices', and managed to have some of these introduced in Windsor and Essex County leagues (in South-eastern Ontario). Hockey and baseball, and subsequently soccer, lacrosse, and basketball, began to emphasize an enjoyable and active experience for all children at the house league level. Rules were introduced to ensure that teams were created with relatively equal levels of skill, and that all players were given equal playing time; and leagues began to emphasize skill development and de-emphasize the outcome. These changes spread throughout Canada, often assisted by pockets of academic criticism (e.g., Cal Botterill in Alberta, Dennis Hyrcaiko in Manitoba, Barry McPherson and Michael Smith in Southern Ontario, and John Pooley in Nova Scotia), and are now the norm for house leagues throughout Canada. Coaches are encouraged (or required) to have their Level 1 certification and, while some house league coaches still attempt to manipulate the player draft or give their best players more playing time, and some house league parents do not behave as well as might be expected, in general the changes have greatly improved the experiences of players.

Creation of alternatives to youth 'sport'

A third solution steps away from the divide of the first two, with less emphasis on the presence of adults, and more on youth-created experiences. These also emerged from the democratizing movements of the 1960s, and began in physical education with the introduction of 'modern educational gymnastics', a system designed to have all children active at the same time, at their own level of ability, in innovative and challenging ways (instead of the traditional line-ups to use apparatus or shoot baskets). Related movements in physical education and children's play – cooperative games (cf. Orlick, 1978, in Canada), and new games (cf. Fluegelman, 1976, in the US) – grew more directly out of countercultural rejection of the damaging effects of competition. Such activities are now a standard part of the physical education curriculum in elementary schools in Canada, and are frequently used in camps and day care settings.

New games such as 'earth ball' also attracted older participants for a time, but older youths and young adults also began to create various other alternative or countercultural activities, i.e. surfing, ultimate frisbee, skateboarding, hot-dog skiing and, more recently, snowboarding, windsurfing, sport climbing, and mountain biking. 'The playful and expressive qualities of these activities were accentuated precisely because the dominant sport forms lacked such characteristics and seemed overly rationalized, technologized, and bureaucratized' (Donnelly, 1988, p. 74). Of course, some of these activities have also lost much of their original oppositional meaning (e.g., 'hot-dog' became 'freestyle' skiing), and have become, at least in part, the dominant sport forms (e.g., Olympic, professional, 'X' Games, adventure racing) they originally opposed. Some of these alternative activities were initiated by adults, others by youths themselves, but in either case they involve characteristics that are similar to the informal, player-controlled games described by Coakley (1998) – action, personal involvement, and opportunities to reaffirm friendships.

Post Montreal Olympics: Consolidation and high performance

Many of the problems outlined in the previous section are still problems, and attempts to resolve them are ongoing. But the 1972 (Munich) Olympics, and to a greater extent the 1976 (Montreal) Olympics heralded the start of a new set of problems for youth sport in Canada and other countries. The 17 year old Olga Korbut, from the Soviet Union, won two gymnastics gold medals in Munich, and became the darling of the media. In Montreal, it was a 14 year old from Romania, Nadia Comaneci, achieving the first perfect scores in gymnastics. It was also in Munich and Montreal that the East Germans came to the fore, especially in sports such as swimming.[10] East Germany finished third in total medals in Munich, and third again in Montreal (90, to the USA's 94, and the Soviet Union's 125), where they were also second in gold medals (40, to the USA's 34, and the Soviet Union's 47). During the 'cold war' era, close competition was expected between the USA and the USSR. Although the USA was far wealthier, the two countries had similar size populations, and the USSR had been a significant force in international sport since the 1952 (Helsinki) Olympics. However, East Germany was a much smaller country, with a population (17 million) that was a little less than that of Canada.

In 1973, Doug Gilbert, a sportswriter, began to explore East Germany's 'miracle system' in a series of articles for the Montreal Gazette, and compare it with the Canadian system in the run-up to the 1976 Olympics (reprinted in Gilbert, 1976). The system, developed from the one in place in the Soviet Union, and then passed on to Soviet satellites in Europe, and Cuba, involved:

- early exposure of children to physical education and a wide range of physical activities;
- a broad base of participants in sport and physical activity;
- early identification of athletic talent;
- intensive and specialized training for those identified.

The success of the East Germans in Montreal, and the fact that Canada was the first Olympic host country not to win a gold medal, triggered some real interest in their system, and prompted a 'youth movement' in Canadian high performance sport. Sport scientists began to conduct research into talent prediction, and early specialization in sport – the younger the better – began to become the norm. The early success of the female gymnasts, and victories for young female athletes in sports such as figure skating and swimming, provided an additional incentive for early involvement and specialization.[11] And it was this early, intensive involvement of talented young athletes (a situation not completely new to Canada because it was already very much in place in ice hockey) that led to a new set of problems.

Problems

By the early 1980s, commentators such as Hart Cantelon (1981) and Ommo Grüpe (1985) were beginning to identify the lost childhoods of these 'child athletic workers' as a social problem. Grüpe (1985, pp. 10–11) noted that children in elite sport programmes:

- are not permitted to be children;
- are denied important social contacts and experiences;
- are victims of disrupted family life;
- are exposed to excessive psychological and physiological stress;
- may experience impaired intellectual development;
- may become so involved with the sport that they become detached from the larger society;
- face a type of abandonment on completion of their athletic careers.

At the same time, writers such as Elkind (1981) and Postman (1982) were beginning to criticize the loss of childhood more generally. Postman focused on childhood loss of innocence through unsupervised exposure to media, while Elkind emphasized the enormous achievement pressures that parents had begun to place on middle-class children (see also the quotation at the beginning of this chapter).

Following Cantelon's lead, and intrigued by a personal encounter with a retired figure skater who claimed a 'lost adolescence', Donnelly began to conduct a series of retrospective interviews with retired high-performance athletes in Canada in 1985 (see Donnelly, 1993, for the final report). All 45 subjects (16 male, 29 female), representing a variety of sports, claimed to have had successful careers; all had intensive involvement in the sport during their childhood and adolescence; all were given every opportunity to address both positive and negative aspects of their careers; and each spent approximately ten times more time on the negative than the positive.

A variety of problems were reported, problems that the subjects connected directly to their early intensive involvement and specialization. These included:

- family concerns – problems such as sibling rivalry and parental pressure;
- social relationships – missed important occasions and experiences during childhood and adolescence;
- coach–athlete relationships – authoritarian and abusive (emotional, physical, sexual) relationships, especially male coach–female athlete;
- educational concerns – any achievements were earned in spite of the sport and school systems, not because of them;
- physical and psychological problems – injuries, stress, and burn out;
- drug and dietary problems – some experiences of drug use, widespread concern about disordered eating;
- retirement – widespread adjustment difficulties, especially when retirement was not voluntary.

These findings have been confirmed by additional research in Canada, and in other countries that adopted the early involvement and specialization model. Information of this type has also been widely reported in more popular sources (e.g., Ryan, 1995).

Donnelly also asked the athletes if they would repeat their careers (10 per cent said 'no', and 65 per cent gave a qualified 'yes' – knowing what they know now); and if they would permit their own children to become involved in intensive training in their sport (40 per cent said 'no', and the 60 per cent who said 'yes', suggested that their experiences and knowledge would help them to protect their own children from the problems and provide them with a more positive experience). This finding has also been confirmed in a number of less formal interviews with retired athletes.

The problems in high-performance sport for children have been intensifying, even attracting the attention of a major children's rights organization, Defence for Children International. In a 1993 report, David noted a number of the problems outlined above, and warned of 'two precise situations that require optimum surveillance and protection: exploitation through sport; and, the traffic and sale of champions' (p. 9). While the latter is directed primarily at arrangements involved in bringing talented young soccer players from Eastern Europe and Africa to various Western European nations, the former applies more broadly – including the exploitation of children in developed nations. Three sports organizations have recently made rule changes because of the intense criticism they have received over their practices regarding children. The Women's Tennis Council raised the age for turning professional to 16 years; and both women's gymnastics and women's figure skating have raised the minimum age for international competition to 16 years. However, Donnelly and Coakley (1997) argue that the new age limits are only token changes and, particularly in gymnastics and figure skating, they have exacerbated rather than alleviated the problems.

Finally, a recently identified, though not a new, problem is the sexual abuse of young athletes by coaches and other adults in sport settings. Two major cases in Canada in 1997 created major concerns about child sexual abuse in sport (see Donnelly, 1999; Donnelly and Sparks, 1997) and, because they primarily involved male victims, left many young women shaking their heads that it had taken the abuse of a high-profile male to provoke any real action. In the first case, Graham James, a hockey coach, pleaded guilty to the sexual abuse of two junior players. Several days later, Sheldon Kennedy – then a player with the National Hockey League Boston Bruins – held a press conference to announce that he was one of the victims. In the second case, the arrest of Graham Stuckless, an equipment manager at Maple Leaf Gardens (a professional ice hockey arena) in Toronto, led to revelations about the existence of a 'pedophile ring' at the Gardens during the 1970s and 1980s. Boys (primarily), lured by tickets to games, visits to locker rooms to meet players, and gifts of equipment, had been coerced into sexual acts. These cases served as a reminder of a number of cases of abuse of female athletes that had passed with little attention; and they provoked a great many calls about abuse in sport to sexual harassment counsellors and the Kids' Help Line telephone hot line from both boys and girls. While sexual abuse may occur at all levels of sport, there is some evidence to suggest that it may be more prevalent at the high performance level.[12] It is there that relationships with adults, particularly coaches, are likely to be intense and involve a great deal of time, where travel and overnight stays are normal, and where young athletes with an enormous commitment to their sport are less likely to make a formal complaint that may jeopardize their careers.

Resolutions

Resolutions to many of the problems created by early intensive involvement and specialization involve a question of balance. The problem is: how to nurture the talent of highly talented children *and* assure their all-round healthy development. Parents, coaches, and other interested parties are concerned that an overemphasis on the child having a 'normal' life may lead to failure to fully develop his or her talent (and miss a chance at the Olympics and/or a career as a highly paid professional athlete); but it is apparent that an overemphasis on the talent can lead to a variety of problems from exploitation to burn out. It is precisely this lack of balance that led Donnelly (1993) to suggest that Canadian national team athletes were the survivors, rather than the products, of our high performance development system, and that we had to find a way to stop 'sacrific[ing] children on the altar of international and professional sport success' (p. 120).

The child sexual abuse issues are clearly illegal, but it has taken far too long for a climate to emerge in which the victims and survivors of abuse may tell their stories, and in which sport organizations and legal authorities act on complaints (Donnelly, 1999; Robinson, 1998). Following a sustained period of high profile criticism from the academic and sport advocacy communities, and in the media, that climate is just beginning to emerge in Canada. However, the other problems noted above are less clearly legal issues, and there are four possible approaches to their resolution. Treat the problems as:

- an educational issue;
- a children's rights issue;
- a child labour issue;
- a child welfare issue.

Each of these has both advantages and disadvantages in attempting to resolve the problems of children in high performance sport. It is probably best not to think of these as choices, but as a four-pronged attack on the problems.

Education

This approach involves the education of all those involved in the lives of elite child athletes – parents, coaches, sport administrators, educators, medical staff, sport scientists, the media, sponsors, and agents – with regard to child development issues, and maintaining a balance in children's lives. With regard to the crisis over sexual abuse and harassment, sport organizations have begun to conduct workshops for coaches on appropriate and inappropriate touching and behaviour. Coach education and certification programmes have also begun to deal with ethical issues, and coaches have been asking for training with regard to social issues. Tinning (1999) cites an Australian coach:

I can't coach kids of today, they're different, they don't respect authority as much. They want to be involved in the decision making; they don't like the sorts of punishment regimes that I've been using for a long time.

Widespread reports of abusive parent-coaches on the Women's Tennis Association (WTA) Tour have led the Women's Tennis Association to initiate counselling programmes for such parents. And a number of television documentaries and public service campaigns have also been aimed at encouraging appropriate and responsible parent behaviour.

Education is the approach most favoured by sports organizations. It is their response to the widespread criticism of problems in their sports (of which they are well aware), but education is also a response which they are able to control. The education approach slows the pace of any changes, thus allowing the *status quo*, with which all those involved, (except the children and their parents) are familiar, to continue. Many estimate that it takes a generation for changes in attitude and behaviour to result from education. The slow pace of change in non-high performance youth programmes, where there are still some examples of the problems that were first identified in the early 1970s, is evidence of this. Thus, while education is necessary, it does not resolve the problems currently being experienced by many young people at present in the system. Criticism, and the resulting education, has brought about some changes[13] but more drastic measures may also be necessary.

Children's rights

The children's rights approach forms a bridge between educational and legal responses to the problems. In addition to Martens and Seefeldt's 'Bill of Rights for Young Athletes' cited previously, there are two other statements of the rights of children in sport. Galasso (1988), who was Dean of Physical Education at the University of Windsor during the 'change agent research' noted previously, was one of the first to address the issue of children's rights in sport. He proposed (pp. 334–6):

- 'the right to self-determination;
- the right to knowledge;
- the right to be protected from abuse;
- the right to try out for a team or position;
- the right to have properly qualified instruction and leadership;
- the right to be involved in an environment where opportunity for the development of self-respect, and to be treated with respect, is imperative'.

More recently, Defence for Children International (David, 1993, p. 9), responding specifically to the problems in high performance sport, proposed:

- 'the right to do as one chooses with one's body;
- the right to be consulted;
- the right to physical and psychological integrity;
- the right to associate freely with whom one chooses;
- the right to education'.

While these charters raise important issues with regard to children's sport, they only have moral rather than legal standing and are, therefore, related more to education.

However, the International Convention on the Rights of the Child (1989) does provide a legally binding constraint on signatory governments (which Canada and 186 other nations are, but the United States is not). At least 18 of the 41 Articles in the Convention touch on issues related to sport and physical activity participation, and identify rights that are routinely violated in children's high performance sport (Kidd and Donnelly, 2000). The Convention provides a legal means to address these violations, but until now legal challenges on the basis of Convention violations remain an unexplored approach in pursuing children's rights in sport.

Child labour

Several Canadian researchers (Beamish and Borowy, 1988; Cantelon, 1981; Donnelly, 1997) have argued that children's involvement in high performance sport is a child labour issue, and that the protections invoked by those laws should be available to young athletes. Bart McGuire, CEO of the WTA Tour, recently acknowledged some concerns about young professionals:

> If you have both parents who have given up their jobs and are living off the earnings of a player on the tour, the pressure gets to be a concern . . . Implicit in the relationship is the fact that if you don't practise for a few days, we don't eat.
>
> (cited by Brunt, 1999, p. S1)

It is also evident that a number of the other categories of adult cited previously (e.g, coaches, administrators, agents) may depend on the labour of young athletes for their livelihood, and would therefore have more of a vested interest in the athlete's performance than in his or her healthy development.

However, while children may be earning incomes, and playing in highly work-like environments, the legal system has been slow to adapt to the rapid changes that have occurred in sport, and this is still an area in which it is possible for authorities to deny that children are working. Thus, there are few protections in the form of limits on training time or the number of competitions, enforcement of the time that athletes devote to compulsory education, securing and investing their incomes, or access to health and safety regulations that govern workers and employers in the workplace. It also appears that such protections are not soon likely to appear. In the entertainment industry (film, television, advertising, dance, music, theatre, and modelling), where it is quite clear that children are workers, there are no protections in most jurisdictions other than the usual laws protecting child employees – which do not appear to be really enforced in the entertainment industry. Donnelly (1997) published excerpts from a draft of a collective agreement for entertainers in Canada and from a draft of the Child Performers' Amendments to the Ontario Labour Code, both of which contain some important items relevant to young athletes. Since neither are yet in force in the entertainment industry, they seem even less likely to be developed for young athletes in the near future.

Child welfare

Another possible legal avenue to pursue is child welfare laws, which have been described as more discretionary than child labour laws. 'When we can reasonably foresee that others will be affected by our actions the law says that we owe them a "duty of care" in terms of how we ought to behave' (Tenebaum, 1996, p. 25). This 'duty' is considerably higher for children because of their special need for care and protection. Child welfare laws are intended to protect children from physical harm, negligence, sexual molestation, emotional harm, and abuse; and to ensure that they receive appropriate medical care. All of these protections have been violated in the case of children in high performance sport. However, the agencies intended to ensure child welfare are usually so overworked with respect to, for example, dysfunctional families, that they are not likely to be eager to investigate complaints involving sport.

From the four possible approaches to resolving the problems of children in high performance sport, only the 'educational' approach is currently in play – backed up to some extent by the moral force of 'children's rights'. Perhaps the threat of legal action, internationally as a Convention challenge, or provincially in terms of child labour or child welfare violations, would be enough to speed up the changes being brought about by education. However, that seems unlikely while adults continue to profit from child athletes, and more direct legal action may be necessary.

Conclusions

For the type of youth sports that became prominent after the Second World War it is clear that there have been a great many improvements – parent and coach education, league restructuring, and the development of alternatives. Many young people, now including large numbers of girls, are participating in adult organized programmes and leagues and enjoying and benefiting from their participation. However, there are some early indications of an unintended consequence resulting from well-meaning parent and coach behaviour. In a recent article, Teitel argues that we may have gone too far in 'changing the adults'; that adults, particularly baby-boomers, now play, and children do not. He goes on the state that: 'Abducting play is only the first part of our crime; holding play hostage, and then returning it to kids in adulterated form, is the second part' (1999, p. 56). Thus:

we're so concerned about our children's emotional safety, their 'feeling good about themselves', that on at least a certain middle-class level, we've gutted play by taking the risk out of it. We've created a vogue for games without winners, games closely supervised to make sure that there is no gloating or bullying – a moratorium on competition in general.

(Teitel, 1999, p. 59)

In essence, Teitel is arguing for a return to the 'get rid of the adults' view, and supports this by noting the excessive surveillance that children are subjected to by parents who are chauffeurs, spectators (at practices and games) and coaches. This reinforces the claims originally made by Devereaux, and supported by Coakley. In New York State in the 1920s, Fredrick Rand Rogers relegated teachers and other adults to the stands during school sports, arguing that the players would not learn to make decisions if adults always made them (Kidd, 1997, p. 128). Perhaps we need to begin to re-imagine a form of children's sport in which adults provide an appropriate level of supervision for safety, but otherwise decline to intervene.

For the type of elite youth sports that became prominent after the Montreal Olympics, the situation deteriorated for a long time. However, it seems that in the last three or four years there has been a levelling off. The situation is not apparently improving in Canada in any marked way, but it is also not getting worse. The sustained period of criticism has led to some educational initiatives, and is beginning to have an effect. But it may take legislation to effect any distinct improvements.

Sociological analysis shows that we can come to understand the social circumstances in which changes occur and problems arise; and that, drawing on such research-based understanding, we are able to intervene. In other words, and as this chapter demonstrates, we can make a difference.

Notes

1. Several researchers have pointed out that the major influence of the Catholic church resulted in a somewhat different pattern of development in Francophone Québec (e.g., Bellefleur, 1986, 1997; Harvey, 1988). Indeed, for the Francophone Catholic hierarchy in Québec, sports under the control of Anglophones posed a danger of assimilation. Unable to prevent the growing interest of Francophones in sport, the clergy took the initiative to create a separate sport system with a less competitive set of values. However, the domination of the clergy was never complete, especially in the larger cities where Francophones were well represented in organized sports. White and Curtis (1990) noted that, in the Francophone school system, there were limited opportunities for interschool sports. However, most commentators point out how the situation has changed in Québec since 1970, as the 'Quiet Revolution' produced a much more secular and modernist society, and a great deal more youth involvement in adult organized sport.

2. It should be pointed out that this 1950s–1960s period of the 'typical' family was short-lived for some and non-existent for many others. However, it was enshrined by a number of US television series (also seen in Canada), and has become a 'golden age' ideal for many conservative and Christian groups who claim an interest in 'family values'. The growth of the women's movement in the late 1960s and 1970s, combined with changes in the economy that made it more difficult for families to thrive on a single income, led to the end of this era of the 'typical' family. Note also that Spock's *Baby and Child Care* was first published in 1945 and, despite many imitators, had sold 28 million copies by 1977.

3. The figures point to a clear increase in female involvement by the late 1980s, but also highlight the adolescent decline in participation for females.

4. One of the first critiques in this period was from the American Association for Health, Physical Education and Recreation (AAHPER, 1968). The report recommended a number of limitations on competitive sport for elementary school children.

5. Other countries (e.g., the UK and the USA) tend to use secondary school sport as the most important development system for professional sport. Community sports, such as Little League baseball in the USA, often prepare students for the secondary school system, and university sports function as a 'finishing school' in the USA. In the UK, professional soccer teams run a 'youth team' in parallel with secondary school programmes.

6. Agreements between the National Hockey League and the Canadian Amateur Hockey Association were signed in 1947 and 1958, initially during a period of financial hardship for the CAHA. They ensured the sponsorship of teams, and the effective ownership of all young hockey players. The agreements ended in 1966 with the expansion of the NHL.

7. Scott (1971, pp. 14–22) cites the full text of a speech given in 1969 to the California State Conference of Athletic Directors by Max Rafferty titled: 'Interscholastic Athletics: The Gathering Storm'. The speech was a popular affirmation of the authoritarian nature of sport, given at a time when that nature was beginning to come into question.

8. Another 'jock-raking' journalist, Leonard Koppett, captured this educational essence of informal play as follows: 'The most important part of play is learning to set up the game, choose sides, agree with your peers, make compromises, figure out answers, submit to self-directed rulings so that the game can continue. These important civilizing functions are bypassed by adult-run leagues' (1981, p. 47).

9. This was a product of the National Task Force on Children's Play, 1974–77.

10. It is now evident that East German success was, in part, due to a secret drug programme. What is not clear is the extent to which US and USSR athletes were also using performance enhancing drugs.

11. Canadian government funding of, and commitment to producing talented athletes led American Olympic researcher John MacAloon to refer to Sport Canada and the Canadian sport system after Montreal as 'the big red machine' (the 'red' being a reference to Canada's flag and to the parallels with Eastern European system).

12. Investigators discovered the existence of a paedophile web site which advocated involvement in youth sports because of the lack of controls that existed.

13. The Canadian women's gymnastics team now boasts that it is the oldest, tallest, and heaviest team in world competition, and that that is preferable to winning medals with 'anorexic children'.

References

● AAHPER (1968) *Desirable Athletic Competition for Children of Elementary School of Physical Education Age*, Washington, D.C.: NEA Publications.

● Barman J. (1984) *Growing up in British Columbia: Boys in Private School*, Vancouver: University of British Columbia Press.

● Beamish R. and Borowy J. (1988) *Q. What Do You Do for a Living? A. I'm an Athlete*, Kingston: The Sport Research Group, Queen's University.

● Bellefleur M. (1986) *L'Église et le Loisir au Québec avant la Revolution Tranquille*, Sillery: Presses de l'Université du Québec.

● Bellefleur M. (1997) *L'Évolution du Loisir au Québec*, Sillery: Presses de l'Université du Québec.

● Berryman J. (1975) 'From the cradle to the playing field: America's emphasis on highly organized competitive sports for preadolescent boys', *Journal of Sport History* 2: 112–31.

● Brohm J.-M. (1978) *Sport – A Prison of Measured Time*, London: Ink Links, (translated by I. Fraser from the 1976 French publication *Critiques du Sport*, Paris: Christian Bourgois Editeur).

● Brunt S. (1999) 'Unlike other games, women's tennis is child's play', *Globe and Mail*, 18 August, p. S1.
● Canadian Council for Children and Youth (1979) *Fair Play Codes for Children in Sport*, Ottawa: Canadian Council for Children and Youth.
● Cantelon H. (1981) 'High performance sport and the child athlete: Learning to labour', in A. Ingham and E. Broom (eds) *Career Patterns and Career Contingencies in Sport*, Vancouver: University of British Columbia, pp. 258–86.
● Cavallo D. (1981) *Muscles and Morals: Organized Playgrounds and Urban Reform, 1880–1920*, Philadelphia: University of Pennsylvania Press.
● Coakley J. (1978) *Sport in Society: Issues and Controversies*, 1st edition, St. Louis: Mosby.
● Coakley J. (1998) *Sport in Society: Issues and Controversies*, 6th edition, Boston: McGraw-Hill.
● David P. (1993) 'Children and sport: Accomplishment or exploitation?', *International Children's Rights Monitor* 10(4): 8–12.
● Devereaux E. (1976a) 'Backyard versus Little League baseball: The impoverishment of children's games', in D. Landers (ed.) *Social Problems in Athletics*, Urbana: University of Illinois Press, pp. 37–56.
● Devereaux E. (1976b) *Two Ball Games* (30 mins.), Consortium of University Films Centre, or Cornell University, Ithaca, NY.
● Dickey G. (1974) *The Jock Empire*, Radnor, PA: Chilton.
● Donnelly P. (1988) 'Sport as a site for "popular" resistance', in R. Gruneau (ed.) *Popular Cultures and Political Practices*, Toronto: Garamond, pp. 69–82.
● Donnelly P. (1993) 'Problems associated with youth involvement in high-performance sport', in B. Cahill and A. Pearl (eds) *Intensive Participation in Children's Sports*, Champaign, Ill.: Human Kinetics, pp. 95–126.
● Donnelly P. (1997) 'Child labour, sport labour: Applying child labour laws to sport', *International Review for the Sociology of Sport* 32(4): 389–406.
● Donnelly P. (1999) 'Who's fair game?: Sport, sexual harassment, and abuse', in P. White and K. Young (eds) *Sport and Gender in Canada*, Toronto: Oxford University Press, pp. 107–28.
● Donnelly P. and Coakley J. (1997) 'Problems resulting from the increased minimum age limits in gymnastics and figure skating', unpublished report.
● Donnelly P. and Sparks R. (1997) 'Child sexual abuse in sport', *Policy Options* 18(3): 3–6.
● Edwards H. (1969) *The Revolt of the Black Athlete*, New York: The Free Press.
● Elkind D. (1981) *The Hurried Child: Growing Up too Fast too Soon*, Don Mills, Ontario: Addison Wesley.
● Fluegelman A. (1976) *The New Games Book*, San Francisco: New Games Foundation.
● Galasso P. (1988) 'Children in organized sport: Rights and access to justice', in P. Galasso (ed.) *Philosophy of Sport and Physical Activity: Issues and Concepts*, Toronto: Canadian Scholars' Press, pp. 324–42.
● Gilbert D. (1976) *Little Giant in the World of Sport: Sports Comparison Study, GDR – Canada*, Toronto: Kontakt Press.
● Grüpe O. (1985) 'Top level sport for children from an educational viewpoint', *International Journal of Physical Education* 22(1): 9–16.
● Hall A., Slack T., Smith G. and Whitson D. (1991) *Sport in Canadian Society*, Toronto: McClelland and Stewart.
● Hardy S. (1982) *How Boston Played: Sport, Recreation, and Community*, Boston: Northeastern University Press.
● Harvey J. (1988) 'Sport and the Québec clergy, 1930–1960', in J. Harvey and H. Cantelon (eds) *Not Just a Game: Essays in Canadian Sport Sociology*, Ottawa: University of Ottawa Press, pp. 69–87.

- Hoch P. (1972) *Rip Off The Big Game: The Exploitation of Sports By the Power Elite*, New York: Anchor Books.
- Holt P. (1984) 'Today's patriotism borders on chauvinism', *Rocky Mountain News*, 25 September, p. 33.
- Howell D. and Lindsay P. (1989) 'Social gospel and the young boy problem, 1895–1925', in M. Mott (ed.) *Sports in Canada: Historical Readings*, Toronto: Copp Clark Pitman, pp. 220–33.
- Howell N. and Howell M. (1969) *Sports and Games in Canadian Life: 1700 to the Present*, Toronto: Macmillan.
- International Convention on the Rights of the Child (1989) [Available] www.unhchr.ch/html/menu3/b/k2crc.htm.
- Izenberg J. (1972) *How Many Miles to Camelot?: The All-American Sport Myth*, New York: Holt, Rinehart and Winston.
- Kidd B. (1997) *The Struggle for Canadian Sport*, Toronto: University of Toronto Press.
- Kidd B. and Donnelly P. (in press) 'Human rights in sports', *International Review for the Sociology of Sport*.
- Kidd B. and Macfarlane J. (1972) *The Death of Hockey*, Toronto: New Press.
- Koppett L. (1981) *Sports Illusion, Sports Reality*, Boston: Houghton Mifflin.
- Lipsyte R. (1975) *Sportsworld: An American Dreamland*, Toronto: Fitzhenry and Whiteside.
- MacGregor R. (1996) *The Seven a.m. Practice: Stories of Family Life*, Toronto: McClelland and Stewart.
- Magill R., Ash M. and Smoll F. (1982) 'Preface to the first edition (1978)', in R. Magill, M. Ash and F. Smoll (eds) *Children in Sport*, 2nd edition, pp. xvi–xvii. Champaign, Ill.: Human Kinetics.
- Mangan J. (1981) *Athleticism in the Victorian and Edwardian Public Schools: The Emergence and Consolidation of an Educational Ideology*, Cambridge: Cambridge University Press.
- Martens R. and Seefeldt V. (1979) *Guidelines for Children's Sports*, Reston, Va.: American Alliance for Health, Physical Education, Recreation and Dance.
- McIntosh P. (1963) *Sport in Society*, London: Watts.
- Orlick T. (1978) *The Cooperative Sports and Games Book: Challenge Without Competition*, Toronto: Random House.
- Orlick T. and Botterill C. (1975) *Every Kid can Win*, Chicago: Nelson-Hall.
- Postman N. (1982) *The Disappearance of Childhood*, New York: Delacorte.
- Ralbovsky M. (1974) *Lords of the Locker Room: The American Way of Coaching and its Effect on Youth*, New York: Peter H. Wyden.
- Redmond G. (1977) 'The first "Tom Brown's Schooldays" (1804) and others: Origins and evolution of "muscular Christianity" in children's literature, 1762–1857', Proceedings of the North American Society for Sport History, p. 16.
- Rigauer B. (1981) *Sport and Work*, New York: Columbia University Press, (translated by A. Guttmann from the 1969 German publication, *Sport und Arbeit*, Frankfurt: Suhrkamp).
- Robinson L. (1998) *Crossing the Line: Violence and Sexual Assault in Canada's National Sport*, Toronto: McClelland and Stewart.
- Rousseau J.-J. (1762) *Émile; ou, De l'éducation*, Amsterdam: Néaulme.
- Rousseau J.-J. (1782) *Considérations sur la Gouvernement de Pologne et sur la Réformation Projettée*, Paris: Cazin.
- Ryan J. (1995) *Little Girls in Pretty Boxes: The Making and Breaking of Elite Gymnasts and Figure Skaters*, New York: Doubleday.
- Sage G. (1990) *Power and Ideology in American sport: A Critical Perspective*, Champaign, Ill.: Human Kinetics.

- Scott J. (1971) *The Athletic Revolution*, New York: The Free Press.
- Seefeldt V. (1982) 'The changing image of youth sport in the 1980s', in R. Magill, M. Ash and F. Smoll (eds) *Children in Sport*, 2nd edition, Champaign, Ill.: Human Kinetics, pp. 16–26.
- Smith M. (1975) 'Foreword', in T. Orlick and C. Botterill *Every Kid can Win*, Chicago: Nelson-Hall, pp. ix–xi.
- Spink K. (1988) *Give your Kids a Sporting Chance: A Parents' Guide*, Toronto: Summerhill Press.
- Spock B. (1946) *Baby and Child Care*, New York: Pocket Books [originally published in 1945 as *The Common Sense Book of Baby and Child Care*, New York: Duell, Sloane and Pearce].
- Stephens T. and Craig C. (1990) *The Well-being of Canadians: Highlights of the 1988 Campbell's Survey*, Ottawa: Canadian Fitness and Lifestyle Research Institute.
- Taylor J. (1975) *How To Be An Effective Coach*, Toronto: Manulife, and Coaching Association of Canada.
- Teitel J. (1999) 'The kidnapping of play', *Saturday Night*, April, pp. 55–60.
- Tenebaum K. (1996) 'Daunted spirits, mangled bodies: Children in high performance sport', unpublished paper, McMaster University.
- Thomas B. and Lewis G. (1994) *Good Sports: Making Sport a Positive Experience for Everyone*, Grand Rapids, Mich.: Zondervan Publishing.
- Thomas J. (1977) (ed.) *Youth Sports Guide for Coaches and Parents*, Washington, D.C.: American Alliance for Health, Physical Education, Recreation and Dance.
- Tinning R. (1999) 'The sports factor: Children and sport', [Available]www.abc.net.au/m/talks/8.30/sportsf/sstories/sf990730
- Vinnai G. (1973) *Football Mania*, London: Orbach and Chambers.
- White P. and Curtis J. (1990) 'English/French Canadian differences in types of sport participation: Testing the school socialization explanation', *Sociology of Sport Journal* 7(4): 347–68.

Chapter Fourteen

Authentic Sociology in Secondary School Physical Education

Doune Macdonald, Greg Naughtin and Naree Wittwer

Introduction

School physical education has been criticized for its failure to adapt to new social, economic and political conditions in the industrialized world. As Rink (1992) observed:

> There is an unwritten assumption in our field that secondary physical education programmes are not good and are endangered. The prevailing view is that most programmes are not meeting students' needs and, in general, are an irrelevant, negative educational experience for many of the youth they serve.
>
> (1992, p. 67)

More specifically, there is abundant evidence which suggests physical education often exists as a marginal and inequitable subject which reflects and reproduces general dissatisfaction with physical education's outcomes, teachers' workplace conditions, and scepticism about the subject's social relevance (Crum, 1990; Evans and Davies, 1993; Macdonald, 1999; O'Sullivan, Siedentop and Tannehill, 1994; Stroot, 1994). The potentially inferior status of physical education has been attributed to its seemingly practical nature in educational contexts which favour overtly intellectual activity and to its failure to generate a population engaged in the movement culture (Macdonald and Brooker, 1997). However, one recently developed Australian physical education syllabus attempts to tackle the issues of the marginality, relevance and impact of physical education through an innovatory approach to the teaching of subject matter knowledge (Shulman, 1986). In particular, the subject matter of sociology is central to the syllabus with the aim being to redefine and extend what it means to be physically educated through having sociology personalized and integrated alongside participation in physical activities.

It is the failure of physical education to meet the needs of students and their present and future communities that is of central concern in this chapter. The rapidly changing social, economic and political milieu of schooling has created new cultural conditions, interests and needs for those who Tinning and Fitzclarence (1992) have termed 'postmodern youth'. Contemporary discussions with respect to the failure of physical education to meet the needs of all secondary students have focused on the nature of young peoples' culture and their rejection of culturally dominant physical activities (Kirk, 1994; Siedentop, 1992; Tinning and Fitzclarence, 1992). In short, Tinning and Fitzclarence (1992, p. 287) have claimed that 'school physical education is irrelevant or boring' for many young people, and criticize its failure to engage with issues such as the impact of the international market in sport, the commodification of lifestyle, and acceptable body images as portrayed in the media. The tendency for physical education's content and pedagogy to undermine inclusivity has also been problematic particularly for those pupils at the nexus of gender, ethnicity and socio-economic status (Evans and Davies, 1993; Kidd, 1995; Siedentop, Doutis, Tsangaridou, Ward and Rauschenbach, 1994).

In parallel with this groundswell of concern, there has been debate over what it means to be physically educated in contemporary terms. Siedentop (1993) suggests that some-one who is physically educated clearly values physical activity, as revealed by their own lifestyle habits, together with 'the degree to which they are involved critically in the sport, fitness, and leisure cultures of their nations' (p. 11). Through being socially *critical*, Siedentop hopes for a physically educated citizen who understands 'structural inequities in . . . local and national cultures which may limit access to sport, fitness, and leisure activ-ity based on irrelevant attributes such as race, gender, age or socioeconomic status' as well as them being 'discriminating consumers of sport, fitness and leisure pursuits' (p. 12). In 1995, the National Association for Sport and Physical Education (NASPE) in the United States published its description of a physically educated person which emphasized an indi-vidual's values, habits and decision making, and lifelong participation in physical activity (NASPE, 1995). Comparing Siedentop's reflection in 1993 with the NASPE charter, the latter could be criticized for failing to sufficiently recognize intellectual and socially critical out-comes for curricula.

Australian and British writers have also foregrounded the social and, in turn, curricular and professional issues underpinning the process of teaching for physical education, while also locating movement as the core of the process supported by interrelated understand-ings of theoretical perspectives and physical skill development (e.g. Arnold, 1979; Brooker and Macdonald, 1997; Kirk, 1988, 1989; Tinning, Kirk and Evans, 1993). Brooker and Macdonald's (1997) review of literature on physical education teaching and curriculum practice reveals key elements that characterize worthwhile physical education and the generation of physically educated pupils. These are a:

- focus on the centrality of movement;
- promotion of a critical perspective on movement;
- promotion of a broader life skills 'through' the medium of physical activity;
- reflective approach to teaching;
- breadth of physical activities;
- task-based approach to teaching and learning.

It is through the teaching of sociology in physical education that the subject's critical potential, both immediate and long term, can be fulfilled. The foregrounding of subject matter addressing, for example, sexuality, gender, violence, and the commodification of the body, can work towards creating a more supportive learning environment within physical education and can stimulate a range of learning experiences which address critical issues for young people such as homophobia, body image, substance abuse, and their alienation from culturally dominant physical activities (Glover, Burns, Butler and Patton, 1998). As these physically educated young people move into communities beyond the school, they are more likely to adopt critical and proactive positions with respect to lifelong participation and enrich the debates surrounding contemporary physical culture. In doing so, physical education is thereby engaging with what Feingold (1997, p. 352) termed 'the current cries from society'. Feingold and colleagues (e.g. Lawson, 1998; Siedentop, 1998), in a special edition of *Quest* have argued the importance of school and tertiary physical education meeting local social needs if they are to remain viable in the twenty-first century and, it should be noted, that many of the fundamental issues to be addressed surrounding schools, young people, families, and health require a sociological sensitivity.

Having suggested that the subject matter of sociology within physical education is imperative if schools are to graduate physically educated students, we will now elaborate how sociology is approached in some Australian senior secondary school physical education syllabi[1] before outlining in more detail that produced by the Queensland Board of Senior Secondary School Studies (BSSSS). Two sociology units, following the BSSSS syllabi, are then presented and discussed in terms of their learning principles, content knowledge and pupil responses with a view to sharing ways in which teachers and coaches can make sociology meaningful for their learners.

Shulman (1986) has articulated a framework for teachers' knowledge which is useful for outlining the types of, and relationships between, knowledge for the teaching of physical education. Within this framework he emphasizes the importance of three dimensions of content knowledge: subject matter, pedagogical and curriculum content knowledge. Subject matter content knowledge includes the material which defines the field of study, the accepted truths of the discipline, together with the knowledge to explain issues related to the field, what is worth knowing, and why. Curriculum content knowledge refers to the syllabi, programmes, materials and resources which shape the scope, sequence and pedagogy of the teaching–learning process. Pedagogical content knowledge, is knowledge of how to most effectively promote learning of the subject matter and, therefore, intersects subject matter (what to teach) and pedagogy (how to teach) as may be stipulated via curriculum content knowledge. The capacity of teachers to transform subject matter into forms of presentation and guidance that are pedagogically powerful, and in keeping with the pupils' abilities and backgrounds, Shulman argues, is central to the act of teaching. As will be discussed further, the Queensland physical education syllabus relies on a particular manifestation of pedagogical content knowledge. It asks teachers to integrate 'practical' (e.g. tennis serves) and 'theoretical' (e.g. impact of technology on tennis performance) content knowledge in order to make the learning experiences more meaningful for the pupils.

Sociology in Australian physical education syllabi

Australian syllabi for senior secondary school physical education include a strong sociological focus following the social justice platform in educational policy, together with the influence of some Australian writers mentioned above. In the state of Victoria, physical education 'examines the biological, social and cultural influences on performance and participation in physical activity' (Board of Studies, 1994, p. 5). In turn, the aims of the subject include for students to, 'understand the social, cultural, environmental and biological factors which influence participation in physical activity' and 'develop a critical perspective on physical activity' (p. 5). In order to fulfil these aims, the areas of study must include subject matter addressing: the influence of sociocultural factors on participation and performance (e.g. gender, ethnicity, income, geographical location); the role of the media and the effects of marketing on participation in physical activity; the changing public image of sporting participants; and the role of ergogenic aids and drugs in sport.

In New South Wales, physical education is positioned within the personal development, health and physical education subject. Approximately 20 per cent of the total subject time addresses the sociology of games and sport in which the 'positive and negative consequences arising from the manner in which sport is organized, promoted, financed and

Table 14.1
Content Area C:
Physical activity in
Australian Society.

Content focus	Possible subject matter
Body, culture and physical activity	● Changing social perceptions and concept of the body and physical activity ● Body image and physical activity ● Mass media representations of the body in physical activity ● Social regulation of the body and physical activity ● Scientific regulation of the body and physical activity ● Social construction of gender

Lifestyle, leisure, recreation and physical activity	● Changing social perceptions and concepts of lifestyle and physical activity
	● Patterns of recreational physical activity
	● Patterns of participation in sport
	● Spectatorship in sport
	● Lifestyle as a commodity
	● Lifestyle, physical activity and
	   – age
	   – socioeconomic background
	   – ethnicity
	   – disability

Money, media, power and physical activity	● Sport as a commodity; the sport industry ● Exercise as a commodity; the exercise industry ● Physical activity and technological change ● Performance enhancing substances ● Physical activity, gender and power ● Physical activity, politics and power ● Equity and physical activity ● Globalization of sport ● National sport policies

Source: BSSSS (1998) Senior Syllabus in Physical Education, p. 17

portrayed are investigated' (Board of Studies, 1995, p. 60). In particular, pupils study Australia's sporting identity, politics and sport, economics and sport, women in sport, and competition in sport using sociological concepts such as socialization, sexism and nationalism.

The physical education syllabus of Queensland lists the subject matter related to sociology in one of three content areas. Table 14.1, outlining 'Content Area C: Physical activity in Australian society', suggests that this syllabus further extends what might be considered as appropriate sociological subject matter knowledge in several ways. It includes a strong focus upon representations and regulations of the body, a more explicit focus than we might see in other syllabi on life-style and leisure thereby moving the pupil beyond the study of sport, and it introduces notions of commodification and globalization. A key text upon which teachers draw for their subject matter knowledge is by McKay (1991), *No Pain, No Gain?*. In this text, McKay's approach is to critically (with 'critical' here suggesting a perspective informed by the socially critical paradigm) examine the role of sport in society and challenge the myths and stereotypes which surround corporatized sports and leisure.

In order to better understand what and how sociology is to be taught and learned in Queensland senior secondary physical education, the following section overviews the Queensland syllabus' key subject matter and pedagogical frameworks.

Physical education syllabus frameworks

The Board of Senior Secondary School Studies' (BSSSS) physical education syllabus has a number of interrelated theoretical and conceptual frameworks which are concerned with the study and practice of physical activity, and focus on 'the complexity of, and interrelationships among, psychological, biomechanical, physiological and sociological factors which influence individual and team performances, and wider social attitudes to physical activity' (BSSSS, 1998, p. 1). The pivotal framework is that drawn from the work of Arnold (1979) which conceptualizes educationally worthwhile knowledge in the physical education syllabus around the dimensions of learning in, about and through physical activity. Supporting frameworks are those of intelligent performance (Kirk, 1989), the subject matter classifications for learning 'in' and 'about' physical activity (Bingham, 1990), the objectives for assessment, and the pedagogy for integration and personalization of subject matter.

The terms learning in physical activity, learning about physical activity and learning though physical activity, reflect three dimensions of movement (BSSSS, 1998). *Learning in physical activity* refers to experiential outcomes, where students directly acquire knowledge, understandings and skills as a result of thoughtful participation in physical activity (e.g. applying tactical arrangements in a game, appraising the physical capacities and requirements of an activity). *Learning about physical activity* refers to a rational form of inquiry, where students directly acquire knowledge and understandings as a result of studying and participating in physical activity (e.g. examining the impact of gender stereotypes on participation in physical activity, planning psychological strategies for pre-match preparation). *Learning through physical activity* refers to instrumental outcomes where students indirectly acquire understandings, capacities and attitudes as a result of studying and participating in physical activity (e.g. increased physical fitness, aesthetic appreciation of a performance, continued participation in a physical activity).

In keeping with the centrality of movement in becoming physically educated, the syllabus prioritizes *action* informed and is shaped by *thought*. It, therefore, aims to develop what Kirk (1988) has described as an intelligent performance, premised on the understanding that the mind and body work together in the production of cognitive and psychomotor skills. In practice, the physical education syllabus positions physical activity ('in', action) as the central concern informed by other relevant sources of information ('about', thought), such as that in the exercise sciences, sociology, and sports psychology, in ways specifically related to the movement itself rather than reified in classrooms. Intelligent performance involves rational and creative thought at a high level of cognitive functioning and engages pupils, not only as performers, but also as analysts, planners and critics in, about and through physical activity. It is this intelligent performance that distinguishes pupils as being physically educated and shapes the objectives and outcomes for the subject.

The syllabus' objectives of acquiring, applying, and evaluating knowledge, understandings, attitudes, and skills emphasize the students as 'decision makers engaged in the active construction of meaning through the processing of information related to the study of physical activity' (BSSSS, 1998, p. 5). More specifically, pupils independently, and in groups, are expected to:

1. acquire knowledge and concepts through gathering, recalling, and comprehending information;

2. apply knowledge and concepts through interpreting, analysing, and manipulating information;

3. evaluate knowledge and concepts through hypothesising, synthesising, justifying, and appraising information.

Clearly, the objectives draw on Bloom's taxonomy (Bloom *et al.*, 1956) and as indicated in Tables 14.2 (page 194) and 14.3 (page 196), learning experiences are organized accordingly.

Pupils are required to acquire, apply, and evaluate subject matter which is drawn from three focus areas, one of which is detailed in Table 14.1 (see page 190), the other two being *learning physical skills* and the *biological bases of training and exercise*. The selection of physical activities underpinning the subject matter (four throughout the two years of study) aims to give students a representative sample of activities available in Australian society on the basis of their structure, form, and strategic features. At least 50 per cent of the allocated time should be devoted to participation in physical activity which encourages the physical activity to be a medium for learning (e.g. record how female and male pupils feel about their bodies as they participate in a water polo unit) as well as subject matter (e.g. developing a range of water polo strategies).

Of particular importance to the presentation of an authentic sociology in physical education is the pedagogical content knowledge suggested by the syllabus. It is enacted through three principles: integration, personalization, and social justice and equity. Integration is closely aligned to the notion of intelligent performance suggested above and refers to the linking of learning about with participation in physical activity. As Kirk, Burgess-Limerick, Kiss, Lahey, and Penney (1999) explain:

> You can better understand your performance of physical activities and enhance the performance itself when you integrate knowledge about movement, such as physiological, psychological, biomechanical and sociological knowledge, with knowledge and practical experience of the physical activity.
>
> (1999, p. xiv)

Physical education, therefore, involves students in closely *integrated* written, oral and physical learning experiences based on the study of four physical activities.

Personalization is the second important principle, and is concerned with learning experiences being made meaningful to the pupil. Constructivist theories inform this thinking. They suggest that enhanced understanding and proficiency occurs when the learner is an active participant, when learning patterns are recognized as unique, and when learning experiences build on learners' previous understandings (Kirk and Macdonald, 1998). Yet, 'Personalisation is not simply a matter of finding some new aspect of information that is recognisable, familiar or comfortable for the learner' (Kirk *et al.*, 1999, p. xiv). It also involves connecting new information to what is already known, distilling what is important information, 'seeing relationships between local, national and global environments and adapting the information to suit the local, national and global contexts in which we live' (p. xiv), together with critical reflection. Therefore, the teacher's role becomes one of a facilitator, encouraging pupils to develop a sense of confidence, independence, and an appreciation of social structures and change processes.

A third principle which shapes both the *what* and *how* of the syllabus is social justice and equity. Embedding social justice and equity in Australian syllabi emerged during the 1980s at a time of federal government intervention in schooling and in a climate of concern for social inequalities (Brooker and Macdonald, 1995). Thus, the syllabus directs teachers' attention to teaching about social justice with respect to gender, disability, age, geographical location, and sexual preference, as well as prescribing learning environments in physical education which are inclusive and supportive of all pupils.

The following outlines of units from two schools are each one of four units that make up the senior physical education subject. Students of physical education are typically 16 to 17 years old, in the final two years of their secondary schooling. The units are described in terms of their subject matter and pedagogy, emphasizing aspects of integration and personalization, together with what we perceived have been the pupils' responses. We believe that each exemplifies an authentic sociology of sport, within a senior schooling context, which might also be instructive for those physical activity leaders working across a range of contexts.

Sample units

Competitive aerobics

The unit outlined below attempts to provide meaningful links between sociological concepts and pupils' experiences in competitive aerobics in a large, suburban, mixed sex, government high school. It is the first unit covered in the course of study. By placing this unit first, pupils are challenged to examine the effects of social and cultural factors that influence individual and community decisions to become involved in, and remain involved in, particular physical activities. Pupils then have the opportunity to apply socio-cultural perspectives to the other physical activities covered in the subject. This unit focuses specifically on the social construction of gender and the power structure that serves to reinforce popular images of gender in physical activity. Pupils consider the influence of popular images of 'femininity' and 'masculinity' in physical activity by examining the beliefs of peers and community members, personal experiences in competitive aerobics and other physical activities, and media portrayals of male and female athletes. Related subject matter draws on aerobic skill development, group psychology, and physiological training principles.

Competitive aerobics was included in the subject because, for many pupils, performance in competitive aerobics has qualities that are in conflict with traditional images of masculinity and physical activity participation. Experiences in competitive aerobics also provide a useful contrast to other physical activities in the course of study (e.g. touch [a non contact variation of rugby football]) which are associated with more traditional images of sport and masculinity.

Immediately prior to the first lesson in competitive aerobics, students are surveyed. In the survey, they are asked to comment on what they believe the unit will involve, how comfortable they are with this type of activity and whether the activity is suited to any particular qualities or groups. The results of this survey are used as a reflective starting point for the examination of the influence of gender stereotyping in physical activity. Students are involved in examining media images, collecting data relating to the beliefs of other pupils in the school, and reading literature regarding gender influences in physical activity. Initially, pupils must prepare and perform a competitive aerobics routine in mixed sex groups. Throughout the unit, pupils reflect on the way their group operates and attempt to analyse the influence of popular images of gender on their group performance and

Table 14.2 Competitive aerobics and the sociology of sport.

Examples of subject matter	General objectives		
Content area C	Acquiring	Applying	Evaluating
• historical and cultural perspectives of physical activity in Australia	• placing physical activity in Australia in a historical and cultural context	• designing, choreographing and performing a competitive aerobics routine	• appraising competitive aerobics routines against set criteria
• media representation of popular belief	• recognising social theory and ideology	• analysing contrasts in media reporting of men's and women's sport	• evaluating the effects of social constructions of physical activity on male and female students' attitudes to, and participation in, physical activity
• sport and the media	• conducting surveys of peers and adults	• analysing popular beliefs regarding physical activity	
• agencies of socialisation	• using personal experience in competitive aerobics classes and physical activity in general as a case study	• applying hegemony theory to an examination of the social context of physical activity in Australia	• evaluating the effectiveness of training activities in the preparation for the performance of competitive aerobics routines
• hegemony and social reality			
• participation in group routine development	• recognising examples of hegemonies in sport at school and Australia	• analysing the effects of male sporting hegemony on participation in aesthetic activities	
• equity in physical activity	• refining and developing aerobics skills and combinations		• justifying strategies for challenging and changing existing beliefs using hegemony and other social theories as frameworks
• social construction of bodies	• performing movement combinations	• devising strategies to change existing beliefs surrounding gender and physical activity	
• body as a symbol			
• social regulation of bodies	• recognising physical capacities specific to the performance of set aerobics routines	• using video feedback in developing and redesigning set competitive aerobics routines	• evaluating the effects of beliefs, images and stereotypes regarding physical activity in Australia on personal and group participation in aerobics activities and other physical activities conducted at school
• patterns of participation in physical activity	• defining and explaining the process of socialisation		
Supplementary subject matter			
• aerobic movement patterns	• locating media images that illustrate the social construction of bodies	• designing appropriate training activities to enhance personal abilities required in aerobics routines	
• movement design principles			• evaluating personal and peer performances towards demonstrating flair in performance and mastery of movement patterns
• feedback and skill learning	• articulating personal understandings of the existence of the body in culture		
• judging and evaluating performance	• observing clothing choices at a local sports centre	• analysing images of the body from a number of sources	
• team building skills	• understanding and recognizing sociological trends and concepts	• analysing attitudes of high school students to the way bodies are portrayed in the media and how this impacts on attitudes to activities such as competitive aerobics	• appraising strategies for the improvement of physical capacities and abilities
• performance capacities for aerobic routines	• developing team building strategies		
• methods to improve physical capacities	• recognising and utilising musical cues in developing aerobic routines		• justifying conclusions regarding the effect of images of bodies on participation in various physical activities

on how their performance is perceived in the wider school community. At the end of the unit, students present their group routine and a written essay based on the influence of popular images of gender in physical activity using competitive aerobics as a personal case study.

Pupils initially find the sociocultural examination of physical activity a difficult task as they generally view physical activity in a strictly physical sense. Furthermore, they often consider that biological and psychological considerations are the main (and only) influencing factors in determining an individual's success and participation in particular physical activities. This observation is reinforced by studies on tertiary students working in the physical activity field, who consider that sociocultural aspects of physical activity are less relevant than the study of biophysical sciences (Abernethy, Macdonald and Bramich, 1997; Macdonald, Kirk and Braiuka, 1999; Macdonald and Tinning, 1995). However, as pupils begin to understand the way that many of the assumptions and beliefs surrounding physical activity are viewed as 'natural' or normal, remain largely unchallenged, and are constantly reinforced by their peers and the media, they become more focused on exposing myths and discussing how things may change. Male pupils are often more reluctant to become involved in discussions and some find the concepts difficult or foreign to their experience. Yet, as they begin to enjoy the cooperative group work involved in competitive aerobics, pupils (particularly male pupils) start to view traditional gender stereotypes as restrictive, not only to females in so called 'male sports' but also to males in the more aesthetic performance type activities. Female pupils, on the other hand, can often contribute more personal experiences of gender restrictions to participation in physical activities to class discussions.

Some of the consequential outcomes of this unit were quite exciting. Pupils on the whole became more cooperative in group work. The personal reflections of students at the end of the aerobics unit served to illustrate the value of an integrated approach to sociocultural studies in physical education. For example, one male student who considered himself as a rugby player and a competitive martial artist recorded in his diary that, 'The girls in my group politely listened to my ideas, tried them once, and ignored them', making the point how, for the first time in his life, he felt marginalized due to his 'intrusion' into stereotypically 'female territory'. Several girls recorded their frustration at having to work with boys who initially felt compelled to demean the activity in order to appear 'tough and cool'. Thus, a sophisticated platform of socially critical awareness was established through the aerobics unit and became evident in the subsequent units, with pupils less confined by the traditional competitive masculine values surrounding sport. What we can learn from this unit are the benefits of having physical activity analysed sociologically alongside participation in physical activity and via questions which are significant to the participants.

Basketball

Basketball provides another rich context for sociological analyses. It is a relatively 'new' physical activity in Australian sporting culture, bringing with it the North American trappings of commercialization, commodification, and entertainment. Through learning experiences such as surveys, audits of school-based participation, videotape and newspaper analyses, and excursions to sporting events, the unit focuses upon the concepts of socialization, hegemony, ideology, and commodification as they relate to sponsorship, spectatorship, gender, and participation patterns in basketball. The body and its representation and comportment (for example, the recent use of body suits for female basketball players) is addressed in terms of the 'Catch 22' of spectatorship, media coverage and equity. In particular, pupils

Table 14.3 Basketball and the sociology of sport.

Examples of subject matter	General objectives		
Content area C	Acquiring	Applying	Evaluating
● patterns of participation in physical activity and sport ● spectatorship in sport ● equity and physical activity ● socialisation, sport socialisation and agents of socialisation ● physical activity, gender and power ● historical perspectives of physical activity in Australia ● social regulation of physical activity attire ● media portrayal of physical activities and their participants ● social learning paradigm ● hegemony and ideology ● Figueroa's framework for social analysis ● sport as entertainment ● participating in separate and mixed sex teams *Supplementary subject matter* ● creating angles for passes ● pass, screen away and roll ● defensive positioning and blocking out ● ball control and shooting accuracy ● man to man offence design and implementation ● feedback and skill learning ● judging and evaluating performance ● team building	● performing basketball skills ● comprehending major game rules ● refining and developing game tactics and strategies ● observing historical changes to sports clothing ● collecting and collating data related to physical activity participation, spectatorship and surrounding influences from surveyed groups ● creating a collage of media images of physical activity ● defining and explaining the process of socialisation ● developing an historical perspective on changes in Australian physical activity and sport ● defining hegemony, ideology and equity ● identifying examples within Figueroa's five dimensions of social analysis	● implementing basketball movements in modified environments ● using or denying space with positioning during modified tasks and game play ● adapting strategies and tactics ● providing feedback to improve teammate performances ● designing and performing a man to man team offensive strategy ● analysing socialising agents and their impact on physical activity participation ● identification of marketing concepts and strategies as applied to basketball competitions ● analysing contrasts in media reporting of male and female sporting endeavours, particularly basketball ● applying a social learning paradigm to personal role learning and in particular, physical activity involvement ● examining the influences surrounding teammate levels of participation in basketball	● selecting and implementing appropriate basketball skills following analysis of game situations ● evaluating teammate performances and interactions ● hypothesising the effects of changes to basketball rules and playing conditions ● appraising media coverage and its transmission of popular belief ● critically reviewing the school and local environments (Figueroa's dimensions) of their transmission of values concerning male and female participation in physical activities, particularly basketball ● justifying strategies for challenging and changing existing beliefs about male and female sporting endeavours

are introduced to the social learning paradigm connecting personal attributes, significant others (agents of socialization), and socialization situations with involvement in basketball. Other subject matter in the unit includes motor learning principles, the development of complex offensive and defensive strategies, and psychological approaches to team building. The pupil cohort for this unit is again mixed sex but the school is a non-government school in a regional, coastal town.

The pedagogical approaches taken in this unit are firmly grounded in integration and personalization. The unit begins with pupils doing a self-analysis of reasons behind their participation in physical activities and comparing their patterns to research data and the profiles (e.g. media coverage, prize money) of those activities. This forms the basis for a wider survey of the pupils' school community, examining pupils' lunchtime activities, and hypothesizing about the lesser female participation in lunchtime sporting activities. Through data collection using videotape analyses, they also become aware of inclusion patterns in their own basketball games during class.

To better understand the social construction of participation in (and exclusion from) basketball, a number of conditions for participation are altered: mixed sex teams; lowered ring and smaller balls (to facilitate dunking attempts of males and females); and dress alterations (males – long trousers, collared shirt with top button done up; females – long dresses/skirts). Each modification provides personal experiences of the impact of social, cultural, historical, and technical discourses on participation. This is supplemented with historical videotape footage and sociohistorical readings. The film *A League of Their Own* (which also links to the softball unit completed earlier in the course), helps to reinforce a number of sociological issues such as player selection, their expected sporting attire and behaviour, media coverage, and spectator reaction.

Pupils also conduct an in-depth study of the media and basketball. They do a media scan of either newspapers, radio, television, or sporting magazines to collect statistics on male and female coverage, and then comment on the implications of such coverage. This is followed by a small group collage of media pictures of basketball to consider the images created and, in turn, the ideologies perpetuated, through such pictures. Towards the end of the unit pupils attend local men's and women's basketball matches to note differences in play together with aspects surrounding the game such as the music, commentary, cheer leaders, and the like. Pupils use this visit to conceptualize the meaning of a 'drawcard' sporting event and to hypothesize strategies for raising the sponsorship and spectatorship profile for women's basketball.

On court participation is generally viewed positively by the pupils. Initial physical performance tasks utilize a maximum of three players per team. Teams are usually mixed sex to enable pupils to recognize and acknowledge one another's contributions. Later in the unit, five against five game situations are conducted against same sex teams, although some mixing of sexes occurs to optimally utilize all players' skills.

The pupils enjoy debating their views with others in the class. They become emotive with respect to some issues such as the spectatorship patterns of traditional male winter sports (e.g. rugby league) as compared to female sports (e.g. netball). The egocentric nature of some pupils makes it difficult for them to view critically the society in which they are immersed, and in part help to replicate, while others resist discussions on issues that challenge dominant ideologies and practices. However, over the two years of study, as the pupils mature and learn to recognize the impact of social, cultural and historical 'taken for granted' factors shaping participation in physical activities, they start to view their world more critically and hypothesize the future impact of these factors. Their willingness to engage in physical activities outside those stereotypical for their sex, and understand the implications of such actions, is indicative of them becoming physically educated.

Conclusion

Physical education, in the senior secondary school context, involves pupils as intelligent performers learning in, about, and through physical activity. It focuses on the complexity of, and interrelationships between, various kinesiological or human movement studies disciplinary knowledge bases which are understood to inform and influence physical performances and participation patterns. Although the BSSSS syllabus has demanded significant shifts in personal understandings and practices, there is general agreement among teachers and pupils that it offers a strong reconceptualization of what it means for senior students to be physically educated, and sociology is significant to this shift.

If physical education is to engage with the physical culture of the community beyond the provision of skills for participation in culturally dominant forms of physical activity, then the sociology component of the subject is critical. In particular, the pervasive and attractive images of sport confronting young people confound the role of physical education and, along with the production of extrinsic outcomes such as fitness and health, position physical education in the curriculum to serve the functional purposes of particular vested interests (e.g. health lobbies, elite sport agencies) which lie beyond those which may be seen as educational (Evans and Davies, 1993; Kidd, 1995; Kirk and Tinning, 1990). Yet, as discussed in Kirk's chapter in this text (Chapter 15), the teaching of sociology to young people has the potential to be alienating. What we have described in this chapter is an approach to content and pedagogy in which the sociological concepts are meaningful to the pupils through being integrated with physical activity and made personally and socially relevant. This constantly challenges teachers to find the 'best' ways of conveying concepts to 16 to 17 year old pupils. Some learning experiences that facilitate an authentic sociology include self-reflective diaries, local surveys, the modification of rules, clothing and equipment, debates, and media and event analyses. However, we also stress the importance of these ways of thinking and teaching being introduced in the lower years of the physical education curriculum and in instructional settings outside the formal curriculum.

These innovatory approaches require teachers to have a range of knowledge and skills: curriculum knowledge, pedagogical content knowledge, as well as sound subject matter knowledge. Research suggests that without confidence in the subject matter, teachers or indeed physical activity leaders more generally, feel less comfortable and less able to present challenging learning experiences and adapt these to the learning needs of the participants (Rovengo, 1995; Schempp, Manross, Tan and Fincher, 1998). As Rovengo (1995, p. 6) summarized, 'The subject matter matters'. It therefore, behoves pre- and in-service physical education teacher education and other professional development providers to adequately address sociological subject matter together with innovative pedagogical strategies which account for the shifting interests and needs of young people. An authentic sociology of sport, founded on the principles of integration and personalization, has the capacity to enrich the life experiences of young people and have a long-term impact upon the generation of physically educated citizens.

Note

1. In this context, a syllabus refers to a legally binding document which outlines how a subject is to be taught and assessed. The syllabi referred to here are for those subjects that are taken as electives in the final two years of schooling and which may be counted towards university entrance.

References

● Abernethy P., Macdonald D. and Bramich K. (1997) 'Undergraduate student subject preferences in human movement studies', *ACHPER (Australian Council for Health, Physical Education and Recreation) Healthy Lifestyles Journal* 44(4): 5–10.

● Arnold P. (1979) *Meaning in Movement, Sport and Physical Education*, London: Heinemann.

● Bingham B. (1990) 'Classifying physical activities for curriculum purposes', unpublished paper.

● Bloom B., Englehart M., Furst E., Hill W. and Krathwohl O. (1956) *Taxonomy of Educational Objectives: The Classification of Educational Goals: Handbook 1, The Cognitive Domain*, New York: Longman.

● Board of Studies (1994) *Physical Education Study Design*, Melbourne: Board of Studies.

● Board of Studies (1995) *Personal Development, Health and Physical Education Syllabus, Years 11 and 12*, Sydney: Board of Studies.

● Brooker R. and Macdonald R. (1995) 'Mapping physical education in the reform agenda for Australian education: Tensions and contradictions', *European Physical Education Review* 1(2): 101–10.

● Brooker R. and Macdonald D. (1997) 'Exploring meanings for physical education', *Journal of Physical Education New Zealand* 30(1): 7–10.

● BSSSS (1998) *Physical Education Senior Syllabus*, Brisbane: Queensland Board of Senior Secondary School Studies.

● Crum B. (1990) *Conventional Thought and Practice in PE and PE Teacher Education: Problems of the Profession – Prospects for Change*, paper presented at the International Association of Physical Education Schools in Higher Education Conference, Atlanta, USA.

● Evans J. and Davies B. (1993) *Equality, Education and Physical Education*, London: The Falmer Press.

● Feingold R. (1997) 'Service-based scholarship: An introduction', *Quest* 49: 351–4.

● Glover S., Burns J., Butler H. and Patton G. (1998) 'Social environments and the emotional wellbeing of young people', *Family Matters* 49: 11–16.

● Kidd B. (1995) 'Confronting inequality in sport and physical activity', *Avante* 1(1): 1–19.

● Kirk D. (1988) *Physical Education and Curriculum Study: A Critical Introduction*, London: Croom Helm.

● Kirk D. (1989) 'Knowledge in movement and the physical education curriculum', *The National ACHPER Physical Education Teacher* 6(4): 1–7.

● Kirk D. (1994) ' "Making the present strange": Sources of the present crisis in physical education', *Discourse* 15(1): 46–53.

● Kirk D. and Macdonald D. (1998) 'Situated learning in physical education', *Journal of Teaching in Physical Education* 17(3): 376–87.

● Kirk D. and Tinning R. (1990) *Physical Education, Curriculum and Culture: Critical Issues in the Contemporary Crisis*, Basingstoke, England: The Falmer Press.

● Kirk D., Burgess-Limerick R., Kiss M., Lahey J. and Penney D. (1999) *Senior Physical Education: An Integrated Approach*, Champaign, Ill.: Human Kinetics.

● Lawson H. (1998) 'Here today, gone tomorrow? A framework for analyzing the development, transformation, and disappearance of helping fields', *Quest* 50: 225–37.

● *A League of Their Own*, film, directed by Penny Marshall. USA: Columbia, 1992.

● Macdonald D. (1999) 'The "professional" work of experienced physical educators', *Research Quarterly for Exercise and Sport* 70(1): 41–54.

● Macdonald D. and Brooker R. (1997) 'Moving beyond the crisis in secondary physical education: An Australian initiative', *Journal of Teaching in Physical Education* 16(2): 155–75.

● Macdonald D., Kirk D. and Braiuka S. (1999) 'The social construction of the physical activity field at the school/university interface', *European Journal of Physical Education* 5(1): 31–51.

● Macdonald D. and Tinning R. (1995) 'PETE and the trend to proletarianization: A Case Study', *Journal of Teaching in Physical Education* 15(1): 98–118.

● McKay J. (1991) *No Pain, No Gain? Sport and Australian Culture*, Sydney: Prentice Hall.

● National Association for Sport and Physical Education (1995) *Moving Into The Future: National Standards for Physical Education*, Virginia: National Association for Sport and Physical Education.

● O'Sullivan M., Siedentop D. and Tannehill D. (1994) 'Breaking out: Codependency of high school physical education', *Journal of Teaching in Physical Education* 13: 421–8.

● Rink J. (1992) 'The plan and the reality', *Journal of Physical Education, Recreation and Dance* 63(7): 69–72 and 77.

● Rovego I. (1995) 'Theoretical perspectives on knowledge and learning and a student teacher's pedagogical content knowledge of dividing and sequencing subject matter', *Journal of Teaching in Physical Education* 4: 284–304.

● Schempp P., Manross D., Tan S. and Fincher M. (1998) 'Subject expertise and teachers' knowledge', *Journal of Teaching in Physical Education* 17: 342–56.

● Shulman L. (1986) 'Those who understand: Knowledge growth in teaching', *Educational Researcher* 15: 4–21.

● Siedentop D. (1992) 'Thinking differently about secondary physical education', *Journal of Physical Education, Recreation and Dance* 63(7): 67–8 and 73.

● Siedentop D. (1993) 'Curriculum innovation: Toward the twentieth century', paper presented at the 36th ICHPER (International Council for Health, Physical Education and Recreation) World Congress, Yokoyama, Japan, August.

● Siedentop D. (1998) 'Regaining the public trust: Complex social problems meet specialized academic disciplines', *Quest* 50: 170–78.

● Siedentop D., Doutis P., Tsangaridou N., Ward P. and Rauschenbach J. (1994) 'Don't sweat gym! An analysis of curriculum and instruction', *Journal of Teaching Physical Education* 13: 375–94.

● Stroot S. (1994) 'Contemporary crisis or emerging reform? A review of secondary physical education', *Journal of Teaching in Physical Education* 13: 333–41.

● Tinning R. and Fitzclarence L. (1992) 'Postmodern youth culture and the crisis in Australian secondary school physical education', *Quest* 44: 287–303.

● Tinning R., Kirk D. and Evans J. (1993) *Learning to Teach Physical Education*, Sydney: Prentice Hall.

Chapter Fifteen

A Task-based Approach to Critical Pedagogy in Sport and Physical Education

David Kirk

Introduction

The notion of a critical pedagogy was introduced to the sport and physical education community in the early to mid 1980s (e.g. Lawson, 1984; McKay and Pearson, 1984; Kirk, 1986). This early work challenged some of the traditional or orthodox ideas and practices in the field. While the notion of a critical pedagogy began to attract attention and interest in the latter half of the 1980s, it was also roundly criticized for being long on criticism and short on constructive alternatives (e.g. O'Sullivan, Siedentop and Locke, 1992). This critical response was, in part, justified. One claim was that critical pedagogy lacked practicality. This criticism was certainly justified in relation to my own teaching.

One of my students' complaints about the curriculum study informed by a critical pedagogy that they did at the University of Queensland, was that the subjects were too abstract and theoretical, too far removed from the nuts and bolts of everyday work in schools compared with their studies of teaching and learning. They convinced me that this complaint was justified, and so I set about trying to theorize an approach to curriculum study that revealed its practical utility to these young student teachers.

The burgeoning interest in critical pedagogy among left-leaning scholars at that time proved to be of great assistance in this task. My reading of the literature produced by these scholars and the influence of my colleague Jim McKay (McKay and Pearson, 1984), led me to develop a position on curriculum study that was focused on educational praxis in the pursuit of social change, informed by the principle of social justice. This work produced a notion of curriculum study as the critique of educational action, identified curriculum issues as 'sites of contestation' where practical educational change could be pursued, and argued for forms of educational research that complemented existing paradigms by including practitioners as genuine partners. Some of this work, at least, began to answer the critics of critical pedagogy by moving towards some practical constructive alternatives to existing orthodoxies.

However, my experience of working with teachers engaged in mid-career professional development courses by distance education at Deakin University between 1989 and 1994, helped me to see that my curriculum and teaching focused approach to critical pedagogy almost completely ignored the learner and learning. This issue was thrown into relief because of the forms of pedagogy that were required by distance education, where student and teacher rarely if ever meet face-to-face. The pedagogies for physical education being developed at Deakin by my colleagues Richard Tinning and John Evans to accommodate the distance education mode (Tinning and Evans, 1994) were influential in my arrival at the use of a task-based approach to critical pedagogy.

In subsequent attempts to theorize this task-based approach to include the learner and learning within the dynamic interplay of the curriculum and teaching, I have been greatly assisted by colleagues such as Inez Rovegno (Rovegno and Kirk, 1995), and Doune Macdonald (Kirk and Macdonald, 1998; Macdonald and Brooker, 1995). The task-based approach to critical pedagogy discussed in this chapter has benefited greatly from these collaborations in terms of its theoretical development. It has also benefited practically by the opportunities presented by the University of Queensland, which I returned to in 1995, to teach large classes of between 100 and 400 students.

The key benefit of a critical pedagogy to young people who are pursuing careers in sport and physical education, is that it seeks to assist them to see beyond the obvious or the surface level of sport. This is important since sport has become increasingly complex through processes of professionalization, mediaization, commercialism and commodification. A critical pedagogy seeks to empower young people in sport by assisting them to make connections between their own life experiences and broader but less visible social processes, such as, the social construction of gender or the relationships between money, media and power in and through sport. It also attempts to bring complex issues to life by locating these issues within young people's practical, everyday experiences of sport and physical activity.

This chapter describes a task-based approach to critical pedagogy in the sociology of sport and physical education, in an introductory subject with just under 400 students, an intermediate level subject with just over 100 (usually second year) students, and in an advanced level professional studies subject with around 40 students. The chapter begins with an outline of some of the key ideas underpinning the notion of critical pedagogy as this term is used here. There then follows a description of the principles informing a task-based approach to teaching and learning. The rest of the chapter provides examples of the application of this approach to the sociology of sport and physical education with students at the University of Queensland between 1995 and 1998. The chapter concludes with some reflective comments on the strengths and weaknesses of this approach.

Critical pedagogy

The notion of critical pedagogy enjoyed considerable popularity among academics on the political left during the 1980s, drawing heavily on the writing of Paulo Friere (1973), Michael Apple (1979), and Henry Giroux (1981) and his collaborators Stanley Aronowitz (e.g. Aronowitz and Giroux, 1985) and Peter McLaren (1988), among others. While many advocates of critical pedagogy loosely aligned themselves with 'new directions' sociology of education (see Whitty, 1985), some, such as Giroux, drew substantially on the work of the critical theorists of the 'Frankfurt School', a diverse group of intellectuals interested in cultural analysis in pre-Second World War Germany (Held, 1980), while others such as Apple grounded their work in post-Marxist perspectives.

The work of this group of mainly male academics and others who followed their lead was criticized at the end of the 1980s by Elizabeth Ellsworth (1989), who asked of critical pedagogy 'why doesn't this feel empowering?'. She claimed that critical pedagogy had taken a 'highly abstract and utopian line which does not necessarily sustain the daily workings of the education its supporters advocate' (Ellsworth, 1989, p. 297). Further critiques noted critical pedagogy's alleged gender and race blindness, and a failure of its advocates to locate themselves reflexively within their analyses (Gore, 1993). However, as Macdonald and Brooker

(1995, p. 102) noted, these critiques informed an approach to critical pedagogy that 'extends the ways in which tertiary education can be discussed' particularly in terms of 'foreground(ing) the social dimensions of professional education'. Macdonald and Brooker (1995) went on to note some of the key components of critical pedagogy that remain useful and important to young people embarking on careers in sport and physical education, including emancipation, empowerment and cultural critique.

Emancipation

The major concern of critical pedagogy is emancipation from unjust and inequitable practices. Examples of such practices are differential treatment of individuals on the basis of their sex, sexual preference, race, skin colour, disability and age when such considerations are inappropriate. For instance, it is inappropriate to pay women a lower wage than men when each group does precisely the same job. It is inappropriate to refuse someone membership of a golf club because of the colour of their skin. In its broadest sense, and in terms of Habermas's theory of knowledge-constitutive interests (Habermas, 1972), human emancipation involves the ability to change and adapt to new challenges and new sets of circumstances. Since change is a common feature of all aspects of life, emancipation in this sense is a vital and necessary human interest and is a practical, day-to-day concern of all who work within the complex social institutions of sport and education.

Empowerment

Critical pedagogy seeks to achieve human emancipation through the empowerment of individuals and groups. Empowerment can take many forms, and does not stop short at merely raising individual consciousness. While increasing self-knowledge is a necessary aspect of empowerment, it is not sufficient in itself. For authentic change to occur at all levels of society, empowerment must incorporate change at institutional and social structural levels as well as change at the level of individuals and groups. Indeed, since each of these levels are interdependent, strategies for empowerment need to account for how these levels of human activity interact. Even though it is a multilevel process, empowerment only becomes authentic when it is realized in the practical daily activities of individuals.

Cultural critique

Critique is one of the main strategies for working towards empowerment and emancipation. Critique is not mere criticism, and is certainly not negative comment. Instead, critique aims to assist people to 'see beyond the obvious', the commonplace and commonsense of the culture of everyday life in order to better understand the interrelatedness of human activity at a range of levels. Critique can take many forms depending on the setting in which it is applied. At the level of the individual, critique can help to enhance your self-knowledge and assist you to act in informed ways. At the level of institutions, critique may take the form of established, evaluative processes that monitor, assess, and modify the work of the organization. At the heart of this notion of cultural critique is an individual's willingness to see beyond surface appearances and to act constructively and positively in meeting new challenges. Critique exposes the complexity of sport and can assist you to develop a better understanding of your own actions, relationships and values.

In addition to these three components, an essential feature of a critical pedagogy is that it is centrally concerned with *education* for social change. In this respect, the term 'pedagogy' should not be interpreted too literally to refer to 'the art and practice of teaching' (following one dictionary definition), nor should it be restricted only to children. Instead, pedagogy should be regarded as a multidimensional concept concerned with the inter-action of learning, teaching and curriculum and their situatedness in social and physical environments. Even though a critical pedagogy begins from the assumption that all human activity is value laden, it does not seek to indoctrinate. On the contrary, with its central concern to bring about social change through education, a critical pedagogy aims to open up possibilities and alternatives, to reveal the complexity of social life and to resist the imposition of simplistic explanations and quick-fix solutions.

A task-based approach to teaching and learning

Central to critical pedagogy as the notion is understood in this chapter is 'caring for and caring about the needs of students' (Macdonald and Brooker, 1995, p. 102). This concern for learners opens up the potential for emancipation, empowerment and critique by shift-ing the focus of education from the mere transmission of information to the social con-struction of knowledge. The term 'task-based' signals an attempt to engage learners in the learning process. In contrast to the tendency for much traditional university teaching to require students to be passive recipients of instruction, a task-based approach attempts to facilitate your active engagement in learning insofar as this is possible with large classes in conventional lecture theatres and classrooms.

Four principles of learning underpin this approach. The first is that learning is an active process in which the individual seeks out information in relation to the task at hand and the environmental conditions prevailing at any given time, and tests out her or his own capabilities within the context formed by the task and environment. The second is that learning is developmental, both in the sense that there are identifiable phases in learning, and that the ways people learn change over time due to growth, maturation and experi-ence. A third principle is that learning is situated and multidimensional in the sense that individuals typically learn more than one thing at a time, often implicitly as in the case of the hidden curriculum. The fourth is that individuals learn in different ways and have preferred learning styles (Kirk, Nauright, Hanrahan, Macdonald, and Jobling, 1996).

The notion of the active learner has been of particular relevance to developing a task-based approach. The use of work sheets illustrates how the principle of the active learner informs this approach. Work sheets take the place of lecture notes or handouts. A typical work sheet would set out the task in terms of what the learners must do, indicate the resources that are needed to complete the task, and provide spaces in which to record information. Sometimes, some key information such as the definition of a concept might be highlighted on the work sheet itself. But unlike the standard 'handout' which contains lots of information, the work sheet directs students to other sources of information such as video, written texts, or the explanations of the teacher and requires them to extract the information for themselves.

So designed, work sheets seek to guide the student's attention to the salient information to be acquired and understood. Underpinning this process, is a belief that learners develop a better and deeper understanding of concepts and information when they actively seek out and extract important material themselves, rather than this being given to them. This 'training of attention' is particularly important when students are unfamiliar with material or are inexperienced in the lecture setting, though the tasks are designed to challenge experienced and more able students as well. This point acknowledges that in any given class there will be a range of levels of intellectual and emotional development.

The tasks that make up the work sheet guide students to extract the required informa-tion in a number of ways and from a range of sources, acknowledging the principle that individuals learn in different ways. Students are asked to listen to the lecturer and to each other, to discuss in small groups, to read from the set text or from other notes provided (always a short passage), to watch slides or video, and to make notes in the spaces provided based on this listening, discussing, reading and watching. Tasks that involve discussion and call for critical reflection attempt to alert students to the principle that more than one thing is being learned at any given moment, and to raise their awareness of the multilayered nature of learning.

A final aspect of a task-based approach is that the learner's own experience is used explicitly as an important resource for individuals to make sense of new information. This key feature acknowledges the principle that learning is developmental, in the sense that learners come to new information with different levels of experience and expertise.

The role of the teacher or lecturer within this task-based approach is that of facilitator. In this role, the teacher's major task is to structure the learning environment in ways which assist learners to acquire information, skills and understanding. A teacher can facilitate learning in a number of ways. These include:

- conducting a situation analysis as part of the planning process
- knowing what the students' current levels of knowledge, skills and understanding are, that is, the likely range of their entry behaviour
- setting challenging and interesting tasks appropriate to the students' current levels of skill and understanding
- using a variety of instructional styles relevant and appropriate to the activity and the students' likely range of stages of development
- motivating students to work hard, and providing a positive environment for learning
- providing relevant and timely feedback to students' on their progress
- setting tasks at new levels of difficulty once particular skills have been learned

Practical applications of a task-based approach

This section includes practical applications of a task-based approach to critical pedagogy in sport and physical education. Three topics have been selected to illustrate the scope of this approach. The topics are gender and sport, the social construction of bodies, and the educational status of school physical education. Examples of applications to the gender and bodies topics are drawn from an introductory level subject in the B.Sc. App. (Human Movement Studies) called 'sociocultural foundations of human movement', which involves lectures to a large class of approximately 350 students, and tutorials to groups of around 30 students. Between one quarter and one third of the students taking this class will pursue a major programme of study in human movement, the rest taking the subject as an elective. The human movement studies specialists typically take the subject in their first year of study, whereas the latter group range across first to fourth year students from a wide variety of degree programmes.

The related example of masculinity and violence in sport is drawn from an intermediate level subject taken by just over 100 second year students intending to complete an applied science degree in human movement studies. In the case of this example, the concern is to apply sociological knowledge as a means of contextualizing young adults' learning in the physical domain. Examples of applications to the educational status topic are drawn from the same introductory level class and also from an advanced level subject called 'curriculum problems and strategies', which is available only to students in the final year of a physical education teaching qualification. Most of the students will have completed a ten week block of teaching practice in schools prior to taking this subject.

Much of the contextual information for the tasks outlined below appears in a textbook written specifically for the introductory and intermediate level subjects just mentioned, titled *The Sociocultural Foundations of Human Movement* (Kirk *et al.*, 1996). The text is used in conjunction with teaching and learning in these subjects, and so frequent reference is made to it throughout the course of discussing the tasks.

Gender and sport

In the introductory level subject, it is assumed that students have no prior knowledge of the topics covered. Consequently, some of the tasks attempt to define and clarify concepts. One example of this, used in relation to the gender and sport topic, is to begin with definitions of sex and gender. The purpose of the task is to assist students to begin to think about gender and sport sociologically, and to appreciate that complex combinations of biological and social factors impact on participation by females and males in specific sports.

Students are first of all asked to read the following statements:

Sex refers to biological characteristics that distinguish females and males. Gender can be described as a socially constructed pattern of behaviour recognized as feminine or masculine. Since it is socially constructed, gender is dynamic, responding to social change. Accordingly, gender differs from one society to another across social classes, ethnic and cultural groups and within the same society.

(Adapted from Ministerial Advisory Committee on Gender Equality, 1992)

Once students have read the statements, they then have an opportunity to ask questions for clarification. It is suggested to them that when the terms female and male are used, it is sex differences that are being invoked. In contrast, when the terms femininity and masculinity are used, it is gender differences that are being invoked. These links between sex and femaleness/maleness, and between gender and femininity/masculinity, are proposed as matters of degree rather than as distinct categories. Students are then invited to work on a task that allows them to apply their understanding of the definitions of sex and gender. The task can be completed either in a small group of no more than four, or by themselves.

The task requires students to discuss and then note whether the following sports segregate females and males on the basis of *sex differences* (due to biological factors), on the basis of *gender differences* (due to social and cultural factors), or on the basis of some combination of each set of factors. They are asked to think of all levels of sport participation, not just the elite level;

- golf
- rugby league
- sailboarding
- snooker
- basketball
- artistic gymnastics
- tennis
- soccer
- synchronized swimming
- netball
- freestyle skiing

Next, students must summarize briefly the arguments for segregation in sports where the basis is:

- sex differences solely
- social and cultural difference solely
- a combination of biological and social factors

Around five to ten minutes is allowed for students to work through the task. When most individuals and groups have finished, the whole group is asked for a show of hands to indicate their response for each sport. This process typically creates considerable controversy in the class. A common pattern of response is for students to select sports such as rugby league (for males) and artistic gymnastics (for females) as clear-cut examples of segregation based solely on sex differences. At the other end of the spectrum, a common pattern of response is that snooker and golf are examples of segregation based solely on gender differences. Most other activities in the list receive an ambiguous and, from the students' responses, somewhat puzzled and arbitrary selection of sex and gender.

It is then pointed out to students that there is no clear-cut and correct response for any of the activities. Certainly, at the elite level of competition in each sport, sex differences may appear to be more obvious factors in segregating males and females, where absolute measures of size, strength and so on are key factors. Students are asked to set the elite level aside and to consider a broader range of ability levels. They are asked to take a further few minutes to discuss or reflect on their initial responses and to complete the summaries of their discussions or reflections when segregation is based on biological factors and on social factors. The task is completed by students being asked to consider whether it is different combinations of sex and gender factors that may be operating across all sports.

A second example of the application of a task-based approach to the topic of gender and sport is masculinity, the media and violence in sport. This example is drawn from a second level subject taken by around 110 students who are pursuing a major course of study in human movement. The purpose of the task is to contextualize young adults' learning in the physical domain. Students are made aware that gender is selected as just one contextual factor among many that could be studied. The issue of masculinity, the media and violence in sport is selected because it touches all students personally.

Students are first of all required to read in class a section of text on 'Media, violence and male sport' in Kirk *et al.* (1996, p. 174) and to note the key issues raised by the authors. This short piece of text is intended to act as a primer for a short group discussion which follows, centred on the question:

Do you believe violence is a problem in male sport? Justify your answer.

Students are encouraged to respond to the text and to clarify their own views based on their experience. They are required to note the various points of view expressed by members of their group.

Students then view two video clips. The first is from journalist Stuart Littlemore's *Media Watch*, a short weekly analysis and critique of the excesses of the print and televisual media. In the clip (*Media Watch*, 1990), Littlemore makes the claim that the media celebrates male violence in sport and uses it as a means of attracting readers and viewers. He focuses particularly on punch-ups and brawls common at the time in rugby league and Australian rules football. The second clip is an excerpt from a late-night variety show hosted by two Australian actors who are well-known for their comedic diatribes on sport, 'Roy Slaven' and 'HG Nelson' (*The Channel 9 Show with Roy and HG*, 1998). This satirical piece by 'Roy' and 'HG' suggests how links are made between masculinity, sport, violence and Australian national identity.

Students find the video clips entertaining. But they are also encouraged to treat them seriously as a source of information. They are asked to note the arguments advanced by Littlemore and 'Roy' and 'HG', particularly the ways in which they suggest links are forged between sport and violence for males, and the role the media plays in this process. Three key focus questions are posed for group discussions following viewing of the video clips:

- To what extent is the source of the problem the sports, or the media, or masculinity, or some combination of these?
- What role does the media play in this process – mere relay or active agent in constructing these relationships?
- How do these relationships form a context for young adults learning physical activities – what are the practical outcomes for what is learned by both females and males, how does the learning takes place, and what are the social consequences of such learning?

These questions generate much animated discussion among students, and the discussion needs to be gently kept on track by occasional interventions calling the whole class together and checking on the groups' progress towards providing a summary of each person's views on each question. The final question is typically the most challenging for students, since it requires them to reflect on their personal experiences and to examine this in light of the information they have collected from the text, the video clips, and from discussion. Part of the difficulty for some of the male students in particular is that they are personally threatened by the issues being studied and struggle to find ways to respond constructively to this critique.

While a degree of discomfort is desirable, since it is indicative that the issue has become problematic for the student, it is important that this discomfort does not result in merely defensive, negative or dismissive responses. In the subject from which this task is drawn, there is an opportunity to follow up these issues in physical activity sessions, where some of the implications of the masculinity and violence nexus can be demonstrated in action and alternatives practised.

The social construction of bodies

The notion that bodies are socially constructed can be a difficult one for students to grasp. Part of the reason for this is the success of the biological sciences in providing explanations of the structure and function of the body. We tend to take for granted that bodies are flesh, blood and bones, and the relevance of biological explanations of the body seem self-evident. The success of biological science has contributed to a naturalistic view of the body, a view that sees the body as a mainly biological phenomenon.

This naturalistic view has sometimes led to claims that differences in sport performance between females and males can be explained solely in terms of biological factors such as strength ('men are stronger') and psychological factors such as motivation ('men are more aggressive'). Similar arguments are made to explain racial differences in sport performance. Individuals who subscribe to a naturalistic view of the body assume that these differences explain variations in behaviour and a wide range of social practices. In other words, differences in sex, colour, size and other physical attributes are seen to be the cause of how people behave and what they believe.

The purpose of the tasks presented below is to challenge this naturalistic view of the body and to assist students to understand that bodies are in large part developed by the society in which people live and the everyday practices they perform. The tasks seek to assist students to grasp the notion that bodies are socially constructed at the same time as they are biologically constructed.

One way to begin this process is to examine and critique an analogy, commonplace in sport, of the body as a machine. The task requires students to read in class the opening paragraph of the chapter on 'The social construction of bodies' in Kirk *et al.* (1996, pp. 159–69), and then to view some images of machine-like bodies. In this particular class, a video clip from the introduction to a television sports show called *Sports Machine*, produced and broadcast by SBS, is used. This clip features the (literal) construction of a heavily muscled male body from a robot-like body, forged from metal. While viewing the clip several times over, students are asked to first of all make a list of machine parts that are intended to relate to body parts; examples include a pump for a heart, electrical wiring for the nervous system, cameras for eyes, hinged levers for limbs and a computer for a brain.

Students are next asked to make a list of the messages about sport and the male body being communicated through the body-as-machine imagery. The intention here is to assist students to make explicit the social values attached to the particular shape, size, and look of the body-machine. In the case of the body-machine shown in the *Sports Machine* video, these values relate to hyper-masculinity and include strength, toughness, power, efficiency and infallibility.

This task is a primer for students to get them thinking about the social construction of bodies, in terms of the attribution of particular social values to the shape, size and look of bodies. It is important that they realize this process of attribution most often occurs at the level of commonsense and that the links between values and bodies are learned through socialization. Students are told that this is why it can be difficult at first to see these connections and, thereby, to grasp the notion that bodies are socially constructed.

The purpose of the next task is to develop students' understanding of the social construction of the body by examining the notion of the 'ideal' body. The task is for students in a small group to discuss and then describe what they think is an 'ideal' body. They are asked to note any differences between the 'ideal' body for females and males. In addition, they are to make particular note of the words used most often to describe 'ideal' bodies.

Students then discuss, describe and note the main features of the ideal body for participating in the following sports, and are encouraged to add their own favourite sport if it is not already listed:

- rugby union prop forward
- netball goal attack
- soccer winger
- downhill skier
- surf lifesaver
- golfer
- gymnast

Students discuss the similarities and differences they have identified for these sports, including any differences for female bodies and male bodies. In a paragraph, they write down what their group discussion suggests about the notion of an 'ideal body' specifically, and more generally about the social construction of bodies.

Students' responses to these tasks vary considerably. Some appear to grasp the notion readily that bodies are in nature and culture simultaneously, and are quick to extrapolate from this core concept a range of implications concerning dress and fashion, make up, sexuality, facial and body hair, and so on. However, by far the more common response from students is that they have known bodies are socially constructed all along, and that the lecturer has simply provided them with a label for their already existing knowledge. This is not an unreasonable reaction; most people understand implicitly that bodies are socially constructed. The challenge that remains for this large majority of students, is to develop additional tasks that assist them to think sociologically about the processes that construct bodies socially. They are then, like the first group, able to see applications of the concept to matters that they would not initially have considered.

Once the core notions of the social constructionist view of bodies have been grasped, they assist students to see that bodies are important to understanding how and why people, as individuals and in groups, behave in the ways they do. People's bodies reflect dominant social norms and values. A naturalistic view of the body stresses only one side of the process, and presents social behaviour as 'naturally' connected to biology. A social constructionist view of the body, in contrast, allows students to analyse how bodies are constructed at different times in history, how body image interacts with self-esteem, the part played by the media in attributing social values to bodies, and the ways in which bodies are involved in the regulation of behaviour.

The educational status of school physical education

It is part of the established body of knowledge generated by educational philosophers and sociologists during the 1960s and 1970s, as well as the conventional folklore of the school, that physical education is marginal to the school's central purposes. These purposes are often described in terms of the intellectual development of young people. Since, according to this conventional wisdom, physical education is concerned primarily with physical activity rather than cognition, its inclusion in the school curriculum and its status as a subject can only be justified on other, non-educational, grounds, such as its contribution to the health and well-being of young people.

Despite some sustained critiques of this patently fallacious thinking, both about the purposes of the school and physical education's place within it, there remains considerable resistance in some quarters to physical education being afforded the same standing as other school subjects. The purpose of the two primer tasks described first in this section is to unsettle some of the taken-for-granted notions individuals harbour about physical education. They are intended for the general, and relatively heterogeneous, class taking the first level 'sociocultural foundations of human movement' subject, and seek merely to prompt the student to begin to give some serious consideration to the question of physical education's contribution to their own and others' education.

A first task is for students to answer the question 'are you physically educated?' They are required to respond to the following statements on page 92 of Kirk *et al.* (1996), adapted from a United States National Association for Sport and Physical Education publication (NASPE, 1995), by scoring themselves on a 1 to 10 scale for each statement.

'A physically educated person:

1. Demonstrates competency in many movement forms and proficiency in a few movement forms.

2. Applies movement concepts and principles to the learning and development of motor skills.

3. Exhibits a physically active lifestyle.
4. Achieves and maintains a health-enhancing level of physical fitness.
5. Demonstrates responsible personal and social behaviour in physical activity settings.
6. Demonstrates understanding and respect for differences among people in physical activity settings.
7. Understands that physical activity provides opportunities for enjoyment, challenge, self-expression and social interaction'.

Students are then asked to note on which of the dimensions they scored highest and on which they scored lowest, and to share these findings with others in their group. Once they have data from a number of class members, students are asked if there are any patterns emerging when the scores are seen together. They are also asked to say what these patterns suggest about their school physical education experiences individually and collectively.

A second task[1] involves students plotting the following factors that relate to their own experience of school physical education across their school career, from year 1 to year 12 on a continuum from 'high' to 'low'. Page 89 of Kirk *et al.* (1996) provides an example.

- student skill levels
- teacher expertise
- student interest and motivation
- proportion of time devoted to physical activity during lessons
- status of the subject

High

Low

Year 1   Year 7   Year 10   Years 11 and 12

Students are then asked to discuss their graph with those of other members of the class and to describe any emerging patterns in school physical education.

These two tasks can assist students to use their own experiences of physical education as a starting point for analysing the social construction of the subject in the school curriculum. A number of points need to be highlighted through these processes, including the variety of people's experiences of physical education, the different forms physical education takes in different contexts, and some of the features of the subject common to different sites, such as the typically low level of teacher expertise in the primary school which is coincidental with the low level of children's skill development. These tasks form a useful starting point for beginning to analyse the educational status of physical education.

The purpose of the second set of tasks developed for a subject taken by around 40 students in the final semester of their physical education teacher education course, is to provide these neonate physical educators with a better and more sophisticated awareness of the kinds of challenges that physical education faces in defending and improving its place in, and contribution to, young people's education. It is assumed that these students have already studied aspects of this issue, such as the purposes of the school, and that they are able to access this broader knowledge and apply it to this more specific and focused issue.

There are two interrelated tasks to be outlined here, the first focusing on the 'crisis' in school physical education, and the second, on setting an agenda for physical education's future. The first task draws heavily on two television documentaries concerned with school physical education, *Fools Gold* made by the Australian Broadcasting Commission's Four Corners team in 1992, and *Going for Gold* made by the ABC's Lateline programme in 1996. It also draws on recent and current newspaper and journal articles, and the students' own experiences in schools as beginning teachers.

The task requires students to view excerpts from each documentary and make notes on the following issues:

- How is the 'crisis' in physical education characterized in each programme?
- Who is given an opportunity to speak? Are there any groups/interested parties missing that you would have expected to hear from?
- What solutions are proposed to the crisis?
- Are there issues that, in your view, the programmes should have addressed but omitted to do so?
- Note the similarities and differences between the programmes with respect to each of the above issues.
- Note any evidence you may have collected during your school teaching practice that suggested to you that there is a crisis in school physical education.

It is significant that both documentaries take as their starting point Australia's likely performance at the Barcelona (1992) and Atlanta (1996) Olympic Games respectively, and that they proceed to frame school physical education within the context of the success and failure of elite sports performers on the international stage. Intermixed with the discourse of sport as a framing category for physical education, is the allegedly deteriorating health and physical fitness of young people. These discourses, of sport and health, are noted by students as two major frames which provide both opportunities and risks for the future development of physical education. They also note that these discourses privilege the voices and interests of some people over others, and they note that teachers of physical education, young people and their parents are key groups missing from the documentaries.

The nature of the problems facing physical education and the solutions proposed, therefore, tend to reflect the experiences and interests of the elite sports performers, health researchers and government officials invited to speak on these issues. When students compare their notes from the documentaries with their own recent experience of teaching in a school during their ten week school teaching practice, they find little evidence of the crisis in physical education in the terms in which it is characterized in the documentaries.

After viewing the documentaries, students discuss their notes in small groups and develop their groups' position on the crisis in physical education. Following a workshop format, each group reports on their discussion to the whole class, and the major issues emerging from this work are noted on the board. Typically, the final year students are more homogeneous in their responses to this task relative to the responses of the students in the introductory and intermediate level subjects, where the classes are much larger and less homogeneous. The major points emerging from the groups form the basis for the agenda setting exercise to be undertaken in the second task.

The second task is concerned with setting an agenda for the future of school physical education. In addition to the work completed in the previous task, students are asked to read a number of short magazine and newspaper articles. Articles by myself (Kirk, 1996), Tinning (1992), Green (1995), Ennis (1984) and others are included. On the basis of this information, students are required to work in a small group to identify five major challenges facing school physical education over the next few years, and potential risks associated with each challenge. Challenges are meant to encompass realistically achievable outcomes that significantly improve the place of physical education in the education of young people, while the associated risks identify potential hazards that may jeopardize the achievement of the outcomes.

Students typically find this second task difficult, particularly the challenge to maximize the opportunities and minimize the risks that arise through the framing discourses of sport and health. This task is, therefore, best viewed as the point of departure in a subject or course of study rather than as a destination, in the sense that students will produce the 'right' answers for physical education's future. Indeed, students are encouraged to view the task as a key theme in their ongoing professional development as teachers, to be revisited and revised throughout their careers.

A critical pedagogy here is concerned to assist students to steer a course between radical pessimism on the one hand, which leads to inaction, and naive possibilitarianism on the other, which leads to radical but strategically ineffective action (Whitty, 1985). The course between these poles is that of educational praxis or informed action. It is important that students are not overwhelmed by the complexity of the issues surrounding physical education's educational status and the difficulties associated with constructing good strategies for change, but are instead provided with some clear examples of practice that already meets the standard of educational praxis. The task, then, is to provide neonate physical educators with a pedagogy of possibility and hope.

Conclusion: Strengths and weaknesses of a task-based approach

This chapter has provided some examples of applications of a task-based approach to a critical pedagogy in sport and physical education. These examples are underpinned by four principles, that learning is active, developmental, situated and occurs through preferred styles. The central purpose of these tasks, within a critical pedagogy, is to educate students for social change by assisting them to 'see beyond the obvious' of everyday life and to begin to think sociologically about sport, the body and physical education. It is important to note that the approach described here is only one way in which a critical pedagogy may be practised, and it is not without its' contradictions and problems. In concluding this chapter, I wish to reflect on some of the weaknesses and some of the strengths of this approach as far as I am aware of them.

One of the key weaknesses of this approach from the point of view of a critical pedagogy, is that it could be viewed as an accommodation to the traditionally dominant form of university teaching rather than a radical alternative to this form. Macdonald and Brooker (1995) note that some versions of critical pedagogy may include several alternative and relatively 'radical' features. These include, among other things, negotiation between teacher and students over assessment requirements and topics to be covered, detailed constructive commentary on students' work, and students contracting to work towards a particular grade or the use of criterion or competency based profiles to describe student achievement rather than grades.

Commenting on the broader context of university teaching, Macdonald and Brooker (1995) go on to observe that intensification of work practices over the past two decades has led to the ongoing specialization and fragmentation of knowledge as it is packaged in the modern university, and to serious difficulties for university teachers to work collaboratively to overcome these structural constraints through the implementation of a critical pedagogy. At many universities like the University of Queensland, the sheer size of classes at introductory and intermediate levels, the facilities (large lecture theatres) made available for teaching and learning, and the requirement to grade student learning according to relatively traditional statistical distributions, make the incorporation of many of these alternative procedures difficult. As Macdonald and Brooker note, to change these structural features of the university curriculum requires political work of a different order in sites additional to the classroom.

Within the approach described here, there can be no question that, while some choice is available to students with respect to how they are assessed and how they study, there is little negotiation at introductory and intermediate levels over the content and sequencing of knowledge, and only slightly more negotiation and self-directed learning in the advanced level subject. This is not a student-centred approach to teaching and learning as advocates of critical pedagogy in physical education might recommend (e.g. Rovegno and Kirk, 1995; Macdonald and Brooker, 1995), and it is not 'democratic' in the sense that all parties have equal say over the curriculum. The sheer size of classes requires that the lecturer, in order to be a facilitator of learning, must remain firmly in charge of the class, highlighting a crucial contradiction for any approach to critical pedagogy implemented within traditional university settings.

From the point of view of some students, this approach has further weaknesses. Those who prefer a didactic mode of pedagogy do not like the task-based approach. There are a range of reasons for this. For example, some students don't enjoy interacting with others in class. Some feel uncomfortable with some topics (e.g. females and the body), even threatened (e.g. males and gender). Others view the teacher-as-facilitator role as an abdication of the teacher's responsibility to supply information in the form of the 'right' answers. A minority simply resent having to 'work' when they come to class, and prefer the didactic mode of pedagogy that allows them to feel that they have done enough by simply being there and taking notes.

Even some of the students who do support a task-based approach can't always be accommodated in terms of differences in their abilities, interests, levels of maturity, and so on. While the work sheets are generally very popular with students, some are not sure how to get the information they need from group discussions. Indeed, unless the learning experiences themselves are very well designed, even the most supportive students find this approach less than useful.

These are just some of the weaknesses I am aware of. Independent and regular evaluations of the subjects where this approach is used, suggest that it also has particular strengths. As I suggested, the work sheets have been very popular with students. The use of multi-media is also attractive to many students, and they prefer the variety that makes classes more interesting for them than the mono-format of the traditional didactic style. In particular, many students like the use of video, especially video clips that draw on popular culture such as television shows, advertisements and movies, although as Aronowitz and Giroux (1985) warned over a decade ago, this material can itself become a less useful vehicle for critique if tasks are not carefully designed to provide students with an appropriate level of analytic distance from what they more typically encounter as entertainment.

Whether this approach fulfills its central purpose of educating students for social change remains to be seen. There is evidence from time to time that individual students have been radicalized by this approach, but also that others have become defensive and dismissive. Given the wide range of abilities, interests and levels of maturity of students, there can be no clear-cut, measurable evidence that this central purpose has been achieved. But this does not suggest to me that the process is any less worth pursuing for that. A task-based approach to teaching and learning in sport and physical education, in my view, makes a small but useful contribution within the range of approaches that might be labelled critical pedagogy.

Note

1. This task was devised by Doune Macdonald, the University of Queensland, see Kirk *et al.*, (1996, p. 89).

References

- Apple M.W. (1979) *Ideology and Curriculum*, London: Routledge and Kegan Paul.
- Aronowitz S. and Giroux H.A. (1985) *Education Under Siege: The Conservative, Liberal and Radical Debate Over Schooling*, London: Routledge and Kegan Paul.
- *The Channel 9 Show with Roy and HG* (1998) ABC Television, 25 April.
- Ellsworth E. (1989) 'Why doesn't this feel empowering?': Working through the repressive myths of critical pedagogy', *Harvard Educational Review* 59(3): 297–324.
- Ennis C. (1984) 'A future scenario for physical education: The Movement for Life curriculum, 2017–2035', *Journal of Physical Education, Recreation and Dance* September, pp. 4–5.
- Friere P. (1973) *Pedagogy of the Oppressed*, New York: Seabury Press.
- Giroux H.A. (1981) *Ideology, Culture and the Process of Schooling*, Lewes: Falmer.
- Gore J. (1993) *The Struggle for Pedagogies: Critical and Feminist Discourses as Regimes of Truth*, New York: Routledge.
- Green K. (1995) 'Physical education, partnership and the challenge of lifelong participation: A shared goal for the 21st century?', *British Journal of Physical Education* Summer, pp. 26–30.
- Habermas J. (1972) *Knowledge and Human Interests*, London: Heinemann.
- Held D. (1980) *Introduction to Critical Theory: Horkheimer to Habermas*, Berkley: University of California Press.
- Kirk D. (1986) 'A critical pedagogy for teacher education: Towards an inquiry-oriented approach', *Journal of Teaching in Physical Education* 5(4): 230–46.
- Kirk D. (1988) *Physical Education and Curriculum Study: A Critical Introduction*, London: Croom Helm.

● Kirk D. (1989) 'The orthodoxy in RT-PE and the research-practice gap: A critique and an alternative view', *Journal of Teaching in Physical Education* 8(2): 123–30.

● Kirk D. (1996) 'The crisis in school physical education: An argument against the tide', *The ACHPER Healthy Lifestyles Journal* 43(4): 25–7.

● Kirk D. and Macdonald D. (1998) 'Situated learning in physical education', *Journal of Teaching in Physical Education* 17(3): 376–87.

● Kirk D., Nauright J., Hanrahan S., Macdonald D. and Jobling I. (1996) *The Sociocultural Foundations of Human Movement*, Melbourne: Macmillan.

● Lawson H.A. (1984) 'Problem-setting for physical education and sport', *Quest* 36: 48–60.

● Macdonald D. and Brooker R. (1995) 'Professional education: Tensions in subject design and implementation', *Educational Research and Perspectives* 22(2): 99–109.

● McKay J. and Pearson K. (1984) 'Objectives, strategies and ethics in teaching introductory courses in sociology of sport', *Quest* 36: 261–72.

● McLaren P. (1988) 'Schooling the postmodern body: Critical pedagogy and the politics of enfleshment', *Journal of Education* 170(3): 53–83.

● *Media Watch* (1990) ABC Television, 21 May.

● Ministerial Advisory Committee on Gender Equity (1992) *Social Justice*, Brisbane: Department of Education, Queensland.

● NASPE (1995) *Moving Into the Future: National Standards for Physical Education*, St. Louis: Mosby.

● O'Sullivan M., Siedentop D. and Locke L. (1992) 'Toward collegiality: Competing viewpoints among teacher educators', *Quest* 44: 266–80.

● Rovegno I. and Kirk D. (1995) 'Articulations and silences in socially critical work on physical education: Toward a broader agenda', *Quest* 47(4): 447–74.

● Tinning R. (1992) 'On speeches, dreams and realities: Physical education in the year 2001', *The ACHPER National Journal*, Summer, pp. 24–6.

● Tinning R. and Evans J. (1994) 'Distance education in physical education: An Australian model for inservice teacher education', *Physical Education Review* 17(2): 126–33.

● Whitty G. (1985) *Sociology and School Knowledge: Curriculum Theory, Research and Politics*, London: Methuen.

General Index

Author Index